# 80 HILLS
## IN NORTHERN SNOWDONIA

# 80 HILLS
## IN NORTHERN SNOWDONIA

*A rambler-friendly guide to*
*26 Hill-Walks in Northern Snowdonia*

**Phil Jones**

ISBN: 978-1-84524-166-7

Cover design: ?????????
Cover Photographs: Phil Jones

First published in 2010 by
Llygad Gwalch, Ysgubor Plas, Llwyndyrys,
Pwllheli, Gwynedd LL53 6NG
tel: 01758 750432  fax: 01758 750438
email: books@carreg-gwalch.com
internet: www.carreg-gwalch.com

# CONTENTS

## SECTION 1

### Carneddau

## SECTION 2

### Glyderau

## SECTION 3

### Snowdon

## SECTION 4

### Nantlle

## SECTION 5

### Moelwynion

# INTRODUCTION

**North**

A hill-walkers' guide book to 80 summits and 26 walks in Northern Snowdonia.
The most popular routes to and from each summit (as well as a few more obscure options) are described in enough detail to encourage even the most wary rambler to head for the hills.

Elvis Costello was once quoted as comparing writing about music to dancing about architecture. Music can only be properly appreciated by listening to it – most who write about it do it scant service. The same analogy could also be applied to hill-walking. It is not a spectator sport. But its enjoyment does take a little more effort than donning a pair of headphones and stretching out onto your sofa. The first step for many people keen to explore the hills is appropriately to arm themselves with a friendly guide book before putting on their boots. And "80 Hills" is as good a place as any to start – the result of a life-long passion I have held for hill-walking, not just in Snowdonia but further afield in Mid and South Wales and the North West Highlands of Scotland.

Committed to an impending move (to set up a permanent home North of the border) before heading up the M6 I decided upon one final challenge of setting foot on every individual summit in North Western Snowdonia that reached above 2000 feet in altitude. It had been my intention to concentrate on this corner of Snowdonia where most of the 'celebrity' summits lie since I intended completing the exercise within 12 months if possible. But as I delved more and more into the logistics of such an exercise I discovered there were substantially more qualifying tops than I had realised. For consistency's sake no hill fitting the criteria was to be omitted no matter how uncharismatic or obscure. So I ended up with my size 10's planting themselves onto a grand total of 80 hills. Some summits consisted of twinned tops – such as Crib Goch or Y Lliwedd – and even though most guides class them as a single summit I have taken the liberty of counting each subsidiary outlier as a separate 'hill' since completing each walk does involve visiting every main and subsidiary summit.

There are actually 101 summits standing within the boundaries of the Snowdonia National Park and reaching above 2000 feet (610 metres) – thus earning the official title of 'mountain' for those who prefer mountain-walking to hill-walking. Conveniently, most of these summits are crammed into the 200 square-mile North Western section of the Park. Bounded by the tourist centres of Bangor, Conwy, Betws-y-Coed and Porthmadog this area is well served by rail and bus links as well as the two major routes – the A5 and A55.

Of the Park's 101 'mountains', 63 lie in this patch – none of them further than 4 miles from a roadside parking spot; little wonder that walkers throng to this corner of North Wales. The 80 hills that make up this guide include those 63 as well as the 8 subsidiary outliers and 3 summits standing outside the National Park itself (in the 'industrialised exclusion zone') but deserving a visit. Finally 6 other tops that fail to reach the 2000ft contour but top 600 metres (1975ft) have also been included since they demand a little more respect. Add them all up and you get **"80 Hills"**.

When first researching how best to approach each mountain I discovered that no single book or magazine gave precise route-finding information where I really needed it. Much of the available literature was inadequate to the point of uselessness. Some, given the haziness of the information presented to the reader, suggested the writer had never actually set foot on the hill in question. Others repeated blatant inaccuracies presumably gathered second-hand from older, misinformed guide-books. And indeed a small number could even prove to be dangerous in the wrong hands.

During the 18 months it eventually took me to complete the exercise I gained a valuable insight into the area, having seen most of the highest hills from every possible angle and under a variety of conditions. I decided this wealth of experience could be put to some use by producing my own guide book to the marvellous hills crowded into this compact corner of North Wales. The resulting book was to provide a mine of information to anyone with an interest in this part of North Wales, and would also hopefully encourage many people perhaps daunted by the thought of heading into 'hill-walking country' to set their sights a little higher.

While many of Snowdon's highest summits merit several visits in order to be fully appreciated, the minor tops have just as much to offer – a little seclusion if nothing else. For anyone keen to broaden their hill-walking knowledge of this beautiful area "80 Hills" is the ideal guide – providing clear directions onto every notable summit, giving safe escape options when necessary, and sprinkling enough intriguing and obscure information en route to add interest to any walk.

Since completing the initial 'challenge' I have revisited most of the 80 in order to verify my first impressions, obtain photographic material and in some cases to enhance the route followed on my original walk in order to ensure that everyone who attempts to follow in my footsteps has a safe and rewarding experience. In the cases of Snowdon and Moel Siabod one single visit was hardly enough anyway, hence their appearance in more than one walk. Setting foot on every summit provided me with a geographical insight far superior to that gained by just 'topping' Snowdon with the tourists or tackling Tryfan's North face with the rock hounds. I quickly came to realise that the knowledge I had gained from standing on top of every peak in this part of North Wales and surveying these magical hills from every angle would make future trips into the hills that bit easier and more fulfilling.

There are better-written books on the subject – compiled by more experienced individuals who have devoted their lives to hill walking in this area. However, "80 Hills" can take its rightful place as an up-to-date guide to the most popular hill-walking area of Snowdonia as well as a mouth-watering menu to the feast of hills on offer here. It provides simple, virtually foolproof directions onto the hill – instructions how to get from start to finish in one piece – an idea of what to expect on the way, what problems to look out for and what escape routes are available.

There are 26 walks described, and all except the final one start and end at the same point regardless of how awkward that can sometimes be. All of these walks can be completed (under favourable weather conditions) by any person with minimal scrambling ability. For those of you already quaking at the knees, each walk has easier options where helpful. Every mountain region also has a section at the start describing family-friendly alternatives. These 'tasters' are intended to provide the inspiration to explore further as experience is gained.

Hill-walking is one of the few activities that benefit you mentally as well as physically. It is enjoyable, exhilarating and empowering. Where else can you witness awesome scenery close-up without an exorbitant entrance fee; or taste real adventure without queuing up for the next ride? You never know, you might get to discover where your own limitations lie and be prompted to stretch them. Whether you have already stood upon most of these hills, or have only driven past en route to the nearest gift-shop, I hope you find something in these pages to entice you closer to at least one particular hill you might have missed.

Anyone who shares my love of hill-walking knows how it can open up a host of new experiences and place you in a variety of situations not encountered in 'normal' life. Some mountains will inspire awe, others fear – some might even cause you to reflect on your place in the cosmos. What is certain is that the efforts taken to reach each summit are repaid in diverse ways.

I'm assuming those of you who do intend completing the main walks have a rudimentary knowledge of this part of Wales, and perhaps already have your own favourite corner but want to discover others. When they might come in handy, I provide precise directions together with a realistic description of the terrain you are likely to come across, and some indication of how long the walk should take. As far as these 'precise directions' are concerned, I've stuck with 6-figure grid references (which any hill-walker ought to be conversant with but are explained further on anyway). Readers should be aware that the route maps in the guide (and on the CD) are purely for illustration and are not an adequate alternative to proper maps (Ordnance Survey 'Explorer' or Harvey 'British Mountain Maps' for example).

The correct compass bearing to follow from each listed reference point is also provided, with the accompanying narrative (and photographs on the CD where relevant) aiding more accurate route-finding. Where the odds of taking a wrong turn are increased, or where the way ahead is not always obvious, a sequence of quite close reference points is recorded with bearings given from one to the next. Where extra compass directions and map references might be helpful these are given within the body of the text, but obviously paths zigzag and meander so irregularly that changing bearings for every step would be confusing rather than helpful.

For those embarking on any of these walks for the first time the accompanying text is there to make things clearer, not to carve in stone one specific route when another might seem more feasible on the day. I hope you have the gumption to eventually put this book aside and follow your own path. After all, that's the fun of hill-walking: the fundamental thrill of pitching your knowledge and experience against the elements and the lie of the land with the help of just a brain and a map. This book is only meant to give you an edge – it's certainly no substitute for experience and common sense. Similarly don't just rely on the map references and compass bearings;

studying the ground and learning to read it is the most important skill any walker can acquire. And of course the most valuable piece of equipment of all is your own judgement. If ever you feel weather or ground conditions demand it, the wiser option is to turn back, confident that on the next attempt you will reach the top in one piece.
Safe walking…..

**Phil Jones (Inverness)**

# HOW THIS GUIDE IS LAID OUT

## TASTERS

*A selection of easier alternatives precedes each Section for those of you averse to heights, who prefer to keep to straightforward paths, or for whom limited time or other constraints make full-blown walks impractical. Each provides a risk-free introduction to the area the main walks cover (and some don't even involve getting out of the car!).*

| WALK No: Hill (s) Name and Hill No. | | |
|---|---|---|
| **Distance walked** | **(Km/miles)** | |
| **Height ascended** | **(m/ft)** | **Brief description of the mountains or route.** |
| **Time taken** | **(hrs/min)** | |
| *This is an informal introduction to the walk – usually including my own personal perspective on the hills visited* | | |

## MAIN TEXT (Route Description)

Each walk is given approach directions to the start point. There then follows a sequential write-up of what to expect during the walk (aided by photographs accessible on the free CD) [identified like this].

A proper map and compass are essential for any walk in the hills, as well as being sound practice, so don't just rely on my sketch-maps. Nor is this guide on its own sufficient substitute for adequate clothing, equipment, experience and common sense. Although it portrays each route in detail when I last walked it – remember that things can obviously change over time.

**1) (123456)** → **Numbered 6-figure map reference point**

   **280°** → **Compass bearing**

**Compass symbol**

SECTIONS OF THE ROUTE THAT NEED PARTICULAR CARE OR THAT COULD POSE PROBLEMS UNDER ADVERSE WEATHER CONDITIONS HAVE ALL RELEVANT WARNINGS CAPITALISED. PARTICULAR LOCATIONS THAT ARE WORTH CLOSER STUDY TO ENABLE YOU TO LOCATE THEM AGAIN ON ANY RETURN LEG ARE ALSO IDENTIFIED IN THIS MANNER.

---

### OPTION 2
These enable you to omit certain parts of the walk, or identify escape routes if conditions prohibit completing the entire walk.

***Time saved is shown where relevant.***

---

## *VIEWS*
*These are intended to give you an idea of what can be seen at various points en route – weather permitting. Don't blame me if cloud hides the lot!*

I was allergic to History at school so far be it from me to ram chronicles of arcane facts down anybody's throat. However, some walkers find a mix of tales and trivia here and there add interest to the day. If you are reluctant to pursue such side-tracks then ignore these brief ramblings and just get on with the walk.

This is a guide to the hills of North Wales, so I make no excuses for using the Welsh names and spellings of the features you will encounter. Consequently, this bit at the very end provides a useful translation into English of all those hills, rivers, valleys, lakes and crags that seem so unpronounceable to the visiting 'Saeson' (Saxons or English people).

The only exceptions are the use of the names **'Snowdonia'** (for 'Eryri') and **'Snowdon'** (for 'Yr Wyddfa'). These are the names by which both are generally shown on the OS maps so I use them here.

# MAPS AND COMPASS

I cannot stress enough the importance of taking a decent map and a compass with you whenever you go out walking in the hills. It should become second nature – as automatic as fastening your seat belt whenever you get into the driving seat of a car. Of course, being able to drive safely is just as important as wearing a seatbelt. Similarly, carrying map and compass are pointless unless you are comfortable with using the two – if only to confirm that you are where you are supposed to be.

## MAPS

The maps best suited for walkers are either those produced by Harvey or the Ordnance Survey,

For the walks covered in this guide Harvey publish one sheet for Snowdonia (**XT40**) specifically with hill walkers and mountaineers in mind. It is printed on durable, waterproof polyethylene and covers the entire area on one sheet at a scale of 1:40,000. 2.5 cms on the map represents 1 Km on the ground.

The old type Ordnance Survey maps at a scale of 1:63,360 used to be the staple of most walkers – 1 inch on the map representing 1 mile on the ground. These have been replaced by the Landranger series at a scale of 1:50,000 (2 cms on the map representing 1 Km on the ground) but the amount of detail crammed onto each map does not always make them easy to decipher. These are better suited for planning sight-seeing tours by road or established footpath than for exploring the great unknown.

Far better for walking or even mountain biking are the new type Ordnance Survey Explorer maps at a scale of 1:25,000 which replaced the old Outdoor Leisure series. Here 4 cms on the map represents 1 Km on the ground (or 2.5 inches to 1 mile). Due to the enlarged scale you need 2 separate maps if you intend following every walk in this guide (despite the fact that many Explorer maps are double-sided).

**OL17** (Snowdon/Conwy Valley) covers most of the area North of Beddgelert. **OL18** (Harlech, Porthmadog and Bala) covers pretty much everywhere else – South of Betws-y-Coed.

## MAP REFERENCES

6-figure map references are given (using Ordnance Survey map gridlines) to pinpoint locations to the nearest 100 metres. Most people are conversant with the use of these grid references no doubt from time spent poring over maps in their Geography lessons at school. Excuse me if I take a moment to explain the method for those who were occupied elsewhere – perhaps staring out of the window at the antics of the netball team.

Every map (OS or Harveys) is divided into kilometre squares by a network of gridlines. These are numbered sequentially left (West) to right (East) and bottom (South) to top (North) – so a kilometre square anywhere on your map can be accurately located by just the simple use of a 4-figure map reference. In the map below, the square containing the tiny lake is **5631** (the square rests in the crook of the **L** formed by the North-South gridline **56** and the East-West gridline **31**.

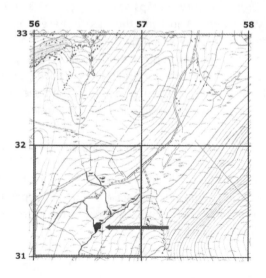

For the purpose of most walkers, sailors and anyone who needs more accurate navigation each kilometre square is divided into 100 smaller 'imaginary' squares (each kilometre square split into 10 columns and 10 rows). In order to pinpoint the tiny lake the map reference would be **565312** (the smaller square rests in the crook of the L formed by the North-South gridline **565** and the East-West gridline **312**.

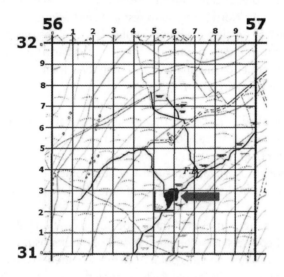

In order to provide even more accurate detail it is even possible to subdivide each imaginary 100x100-metre square into a further 100 squares – giving 8-figure grid references which pinpoint a location to the nearest 10 metres. But for the purposes of most route finding (and certainly for the walks in this book) a 6-figure reference is perfectly adequate.

## COMPASS

There are many books available detailing how to use a combination of compass and map – how to identify your location on the map from the features visible on the ground – the easiest method of measuring the distance you have walked by counting your paces – techniques for navigating in zero visibility in order to follow a bearing from one grid point to another. These skills are certainly a boon for anyone venturing into the wilder corners of Snowdonia, but for the purposes of this guide I shall concentrate on how to head off in the right direction from each compass direction given in the book.

The planet is a huge magnet thanks to the enormous blob of molten iron located at its core. Because of this every compass needle will align itself towards 'magnetic North', coming to rest in a North-South direction (unless the rocks nearby are also magnetic – but in North Wales this problem does not arise). Unfortunately, because it is molten, the Earth's iron core tends to wobble. Consequently 'magnetic North' wanders slightly from 'true North' which is what the maps show.

At the time of writing (2009) this magnetic variation means that your compass needle will actually point 2° West (to the right) of grid North (the North on your map). This variation is decreasing by about 1° every 6 years, so by 2021 magnetic North and true North should coincide – before the former wanders off East of North for a period of time.

Thankfully, for the purposes of this guide such variation will not send you seriously off course since the narrative and photographs provide sufficient back-up. I merely mention this point since many guidebooks make a big deal of magnetic variation. It is only really a problem if navigating in hazardous locations where the terrain is completely obscured by fog, snow, darkness, etc. Also in orienteering (where pinpoint accuracy is part of the deal) or sailing (where landmarks are few and far between) veering 2° off course can of course involve you finishing up quite a distance away from your intended destination.

In order to follow the bearings given in the guide the first point to mention, of course, is that bearings should only be relied upon if you know where you are to begin with. If you are ½ a kilometre or so from where you should be according to the book then obviously heading off on a compass bearing I have given you is unlikely to lead you to the next point.

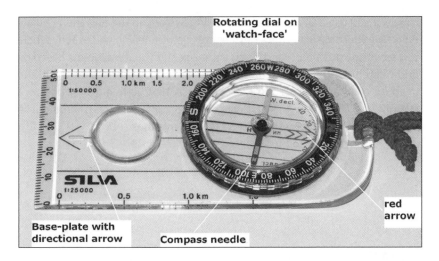

Rotating dial on 'watch-face'

Base-plate with directional arrow

Compass needle

red arrow

So, having ensured you are where you should be, hold the compass in front of you close enough so you can read the numbers set around its rotating dial. Now if you want to head off on a bearing of say 170° all you need to do is rotate the dial surrounding the 'watch-face' of the compass until the long shaft of the 'directional arrow' on the base plate lines up with 170 on the dial. At this point it doesn't matter if you jiggle the compass.

Next, in order to get your bearings – hold the compass in front of you and as level as possible so that the compass needle is free to rotate. Now adjust the direction the compass is facing until the compass needle (which will point towards 'magnetic North') rests inside the large red arrow on the 'watch-face'. The 'directional arrow' on the base plate of the compass will now point in the direction you need to follow. There's nothing particularly scientific about it, and certainly no need to continue holding the compass in front of you as you set off. As long as you have been able to determine whether you need to set off to your right, your left, straight ahead or whatever, then the compass has done its job.

Remember – for the purposes of the walks in this guide keeping an eye on your surroundings is more important than checking map and compass every five minutes. If you have already read up on the walk and consulted a map beforehand then you will already have visualised the route in your mind anyway and have a good idea of what to expect on the ground.

Finally, if you use a GPS (Global Positioning System) in the hills then you are unlikely to become lost. These devices are useful in telling you exactly where you are at any one time – and if you enter a sequence of waypoints based on grid references they will theoretically guide you from A to B to C without need for compass or map. **EXCEPT**, of course, that getting from A to B in a straight line is not always the wisest course to follow when a 100-metre cliff separates the two – something GPS's tend to overlook.

# THE HILLS

| # | | Hill Name | feet | metres | | # | Hill Name | feet | Metres |
|---|---|---|---|---|---|---|---|---|---|
| 1 | | Cefn y Capel | 1509 | 460 | 48 | 62 | Garnedd-Goch | 2297 | 700 |
| 2 | | Crâs | 1558 | 475 | 49 | 59 | Trum Y Ddysgl | 2326 | 709 |
| 3 | | Crimpiau | 1558 | 475 | 50 | 75 | Moelwyn Bach | 2329 | 710 |
| 4 | | Cefn Coch | 1591 | 485 | 51 | 44 | Llechog | 2355 | 718 |
| 5 | | Moel Bowydd | 1617 | 493 | 52 | 39 | Moel Eilio | 2383 | 727 |
| 6 | | Manod Bach | 1676 | 511 | 53 | 61 | Craig Cwm Silyn | 2408 | 734 |
| 7 | | Gyrn | 1778 | 542 | 54 | 16 | Craig Eigiau | 2411 | 735 |
| 8 | | Craig Wen | 1797 | 548 | 55 | 53 | Yr Aran | 2451 | 747 |
| 9 | | Clogwyn Bwlch-y-Maen | 1797 | 548 | 56 | 14 | Drosgl | 2487 | 758 |
| 10 | | Foel Rudd | 1870 | 570 | 57 | 28 | Gallt Yr Ogof | 2503 | 763 |
| 11 | | Moel Farlwyd | 1893 | 577 | 58 | 74 | Moelwyn Mawr | 2527 | 770 |
| 12 | | Moel Wnion | 1902 | 580 | 59 | 4 | Drum | 2529 | 771 |
| 13 | | Foel-fras (Moelwynion) | 1922 | 586 | 60 | 66 | Moel Hebog | 2566 | 782 |
| 14 | | Carnedd Y Cribau | 1938 | 591 | 61 | 10 | Bera Mawr | 2604 | 794 |
| 15 | 73 | Foel Boethwel | 1975 | 602 | 62 | 36 | Elidir Fach | 2608 | 795 |
| 16 | 1 | Foel Lwyd | 1978 | 603 | 63 | 23 | Pen Llithrig Y Wrach | 2622 | 799 |
| 17 | 41 | Foel Goch | 1985 | 605 | 64 | 27 | Y Foel Goch | 2641 | 805 |
| 18 | 71 | Moel Meirch | 1991 | 607 | 65 | 9 | Bera Bach | 2647 | 807 |
| 19 | 54 | Craig Wen | 1994 | 608 | 66 | 37 | Mynydd Perfedd | 2664 | 812 |
| 20 | 48 | The Cwm Dyli Horns | 1998 | 609 | 67 | 51 | Lliwedd Bach | 2683 | 818 |
| 21 | 63 | Mynydd Graig Goch | 2000 | 610 | 68 | 38 | Carnedd Y Filiast | 2694 | 821 |
| 22 | 2 | Tal Y Fan | 2000 | 610 | 69 | 31 | Tryfan (Far South Peak) | 2709 | 826 |
| 23 | 52 | Gallt Y Wenallt | 2032 | 620 | 70 | 34 | Foel-Goch | 2726 | 831 |
| 24 | 24 | Craiglwyn | 2043 | 623 | 71 | 22 | Pen Yr Helgi Du | 2733 | 833 |
| 25 | 77 | Moel Penamnen | 2043 | 623 | 72 | 12 | Llwytmor | 2785 | 849 |
| 26 | 15 | Pen Y Castell | 2044 | 623 | 73 | 8 | Yr Aryg | 2837 | 865 |
| 27 | 39 | Foel Gron | 2063 | 629 | 74 | 80 | Carnedd Moel Siabod | 2861 | 872 |
| 28 | 57 | Y Garn | 2077 | 633 | 75 | 50 | Y Lliwedd (E top) | 2929 | 893 |
| 29 | 26 | Creigiau Gleision (N top) | 2080 | 634 | 76 | 49 | Y Lliwedd (W top) | 2947 | 898 |
| 30 | 64 | Moel Lefn | 2094 | 638 | 77 | 32 | Tryfan | 3010 | 817 |
| 31 | 13 | Gyrn Wigau | 2110 | 643 | 78 | 47 | Crib Goch (E top) | 3021 | 921 |
| 32 | 76 | Moel-yr-Hydd | 2125 | 648 | 79 | 46 | Crib Goch (W top) | 3028 | 923 |
| 33 | 60 | Mynydd Tal-Y-Mignedd | 2142 | 653 | 80 | 35 | Elidir Fawr | 3031 | 924 |
| 34 | 65 | Moel Yr Ogof | 2149 | 655 | 81 | 6 | Garnedd Uchaf | 3038 | 926 |
| 35 | 79 | Graig-Ddu | 2158 | 658 | 82 | 55 | Clogwyn Du | 3054 | 931 |
| 36 | 78 | Manod Mawr | 2169 | 661 | 83 | 5 | Foel-fras (Carneddau) | 3091 | 942 |
| 37 | 70 | Ysgafell Wen (unnamed top) | 2194 | 669 | 84 | 33 | Y Garn | 3107 | 947 |
| 38 | 69 | Ysgafell Wen | 2205 | 672 | 85 | 21 | Yr Elen | 3156 | 962 |
| 39 | 42 | Moel Cynghorion | 2211 | 674 | 86 | 18 | Carnedd Fach | 3165 | 965 |
| 40 | 68 | Moel Druman | 2218 | 676 | 87 | 7 | Foel Grach | 3202 | 976 |
| 41 | 25 | Creigiau Gleision (S top) | 2224 | 678 | 88 | 17 | Pen Yr Ole Wen | 3208 | 978 |
| 42 | 3 | Carnedd Y Ddelw | 2257 | 688 | 89 | 30 | Glyder Fach | 3262 | 995 |
| 43 | 72 | Cnicht | 2260 | 689 | 90 | 29 | Glyder Fawr | 3283 | 1001 |
| 44 | 11 | Llwytmor Bach | 2264 | 690 | 91 | 19 | Carnedd Dafydd | 3425 | 1044 |
| 45 | 58 | Mynydd Drws Y Coed | 2280 | 695 | 92 | 20 | Carnedd Llywelyn | 3491 | 1064 |
| 46 | 67 | Allt-Fawr | 2289 | 698 | 93 | 45 | Carnedd Ugain | 3493 | 1065 |
| 47 | 56 | Mynydd Mawr | 2290 | 698 | 94 | 43 | Yr Wyddfa (Snowdon) | 3561 | 1086 |

Hills visited in this guide in ascending order of altitude
Numbers in bold print relate to individual hill numbers used in guide

# THE WALKS

| Walk | No. | Peak Name | H't (ft) | H't (m) | Ascent (metres) | Distance (Km) | Time (min) |
|---|---|---|---|---|---|---|---|
| Carneddau | | | | | | | |
| 1 | 1 | Foel Lwyd | 1978 | 603 | 315 | 5.90 | 120 |
| | 2 | Tal Y Fan | 2000 | 610 | | | |
| | 3 | Carnedd Y Ddelw | 2257 | 688 | | | |
| | 4 | Drum | 2529 | 771 | | | |
| | 5 | Foel-fras (Carneddau) | 3091 | 942 | | | |
| | 6 | Garnedd Uchaf | 3038 | 926 | | | |
| | 7 | Foel Grach | 3202 | 976 | | | |
| | 8 | Yr Aryg | 2837 | 865 | | | |
| | 9 | Bera Bach | 2647 | 807 | | | |
| 2 | 10 | Bera Mawr | 2604 | 794 | 1130 | 21.25 | 465 |
| 3 | 11 | Llwytmor Bach | 2264 | 690 | 795 | 9.60 | 270 |
| | 12 | Llwytmor | 2785 | 849 | | | |
| | | Crâs | 1558 | 475 | | | |
| | | Moel Wnion | 1902 | 580 | | | |
| | | Gyrn | 1778 | 542 | | | |
| | 13 | Gyrn Wigau | 2110 | 643 | | | |
| 4 | 14 | Drosgl | 2487 | 758 | 815 | 16.40 | 345 |
| | | Cefn Coch | 1591 | 485 | | | |
| | 15 | Pen Y Castell | 2044 | 623 | | | |
| 5 | 16 | Craig Eigiau | 2411 | 735 | 750 | 19.50 | 360 |
| | 17 | Pen Yr Ole Wen | 3208 | 978 | | | |
| | 18 | Carnedd Fach | 3165 | 965 | | | |
| | 19 | Carnedd Dafydd | 3425 | 1044 | | | |
| | 20 | Carnedd Llywelyn | 3491 | 1064 | | | |
| 6 | 21 | Yr Elen | 3150 | 960 | 1370 | 18.70 | 490 |
| | 22 | Pen Yr Helgi Du | 2733 | 833 | | | |
| 7 | 23 | Pen Llithrig Y Wrach | 2622 | 799 | 890 | 13.70 | 330 |
| | | Crimpiau | 1558 | 475 | | | |
| | | Craig Wen | 1797 | 548 | | | |
| | 24 | Craiglwyn | 2043 | 623 | | | |
| | 25 | Creigiau Gleision (S top) | 2224 | 678 | | | |
| 8 | 26 | Creigiau Gleision (N top) | 2080 | 634 | 830 | 16.50 | 345 |

| Walk | No. | Peak Name | H't (ft) | H't (m) | Ascent (metres) | Distance (Km) | Time (min) |
|---|---|---|---|---|---|---|---|
| | | Glyderau | | | | | |
| | | Cefn y Capel | 1509 | 460 | | | |
| | 27 | Y Foel Goch | 2641 | 805 | | | |
| 9 | 28 | Gallt Yr Ogof | 2503 | 763 | 790 | 9.75 | 270 |
| | 29 | Glyder Fawr | 3283 | 1001 | | | |
| | 30 | Glyder Fach | 3262 | 995 | | | |
| | 31 | Tryfan (Far South Peak) | 2709 | 826 | | | |
| 10 | 32 | Tryfan | 3010 | 917 | 1065 | 9.20 | 330 |
| | 33 | Y Garn | 3107 | 947 | | | |
| | 34 | Foel-Goch | 2726 | 831 | | | |
| | 35 | Elidir Fawr | 3031 | 924 | | | |
| | 36 | Elidir Fach | 2608 | 795 | | | |
| | 37 | Mynydd Perfedd | 2664 | 812 | | | |
| 11 | 38 | Carnedd Y Filiast | 2694 | 821 | 1380 | 16.25 | 470 |

| Walk | No. | Peak Name | H't (ft) | H't (m) | Ascent (metres) | Distance (Km) | Time (min) |
|---|---|---|---|---|---|---|---|
| | | Snowdon | | | | | |
| | 39 | Moel Eilio | 2383 | 727 | | | |
| | 40 | Foel Gron | 2063 | 629 | | | |
| 12 | 41 | Foel Goch | 1985 | 605 | 680 | 10.40 | 270 |
| | 42 | Moel Cynghorion | 2211 | 674 | | | |
| | 43 | Yr Wyddfa (Snowdon) | 3561 | 1086 | | | |
| 13 | 44 | Llechog | 2355 | 718 | 1275 | 17.30 | 450 |
| | 43 | Yr Wyddfa (Snowdon) | 3561 | 1086 | | | |
| | 45 | Carnedd Ugain | 3493 | 1065 | | | |
| | 46 | Crib Goch (W top) | 3028 | 923 | | | |
| | 47 | Crib Goch (E top) | 3021 | 921 | | | |
| 14 | 48 | The Cwm Dyli Horns | 1998 | 609 | 1100 | 11.80 | 360 |
| | 49 | Y Lliwedd (W top) | 2947 | 898 | | | |
| | 50 | Y Lliwedd (E top) | 2929 | 893 | | | |
| | 51 | Lliwedd Bach | 2683 | 818 | | | |
| 15 | 52 | Gallt Y Wenallt | 2032 | 620 | 1035 | 13.80 | 360 |
| | 53 | Yr Aran | 2451 | 747 | | | |
| | 54 | Craig Wen | 1994 | 608 | | | |
| | 55 | Clogwyn Du | 3054 | 931 | | | |
| 16 | 43 | Yr Wyddfa (Snowdon) | 3561 | 1086 | 1265 | 16.00 | 435 |

23

| Walk | No. | Peak Name | H't (ft) | H't (m) | Ascent (metres) | Distance (Km) | Time (min) |
|------|-----|-----------|----------|---------|-----------------|---------------|------------|
| | | | | | | | |
| Nantlle | | | | | | | |
| | | Foel Rudd | 1870 | 570 | | | |
| 17 | 56 | Mynydd Mawr | 2290 | 698 | 560 | 6.80 | 190 |
| | 57 | Y Garn | 2077 | 633 | | | |
| | 58 | Mynydd Drws Y Coed | 2280 | 695 | | | |
| | 59 | Trum Y Ddysgl | 2326 | 709 | | | |
| | 60 | Mynydd Tal-Y-Mignedd | 2142 | 653 | | | |
| | 61 | Craig Cwm Silyn | 2408 | 734 | | | |
| | 62 | Garnedd-Goch | 2297 | 700 | | | |
| 18 | 63 | Mynydd Graig Goch | 2000 | 610 | 1355 | 28.00 | 570 |
| | 64 | Moel Lefn | 2094 | 638 | | | |
| | 65 | Moel Yr Ogof | 2149 | 655 | | | |
| 19 | 66 | Moel Hebog | 2566 | 782 | 795 | 9.10 | 270 |

| Walk | No. | Peak Name | H't (ft) | H't (m) | Ascent (metres) | Distance (Km) | Time (min) |
|------|-----|-----------|----------|---------|-----------------|---------------|------------|
| Moelwynion | | | | | | | |
| | 67 | Allt-Fawr | 2289 | 698 | | | |
| | 68 | Moel Druman | 2218 | 676 | | | |
| | 69 | Ysgafell Wen | 2205 | 672 | | | |
| | 70 | Ysgafell Wen (unnamed top) | 2194 | 669 | | | |
| 20 | 71 | Moel Meirch | 1991 | 607 | 930 | 16.25 | 360 |
| | 72 | Cnicht | 2260 | 689 | | | |
| 21 | 73 | Foel Boethwel | 1975 | 602 | 575 | 9.00 | 210 |
| | 74 | Moelwyn Mawr | 2527 | 770 | | | |
| | 75 | Moelwyn Bach | 2329 | 710 | | | |
| | 76 | Moel-yr-Hydd | 2125 | 648 | | | |
| 22 | | Moel Bowydd | 1617 | 493 | 820 | 11.00 | 300 |
| | | Foel-fras (Moelwynion) | 1922 | 586 | | | |
| | 77 | Moel Penamnen | 2043 | 623 | | | |
| 23 | | Moel Farlwyd | 1893 | 577 | 500 | 9.50 | 210 |
| | 78 | Manod Mawr | 2169 | 661 | | | |
| | 79 | Graig-Ddu | 2158 | 658 | | | |
| 24 | | Manod Bach | 1676 | 511 | 785 | 9.50 | 270 |
| 25 | 80 | Carnedd Moel Siabod | 2861 | 872 | 775 | 10.00 | 270 |
| | 80 | Carnedd Moel Siabod | 2861 | 872 | | | |
| | | Clogwyn Bwlch-y-Maen | 1797 | 548 | | | |
| 26 | | Carnedd Y Cribau | 1938 | 591 | 985 | 20.00 | 410 |

# FURTHER READING

Some of the publications that I found most helpful and instructive are listed below, as are the ones I dipped into after completing the walks to make sense of what I had just seen.

| | |
|---|---|
| Steve Ashton: | HILLWALKING IN SNOWDONIA *(Cicerone)* |
| Steve Ashton: | RIDGES OF SNOWDONIA *(Cicerone)* |
| | |
| H M S O: | SNOWDONIA NATIONAL PARK *(H M S O)* |
| | |
| Dorothy Hamilton: | BUS AND RAIL WALKS IN AND AROUND THE CONWAY VALLEY *(Gwasg Carreg Gwalch 'Walk With History Series)* |
| | |
| K Mortimer Hart : | THE CONWY VALLEY & THE LANDS OF HISTORY *(Landmark Publishing)* |
| | |
| G M Howe +:<br>P Thomas | WELSH LANDFORMS & SCENERY *(Macmillan)* |
| | |
| Dewi Jones: | TYWYSYDDION ERYRI (The Guides of Snowdonia) *(Gwasg Carreg Gwalch)* |
| | |
| Iwan Arfon Jones: | ENWAU ERYRI (Place-names in Snowdonia)) *(Y Lolfa)* |
| | |
| Jonah Jones: | THE LAKES OF NORTH WALES *(Y Lolfa)* |
| | |
| David Kirk: | SNOWDONIA – A HISTORICAL ANTHOLOGY *(Gwasg Carreg Gwalch)* |
| | |
| Bryan Lynas: | SNOWDONIA ROCKY RAMBLES *(Sigma Leisure)* |
| | |
| Frances Lynch: | GWYNEDD : A GUIDE TO ANCIENT AND HISTORIC WALES *(CADW – HMSO)* |

Terry Marsh:        THE MOUNTAINS OF WALES
                    *(Hodder + Staunton)*
Terry Marsh:        THE SUMMITS OF SNOWDONIA
                    *(Robert Hale)*

R Millward +:       LANDSCAPES OF NORTH WALES
A Robinson          *(David + Charles)*

Ordnance Survey:    SNOWDONIA AND NORTH WALES
Leisure Guide       *(O. S.)*

Carl Rogers:        WALKING IN SNOWDONIA –
                    VOL 1 THE NORTHERN VALLEYS *(Mara Books)*

Not forgetting my monthly fix of 'TRAIL' magazine *(Emap Publishing)*

2 useful Web addresses :
***www.metoffice.gov.uk/loutdoor/mountainsafety/***
***www.traveline.org.uk***

# CARNEDDAU

*Most visitors to North Wales approach Snowdonia from the East – either along the A5 which pierces the flanks of the hills before emerging at the end of Nant Ffrancon, or along the more popular A55 which opts for a line closer to the coastal lowlands. This latter approach promises little of the majestic views to come until it begins the snaking run down Rhuallt Hill East of St. Asaph.*

*Then suddenly, on the horizon, if you are lucky enough to have clear conditions, you may catch your breath. What's that isolated top on the distant horizon, vaguely shaped like a shark-fin? It can only be Moel Siabod. Tucked further back to the right – the Snowdon 'Horseshoe', and Tryfan's bristling crest. And finally, that grey mass creeping towards the cliff tops of Penmaenmawr; the Carneddau.*

*The Carneddau massif is the second largest area of consistently high ground in the United Kingdom – second only to the Cairngorms. Yet its hills are approachable even to the least experienced hill-walker.*

## TASTER 1

*Anyone interested in taking a closer look at these hills but with only limited route-finding skills or hill-walking experience could do a lot worse than spend some time getting acquainted with the North Wales Path.*

*The most scenic section runs from the outskirts of Bangor to Conwy and can be consumed in simple bite-sized units – anything from two to five miles at a time.*

*For example, if you have a couple of hours to spare, drive past Hendre Farm (just off the A55 – Tal-y-Bont exit) up the steep hill to the start point of **Walk 4**. You can then explore the North Wales Path as it runs West to East.*

*One enjoyable section follows the same route as **Walk 4** and you can continue along the path beyond **point 3** until you reach the high slopes overlooking Abergwyngregyn. From there you can turn back and retrace your steps or press on, following the steep descent that exits the main footpath left. This short-cut drops down to the minor road heading up this side valley (to the start of the path serving the Aber Falls). The village of Abergwyngregyn is only a short distance down the road on your left – in the lay-by opposite the Aber Falls Hotel a bus-stop provides transport back to Hendre Farm.*

**Distance – about 4 miles**

## TASTER 2

*This is an easy one to recommend.*

*From the village of Abergwyngregyn continue up-valley as if approaching the start point of **Walk 3**. If there is space, park in the roadside bays before reaching the bridge at Bont Newydd (now cursed with 'Park + Display' status). From here follow the well-signposted path along the valley of the Afon Rhaeadr-fawr to the foot of the Aber Falls.*

*This is a walker-friendly path that attracts mountain bikers, hikers, nature lovers and families looking for a picnic spot when the sun is out.*

**Allow about 2 hours for the walk to the falls and back, although a straight hike there and back will take no longer than 1½.**


## TASTER 3

*Start again as if heading for Llwytmor – but from the start point of **Walk 3** continue along the low level path leading to Llyn Anafon. There's enough here to draw the eye and feed the senses without need to labour across any contours.*


## TASTER 4

*You have a choice to make here.*

*Follow the directions for the approach to **Walk 1** and after parking at the start point it is easy enough to hike as far as the highest point of Bwlch y Ddeufaen. That in itself gives a feel for this neck of the woods.*

*Alternatively use the path from the roadside at **point 7** to walk directly to the top of Tal Y Fan. There's a bit of clambering over rocks, but if the ground is dry and visibility clear it's a piece of cake and gives an airy perspective of the North Wales coast.*

**45mins up – 30mins down.**

# TASTER 5

*From the map, Llyn Eigiau looks worth a visit. Well it's not much to write home about, unless you are prepared to go beyond the head of the shrunken lake into Cwm Eigiau itself. The desolate valley that lies beyond the reservoir is certainly worth walking the extra couple of kilometres for. In summer or winter it is a magical place.*

*Otherwise, if you are after a pleasant spot in which to picnic, head along* **Walk 5** *as far as* **point 2**, *but instead of turning right, go straight ahead between the two large rocks, following the path as it zig-zags uphill (***Option 2** *in reverse, basically). The path soon sweeps left into the broad valley of Pant Y Griafolen. The outcrop of Cerrig Cochion on the right-hand side of the path provides a wonderful spot to relax, enjoy the scenery and perhaps mess about on the bare rock.*

**Cerrig Cochion are less than ½ an hour's walk from the car park.**


# TASTER 6

*The high tops of* **Walk 6** *are strictly for the experienced hill-walker – or at least someone committed to spending a full and probably exhausting day on the hills.*

*However, making use of the parking bays strung out along this section of the Ogwen valley, anyone can leave their vehicle for a half hour or so and wander along the shore of Llyn Ogwen to take a closer look at the Carneddau.*

*From Ogwen Cottage to Glan Dena there is more than enough of the lake shore to investigate. The setting could not be more dramatic – particularly in winter when the tops are snow-covered.*


# TASTER 7

To get a closer feel for Carnedd Llywelyn and its neighbours, however, there is a relatively pain-free option. Following the service road to the reservoir of Ffynnon Llugwy should not be beyond the ability of most unseasoned walkers – although it is a horribly steep slog for the first couple of kilometres.

But once you cross the waterway or leat (at **point 3** of **Walk 7**) it becomes less of a climb. And if you follow this Landrover track as far as the shores of Ffynnon Llugwy you will feel you have reached the heart of these mountains.

There are also superb views behind you across Nant y Benglog towards the Glyderau.

**Distance – less than 4 miles**


# TASTER 8

There is a perfectly pleasant circular walk from the car park behind the shops where **Walk 8** begins.

Once on the A5 follow it towards Betws-y-Coed for about 700 metres. On the left hand side of the road there is a private car park and campsite entrance just before you reach the driveway to the Youth Hostel.

Follow the sign-posted path towards the campsite, passing buildings on the left before turning right towards the main campsite – there is a ladder stile on your left giving access to a meadow with another ladder stile ahead. Cross this second stile to join a path which climbs gently across another meadow to a third ladder stile. In early summer these meadows are a sea of bluebells. Wherever you pause along this walk, look behind you and there are brilliant views, in particular of Moel Siabod.

Once you cross the third ladder stile a path on your left leads back to the A5 and emerges opposite the shops behind which you parked.

**This walk will take no longer than 45 minutes.**


*If you managed any of these without a problem and would like to explore more, how about tackling some of the 'real' walks that follow?*

# Foel Lwyd [1] / Tal y Fan [2]

| | |
|---|---|
| 5.9 Km (3.7 miles)<br><br>315m (1033ft)<br><br>Time : 2hrs | Two tops that form the first links in a chain of summits that runs between the valleys of the Conwy and Ogwen |

From the Eastern banks of the Conwy estuary, particularly in the vicinity of Deganwy, Tal y Fan assumes a prominent position on the skyline above Conwy Castle. But it is a green hill flanked by verdant fields not a grey, barren hump, littered with rocks. So although this and its lowlier neighbour belong to the Carneddau range, they hardly look the part. I had never considered setting foot on their slopes despite visiting most of the neighbouring peaks on several occasions. In fact, it was only when researching this book that I realised how high they were.

Carnedd Llywelyn, the third highest mountain in Wales, is surrounded by more ground above 3000ft than the rest of England and Wales combined. In such a setting, it is understandable why Foel Lwyd and Tal y Fan fail to appear on most 'must-visit' lists. But if you have a couple of hours to spare then put them on yours and get out there. Like many of the walks in this book, they provide a fresh outlook on Snowdonia. Whether you are looking for a quick hike on a sunny afternoon or an easy 'walk on the wild side' for children not yet bitten by the hill-walking bug, these two are guaranteed to fit the bill.

**North**

**Don't forget**

**map/compass**
**whistle/torch**

**suitable footwear**
**+ clothing**

**food/drink**

**brain**

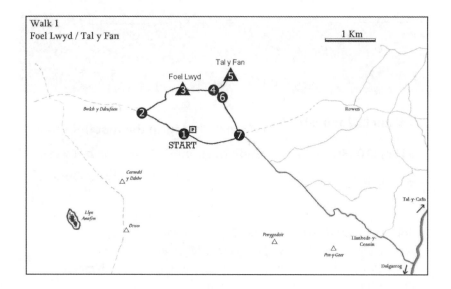

Walk 1
Foel Lwyd / Tal y Fan

1 Km

## APPROACH

From the A55, at the main Llandudno exit take the A470 South signposted Llanrwst. Follow this road for about 7Km then as you pass the Tal-y-Cafn public house on your right, turn right (sign-posted Ty'n y Groes and Dolgarrog). This road crosses a railway line then the bridge over the Afon Conwy. It then takes a sharp left and after a short set of twists and turns eventually climbs to a T-junction (more a staggered cross-roads actually). Turn left at this junction onto the B5106.

Pass two turnings right (sign-posted Rowen), followed by the cemetery, then on entering Tal-y-Bont village take the first turning right (signposted Llanbedr-y-Cennin) with 'Y Bedol' ('The Horseshoe') inn and the village school just beyond the junction.

From the A5 at the South Eastern outskirts of Betws-y-Coed, take the main exit North (signposted Llanrwst and Conwy – A470) practically alongside the Waterloo Bridge. Follow this road for about 6Km until you reach Llanrwst. Upon entering the town the road bears left across a railway bridge after which you must take the first junction left before entering the main shopping street. This road to the left, only wide enough for traffic to proceed one way at any one time, transports you across the arched bridge spanning the Afon Conwy (signposted Trefriw).

At the T-junction on the opposite bank of the Conwy turn right and continue along this road, passing through Trefriw and Dolgarrog. About 1Km after passing the Dolgarrog aluminium plant on your right, having entered the village of Tal-y-bont, go past the village school on your left, followed by 'Y Bedol' inn, and on your left is a side-road signposted Llanbedr-y-Cennin.

You are now on a narrow road that climbs pretty steeply onto the shelf of high ground overlooking the Conwy valley. Shortly you will reach 'Ye Olde Bull Inn' on your left – continue beyond it uphill rather than taking the side-road right.

*After one particularly steep climb, the views open out slightly revealing the first bit of high ground on your left – Pen-y-Gaer then Penygadair.*
*On your right is a long, fairly level ridge – the bumpy top of Tal Y Fan, and further left the shorter stretch to Foel Lwyd. From this point along the road they look a bit of a handful – distance rather than height.*

But there's a bit more driving to do yet. Pass a minor road on the right, then drop down to cross a bridge in the incised valley of the Afon Tafolog. As the road climbs again you pass another minor road on the right (to Rowen), followed by the unmetalled road on your right to Rhiw Youth Hostel at the point where your road veers slightly left. A footpath on the right just past the Youth Hostel driveway gives direct access to Tal Y Fan's summit. But to combine the two summits it is best to continue along the road, cross the cattle grid and park at a pull-in point where a gate prohibits one driving any further [1-01].

There is space here for between fifteen and twenty vehicles, primarily because this is a convenient starting or finishing point for walkers doing the '15 Peaks Challenge' which combines all the official 3000ft tops of Wales – starting with Foel-fras (by way of Drum) and ending with Snowdon.

# START

1)    (721715)        →

     275°             →

As if this walk wasn't easy enough, its starting point at 414 metres above sea-level is the highest in the guide. A ladder stile alongside a gate gives access onto the broad track that continues up-valley. This follows the high pass of Bwlch y Ddeufaen, a high level route of significant importance from as far back as the Bronze Age.

Bwlch y Ddeufaen has long been a strategically important inland route linking Anglesey and the West to the more populous lands East of the Vale of Conwy.

Until the last 250 years or so anyone crossing North Wales had the choice of following this bleak, high level route or risking a more treacherous passage along the coastal lowlands. The latter involved negotiating the dangerous, precipitous headlands of Penmaen-bach and Penmaen Mawr.

Crossing the Afon Conwy at its estuary was also a more hazardous operation due to unpredictable tides. The safer option was to utilise the ferry at Tal-y-cafn (close to where the Bwlch y Ddeufaen route drops down into the main valley). As recently as 1800, before the upper reaches of the Conwy began to silt up, sea-going vessels were able to sail upstream as far as Tal-y-cafn.

In the heyday of droving, the route across Bwlch y Ddeufaen to the ferry crossing at Tal-y-cafn was a major drovers' road. Traffic in livestock through local centres such as Llanrwst was considerable. In 1810 some 6000-8000 cattle and four times as many sheep were driven from Anglesey to the middle of England or the outskirts of London. Significantly, during the Glyndŵr 'rebellion', there was an embargo on Welsh livestock – but even so, cattle from North Wales were still illicitly traded in parts of Cheshire.

I am fascinated by the notion of huge droves of livestock being walked from North Wales to the markets of Mid- or Southern England along what are now little more than hill tracks (the journey usually taking two or three weeks to complete). Each drove consisted of several hundred cattle and sheep as well as pigs and geese. In the days before Vibram, to avoid wear and tear to their feet, the cattle were shod in metal 'shoes'. Pigs and sheep wore boots of wool and leather, and the feet of the geese were protected by a mixture of tar and sand. Small dogs were employed to keep the herds together, while most of the drovers from hereabouts rode Welsh ponies (no doubt equine ancestors of the ones still found grazing in the more sheltered valleys of the Carneddau).

As you pass under the overhead transmission lines for the first time you get a fairly good view of the way ahead with the slopes leading up onto Carnedd y Ddelw on your left and the steep flanks of Foel Lwyd on your right. On the horizon immediately ahead of you stands a wall with a distinctive gap in it [1-02]. That's **point 2** – just so you know in advance. Drawing closer to this wall you will notice a massive, pointed standing stone adjacent to your path on the left, and further ahead on its right a slightly larger more rectangular standing stone. These are the two stones that give the pass its name [1-03].

**2)**     **(712719)**     →

        **60°**     →

The dry-stone wall ahead of you is the highest point of Bwlch y Ddeufaen (close to the 430-metre contour) [1-04]. Cross it by the gate or ladder stile then exit right to descend along the lee of the wall towards an electricity pylon posed on a little patch of green [1-05]. A path skirts the left-hand side of this metal monstrosity before veering to the right along the lower margins of a pile of loose rock towards the wall again. Take time to look at the views behind you as you gain height; perhaps to get your bearings for future reference with regard to the rest of the Carneddau massif further South [1-06 looking back downhill].

        **0°**     →

Loose rock merges into a small heap of waste (just the other side of this wall is an abandoned quarry – probably the work of the small-holder who once farmed this side of the hillside). Keeping within touching distance of the wall, your path climbs up steep vegetated slopes to a ladder stile occupying the corner where the main wall angles left and a second wall joins it from the right-hand side. Keep on the same side of the main wall and continue uphill to where it abruptly turns right (close to **717724** where the angle of slope also relents briefly). As you scan the horizon to the North you are confronted by evidence of quarrying on a much vaster scale – the monumental rock workings atop Penmaen Mawr [1-07]. Much of the vast excavation is hidden from the A55 that runs beneath the beetling slopes of this bulky headland but from here you begin to get some idea of the scale of the operation.

75°    →

*A number of massive boulders lie sunning themselves on the turf-covered slopes facing West. Perhaps it's a hint to stop a while and take in the scenery [1-08]. From here there are excellent views across to Carnedd y Ddelw and Drum. It is possible to follow the Bwlch y Ddeufaen track Westwards to where it eventually joins the North Wales Path (linking Bangor to Prestatyn). Further right the cliff-tops of Penmaen Mawr stand level with blue horizon, while closer at hand to their left is the nameless mound (grassed on top but walled with grey scree) above Llanfairfechan's valley road – the site of an Iron Age settlement [1-09].*

More steep grass quickly leads you onto the first top of the day. There is nothing here to mark the actual summit, but large rocks on the other side of the wall (on your right-hand side) are probably the highest point of **Foel Lwyd** (at **720723** – 603m/1978ft).

There are protruding step stones set in the dry-stone wall allowing you to cross over and set foot on the highest point if you so wish.

3)    (720723)    →

90°    →

*Back on the left-hand side of the wall the rocky summit of Tal y Fan is clearly visible immediately to the East across the slight dip ahead of you.*
*It is also worth taking another look seawards – Anglesey, Puffin Island and Traeth Lafan can now be clearly picked out as well as the massive quarry hollowing out the top of Penmaen Mawr.*

A narrow path heads away from the wall, weaving its way downslope through clumps of heather. In places it has been incised into the peat and no doubt gets wet following periods of heavy rain. On reaching the broad, level saddle separating Foel Lwyd from Tal y Fan, another path runs left to right to a ladder stile in the wall on your right [1-10]. Cross this stile to gain the Southern slopes of Tal y Fan's main ridge.

**4)     (727724)     →**

       30°          →

From here you will see a dry-stone wall snaking its way up the steep face of Tal y Fan. Follow the line of this wall uphill all the way – crossing a series of grassy platforms connected by patches of large angular blocks and boulder piles that provide a more intriguing challenge than Foel Lwyd's ascent. You may even have to take your hands out of your pockets before you are able to set foot on the actual summit.

From the last shelf of deep heather you are finally greeted by the welcome sight of a proper summit cairn [1-11] a short distance ahead – a squat, square tower topped by a few rougher blocks [1-12] marking the top of **Tal y Fan** (at **729726** – 610m/2001ft).

*The highest point of the day provides a worthy viewpoint. Due East stretches the Conwy valley – the river, bordered by fields and trees and a small lake which according to the OS map didn't seem to exist!\* Turning clockwise, the shapely ridge of Pen-y-Gaer – Penygadair – Pen y Castell. The higher summits to the right partly obscured by Drum. Then facing North – across the ladder stile set in the dry-stone wall – the mass of Penmaen Mawr, Foel Lûs, Penmaen-bach just beyond the Sychnant Pass, and finally Conwy Mountain with Conwy Sands and the Great Orme poised above.*

If you have time on your hands it is possible to spend another quarter of an hour or so exploring the Eastern section of this long ridge in order to maximise the views on offer. But beyond **734729** the slopes begin to descend perhaps a little too steeply South and East towards Rhiw Youth Hostel. The best option is to retreat to the top itself before attempting any descent route.

**5)**   **(729726)**   →

   210°   →

Retracing your steps is an easy jaunt back to the ladder stile at **point 4**. From there, facing South, a clear path (dried mud studded with rocks) heads towards a slender marker post on the immediate skyline. Beyond this post the ground eases itself downslope. The dry-stone wall on the right-hand side of your path meets another wall running across slope left to right.

Before the two walls meet, a ladder stile allows you to cross the wall on your right and join a clear path heading downslope [1-13]. On the Explorer map this path is shown crossing the wall that stands immediately ahead of you rather than the wall on your right. I know. I'm just being picky but the most practical route is along the only visible path, the one crossing this stile.

**6)**   **(727723)**   →

   160°   →

Another marker post identifies the route ahead but the path is never in doubt [1-14]. Crossing rough pasture and cutting a broad swathe through the heather, it eventually leads you to another wall (with ladder stile). Beyond this a clear footpath leads to a dry-stone wall where a ladder-stile deposits you at the road alongside a public footpath sign.

You will notice the wide grass verge has been eroded in places by vehicle tyres – a clear sign that it's a popular parking spot for those walkers opting to reach Tal y Fan by the more direct approach without a diversion to Foel Lwyd first.

**7)**    **(731715)**      →

       **245°**      →

You don't really need detailed compass directions back to the car. Once you have crossed the stile turn right and head uphill and within just over 1 Km you are back at the starting point.

   * Oh – that mystery lake visible from the summit of Tal y Fan? As I drove back in the direction of Ty'n y Groes, there it was on the right hand side of the road – a recently furrowed field covered in long strips of polythene. Perhaps I should give the map makers more credit.

**END**

# Carnedd y Ddelw [3] / Drum [4] / Foel-fras [5] / Garnedd Uchaf [6] / Foel Grach [7] / Yr Aryg [8] / Bera Bach [9] / Bera Mawr [10]

**21.25 Km (13.3 miles)**

**1130m (3706ft)**

**Time : 7hrs 45min**

**The Northernmost Carneddau are often shunned by the Dyffryn Ogwen brigade, but are worth exploring for the splendid views, and a change of perspective on one of the consistently highest mountain regions outside Scotland.**

What's the windiest bit of Snowdonia? If you ask me, it's this Northern section of the Carneddau without a doubt.

I've frequently nibbled the edges of this cracker – a foggy encounter on Bera Mawr and Bera Bach one wet Sunday – a quick dash onto Drum during the Christmas break when hoar frost clung like tinsel to the wire fencing – an unseasonably balmy February day – and I have yet to experience a calm day here. I've had the breath snatched from my lips fiercely enough to fear asphyxiation, and once had to abandon any attempts at crossing over a stile due to the remorseless gale. Even when I chose an incredibly sunny May day to finally complete all eight tops following a favourable weather forecast there was no let up. Hot and sunny on the beach – brisk and blustery on the tops. You have been warned.

It's a big day out in semi-wilderness, with your navigation skills tested to the limit if the cloud should drop – but it can be easily adapted to suit the weather conditions or each individual's stamina level.

**North**

**Don't forget**

**map/compass whistle/torch**

**suitable footwear + clothing**

**food/drink**

**brain**

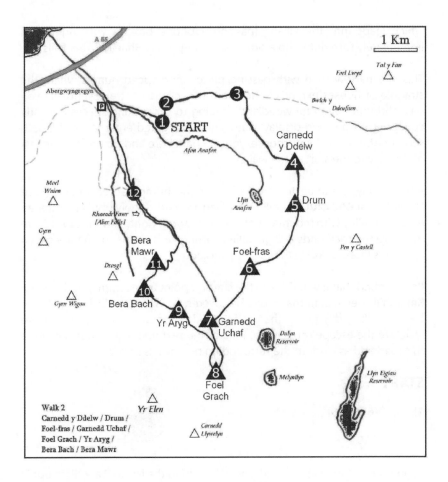

## APPROACH

If you have already had occasion to study the approach directions to the neighbouring summits of Llwytmor Bach and Llwytmor **(Walk 3)** then this bit is identical as far as Bont Newydd.

From the A55 expressway take the Abergwyngregyn (Aber) exit. If driving from the direction of Bangor, bear right under the dual-carriageway and at the T-junction turn left towards the Aber Falls Hotel. If driving from the direction of Llandudno, the slip road brings you to a T-junction with the Aber Falls Hotel opposite you on your left. Take the road to the right of the hotel which leads into the village (passing a phone box on your right) and immediately turn right into a side road (sign-posted 'Rhaeadr Aber Falls').

This is a narrow road with passing places (and speed humps where the straggle of houses extends South from the village centre). Eventually you pass through delightful woodland, leading to car parking spaces (recently converted to 'pay-and-display' status) near the gated entrance to the path serving Aber Falls. If you choose, you can park here and go on foot the rest of the way to the start of the walk.

Alternatively, continue to drive left over the hump-backed bridge (Bont Newydd – at **663720**) and follow the narrow road steeply uphill to enter an enclosed valley with mountains ahead and to your right. Continue for 1.5 Km to where the road ends in a gravelled cutting with ample room for a dozen or so cars (at **676716**) [2-01 from the path above]).

Bear in mind that if you drive to the starting point as recommended, this 1.5 Km uphill stretch of tarmac has to be covered on foot at the END of what can be a gruelling day rather than at the START. The decision is yours. But to facilitate the escape routes described in the text your car is best parked at this road end as close to the surrounding hillsides as possible.

## START

1)      (676716)      →

        350°          →

Facing this cutting in the hillside, head left along the North Wales Path uphill as it follows a dry-stone wall, aiming for the pylons on the skyline. A wire fence close to the beginning of this path is easily crossed by way of an antiquated, cast-iron ladder stile (minus its top rungs) [2-02]. Beyond this piece of gymnastic equipment the grass track climbs quite steeply to the 250-metre contour where it broadens into a gravelled cart track. Shortly, as the angle relents, this track takes a distinctive turn right beneath a convoy of overhead power lines heading towards Bwlch y Ddeufaen.

Bwlch y Ddeufaen is a significant, high-level gap in the landscape between the Conwy valley and all areas to the West. The coastal lowlands were impassable until the last 250 years or so when transit improved (barring Bank Holiday weekends when gridlock is now the problem, rather than marshland, rocky headlands, unpredictable tides and impenetrable forest).

The Romans built a road using part of the col; the main thoroughfare between the copper mines of Parys Mountain on Anglesey and the port of Bridlington! But it is quite likely that a route existed here much earlier for the export of stone axes from Graig Llwyd (nearby on the flanks of Penmaen Mawr) to the continent.

Many marker stones and burial cairns from the Iron Age and Bronze Age testify to its strategic importance prior to the arrival of the Romans. The route was also used by Cromwell's forces when they rode to Caernarfon some 500 years ago.

Some of you may wonder why so much electricity is needed in this empty corner of North Wales. The overhead power lines for the most part run from the Wylfa nuclear power station on Anglesey (soon to be decommissioned) to feed the voracious appetite of the aluminium refinery in Dolgarrog (historically a major employer in the Conwy valley to the East but under threat of closure at the time of writing). One line continues beyond this valley to supply the domestic requirements of the more populated areas East of the Denbigh Moors.

2)    (676720)      →

      70°            →

It is straightforward enough from here on as the cart track skirts the Northern slopes of Foel Dduarth and Foel-ganol.

*To the North the proximity of the sea is suddenly evident – the vast flats of Traeth Lafan (sandbanks clearly visible at low tide), Puffin Island and Penmon lighthouse at the Eastern tip of Anglesey. And the occasional container ship floating like a Lego brick on the horizon en route East to Liverpool. To the right, the bulky promontory of Penmaen Mawr rises sheer above the shore. 4500 years ago its summit was a hive of activity – the ancient quarries of Graig Llwyd being the site of a Stone Age axe factory. Now most of the rock is carted away by tipper wagons to surface our motorways.*

*Further East, a few miles offshore of Y Rhyl and Prestatyn, stands a row of 30 white towers comprising a wind farm. Much local debate has been held regarding their aesthetic impact on the seascape (particularly with the threat of a further 270 to be located offshore closer to Llandudno). Perhaps in the long run they are a reasonable alternative to the jumble of wire and metal that scars the hillsides beside and ahead of you now.*

**3)**  **(693722)**  →

   105°  →

Uncertain if this cart track is heading anywhere? Fear not. A signpost stands at the crossroads in the paths [2-03]. Aber behind you, Rowen ahead (along the Roman Road crossing the bleak expanse of Bwlch y Ddeufaen), Llanfairfechan left (maintaining the North Wales Path's link to the coastline) and Drum to your right. Go right [2-04], and follow the broad track as it threads its way between Pen Bryn-du and Blaen y Ddalfa.

---

### OPTION 1

The day's first summit can also be reached by following the overhead power lines (and the Roman Road) East as far as **712719** where you meet a stone wall descending from the slopes to the right.

Follow the line of this wall uphill (the side of the wall you choose to follow is up to you – and the direction of the prevailing wind). In places the going is wet underfoot, but substantial stepping stones make the worst sections easily bypassed.

The wall tops out at 665 metres (**705708**) at a small cairn.

Bear left here and Carnedd y Ddelw is immediately to your left again at the highest point of the ridge so far, overlooking the featureless ground to the East.

***Additional time for this alternative route is negligible. But the going underfoot is considerably more difficult, particularly after heavy rain.***

---

Ahead of you, the twin humps of Carnedd y Ddelw and Drum lie low on the horizon [2-05] before the upper Afon Anafon valley eventually opens out at your feet [2-06]. Tucked into the head of the valley, the Llyn Anafon reservoir at the base of Llwytmor draws the eye like a magnet. Bear left and continue along the broad path, heading right and rising gradually towards the main summit of Drum. As the track begins to show signs of erosion, it is worth veering left to attain the day's first summit; a small cairn marking the top of **Carnedd y Ddelw** (at **707705** – 688m/2257ft) perched above the upper Tafolog valley.

**4)**      **(707705)**      → 

        180°           →

There's not that much to detain one here, particularly with so much still to do. You can either contour South to rejoin the eroded track and follow it uphill, or stick to the coarse grass and follow the fence-line. As the gradient eases locate the step stile in the wire fence on your left beyond which stands a small stone windbreak marking the top of **Drum** (at **708695** – 771m/2529ft) [2-07].

An alternative name exists for this summit – Carnedd Pen-y-dorth Goch on older OS maps has been replaced by Carnedd Penyborth-Goch on the current Explorer map. The former name is probably a printing error, since Pen-y-dorth Goch translates as 'Summit of the red loaf' – an unlikely title for this particular top.

**5)**      **(708695)**      →

        235°           →

Having made the most of the limited protection from the wind offered by this shelter, recross the step stile and turn left, keeping to the broad track as it dips towards a shallow col. Foel-fras dominates the skyline ahead, with its cliffs to your right looking particularly imposing. If the wind persists you may be grateful for the two sets of crags on the left of your path that provide some protection from the Eastern tundra. Too soon the hillside opens up again, an expanse of golden turf as far removed from Grade 1 as is possible (unless we are talking haircuts rather than scrambles).

The ground is boggy in places, particularly in the col of the aptly named Bwlch y Gwynt (at **707691**) [2-08] but much of the path is paved here [2-09]. As this sinewy track begins to attack the slope direct, a spongier option runs parallel to it on the left where a faint line of trampled grass runs closer to the wire fence. Keep to the right of this fence as it transforms into a stone wall [2-10] which eventually crests the summit (with ladder stiles at either end – ignore both). Take one last glimpse behind you at the path you have just followed from Drum [2-11]. Now turn to confront this newly-gained top – a mass of frost-splintered rock [2-12], with a trig point set into a small rock pillar [2-13] identifying the summit of **Foel-fras** (at **697681** – 942m/3091ft).

*This is where the views are worth the effort of the walk for perhaps the first time – Carnedd Llywelyn and Carnedd Dafydd loom large, but pride of place is taken by the truncated prow of Yr Elen.*
*Further right across the deep valley of Nant Ffrancon, the guillotined flanks of Mynydd Perfedd and Carnedd y Filiast point North, with the graceful pyramid of Elidir Fawr surmounting both in the distance.*

In September 2009 the Ordnance Survey, after being petitioned by members of the 'Gwenllian Society', took the unprecedented step of agreeing to add Carnedd Gwenllian as an alternative name for Garnedd-Uchaf on any future maps covering this area.

Princess Gwenllian, the daughter of Llywelyn ap Gruffudd and Eleanor de Montfort, was born in June 1282 at Abergarthcelyn (later renamed Abergwyngregyn). Her mother died shortly after giving birth.
Wales came under Norman control when Llywelyn was killed in December 1282. The baby Gwenllian was Llywelyn's natural heir but Edward I, King of England, was afraid that one day she might have children who could rebel against him, so at the age of a little over one she was taken to the convent at Sempringham in Lincolnshire. She spent the rest of her life there and died there in June 1337 aged 54.

The Gwenllian Society fought to have her name immortalised in the mountains that already bear the names of her father and uncle (Carnedd Llywelyn and Carnedd Dafydd respectively). Now finally the Princess has been reunited in spirit at least with her father and his brother in their homeland.

**6)     (697681)     →**

**225°          →**

It is a pleasant stroll from here to the next summit once the rocks give way to grass again. Downhill most of the way – an outcrop of boulders [2-14] in the shape of any number of Dartmoor's numerous tors makes a feeble attempt at guarding access to the flat summit with its cairn a short distance West – the top of **Garnedd Uchaf** (at **687669** – 926m/3038ft).

**7)     (687669)     →**

**170°          →**

Little time to loiter here – and there are better spots to linger later. But Yr Elen is sure to draw the eye [2-15] before you are forced to scrutinise the track climbing Foel Grach to your left [2-16] with the backdrop of Carnedd Llywelyn beyond.

A broad depression separates Garnedd Uchaf from Foel Grach, and as you reach its lowest point take a moment or two to savour the shapely lines of Yr Elen and Cwm Caseg on the right [2-17].

From here the gradient increases significantly but the path covers easy ground before finally bringing you up against grey turrets of rock. A small roofed shelter occupies the Northern lee of this jumble of crags [2-18 and 2-19], but the fun lies ahead in picking a line through the jagged outcrops. Whether you head to the left or right of the shelter you may be inclined to remove your hands from your pockets for the first time today. With minimal effort, you reach an extensive boulder-field on which stands the summit of **Foel Grach**, the highest point you will reach today (at **688658** – 976m/3202ft).

This is one of the most exposed tops of the Carneddau, particularly when the weather is unfavourable, as there is little shelter to be found amongst the splintered rocks that make up the summit plateau [2-20].

One stormy May day when I visited these tops some years ago I was waylaid by a gentleman enquiring whether or not I had come across any dotterels. He was looking for a pair that he believed was in the vicinity. Given the wind, I would guess that any right-minded dotterel would more likely than not be found wading at the beach rather than searching for grub up here, although I later learned that these wading birds do actually favour higher ground. The fact that he had travelled here from Hoylake in search of these elusive birds spoke volumes.

**8)     (688658)     →**

      **350°          →**

From this summit, the half-way point of the walk incidentally, you now have to retrace your steps in the direction of Garnedd Uchaf. It is, however, worthwhile dropping downslope to your left to maximise the close-up views of Yr Elen. There is no finer spot from which to study this shapely peak [2-21]. Once you reach the broad col at **688664** a clear path strikes left. This leads you to the next section of the walk, on terrain subtly different from that you have covered so far.

---

**OPTION 2**
If the weather conditions are such that you are relying on map and compass for route-finding, the more prudent among you might consider a simple reversal at this point, omitting the final three peaks.
*Time saved on retracing your steps from here, approximately 1½ hrs.*

---

The remaining peaks are quite different in character to the five already visited, largely due to the change in geology to a more resistant material. The first half of the walk involved broad paths and a rolling landscape, with one wave of rising ground succeeded by another at slightly higher altitude. The second half is pretty much an improvised slog, punctuated by jagged outcrops that emerge from the featureless, occasionally boggy surroundings like bony growths [2-22].

The faint path contouring the Southern flanks of Garnedd Uchaf eventually leads to Bera Bach (which can be seen in the distance), but it is worthwhile bearing further right towards the nearby outcrop of Yr Aryg (which barely pokes above its surroundings yet is less than 50 metres below the magical 3000ft mark).

Resembling a geological Acropolis plonked onto the gentle terrain surrounding it, Yr Aryg screams and swears at you to climb it – or at least give it a hug since you're passing so close. It looks interesting. It certainly needs some hands-on work, so how can you possibly resist? And it's an excellent way to get into mountain-goat mode that might be needed for later in the day. Reaching the flat, square patio of bare rock that forms **Yr Aryg**'s 'summit' (at **681674** – 865m/2837ft) is an exhilarating, but simple scramble. Standing king-of-the-castle on its top, the two remaining summits cannot be mistaken (unless the cloud is closing in, in which case this is your last opportunity to return to the main path and retrace your steps North).

THE NEXT SECTION IS A SERIOUS UNDERTAKING IN LOW CLOUD OR UNDER SNOW DUE TO THE LACK OF CLEAR PATHS. THE ESCAPE ROUTE OF THE NORTH WALES PATH IS ONLY A SHORT DISTANCE NORTH, BUT THE CONVEX SLOPES YOU MUST TRAVERSE TO REACH IT ARE TAXING AND GOOD NAVIGATIONAL SKILLS ARE ESSENTIAL FOR MUCH OF THE WAY.

9)  (681674)  →

    295°  →

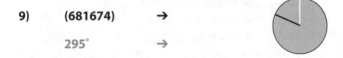

Heading on the same bearing, Bera Bach on the low skyline ahead of you looks close enough to touch – a small cock's-comb of rock on the horizon. The ground you must cross to reach it is relatively easy as long as you steer clear of the peaty hollows (some waterlogged) and the prolific evidence underfoot of the feral ponies that graze this part of the Carneddau. **Bera Bach** (at **672677** – 807m/2647ft) is in fact the higher of the pair, but gains its misnomer by virtue of its relative size [2-23]. Again, it's a little gem to climb, and reaching its summit reveals outstanding views, particularly to the West.

*Anglesey and the Menai Strait are still there to the North. Caernarfon and the hills of Llŷn (principally Yr Eifl) are clearly visible to the West. And alongside, the Southern Carneddau rise majestically with their neighbours across Nant Ffrancon.*

**10)  (672677)        →**

**70°              →**

In comparison, Bera Mawr on your right looks like its neighbour's evil, overgrown twin – an almost insurmountable monolith of grey rock; enormous when compared to this tiddler under your feet [2-24]. The easiest approach as you descend from the highest spot is to circle Bera Bach in an anti-clockwise direction heading West then North before creeping up on Bera Mawr's South Western flanks.

---

### OPTION 3

A less exhausting escape route, by-passing Bera Mawr totally, can be utilised by heading South West from Bera Bach beneath the slopes of its neighbour Drosgl. On this heading you will meet with a path going downhill all the while and eventually branching North (at **652690**).
This path contours the Eastern slopes of Moel Wnion.
For clearer details refer to **Walk 4**.
Exit stage right from this path down steep slopes (the left bank of the Afon Gam complete with waterfalls) to join the North Wales Path in the vicinity of **661701**.
Once you emerge on this clear track, continue right all the way to the foot of the Aber Falls. Cross the river nearby by a wooden footbridge below this path then rejoin the main gravelled 'tourist' path that heads away from the Falls along the valley floor and rejoins the main walk at **point 12 (668702)**.

*Time saved approximately 1hr – as well as a good deal of exertion.*

---

As you turn your back on the scrappy boulder fields that litter Bera Bach's lower slopes, make a bee-line across tussocky grass to the left edge of Bera Mawr. Climbing the first few layers of slab is easy, and you quickly gain the heart of this rocky citadel until only the final tower remains. Again, approaching from the West is the most practical route.

Leave trekking poles and rucksack on the ground here as you will need both hands to haul yourself onto Bera Mawr's top. But the climb up along a five-metre groove has excellent handholds, and if you have already done a bit of scrambling you should take to this challenge like a duck to . . . orange sauce. In no time at all you are on the splintered top of **Bera Mawr** (at **674682** – 794m/2604ft), where logistically there is just enough room to crouch and reflect [2-25 from approach to Foel-fras].

**11)    (674682)    →**

   **40°         →**

Make the most of the views and the chance to picnic among the boulders. It's all downhill from here – particularly during the next hour when the going is punishing due to the nature and angle of the terrain. The aim is to reach the bottom of the valley North East of this summit – the floor of the Afon Goch. There's no point recommending one particular line of approach rather than another since you will eventually reach the river whichever route you take as long as you maintain Llwytmor's Southern face in front of you. But I suggest you try to cross the river upstream of **678691** where a waterfall cuts a notch through thick layers of rock.

Then once the Afon Goch has been crossed it is a matter of following any available path downstream.

   **300°         →**

If in doubt always choose the option closest to the water's edge to avoid getting side-tracked onto the imposing Western flanks of Llwytmor.

A large stone enclosure appears to bar the way ahead at **671696**, but the path squeezes past a large boulder forming one of the enclosure's corners then edges between its stone walls and the river below.

Soon after this section, the path becomes more distinct – crossing a damp declivity then scrambling onto crags that give a grandstand view of the river below you on your left. From this point on, river and path become suddenly more 'attention-seeking'. The river, confined now into a narrow chasm takes a suicidal plunge of 60 metres – the Aber Falls (Rhaeadr Fawr). Fortunately the path was not created by lemmings and does not take quite the same route. Instead, it clings to the steep Eastern slopes, teasing you with a degree of exposure that tired legs are often less able to take pleasure from [2-26 taken from **Walk 4**].

THIS DAMPEST SECTION OF PATH IS BEST AVOIDED IN ICY CONDITIONS UNLESS YOUR BOOTS ARE SKID-PROOF. A SLIP AT THIS STAGE COULD HAVE SERIOUS CONSEQUENCES.

On your left the valley suddenly spreads out below in a vast bowl. Ahead, the path crosses a rocky ledge where a steady tread is essential. At either end of these sloping slabs the going is easy (unless greasy after rain) but the central five metres or so rarely dry out, the tilt of the ground is never quite level enough to aid controlled progress, and there is absolutely nothing substantial to hold on to.

After this 'bad step' the next obstacle is a tree-choked gully that cuts directly across the path. The more obvious route seems to trend down to your left, but that heads to a dead end. Instead, climb easy rock on your right to gain a higher path skirting the rim of this chasm.

*Now that the adrenaline has had time to wear off, it is worth spending a few minutes admiring the wooded vale of the Afon Rhaeadr-Fawr laid out at your feet; the falls themselves still hidden to your left at this point.*

The path now becomes more walker-friendly, although there is still an excruciating scree slope to cross – made up of extra-large, angular blocks that are not especially easy on the ankles. But sections have been raked level to provide a track of sorts. Follow one of these until steep-sided grassland is reached with a large forest plantation beyond. Aim left now, dropping directly downslope to join the main path – this entails doubling back to head up-valley for a short distance to reach a fence at the valley bottom with a stile. Cross this and join the main thoroughfare at **668701**.

*Go on – take a look over your left shoulder before heading down to the road [2-27 and 2-28]. Wasn't all that effort worth it? You can almost picture Sherlock Holmes and Professor Moriarty perched somewhere above the plumes of thundering white water in a fight to the death.*

**12)    (668701)        →**

No compass directions needed for the final 3.5 Km of the walk.

Turn right, away from the Falls, and follow the day-trippers and picnickers through a mix of pasture, woodland and brazen banks of bluebells towards the car parks at the end of the trail. En route you pass an information centre on your right – and further on a large, flamboyant notice board (when I passed here on that May afternoon it was advertising 'Clychau'r Gog' – 'Cuckoo's Bells' – not a Welsh pop group but the blue-bells flourishing on the slopes all around). Eventually a gate and footbridge deposit you onto a metalled road.

Do not turn right here – this particular bit of tarmac leads nowhere (a car park with a toilet block but little else). Instead, turn left and shortly you will reach Bont Newydd (at **663720**), where a house faces you at a T-junction. Assuming you drove to the end of the road before starting your walk, you now take the right branch and begin the hard 1.5 Km slog back to your car.

If the weather is fine take your time. It's a quiet neck of the woods. Uphill all of the way, you first pass a small farmyard (with black bantams feeding at the verge when I last walked past – and yes, I do know my bantams from my dotterels). Then following the steepest section, the road begins to mirror the power lines as they finally lead you back to your car.

*As you motor back along the A55 take one final look at the high ground inland. A few hours ago you were traipsing those tops, possibly level with the clouds even. Something you can surely look back upon with a degree of pride.*

**END**

# WALK 3

## Llwytmor Bach [11] / Llwytmor [12]

| | |
|---|---|
| 9.6 Km (6 miles)<br><br>795m (2608ft)<br><br>Time : 4hrs 30min | **A discrete block of high ground set above the secluded Anafon valley giving stunning views of the North Wales coastline** |

Some mountains draw the walker onto their summits like magnets draw iron filings. Others, like Llwytmor, despite their nagging presence on the skyline are more often than not put off for another day. I certainly took my time getting round to 'the big grey one' – a slab of mountain like an over-turned boat marooned upon the forested hills above Aber, with an attention-grabbing rudder of broken crags at its Eastern end.

I have tacked it at the end of a Drum ➔ Foel Grach circuit before now (a superb walk but with a good deal of back-tracking). And based on a cursory glimpse of the map you might consider combining it with Bera Bach and Bera Mawr (until you are faced with the hideous slog from Cwm yr Afon Goch).

But I have made the effort to summit this twin top on two subsequent occasions purely to admire the views out to sea. Consequently I feel it deserves half a day all to itself. It might be the last of the Carneddau you consider climbing, but don't by-pass it just because it lacks the glamour of its neighbours. It's worth 4½ hours of anyone's time.

**North**

**Don't forget**

**map/compass**
**whistle/torch**

**suitable footwear**
**+ clothing**

**food/drink**

**brain**

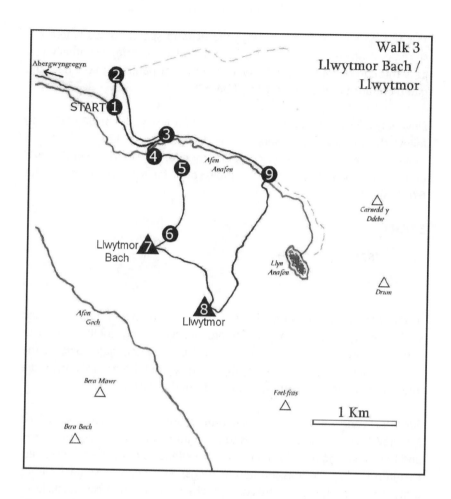

## APPROACH

From the A55 expressway take the Abergwyngregyn (Aber) exit. If driving from the direction of Bangor, bear right under the dual-carriageway and at the T-junction turn left towards the Aber Falls Hotel. If driving from the direction of Llandudno, the slip road brings you to a T-junction with the Aber Falls Hotel opposite you on your left. Take the road to the right of the hotel which leads into the village (passing a phone box on your right) and immediately turn right into a side road (signposted 'Rhaeadr Aber Falls').

This is a narrow road with passing places (and speed humps where the straggle of houses extends South from the village centre). Eventually you pass through delightful woodland, leading to car parking spaces near the gated entrance to the path serving Aber Falls.

Drive left over the hump-backed bridge (Bont Newydd – at **663720**) and follow the narrow road steeply uphill to enter an enclosed valley with mountains ahead and to your right. Continue for 1.5 Km to where the road ends in a gravelled cutting with ample room for a dozen or so cars (at **676716**).

## START

1)      (676716)        →

      350°             →

A gravel track through a metal gate (with a sign prohibiting unauthorised vehicle entry) exits this car park before shortly turning uphill. A footpath continues South along the lower ground beyond this gate towards the Anafon valley – this is the route of the return leg but there is a slightly more interesting approach worth seeking out from the North.

Turn North and you will find a track running uphill along what is part of the North Wales Path. This track keeps to the right hand side of a dry-stone wall and to reach it you have to climb over a wire fence by way of an antiquated, cast-iron ladder stile (missing its top rungs). Beyond, a grass track climbs quite steeply to the 250-metre contour where it is met by a cart-track. Keep on the grass track aiming for the line of pylons on the skyline (still resisting the temptation to turn right in the direction of the Anafon valley just yet).

2)     (676720)       →

    155°            →

Once you top out on level ground, a view of the coastal strip with Anglesey and Puffin Island opens up ahead of you. This alone is worth that little bit of extra effort. Now locate the grass-covered cart-track at the base of the first pylon on your right [3-01]. Follow it with your eyes as it contours the slopes of Foel Dduarth in the direction of the Anafon valley – a ribbon of green carpet, hopefully sunlit and dry on the day you visit [3-02].

This track is actually an ancient by-way – linking an Iron Age settlement (c1000 BC) at 677717 and a Bronze Age cairn or burial site (c2000 BC) at 678717. At this point in the walk it runs alongside an extensive area of cultivation ridges; evidence of ancient ploughing. The aforementioned ladder stile is not thought to date from the same period.

Barely crossing a contour, this broad footpath gradually transforms into a rocky track (joining the cart-track you by-passed on the way uphill). This is the access road serving the Llyn Anafon reservoir at the head of the valley. After squeezing between some wooden posts next to a chained five-bar gate you begin to notice the track's gentle ascent as it bears left to enter the broad valley of the Anafon [3-03].

95°          →

This is a beautiful, tranquil valley worth half a lazy day to itself so you can explore the remnants of prehistoric settlements, evidence of quarrying on the hillsides, and the river itself as it boulder-hops its way seaward. But facing you directly across this valley are the steep slopes leading up onto Llwytmor. From here you become instantly aware that the map does not lie – a relentless barrier of contour lines, closely spaced enough to twang the most elastic hamstring.

The nightmare flanks of this mountain are cloaked by a forest plantation – rapidly diminishing as the trees are being actively harvested. Prior to my first visit here my plan back at base-camp had been to cross the river close by and in the absence of any path attack the slopes directly (with the plantation edge as a handrail to my right) [3-04]. However, one look at the reality of the situation gave me second thoughts [3-05]. Besides, looking up-valley I could make out a network of paths climbing high up above the river terraces on the opposite river bank in the general direction of the day's target. That's the beauty of a walk like this – you are encouraged to improvise; modifying the route as you go along in line with what you encounter on the ground.

No harm in reading on to find out how I got to the top though, is there?

As the track begins to descend slightly in a more Westerly direction, a large, complex stone enclosure comes into view on the low floodplain at the river edge [3-06, and 3-07 taken from the opposite valley side]. It appears to be a series of sheep-pens, but I cannot help but be reminded of one of those American TV detective programmes where the dead body is outlined in chalk (in this instance they used dry-stone walls instead).

**3)      (682713)      →**

            270°            →

Keep your eyes peeled for a narrow path (wide enough for a slim sheep) that drops to your right off this track and winds through gorse bushes as it heads back down-river [3-08]. This descends onto a terrace still some distance above the banks of the Anafon but if you stick to the path it provides a relatively easy way down to the banks of the stream. Unless there has been heavy rainfall recently, crossing the river hereabouts should not present any difficulties [3-09].

Failing that, one can find somewhere further upstream to remove boots and stockings, roll up trouser legs and wade across – I have done so even in mid-February and lived to tell the tale.

            180°            →

Once you reach the opposite bank the best option is to tackle the initial bit of steep slope ahead of you in a direct line. In this way you will gain the top of the terrace that stands above the flood plain, almost level in altitude with the main track on the opposite bank [3-10 from across the river].

**4)    (681711)    →**

**100°    →**

Although not shown on the Ordnance Survey map, a clear path heads up-valley, parallel to the river and gaining height steadily. At the first obvious split in this path, take the rightmost (higher) branch which proceeds towards the skyline of the spur probing into the valley from the bulk of the mountain. Close to the 400-metre contour the view ahead opens up – a section of uneven ground, bunged up with crags and riven by streams feeding the main river below. Not the most encouraging of prospects.

**5)    (684709)    →**

**200°    →**

Now it is simply a case of gaining height by the least painful means. Fortunately, heading upslope to your right is the most direct and practical approach. Underfoot, the low bushes of bilberry and clumps of moss carpeting the slopes are preferable to the obstacle course of heather and boulder-field further along the valley side (unless done in winter when the heather is at its shortest). Boggy bits are few and far between, and there is a good deal of sheep-shorn pasture to assist your passage.

In terms of keeping tight control on one's bearings, the crags on the skyline ahead marking Llwytmor's main summit quickly become hidden by the angle of the slopes above you, so you'll get no more help there then. But just below the skyline far to your right there are other crags, together with a small boulder-field (square-ish in outline). Perched on the skyline some distance above this boulder-field stands a large, isolated block of stone [3-11] clearly visible from some distance. These two features will provide you with something to aim for should you find the relentless climb rather disorientating. In poor visibility, of course, they might well be missed. The only advice then is to face uphill and keep walking until the angle levels off.

One summer morning when I found myself up here the bright sunshine brought out the skylarks and a solitary red kite – no real help in direction-finding, but something else to add to the day's list of bonuses.

Keeping the aforementioned boulder-field to your right you will eventually reach rockier ground as you draw level to it. Now bear left towards that isolated block – a huge tusk of rock (more of a molar than an incisor). Beyond this point there is still some distance to cover, but the angle at last relents as the ground begins to level out.

Raised above this sea of moorland like a table of rock, Llwytmor dominates the skyline ahead and to your left. Its slopes are draped with a patchwork of grey boulder-fields, and its flat top eventually disintegrates to your left into a series of frost-shattered columns and pinnacles. In contrast, the summit cairn at the rightmost end of the table-top barely registers. Across to your right the adjacent summit of Llwytmor Bach is closer at hand (although still hidden from view) and it is well worth a momentary diversion to seek out this upland area's Westernmost peak. Besides, at a height of 690 metres (the same as Cnicht) it merits exploration.

---

### OPTION 1

Those in a hurry, and with no sense of adventure, can set off left at this point and aim for ground roughly 2/3 of the way along Llwytmor's base (counting from left to right). This should place you close to the crags described towards the end of **point 7**'s narrative.

***Time saved – about ¾ of an hour.***

---

6)  **(683701)**     →

     **260°**     →

Rocky outcrops immediately to your right give you something concrete to aim for (although if the truth be known, they are composed of a volcanic tuff, not concrete). This set of rocks is sure to have tricked many into believing they have reached the minor summit at last. But then, as the ground levels finally and your boots scrape onto these rocks, you spy a mound of stones even further West – **Llwytmor Bach** (at **681699** – 690m/2264ft).

The map does Llwytmor Bach no favours at all, and falls far short of telling the whole story. Llwytmor Bach's summit is a compact pyramid of boulders, complete with a sturdy windbreak facing the East. There used to be a tiny roofed shelter alongside it with enough room inside for one, but on a more recent visit I discovered that it had been removed. Why? Who knows?

*The views are what this walk is all about really.*

*At every stage of the slog up Llwytmor's slopes, as you are forced to pause for breath, instinctively you turn back to face the Anafon valley to gauge how much height you have gained. But the magnificent views at your feet remove any lingering frustration at how much remains to be climbed.*

*From Llwytmor Bach you are, for the first time, able to see what lies beyond the Northern skyline – Moel Wnion and the rocky stub of Gyrn – the city of Bangor to their right (Penrhyn Castle easily identifiable close to Llandygai).*

*The expanse of the Lafan Sands or Traeth Lafan (formerly Traeth Llefain) separates Anglesey from the mainland and at one time provided the only available crossing by foot. Flashes of white on the island mark the houses of Beaumaris and Llandegfan beyond, while those out to sea are more likely to be sailboats plying close to harbour.*

*Further East, Anglesey's serrated shore is indented by numerous rocky headlands and sandy bays – the hinterland an expanse of flat farmland with just a smudge of higher ground marking Parys Mountain.*

*Continuing along the coast, the bulky headlands of Penmaen Mawr, the Great Orme and Little Orme, put feelers out into the expanse of blue.*

*Closer across the valley, the hog's back of Foel Dduarth, Foel-ganol and the rust-red slopes of Yr Orsedd stand guard over the track following the opposite valley side [3-12 and 3-13].*

*To the immediate South the only easily identifiable peak is Bera Mawr like a ruined castle, solitary and desolate (Bera Bach being hidden behind it), while to the East Llwytmor beckons.*

7)      (681699)        →

        115°            →

If you pause at this summit to study the flat ground between Llwytmor Bach and the grey walls of Llwytmor, a faint path can be clearly seen bearing slightly left of your desired line [3-14]. Follow this easy path, passing a series of peaty pools before heading right to the crags at the foot of the mountain. From the base of this grey wall you are spoilt for choice since every conceivable route appears to lead uphill.

A number of serviceable paths thread their way through blocky boulder-fields and heather-clad slopes, all eventually depositing you on the flat summit with a line of small crags ahead and a sizeable windbreak to their right marking the top of **Llwytmor** (at **688693** – 849 metres/2785 ft) [3-15 and 3-16].

> *North, the solitary clump of Llwytmor Bach still catches the eye [3-17]*
> *Gyrn's mini-pyramid further left pokes above the low moorland [3-18].*
> *The sweep of the Carneddau fills the skyline to the East, looking strangely restrained from this height – Drum furthest left – Foel-fras – Carnedd Llywelyn and Carnedd Dafydd with a truncated Yr Elen beneath their gloomy ramparts.*
> *The gap between Pen yr Ole Wen (peeking over the right shoulder of Carnedd Dafydd) and y Garn is filled with Snowdon (Yr Wyddfa) and Crib Goch. Further right, Mynydd Perfedd, Elidir Fawr and Carnedd y Filiast form a Western barrier to Nant Ffrancon while beyond, Yr Eifl stands in superb isolation at the sea's edge.*
> *In the foreground Bera Bach can now be clearly picked out left of the towers of Bera Mawr [3-19 and 3-20].*
> *A vantage point worth spending time to savour if the weather is kind – somewhere to grab a bite, even perhaps a place to return to late in the day at the height of summer when a spectacular sunset is likely. But no matter what time it is, on a clear day the views from this top are spell-binding [3-21].*

8)      (688693)         →

        135°             →

A small cairn can also be found at the Easternmost end of Llwytmor's plateau summit [3-22] and is worth the detour for a close-up view of the shallow gap separating it from Foel-fras [3-23].

0°    →

From the boulder-fields, turn North to drop gradually downhill. All too soon 'gradually' becomes 'rapidly' and it is not always possible to maintain contact with a path of any sort. If you look at the map, the reservoir [3-24 from **Walk 2**] and its service road look the most favourable targets in order to regain the track back to the car park, but there is no obvious route down to its shoreline. Less difficult terrain lies further left some distance downstream of the reservoir [3-25 from **Walk 2**].

Like many lakes draining into the more densely-populated areas of Snowdonia, the Anafon reservoir currently supplies drinking water to Llanfairfechan. Unfortunately, in early summer 2008 the dam holding back the waters was found to have a crack in it, and much of the water had to be drained away to avoid an uncontrolled deluge downstream. At the time of writing, the lake is in a much sorrier state than it was when I first walked in this region. Hopefully Dwr Cymru (Welsh Water) will be able to effect repairs sooner rather than later, ensuring not only a vital supply of water to the local livestock, but also restoring the lake's tourist-appeal.

320°    →

LLWYTMOR HARDLY WARRANTS WARNINGS OF ANY SORT, EXCEPT THE USUAL REMINDERS FOR CAUTION IN POOR VISIBILITY OR THE DIREST WEATHER CONDITIONS. BUT BEWARE POTHOLES HIDDEN BY THE LUSH UNDERGROWTH – TRAPS DESIGNED TO SNARE AN UNWARY BOOT, HOLD IT FAST AND INVITE A TWISTED ANKLE OR WORSE.

Eventually the reservoir comes into view with a tempting series of slopes leading down to a shoulder of high ground cradling its North Eastern shores. But of course, things never turn out to be as straight-forward at ground level as they appear from high above or on the map. An easier line involves heading left sooner or later, taking advantage of the swathes of grassland that cushion your descent. The significant barrier of crag that emerges on your left as your path turns the corner to face downriver is easily by-passed below, still trending down-valley and down-slope. Some wet ground has to be crossed beyond this point, but again the discomfort level is tolerable.

Finally, with the river and the service road from the reservoir clearly in view still some distance below, locate a dilapidated rectangular stone enclosure at the river edge alongside a small patch of spindly trees (close to **694708**). Aim to reach the floodplain of the river as close to here as possible in order to then cross the Anafon by way of the small island (at **693708**). The river is easily forded at this point, and the main track is a short distance up the opposite bank. Once you reach that head left and down-valley (an easy 2.5 Km walk back to the car).

9)     (694709)      →

        290°         →

A glorious 45 minutes or so can now be enjoyed dawdling alongside the river. The track is straightforward (if a little hard on the soles after the relatively soft ground of the mountain). Two large stone enclosures lie to your left on the valley floor, one close to the path and the second (our murder victim) much further below.

It is worth dropping down towards the lower ground after you pass **point 3** in search of that narrow sheep path again. This avoids an unnecessary slog back uphill towards **point 2** and once you reach the terrace perched above the river aim for the fence just over the brow of the large spur directly ahead of you [3-26].

Turn right once you meet this fence and follow the path that runs alongside it [3-27]. The fence is soon replaced by a substantial wall, topped by a fence to presumably dissuade entry into the pastureland on its left-hand side.

Although several well-worn paths run off to the right, the best route remains in the lee of this wall, keeping downslope of a large slab of grey rock as the wall makes a dog-leg turn to gain lower ground on your left [3-28].

Evidence can be seen of a pair of farmsteads or round houses (dating from the Iron Age or early Roman times) either side of this wall. They are surrounded by a thick stone wall with a clear entrance on the North West. The building on the left side of the wall has been cut into the hillside.

There are also levelled fields alongside these dwellings; evidence of ancient agriculture [3-29 from across valley].

Turn right and follow the path that continues to run along the entire length of the wall before joining a short section of cart-track with gate beyond [3-30]. The car park is through this gate immediately to your right.

**END**

# WALK 4

# Gyrn Wigau [13] / Drosgl [14]

| 16.4 Km (10.25 miles) 815m (2673ft) Time : 5hrs 45min | A relaxing interlude in the North Western foothills of the Carneddau. |
|---|---|

If, rather than working your way through this book in 'walk' order, you are merely looking for an easy introduction to the Carneddau then this is it.

Although it follows the entire Northern seaboard from Penrhyn Port on the outskirts of Bangor to the flat sprawl of Prestatyn, the most impressive section of the North Wales Path runs between the village of Tal-y-Bont and Conwy. I have walked this stretch on numerous occasions, transfixed by the close-up views of the Menai Strait, the stunning scale of the Aber Falls and the alien beauty of the Sychnant Pass.

To be honest, first impressions along this particular section would suggest that the adjoining hills are fairly inconspicuous, inviting little investigation. But anyone looking for a walker-friendly introduction to this corner of Snowdonia should get onto the North Wales Path here and take this short detour South. In dry weather you don't even need to bother with your walking boots.

**North**

**Don't forget**

**map/compass whistle/torch**

**suitable footwear + clothing**

**food/drink**

**brain**

## APPROACH

Following the A55 West-bound (from Conwy) – exit 3Km West of Abergwyngregyn (sign-posted Tal-y-Bont). Immediately go right at the T-junction and left at the next (alongside Hendre farm).

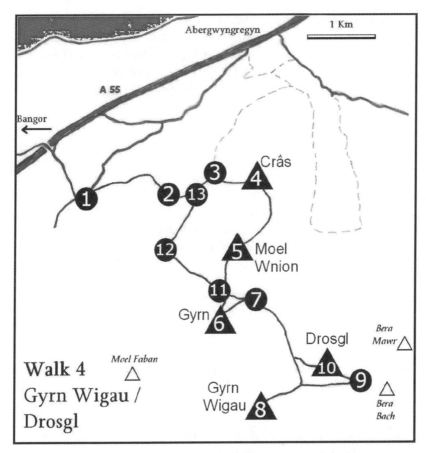

You are now on an extremely narrow road which soon begins to climb steeply through primordial woodland. Where the road emerges from the trees you will see a sign for the 'Slate Trail' footpath, and a short distance beyond that you come to a T-junction. The walk starts nearby and the best place to leave your car is on the right-hand grass verge (or left as you face back downhill) if space permits.

Following the A55 East-bound (from Bangor) – exit 3Km East of the Llys-y-Gwynt services on the outskirts of Llandygai (sign-posted Tal-y-Bont). If you bear left you eventually reach Tal-y-Bont village. But instead, turn right to cross the A55 – passing Hendre farm on the left (ignore the side road left just before it) and continue steeply uphill to the T-junction where there is space to park.

There is also room for a car or two if you turn left at the T-junction, adjacent to a gateway 150 metres on the right where the North Wales Path abandons the tarmac [4-01]. Assuming you park at the T-junction, face uphill and take the left-hand road. Follow it for some 150 metres, approaching a stand of tall straggly conifers. On the right is a gate, with ladder-stile alongside where the real walking starts.

## START

1)      (627705)        →

        70°              →

This stile gives access to a broad cart-track crossing an expanse of pastureland to the right-hand side of a dense stand of forest [4-02].

> This section of the long-distance 'North Wales Path' corresponds with an old pack-horse track which ran from Llanllechid on the outskirts of Bangor to Llanbedr-y-Cennin in the Conwy valley.

The landscape hereabouts gives the appearance of having been manicured (so different in nature to much of the ground covered in the rest of this volume).

Ignore the track bearing right after passing through the gate – this is an access road to the nearby farm. Keep to the clear cart-track running across these gentle slopes, first skirting close to the dense forest plantation on your left, then crossing grassland before drawing closer to the forest margins again. A gate with ladder-stile alongside it gives access to open pasture now. The track can be seen traversing this grassland, barely crossing a contour line as it approaches the trees in the middle distance.

*You will already have spotted Conwy Bay on your left. Even at this modest altitude there is a distinct element of being lord and master over all you survey. Now turn properly to face the sea and the shoreline stretched out beneath you [4-03].*
*First there's the Menai Strait between Anglesey and the mainland, with the*

white buildings of Llandegfan seemingly perched above the battlements of Penrhyn Castle [4-04] which dominates the foreground. Ignore this side of the water for the time being, instead following the straits further right – a straggle of more white houses where Beaumaris is squashed tight against the shore. At that village's Eastern end the castle is clearly visible; then further along the shoreline finally peters out at the promontory of Trwyn Penmon with its unmanned light-house facing Puffin Island. From here you can even see the marker buoy identifying Perch Rock roughly midway between the two islands.

And between the mainland and Puffin Island lies Traeth Lafan which once provided a more risky crossing of the straits when the tide was out.

Further East again Great Orme's Head is visible probing the blue with its craggy slopes; it's name a relic of Viking visits when its headland of rock no doubt resembled the snout of a sea-serpent ('worm' or 'orme') to ships sailing past in the mist.

Meanwhile, practically beneath your feet lie the flatlands marking the point where the Afon Rhaeadr-fawr running through Abergwyngregyn bisects a small rectangle of conifers before entering the sea.

At this point, following this track is hardly more taxing than a stroll on the beach (a marker stone half way along on the left-hand side is presumably not intended as a navigation aid since none is necessary even in dire visibility) [4-05]. You climb another ladder stile alongside a gate before approaching more woodland (separated from the pasture at first by slate-fencing, then a tidy, dry-stone wall). The wooded ground ahead of you and to your left falls away into the valley of Nant Heilyn but the path maintains progress along level ground to cross this dip in the landscape well above the tree-line.

Overhead transmission lines carried aloft on a variety of pylons cross the path ahead of you (2 sets – not 3 as shown on most maps).

2)     **(639705)**     →

       90°        →

As the path bears left at the head of Nant Heilyn, approaching the first of the pylons, a recently constructed causeway of stone blocks and gravel, complete with metal gate, ensures smooth passage across this tributary valley which was subject no doubt to considerable erosion in the past [4-06].

Much of the heather clad hillside on your right is now separated from the grassland by a stone wall, fence or combination of both. As you keep to the broad track (now distinctly fading) that crosses this green pasture you pass over another pair of ladder stiles with gates alongside, both within a short distance of each other.

IMMEDIATELY AFTER CROSSING THE SECOND STILE IT IS WORTH LOOKING OUT FOR A GATE IN THE WALL ON YOUR RIGHT AT **644706** GIVING ACCESS TO THE HILLSIDE. THIS IS WHERE YOU REJOIN THE NORTH WALES PATH ON THE RETURN LEG AT **POINT 13** [4-07].

A final gate/ladder stile combination places you close to the foot of a pylon where the path ducks under the power lines again at **646708**. This is where you abandon the security of a proper track for the time being [4-08].

3)    (646708)        →

      160°            →

Beyond this ladder stile, turn right to face the wall marking the boundary between lush pasture and more scrappy pickings uphill. A gate with yet another ladder stile some distance to its left provides access to the first slopes of the day. Off you go then!

Once you reach the other side of this wall you are faced with more pasture on your right in the lee of the wall, giving way to heather further left, while the slopes of Moel Wnion immediately ahead and to your right are covered in coarser grass and little else [4-09].

Keep to the lee of this wall as you progress uphill, aiming for a point where the heather on your left almost meets with the wall on your right. A series of depressions in the ground resembling a cart track extends beyond this point, crossed at numerous places by sheep trods and faint paths worn into the turf.

For the first diversion of the day bear left (directly up steeper ground),
keeping your eyes open for the clear footpath that winds its way between
substantial clumps of heather. In places it's a case of carefully wading
through the undergrowth until you reach easier slopes where coarse grass
replaces much of the densest vegetation. But shortly on the skyline to your
left you will stumble across two significant aggregations of boulders [4-10].
The one on the right resembles a section of collapsing wall; the one on the
left looks the more natural of the pair despite the small pyramid cairn on top
marking the summit of **Crâs** (at **654709** – 475m/1558ft). OK, so it's not
exactly one of Snowdonia's more significant summits and obviously does
not feature in the main list of 80 hills that make up this volume. But it
provides a cracking vantage point from which to drink in the views, and
perhaps an opportunity to regain your breath before having to hurdle more
serious contours ahead.

*With the sea ahead of you, in sequence from left to right, if conditions are
amenable you are presented with a panorama that extends from the
Northern coastline of Llŷn to the muzzle of the Great Orme.*
*First, the pyramids of Yr Eifl poke above the forested slopes of Mynydd
Llandegai – and across the short stretch of sea, the Western end of the Menai
Strait, the sand dunes of Newborough Warren are clearly visible*
*Closer at hand the A55 can be seen running almost parallel to the North
Wales Path – followed by the city of Bangor and the patchwork fields
fringing the coastline between Tal-y-Bont and Llanfairfechan. Then comes
the South Eastern promontory of Anglesey, Traeth Lafan and Puffin Island,*

*with Red Wharf Bay partially hidden beyond – while on this side of the water Llanfairfechan clings desperately to the slopes beneath the cliffs of Penmaen Mawr with the neighbouring Great Orme winning the race to reach the sea by a clear head.*

*Foel Dduarth guards the entry into the Anafon valley – fronted by the harvested forests on the North Western flanks of Llwytmor Bach [4-11] in contrast to the near-vertical fans of scree on its Western slopes where they plunge into the valley of the Afon Rhaeadr-fawr [4-12].*

*Then finally the Aber Falls themselves make an appearance with Bera Mawr perched on the skyline above. Enough to make anyone dizzy.*

**4)**     **(654709)**       →

     **200°**         →

From this little patch of high ground a faint path runs easily down to contour the Eastern slopes of Moel Wnion. Ever so gradually this path begins to climb again. Keep heading along this clear footpath, choosing the right-hand fork as the angle increases and the horizon approaches [4-13]. A faint notch on the skyline identifies where the correct path reaches a level section again close to the 500-metre contour. Where the path begins to level out in its determined efforts to circle Moel Wnion, a fainter path runs off to the right (close to **655702**). It's a barely discernible scuff mark threading through the tussocky grass but it runs easily upslope onto the very broad, almost flat summit of Moel Wnion [4-14].

---

### OPTION 2

Those on a mission to reach Gyrn Wigau and Drosgl no matter what, or too impatient to humour my rambling diversions, should keep to the level path skirting Moel Wnion. This soon reaches the flatlands at the foot of the two higher peaks at **652689**. From there, proceed as at **point 7**.

*Time saved – 45mins at most*

---

The only distinguishing feature on this hilltop is the low, sprawling cairn at the South Western corner of the hill with a shattered stone column (once a trig point) marking the summit of **Moel Wnion** (at **649697** – 580m/1902ft).

*From any angle, Moel Wnion bears the profile of an insignificant Pennine*
*outlier, or at best the abandoned offspring of Dartmoor. You are hardly likely*
*to meet many other walkers on this summit, but it provides as good a spot as*
*any to study the surrounding terrain. From here you get the first clear view of*
*the Western Glyderau above Nant Ffrancon (their Northern spur truncated*
*by the scars of Penrhyn Slate Quarries). You also get a closer look at the main*
*menu – but first another little appetiser…..*

**5)**    **(649697)**    →

       195°           →

A grassy track runs down the South Western slopes of Moel Wnion (not
marked on the OS map). Follow this to a broad saddle at **648691** just below
the 500-metre contour.

---

### OPTION 3

This is where I wander off the more obvious route once again. For those
of you with less time to squander, read on….. From this col follow the
main path left until you reach a small series of pools beyond which a
clear path climbs onto the shoulder of Drosgl – see **point 7**.

#### *Time saved – less than 30mins*

---

A series of paths congregate at this col – including one track that can be
driven along by all-terrain vehicles as far as the foothills of Bera Bach and
probably beyond.

Much of the landscape hereabouts bears scars relating to its industrial past
– quarrying and small scale mining in particular. Opposite the bland slopes
of Moel Wnion stands a set of low, shapely, conical hills forming a backdrop
to the less attractive hinterland of Bethesda. Chief amongst these is Gyrn [4-15],
a prominent hillock, covered in a scatter of grey boulders and bearing a
substantial dry-stone-wall enclosure at its base.

To reach the summit is just a matter of crossing the main path running left to right across the broad col and picking your way forwards and upslope between rocky patches. In no time at all, with a minimum use of hands, you reach the small, circular windbreak identifying the summit of **Gyrn** (at **648688** – 542m/1778ft) [4-16].

If you have kept up with me so far then I admit that we're still a paltry 70 metres or so above Crâs. Almost an hour since we left that molehill we are still no nearer the first real mountain top of the day. But with a choice of starters like this, why rush to devour the main course?

6)  (648688)    →

  55°         →

Gyrn is probably the airiest top of the day so far; an insignificant peak which still gives the impression of being close to the heart of more mighty mountains.

> SouthWest a descending spine of hillocks, Llefn and Moel Faban, leads the eye to the lower Ogwen valley. But to the immediate South stands a wall of pale pastureland comprising the ridge of Gyrn Wigau and Drosgl [4-17], beyond which can be seen the loftiest tops of the Carneddau.
>
> Gyrn Wigau and Drosgl stand at the Westernmost end of the spur extending seawards from Garnedd Uchaf – separated from the main top by Yr Aryg and Bera Bach (see **Walk 3**).
>
> For now it is worthwhile studying the way ahead. The lower slopes of Gyrn Wigau are uniformly gentle, and are striated by a series of runnels and paths. One apparent path runs the entire length of the ridge, barely crossing the 500-metre contour. This feature is in fact an abandoned waterway constructed when much of the area was mined [4-18].
>
> This is eventually crossed by a valley cut into the lower slopes of Drosgl, a short distance to the right of the summit when viewed from Gyrn. Follow the line of this valley uphill and you will see another path approach the main ridge from the left. This is the path you will follow to reach the higher ground.

Firstly you need to regain low ground. You can either retrace your steps to where you exited Moel Wnion, or you can descend the rocky slopes to the right of the stone enclosure directly below you to meet one of several paths that cluster around the pool-studded col at **652690** [4-19].

**7)**      **(652690)**     →

        **135°**          →

Facing the North Western slopes of Drosgl it is possible to pick out a clear track climbing to a small cluster of stone workings half way up the slope [4-20]. Follow this path easily until you reach these workings (at **657686** – enigmatically marked on the map as 'Pile of Stones').

From here a stone track trends to the right [4-21], gaining height more rapidly now until it reaches the flat crest of the ridge. To your right the spiny tops of Gyrn Wigau can be seen peeping above the flat expanse of tussocky grass [4-22].

The main track swings to the left, but a small cairn at **659678** marks a crossroads of tracks and the exit point right of a faint path following the broad ridge towards the rocky spines that mark the two tops of Gyrn Wigau. The first set of vertical rocks, easily topped, is the true summit of **Gyrn Wigau** (at **654675** – 643m/2109ft).

If you listen closely, the sounds of a fanfare can be heard on the wind as you finally get to set foot on one of the 80.

> *Take a look at the awesome cliffs of Carnedd y Filiast, Mynydd Perfedd and Foel-goch at the head of Nant Ffrancon. Or closer still the elegant lines of Yr Elen and the rock face of Ysgolion Duon to the left of Carnedd Dafydd. If you have yet to visit those tops at least you can inspect the treat you have in store from gentler surroundings.*

**8)**      **(654675)**     →

        **65°**          →

An easy plod retraces your steps back to the cairn at **659678**. Ignore the narrow track to the right. Instead follow the broader one almost straight ahead heading towards a line of rocks on the skyline [4-23]. This temporary road eventually degenerates into a wet, grassy track that circuits the Southern flanks of Drosgl. Suddenly dominating the landscape ahead is the summit of Bera Bach; an imposing fortress of weathered grey rock surmounting a field of boulders and crags. Do not be misled into thinking this monolith is Drosgl's summit.

As you follow the grassy track across the level ground at the base of Bera Bach you eventually come upon a series of pools nestling in the well of the saddle separating the two tops. Look over your left shoulder and you will make out a faint path leading through grass then boulder-fields to the nondescript top of Drosgl.

---

### OPTION 4
Rather than yet another shortcut – if you have time on your hands like I did the last time I was here, the summit of Bera Bach is less than half an hour away (there and back). It's simply a matter of picking your way through the rock litter to gain higher ground.
One fine rocky spur on your right overlooks the valley of the Afon Caseg and the silvery slopes of Yr Elen. But the main summit lies further left where easy scrambling gains the rock-bound top.

---

**9)**    **(668678)**    →

      **295°**    →

The approach onto the day's final hill is gentle and less than 40 metres of ascent leads you onto the boulder-strewn, cairned summit of **Drosgl** (at **664679** – 758m/2586ft) [4-24] – officially the highest point of this walk unless you dragged yourself onto Bera Bach.

If you are tempted to investigate the burial cairns on Drosgl more closely, it is better done in daylight than at dead of night. The largest of the three dates from about 2000 BC (based on stone fragments and other artefacts found within). A smaller one close by (no longer standing) reportedly contained the remains of a young woman.

The third has a less morbid origin – geological detritus rearranged into piles by walkers anxious to leave their mark.

10)     (664679)          →

        275°              →

To regain the broad track that led you onto the ridge it is possible to descend the Western flanks of Drosgl (although there are no clear paths on this side of the hill). As long as you keep bearing left your line of descent will eventually intersect with your main route of ascent.

If visibility permits, it is possible to make out the crossroads of paths a long way downslope of Drosgl's summit, and there is a discernible path heading directly downhill the entire way to the col. But, whichever descent route you take, you will eventually meet the main track as it crosses the lowest point between Moel Wnion and Gyrn at **648691**. There is no guarantee that you will find exactly the same path you followed on the way up, but whichever route you employ should eventually lead to this junction of paths.

11)     (648691)          →

        300°              →

Now continue straight ahead along the col separating Gyrn from Moel Wnion. A stony track, often resembling a dried stream bed loops around the South Western edges of Moel Wnion, dropping quite steadily as it does so. At one point this path splits in two, a better constructed offshoot heading to the left (and seemingly in the wrong direction). But it is safe to follow the better of the two paths as they join up again shortly after.

The path maintains a fairly high line above a small reservoir on the left [4-25]. Then Bangor pier comes to view as the path reaches open pasture where a number of options are laid out on the ground before you. Paths run downhill in most directions from here offering more direct access to the North Wales Path and the road beyond. But most cross enclosed fields where walkers are rarely welcome.

**12)**     **(639698)**     →

      30°          →

Instead, bear right where an opportunity to contour the Northern face of Moel Wnion presents itself. If you find this path to the right suddenly climbing towards spoil heaps of rock you have turned right rather too soon and are approaching the disused quarry marked on the map at **642697** [4-26]. If you have reached the disused quarry, drop some 200 metres North to join a fairly clear path heading to your right across open grassland.

This soon turns left to reach a series of stone walls beyond which the North Wales Path can be clearly seen. Go through one gate, then another shortly afterwards in the wall directly ahead (at **644706** – the one I advised you to take note of earlier in the walk). This gate gives access to the North Wales Path a short distance below.

**13)**     **(644706)**     →

      245°         →

From here it is a simple case of turning left and retracing your steps to the road.

Surprisingly, on the last two occasions when I completed this circuit I have only ever met two groups of walkers hereabouts despite fine walking weather.

The first group comprised three teenage boys (laden with enormous rucksacks) and a teenage girl on a mountain bike chaperoning them along the final stretch of the North Wales Path. They had set off on foot from St David's College in Llandudno sometime that morning and were heading to a camp site in the Ogwen valley where they would spend the night – as part of the Duke of Edinburgh Award. Full marks for endurance and stamina, but I hope their adventure allowed them to set foot on at least one summit during the weekend.

The second, a group of four 'ramblers' had followed the path past the foot of Moel Wnion onto the low ridge between Drosgl and Gyrn Wigau and were then intending heading East, by-passing the base of Bera Bach en route to the Aber Falls. They had wandered this far into the foothills of the Carneddau yet had no plans to set foot on a single summit. Beats me!

**END**

# Pen y Castell [15] / Craig Eigiau [16]

| | |
|---|---|
| 19.5 Km (12.92 miles)<br><br>750m (2460ft)<br><br>Time : 6hrs | **A long trek in the Carneddau into the vast corrie of Cwm Eigiau that also reveals a bird's eye view of the lakes of Dulyn and Melynllyn.** |

Approaching the end of one of the chilliest, wettest May weeks in ages might not seem the perfect time to venture out onto the hills – especially into a region resembling an extensive bog. But the day's forecast promised plenty of sun. So with a wet Bank Holiday looming I had no hesitation in setting my alarm, dreaming of the wilder side of the Carneddau, and electing to avoid hitting the snooze-button for once.

Many hill-walkers look no further East than the line of peaks extending from Carnedd Llywelyn to Drum. Anyone who has followed that ridgeline will have seen little in this corner to whet the appetite. But a closer look at the map reveals two hidden pearls invisible from the loftier tops – the two cirque-enclosed lakes of Dulyn and Melynllyn.

What better way to explore these two, with the added treat of a visit to the heart of Cwm Eigiau, than by an airy walk joining two much-neglected summits – Pen y Castell (perched some way East of Drum), and Craig Eigiau (the highest point of the vast cliffs plunging into the Llyn Eigiau reservoir). On the map, much of the walk looks like a navigational nightmare – but on the ground it's a different matter as long as the weather chooses to cooperate. This refreshing walk provides a pleasant interlude for someone in search of views rather than height for a change.

**North**

**Don't forget**

**map/compass whistle/torch**

**suitable footwear + clothing**

**food/drink**

**brain**

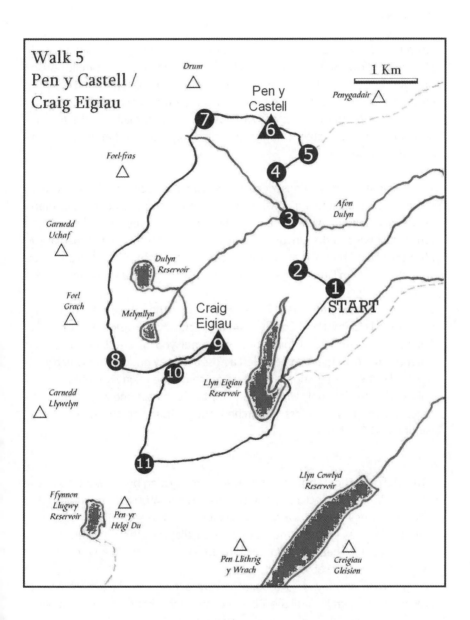

Walk 5
Pen y Castell /
Craig Eigiau

Drum

1 Km

Pen y Castell

Penygadair

Foel-fras

Garnedd
Uchaf

Dulyn
Reservoir

Afon
Dulyn

Foel
Grach

Melynllyn

Craig
Eigiau

START

Carnedd
Llywelyn

Llyn Eigiau
Reservoir

Ffynnon
Llugwy
Reservoir

Pen yr
Helgi Du

Llyn Cowlyd
Reservoir

Pen Llithrig
y Wrach

Creigiau
Gleision

## APPROACH

From the A55, at the main Llandudno exit take the A470 South signposted Llanrwst. Follow this road for about 7Km then at the Tal-y-Cafn public house on your right turn right (sign-posted Ty'n y Groes and Dolgarrog). The road crosses a railway line then the bridge over the Afon Conwy. It then takes a sharp left and after a series of twists and turns eventually climbs to a T-junction (more accurately a staggered cross-roads). Turn left at this junction onto the B5106.

You will pass two turnings right (sign-posted Rowen), followed by the cemetery, then on entering Tal-y-Bont village another turning right (signposted Llanbedr-y-Cennin) with 'Y Bedol' ('The Horseshoe') inn and the village school just beyond the junction. Ignore all these junctions, but immediately after the village school is an unsignposted turning right. This is the one you want. If you reach Dolgarrog you have gone a kilometre or so too far.

From the A5 at the outskirts of Betws-y-Coed, take the main exit to the North (signposted Llanrwst and Conwy – A470) practically alongside the Waterloo Bridge. Follow this road for about 6Km until you reach Llanrwst. Upon entering the town the road bears left across a railway bridge after which you must take the first junction left before reaching the main shopping street. This road to the left, only wide enough for traffic to pass one way at any one time, transports you across the arched bridge spanning the Afon Conwy (signposted Trefriw).

This arched bridge, Pont Fawr, replaced a pre-existing bridge crossing the Conwy which was declared unsafe in 1626. The new bridge was designed by Inigo Jones. Ten years after it was first commissioned, on the very day the bridge was opened, the central arch collapsed (the central locking stones having been put in upside down – due to the workmen's predilection for mead allegedly).

The men employed to rebuild it were allowed to drink only 'non-alcoholic' buttermilk until the job was completed – hence it is also known as the Buttermilk Bridge. In 1702 the central arch collapsed again following floods and it was re-erected in its present form.

At the T-junction on the opposite bank of the Conwy turn right and continue along this road, passing through Tefriw and Dolgarrog. About 1Km after passing the Dolgarrog aluminium plant on your right, having entered the village of Tal-y-Bont, take the first side road left (not signposted and easily missed). If you see a school on your left, followed by 'Y Bedol' inn and a sign for Llanbedr-y-Cennin, you have gone a wee bit too far.

Whichever route you take to reach this side road into the hills, be careful once you start to follow it. It is extremely narrow in places and also climbs quite steeply, 250m in less than 2Km (much of the time by way of staggeringly steep S-bends). Eventually the gradient does ease and the road takes a sharp turn left at a point where a narrower side-road runs straight ahead. Continue ahead along this side-road.

Shortly you come to a gate – open it, drive through, and close it after you (assuming it was closed when you reached it). To the left, heading back towards the Conwy valley, you should be able to make out a water-filled channel which provides a supplementary feed to the Coedty Reservoir. The main supply for this small basin comes from the Llyn Eigiau Reservoir that lies at the end of this road.

You then pass 'Rowlyn Isa' farm on your right followed by another gate. Beyond is a switchback section of road running through sparse woodland before emerging into the open again with a third gate still to pass through. Ahead of you now the landscape is remarkably rugged; a vast expanse of rough pastureland closed in on three sides by hills of varying stature. Prominent on the skyline ahead stands the magnificent headwall of Cwm Eigiau enclosing the dammed waters of Llyn Eigiau. This view alone is worth the drive into such an isolated corner of Snowdonia.

The circuit of the Cwm Eigiau Horseshoe is a popular hill-walking challenge despite its remote approach. From left to right the walk takes in Pen Llithrig y Wrach, Pen yr Helgi Du, Carnedd Llywelyn and Foel Grach, as well as crossing the prominent gaps of Bwlch y Tri Marchog and Bwlch Eryl Farchog.

The steep drop (200 metres within less than ½Km where the Afon Porth-llwyd tumbles from this upland area to the floodplain of the Conwy) provided a sufficient head of water to power turbines and thus generate electricity that was originally consumed by the aluminium works in Dolgarrog. The Llyn Eigiau and Llyn Cowlyd reservoirs together with the waters of the Afon Dulyn were linked by underground pipe and overground leat to maintain a regular flow of water into the Coedty Reservoir (dammed in 1922 to feed the Aluminium Works and Hydro-Electric power station at Dolgarrog).

The Eigiau in particular has a tragic history. The original dam was built in the 1890's but was enlarged in 1908 – massive stone and concrete foundations were laid at some depth with a stone wall set on top of them. However the foundations did not go down as far as the bedrock base. On the night of Monday 2nd November 1925, following exceptionally heavy rain, the runoff was of such quantity that it tunnelled beneath the foundations of the Eigiau dam, breached the overflow lake of the Coedty and completely obliterated the tiny village of Porth-llwyd downstream. The aluminium works at Dolgarrog were also inundated, causing the furnaces to explode.

16 souls sadly perished, but the majority of the villagers survived having turned out to watch a film being shown in a travelling cinema which was fortunately parked outside the inundated area. The 'Dolgarrog Disaster' as it was called led to changes in the design and inspection of dams, and a reappraisal of recognised methods of dam construction worldwide.

Beyond this third gate a relatively straight and level stretch of road leads to a final gate which provides access to the reservoir service road and the remote farm of 'Hafod-y-Rhiw'.

Park this side of the final gate [5-01] (there is ample space on the right hand side for twenty or more vehicles without anyone having to block the way through).

At more than 370 metres above sea level, this is one of the highest starting points for any of the walks covered in this volume. But even a cursory glance at the skyline surrounding this outlandish spot shows that there are still plenty of contours to tackle.

Even before setting off on this walk I was reminded of how this area has managed to retain some its wild character despite man's clumsy attempts to harness what little natural resources it offered in the past. As I drove up to the third gate I slowed down to gaze in amazement at a hare sniffing the air at the roadside. And while I was putting on my boots I heard the summer's first cuckoo. Good signs that all was well with the world up here.

## START

1)      (732663)      →

      290°              →

On entering the parking area you pass a wire fence on your right with a locked gate and ladder stile [5-02]. Cross this stile to join an occasionally wet, but straightforward, track that crosses the relatively level Northern banks of the Afon Porth-llwyd.

Steeper slopes grow closer as you approach another gate with ladder stile alongside [5-03]. Cross the stile and immediately take the narrower right fork in the track alongside a large outcrop of grey rock (one of a pair between which the main track continues its leisurely way uphill towards the Melynllyn reservoir) [5-04].

2)      (726667)      →

      90°              →

The narrow track you have taken descends for a while as it skirts the high ground for now. Although it is constantly wet underfoot, it is never boggy or even muddy, and for much of its length a narrow stream runs in a ditch along the path's left verge. Another gate and ladder stile lead past the ruin of a smallholding at **727674** ('Maeneira' on the map).

*This is a wonderful spot to stop for a moment or two to drink in the atmosphere. On your left are slopes covered in coarse grass and a variety of boulder and crag. On the right and ahead as the view enlarges is an open area of rough pasture, patches of heath and a network of dry-stone walls and the Afon Dulyn. And right alongside your path are the sad remains of what was once someone's livelihood with its collapsed walls, abandoned paddocks and few surviving trees that provided scant shelter when the East wind did its worst. There is abundant evidence that much of this area was inhabited during the Bronze Age (some 4000 years ago) yet now man's passage barely registers on the scene.*

**305°**              →

From here the path becomes less rocky underfoot as it bears left and climbs to pass through a gate [5-05]. Once through the gate the path is less distinct as you make your way across a patch of rough pasture bounded by a wire fence ahead of you that drops to the right towards the valley floor.

As you also trend downslope to the right, an ugly concrete dam appears with a fenced walkway providing one means of crossing the Afon Dulyn. The Afon Dulyn and Afon Ddu combine just to the West of this dam, become the Afon Dulyn proper and eventually reach the Conwy at the village of Tal-y-Bont. Even this stream is not allowed to run unfettered – the channel you saw as you closed the first gate on your drive up-valley is supplied with water hijacked by pipeline from where the Afon Dulyn passes close to 'Rowlyn Isa' farm.

**3)**     **(725675)**     →

       **0°**                →

There is a better way of crossing the Afon Dulyn than by the concrete walkway. Just beneath the dam a crude causeway of boulders and gravel leads across the stream [5-06] to a clear track leading left to a metal gate (impossible to open unless you possess the metacarpals of the Incredible Hulk) with a rickety little stile alongside it.

Gingerly cross this stile and follow the track a short distance upslope. The track meets a ladder stile after crossing the Afon Ddu (here retained in a set of metal tubes set under a causeway) which feeds the tiny reservoir on your left [5-07]. But ignore the stile because your route goes up to the right before this river crossing, a rise along a grassy footpath between dense clumps of gorse and heather.

Ahead is a level area of grass (complete with weather-recording equipment set on a tripod concreted to the ground – possibly a temporary installation nevertheless, so don't worry if you are unable to find it when you're next there). To the right of this is a wooden five-barred gate. This opens easily leading to an embankment on your left overlooking a stone-lined ditch with a concrete weir crossing it. Assuming the ditch is not overflowing (it was bone dry when I was last there) use this concrete weir to reach the opposite bank.

Immediately ahead of you now is a wire fence with a wooden step allowing you to cross into a narrow paddock of long grass. Another fence separates you from a larger area of grassland beyond but this fence is almost flattened and can be easily walked through [5-08 looking back]. There is no clear path across this rough pasture but as long as you can see the long ridge of Cefn Coch and Craig Cefn Coch on the skyline ahead of you there is no doubt in which direction you should head – continue towards the higher slopes [5-09].

At one stage you pass across a series of low boulders set into the ground. These in fact make progress easier – particularly if the ground is wet after a period of rainfall. Beyond these is more coarse grass, seemingly pathless. But if you listen out for the hidden stream running in practically a straight line through the long grass, a path runs alongside its right hand bank as you look upstream.

The grass shortens and the ground becomes drier as the angle of slope increases and you reach the rock-strewn top of **Cefn Coch** [5-10] (at **723681** – 485m/1591ft) which barely registers on the map. Pen y Castell is still some distance away on the right-hand skyline, with the more prominent outline of Craig Cefn Coch away to its right. A dry-stone wall sweeps down from higher ground to the left crossing the broad slope between you and your destination, and a substantial track runs left to right, undoubtedly placed there to facilitate your passage.

**4)**     **(723681)**     →

    0°                →

It's not much of a drop to this track.

    60°               →

Once you reach it turn right and pass through the wall by way of a ladder stile to the right of a gate. The track is now a rutted, turf-covered lane running beneath the fenced-off slopes of Craig Cefn Coch on your left. Shortly the track passes through an ungated gateway in a section of fallen wall – a slender, pointed column of slate on the left supposedly once acting as a rudimentary gatepost. A few yards further on cross the ladder stile on your left which gives access over the fence onto the slopes of Craig Cefn Coch.

**5)**     **(727685)**     →

    345°              →

The heather-clad slopes become increasingly rocky as the vertical crags topping Craig Cefn Coch grow closer. Unless you want to set foot on the minor, rock-littered summit of **Craig Cefn Coch** (at **726686** – 570m/1870ft), bear to the right and cross a broad saddle of tussocky grass leading to the smoother grey outcrop of **Pen y Castell** (at **721688** – 623m/2043ft).

*Now that you have reached the first significant top of the day it is worth taking a few moments to scan the views.*
*First face South to pick out the route you have just followed. At the opposite side of the flat valley of the Afon Porth-llwyd stands Moel Eilio (a different peak to the one crouching above Llanberis – this one barely reaching 546*

metres in height). This hill falls away steeply to the left to the tiny Coedty Reservoir which is a feeder for the hydro-electric power station at Dolgarrog. Now turn a few degrees clockwise to where three ridges lie en echelon – Creigiau Gleision the furthest back, Pen Llithrig y Wrach in the middle, and closest at hand the Northern ridge of Cwm Eigiau upon which is perched the day's second target, Craig Eigiau. From this high point the flat plateau of Gledrffordd leads further right to the headwall of the corrie containing Melynllyn.

Further right again along the skyline runs the ridge comprising Carnedd Llywelyn (when I was last here it still held a withered cornice of snow this late in the Spring), Garnedd Uchaf, Foel-fras and finally Drum fronted by the headwall of Cwm Dulyn.

Due North the shallow trough of Cwm y Ddeufaen can be seen stretched out between Carnedd y Ddelw on the left and Foel Lwyd on the right. Set within the Northernmost opening you may be lucky enough to be able to pick out the towered summit of Penmaen Mawr (the largest block is actually the quarried face of the hillside below which much of the present day excavations are carried out).

To the right of Foel Lwyd stands the flat-topped ridge of Tal y Fan. Further East lies the trench of the Conwy valley, fronted by the conical peak of Penygadair and its lower, more rounded neighbour Pen-y-Gaer.

Although Penygadair has a distinctive outline, it is Pen-y-Gaer that has the more interesting history. It is the site of what was once an Iron Age hill fort – one of a number in the area. Pen-y-Gaer is particularly noteworthy for the inclusion of 'chevaux de frise' (a 'minefield' of small, angular stones laid out on the ground in such a way as to break up any attack by tripping up unwary invaders or their mounts). I have never set foot on its slopes, but I can think of several hills in North Wales and further afield that have similar defences, though usually supplied by nature.

6)      (721688)        →

        280°            →

Look more closely West and you will see a fence running in a fairly straight line towards the skyline just to the right of Drum's summit. At the lowest point between Pen y Castell and Drum another fence runs left to right, breached by a ladder stile beyond which a sinuous path runs uphill parallel to and some way left of the first fence [5-11]. Your route involves crossing the ladder stile, following the path uphill until you are roughly level with the top of the rocky outcrops on the left of Drum's lower flanks, then trending left and upwards to gain the peat-scarred slopes beneath the col separating Drum from Foel-fras.

Although there is no obvious path from Pen y Castell to the ladder stile, the hummocky ground you must cross to reach lower ground is relatively easy going. Then after crossing the stile and starting up the grassy path, a closer study of the skyline above the grey outcrops of rock on the left will eventually reveal a small notch. Aim for this, exiting the main path left as the angle of ascent increases. An indistinct footpath dawdles in the same direction, but for a while the going underfoot is uneven as angular boulders litter even the higher slopes.

Not far below this notch is a grassy patch on which are scattered rusted metal fragments – possibly some discarded piece of farm equipment you might think.

But from further reading, it is more likely to be the wreckage of a crashed aircraft – not uncommon on the East-facing slopes of the Carneddau. For example, a Whitley MkV BD232 came down on 26th September 1942 close to 'Dulyn bothy' which stands beside the outflow of the lake.

7)      (710690)      →

        240°      →

This notch is little more than a shallow cutting in the almost level plateau. Beyond it open grassland sweeps relentlessly South across the massive headwall of Cwm Bychan (the source of the Afon Ddu). A pair of rocky spines crests the skyline above you in the col separating Drum from Foel-fras but resist all temptation to head in their direction. Instead, contour the valley head gaining a minimum of height (just enough to skirt the worst of the peaty scars that tattoo the Eastern flanks of Foel-fras). Fortunately most of the ground is covered in coarse grass rather than impenetrable heather. Bear in mind that the flatter the ground is, the wetter it is more likely to be (particularly at the lowest point of the col). And downslope of the larger peat scars the ground is generally waterlogged – sodden turf squeezing out groundwater like a compressed bath-sponge.

As you reach the flanks of Foel-fras a fence runs downslope across your path. This fence is easily crossed by way of any number of stone blocks set close enough to provide a leg-up. Beyond it grassy slopes abut against an extensive patch of large boulders. The best option is to bypass this boulder-field on its upslope side. Besides, height gained by this stage comes in useful later on. Another fence cuts across your route – again not difficult to overcome (in this case it helps to select a section of fence to cross where the topmost strand of wire is barb-free).

Garnedd Uchaf is visible as a grey row of crags on the skyline, whilst ahead of you grassy slopes lead onward. But now at last a substantial wall of dark rocky ribs and slabs can be seen dropping steeply into a hidden hollow where the ground dips out of view.

> Look out for a small, circular sunken pool on your left [5-12]. Beyond it a spur of rugged ground can be seen probing into the hidden valley with the arm separating Dulyn from Melynllyn prominent beyond.
> Above this scene Pen Llithrig y Wrach can be seen peering over the horizon.

You may feel it is perverse to be within touching distance of classic peaks such as Foel-fras, Garnedd Uchaf and Foel Grach yet choose to tip-toe past them in search of a hole in the ground filled with water. But as you contour the convex slopes and that water-filled hole begins to take shape far below on your left perhaps you will realise that contours are not everything. I have read of hill-walkers who purposely shun the summits themselves because they dislike the concept of 'bagging' a peak. Perhaps that's taking denial a bit too far.

As you circle the headwall of Cwm Dylun you have the choice of a variety of platforms from which to study the rock basin, a series of broad, rocky steps. Dulyn is an almost circular corrie lake, drawn out to a slight kink where the river exits [5-13]. A large embankment of glacial debris forms a natural dam on the left side of the outflow. In contrast on the right steep cliffs plunge to the water's edge, and by all accounts beneath.

Cwm Dulyn, like every cirque, cwm or corrie in Snowdonia, owes its existence to the localised erosive power of ice during the final stages of the last Ice Age. Ice and snow accumulating on the more shaded slopes of the hillside eventually grew thick enough to form a small, local glacier. Over time the weight of ice was sufficient for the lowest layers of ice to change texture and flow downslope rather like icing flowing from the top of a cake. The constant slither of rock-laden ice at the base of the glacier gouged out a significant hollow on the face of the slope. Over the hundreds of years involved this hollow became deepened and steepened to form the distinctive rock basins found throughout most of Highland Britain today.

An amazing depth of 55 feet has been measured less than a metre from the shore beneath Dulyn's headwall. For those with a thirst for even more trivial information, water from this lake supplies Llandudno.

You might think any traverse of this lake's headwall is a daunting prospect when approaching from the North – a sheer wall of wet rock and sparse vegetation with a number of cataracts plunging vertically into the lake from a series of slabby ramparts. But as you slowly circle the cirque's airy lip, you will find that crossing the first three water-courses at least is straightforward.

Some of these streams have cut notches into the headwall but none are difficult to get across. Their gullies are narrow, bordered by either rocky steps or grassy banks which enable you to step across.

*There are few things more mesmerising than running water. Perched at such altitude it is tempting to follow each tributary stream's progress downslope until the point at which it reaches more resistant rock and plunges into the invisible chasm below. I was first here following a period of relatively extreme*

*rainfall and although the boggiest ground had dried up, some of the smaller
streams continued to bubble out in a series of gushing white springs from
beneath half-buried boulders.*

As you reach one of the larger cataracts, with a massive slab of grey rock
forming its furthest bank, there comes a welcome change in the nature of
the headwall beyond. Grassy slopes, scattered with a few loose rocks,
beckon you towards higher ground well above the cliffs ahead [5-14]. A low
collapsed wall leads up this steep ground and directs you without too much
exertion to the immediate skyline.

On gaining the highest ground directly opposite Dulyn's point of outflow
you will be tempted to have a breather no doubt. It provides a superb spot
from which to take a retrospective look at the corrie wall. More than likely
you will ask yourself how on earth you managed to get across it. On my first
visit here a helicopter entered the valley and hovered for a few minutes
above the lake's surface – some 200 metres beneath my boots. I have visited
the valley twice since and on each occasion a helicopter made a brief
reconnaissance of this lake so unless I am being stalked from the sky the area
must be part of a regular run (by RAF Mountain Rescue so I am reliably
informed). As you continue to contour the lake in an anti-clockwise direction
you reach another grassy embayment that has to be crossed and ascended
at the same time.

*In a short time you are on the high rim of the corrie with the main valley of
Pant y Griafolen stretching ahead of you. From this higher viewpoint it is
possible to see the small refuge hut ('Dulyn Bothy') on the left-hand bank of
the stream draining out of the lake (**705664** on the map).*
*Pen y Castell and its neighbours form a low barrier on the left and the slopes
of Cefn Tal-llyn Eigiau mirror the same scene on the right.*
*Further right above this valley side is your first clear view of the high plateau
of Gledrffordd, perched above the elevated basin enclosing Melynllyn. And
cresting the skyline of this extensive platform in stark contrast are the
serrated teeth of Craig Eigiau.*
*The hump of ground between the two lakes still hides Melynllyn's waters
from view, although the track leading from this secluded lake to the service
road of Llyn Eigiau can be clearly picked out.*

The slopes beyond consist of a selection of large grey boulders, coarse grassland, some smaller boulders and 'interesting' outcrops of bedrock. Since your intention is to gain height as you contour these slopes you may decide to make use of a little treasure of a rock climb.

On your right is a particularly sizeable block of rock, darker than most perhaps because it casts quite a shade. If you can be bothered to approach closer, and pick your way through the large angular blocks that lie at its feet, you will find a slab of wet rock beyond it. This gives an excitingly wet, greasy route to the immediate skyline.

But if you prefer to by-pass this barrier, continue along easy grass slopes to gain a fairly flat area leading to the slopes above Melynllyn [5-15].

Melynllyn lying some 100 metres higher than its neighbour is about half the size of Dulyn, and rectangular rather than circular. Its headwall is much smoother than Dulyn's – a series of grass-covered slopes set back some distance from the floodplain and the lake shore [5-16]. Unfortunately to gain the immediate skyline and access to the plateau of Gledrffordd involves another substantial ascent – but the ground is easy underfoot and the direct approach is preferable to contouring. Aim for the horizon to your right and you will soon reach a broad spur extending from the shoulders of Carnedd Llywelyn [5-17].

*Beyond this spur its grey corrie walls tower high above the hidden basin cradling Ffynnon Llyffant [5-18 taken from* **Walk 6***] – Wales's highest lake at 820 metres above sea level – a secluded body of water situated at an altitude greater than all but 27 of the summits covered in this book!*
*Dominating the scene to your left is the broad platform of Gledrffordd, pock-marked by the occasional drinking-hole. Right of this are the sheer walls of the Gallt Cedryn cliffs of Pen Llithrig y Wrach, scarred by steep runnels of scree.*

8)     **(696653)**        →

       130°              →

A short way ahead across easy slopes you come upon an intermittent footpath heading from the higher ground behind (on your right – the ridge between Carnedd Llywelyn and Foel Grach) to the flat shelf stretching out ahead and to your left. Your route lies to the left – following what can be used as an alternative high-level return leg for those completing the Cwm Eigiau Horseshoe.

The path crossing the flat top of Gledrffordd is not marked on the Explorer map but it is clear enough on the ground [5-19]. For much of the way it is a broad, continuous scuff-mark in the coarse turf covering this plateau. In many places the grass has been worn away to reveal pale patches of thin soil and gravel.

ADJACENT TO ONE OF THE LARGER PATCHES OF BARE GROUND [5-20] LIES AN ELONGATED POOL [5-21] (ON THE RIGHT-HAND SIDE OF THE PATH DIRECTLY BENEATH THE HIGHEST POINT OF PEN LLITHRIG Y WRACH AS YOU FACE SOUTH). ON THE LEFT HAND SIDE OF THE PATH ALONGSIDE THIS BARE PATCH STANDS A SLIGHTLY RAISED HUMMOCK ALMOST RESEMBLING A TURF-COVERED CAIRN [5-22]. KEEP THIS LOCATION IN MIND FOR LATER (**POINT 10**) AS IT IS THE BEST SPOT FROM WHICH TO DESCEND GLEDRFFORDD, WHICHEVER VALLEY YOU CHOOSE TO DROP INTO.

---

OPTION 1
If you intend to leave Craig Eigiau for another day, this is the point at which to drop down into Cwm Eigiau. Continue as if at **point 10**.

*Time saved – some 45mins*

---

Continue along the faint track and as you crest the flat rise ahead you should be able to see the cock's comb of Craig Eigiau on the near horizon – perched like a tiara on a leg of pork. The ground falls away ahead of you across small outcrops of rock to another flat area – with a series of small pools on the left and drier ground on the right.

The path has already split on this rise – the left fork contouring the slopes of Cefn Tal-llyn Eigiau to the left of the pools, the right fork heading for the rocks and splitting again giving you a choice of at least two possible approaches.

But before dropping off this inconspicuous mound it is worth studying the map. This patch of raised ground is actually the highest point of Gledrffordd and so officially should qualify as the summit of **Craig Eigiau** (at **709654** – 738m/2421ft) [5-23]. You will not stand here too long to savour the scene when more charismatic rocky heights beckon within touching distance. Head to the right of the dampest ground and soon you are facing the barrier of grey rock [5-24]. You have a variety of choices, but reaching the highest tip of this rocky crest presents no difficulties (at **712655** – 735m/2411ft). One path weaves its way through the crags but by diverting right you may easily clamber across smooth, bare rock and rounded boulders to reach your goal.

From these Western approaches I have always thought that this sinister wall of rock would be more fitting as a barrier to the darker fringes of Middle Earth than as a fairly insignificant top in this corner of North Wales. Indeed a number of guidebooks, perhaps overcome by the dramatic setting, incorrectly identify this spot as the real summit of Craig Eigiau, but of course the contours never lie.

*As you took a leisurely stroll along the flat top of Gledrffordd you no doubt turned around to admire the dramatic skyline of the Cwm Eigiau Horseshoe. Left to right as you look back are Pen Llithrig y Wrach – the col of Bwlch y Tri Marchog with its distinctive bulge – Pen yr Helgi Du – the flat saddle of Bwlch Eryl Farchog – the cliffs of Craig yr Ysfa leading up to Carnedd Llywelyn – and the enormous cairn (said to contain the bones of Tristan – one of the Knights of the Round Table) perched out on a limb to its right separating the highest point from Foel Grach.*

*A closer look across the shallow trench of Bwlch Eryl Farchog reveals the Southern face of Glyder Fach, with the descent path of the Bristly Ridge, and the striated turret of Tryfan barely visible against the grey rocks of its loftier neighbour [5-25].*

*From the crest of Craig Eigiau itself you also get your first glimpse into Cwm Eigiau [5-26] – the boggy remnants of the reservoir close to the breached dam, the track up-valley and the service road back to where you parked. Unfortunately the main body of the reservoir is still hidden.*

*On its opposite valley side – a high level approach onto Pen Llithrig y Wrach is overlooked by the bare ridge of Creigiau Gleision.*

Craig Eigiau's smooth, grey, fractured rock is in complete contrast to the rest of the ridge – no doubt a quirk of geology. It actually marks the line of contact between a resistant outcrop of dolerite (a volcanic rock) and a softer mass of siltstones and mudstones.

The last ice sheets to cover this region buried the entire ridge and were able to smooth and sculpt even the toughest bits of Craig Eigiau (without actually wearing them away completely).

In total contrast, resistant rock bands on the summits of the higher Glyderau close by were sufficiently elevated to poke through the surface of the same ice sheets for much of the last Ice Age. Consequently these rocks were exposed to hundreds of years of daily freeze-thaw weathering which has resulted in what is now a massive scrap-yard of angular rock fragments with no smoothing evident.


9)      (712654)      →

        270°      →

It is now a case of retracing your steps along the level terrain towards the lower slopes of Carnedd Llywelyn.

---

OPTION 2

However, it is possible to return to the start point of the walk without entering the head of Cwm Eigiau. This is a useful alternative should the weather take an unfavourable turn.

Pick your way Northwards along a faint path that crosses to the Eastern side of this rocky spine for a while before emerging on the West side again close to where the main backbone disintegrates into separate blocks laid down on more level, heather covered terrain.

You will notice a path continuing downhill (North) along the left-hand side of a fence. Join this path and follow it downslope as it veers closer to the fence to skirt to the right of a series of low crags.

Ahead of you a dry-stone wall emerges from the hidden side of this ridge on your right. Keep to the left-hand side of this wall.

As you enter the broad valley of Pant y Griafolen a clear track can be seen heading down-valley, quite some distance from the wall. Ignore the path running in the lee of the wall, and the ladder stile part of the way along it. Instead head for easier ground by dropping down the slopes on your left to join the main track – an old service road that can be seen running up the valley [5-27] (all the way to the shores of Melynllyn). Once you join this track turn right – crossing a wire fence by way of a ladder stile alongside a gate, and a wall further along the same way. The track now takes a swing to the right around the stump of the ridge, passing the smooth fin of Cerrig Cochion [5-28] on your left, a pleasant spot from which to appreciate your general surroundings.

Keep following this track as it descends a couple of shallow zig-zags. Then after passing a series of stone enclosures on your left you reach a patch of open ground with feeding stalls set out for the sheep. On your right a gate gives access through a dry-stone wall to a path which peters out by the time it reaches the Northern shoreline of Llyn Eigiau. But ahead of you the track passes between two large stone outcrops to meet a locked gate with ladder stile – the same one you encountered at **point 2**. Cross the ladder stile and head for the car park at the end of the service road a short distance away.

*Time saved – approximately 1hr*

Some way before the flat ground begins to rise towards the flanks of the Carneddau's highest point you will hopefully come across the large patch of worn turf again with the pool now on your left and the hump disguised as a turf-covered cairn close by on your right.

**10**   **(705651)**   →

   205°   →

To reach the head of Cwm Eigiau bear South (left) just beyond this pool, crossing a substantial area of flat ground where the turf is less luxuriant. If visibility is good, just aim for the gap of Bwlch Eryl Farchog between Pen yr Helgi Du and Carnedd Llywelyn and start walking.

OPTION 3 THAT FOLLOWS PROVIDES AN INTERESTING ALTERNATIVE RETURN TO THE SERVICE ROAD AT THE HEAD OF LLYN EIGIAU, JOINING OPTION 2 FOR THE FINAL FEW KILOMETRES. IT CAN BE PURSUED AS SOON AS YOU FIRST REACH THIS EXIT POINT, OR AFTER FIRST VISITING CRAIG EIGIAU.

THE IMPORTANT POINT IS THAT THIS ROUTE SHOULD NOT BE ATTEMPTED UNLESS WEATHER CONDITIONS, AND IN PARTICULAR VISIBILITY, ARE FIRST CLASS. THE REASONS FOR THIS WILL BECOME OBVIOUS AS YOU READ ON.

## OPTION 3

To reach the track that heads down the valley from the basin of Melynllyn involves following a very steep path clinging to the left edge of a series of massive mine workings. In poor visibility it is not inconceivable that you could wander directly over the rocky cliffs towering above the lake's South Eastern shore and plunge into one of the dark chasms cut into the crags [5-29 seen from below].
To ensure you reach the path in one piece keep an eye on the views ahead and adjust your course if necessary.
To begin with, locate the hump to the right-hand (North) side of the path – as you face it you will see the dark cliffs of Dulyn's headwall behind and slightly to its right. Begin to walk North, keeping slightly to the right of the hump. A faint track can be picked out leading directly downslope – little more than a sheep trod. As the gradient increases, a convex slope which means that much of what lies below is hidden, look out for Dulyn's dark waters below to your left. You will note the large, rock-covered face of the natural dam to the right of its outflow and much further right an isolated stand of trees. Continue downhill aiming for these trees [5-30].
Shortly you will cross a clearer path – a very narrow slot cut into the sloping turf – that runs from the direction of Craig Eigiau towards the waters of Melynllyn (which are by now visible to your left).
To steer clear of the mine workings head left along this footway and pick your way down the slightly less steep slopes to the lake shore.
However, you can opt to continue ahead by slowly dropping downhill to reach a set of large grey rocks laid out on the turf to your right. Directly ahead on the valley floor you cannot fail to pick out the track from Melynllyn's shore with a ruined building alongside it [5-31]. Aim for

this building (keeping to the same bearing as before – the solitary coppice of trees stands directly beyond these ruins).

Now suddenly the gradient increases. To your right a massive crag of rock plunges into the valley. And closer at hand a huge void opens up as the ground falls away. But straight ahead of you, to the left of this void, a perfectly straightforward staircase of rock and turf leads down to the floor of the valley.

Once you reach the relative safety of one of the numerous platforms that keep your descent in check, you can confidently cast your eyes to the right at what lies beyond the edge of the path. A massive man-made cavern has been cut into the hillside, now flooded and silent except for the eerie sound of dripping water and rustling vegetation. Little light filters into the depths of these workings – just enough to make out the collapsed roof and slime-covered walls of the shaft where men once laboured for slate (stone mainly used as honing or sharpening-stones in the case of this particular mine).

A smaller shaft lies some distance below this one, narrower and with too much unstable debris to attract closer investigation.

Level ground is close by now, wet where a sluggish stream escapes the open shafts and drains towards the ruined workings. The wheel powered by this diverted stream, and utilised to drive the saws that cut the slate into blocks, now sits frozen by rust in the stone walls.

It defies imagination in this modern metro-centric age that such a wild, secluded area, far from the nearest road, was once an industrial site (albeit a relatively minor one)

The well-constructed track at the side of these ruins runs down-valley to your right, crossing the two ladder stiles as already described in the alternative return leg from Craig Eigiau before swinging right, to eventually reach the service road to Llyn Eigiau [5-32].

*Time saved – approx 30mins*

From the level tract of Gledrffordd the gradient eventually begins to increase as you get closer to the descent path South marked on the Explorer map (in the vicinity of the 650-metre contour at **702644**). The best route keeps to the left hand bank of the stream running into the head of Cwm Eigiau for most of the descent [5-33]. In places the path disappears, and there are numerous wet patches that are most easily avoided by keeping close to the stream itself.

*From this lower vantage point the huge cliffs of Craig yr Ysfa look particularly intimidating. Funnels of scree spilling from the fissures cleaving the near-vertical headwall of Cwm Eigiau appear to give access onto the ridge linking Pen yr Helgi Du and Carnedd Llywelyn. However, this wall of rock is best left to rock-climbing experts [5-34 to 5-36].*

This region is deservedly more popular now with hill walkers and climbers than it was a century or so ago. Part of the lore relating to Craig yr Ysfa is that its great crags were only 'discovered' by rock climbers peering South through a telescope from the summit of Scafell in the Lake District.

*The adjacent slopes beneath Pen yr Helgi Du look similarly daunting, but in this case a scree chute does provide direct but gruelling access onto the skyline [5-37]. This path emerges where the Southernmost end of Bwlch Eryl Farchog abuts against Pen yr Helgi Du. Most guidebooks suggest this route be used only as a means of ascent (preferably when not iced-over).*

As you approach flatter ground it now pays to cross the stream on your right to its opposite bank in order to reach a grass-covered dyke by way of a faint path running along the stream bank. Where the dyke veers further right you should bear left across a lower embankment that leads to a set of ruined quarry buildings close to the floor of Cwm Eigiau. Beyond these a stream runs along the margins of the waste heaps bearing witness to the extensive excavations that have hollowed out the Northern flanks of Pen yr Helgi Du [5-38].

A distinctly dilapidated stone bridge carries a track across this stream should you wish to gain a closer look at the slate heaps, but the old quarry workings are best studied from a distance. The track continues from the bridge crossing to the right of the quarry where a path can be seen heading uphill onto the skyline. This path is notoriously loose underfoot and is not one of the recommended routes onto Pen yr Helgi Du.

**11**   **(700636)**   →

   **95°**   →

If you happened to cross this bridge, return now to the left bank of the stream (facing down-river) and continue walking down along the valley floor towards a larger group of ruins close by [5-39]. Look out for an extensive embankment of hewn slate that extends from the valley side on your left – just beyond this you meet with a broad track, the main route from Cwm Eigiau to the Eastern shoreline of Llyn Eigiau.

This is a pleasant and relatively level walk now – passing along the broad valley of the Afon Eigiau [5-40 looking back up-valley]. Close to **713638** a fence crosses the path – with a gate and ladder stile offering a choice of ways though [5-41].

> *Just beyond stands the tiny cottage of 'Cwm Eigiau' [5-42] – now a refuge hut owned by a Midlands based Mountaineering Club – perched beneath the steep face of Craig Eigiau. Large stone enclosures cover much of the pasture on the valley floor hereabouts, whilst across valley the slopes bear more scars of abandoned quarrying [5-43].*

The path takes a right-angled turn right, crosses a ladder stile alongside the gate in the wire fence, and a flat wooden bridge before turning sharp left again to continue down-valley. This bridge crosses the Afon Eigiau which by this point has become quite deep [5-44]. Beyond here gentle meanders cut through grass-covered banks before entering the lake, which still looks unimpressive despite the vast area it covers.

From this point the path adheres to the Eastern side of the valley, passing by a track running off to the right, back up-valley towards the small-holding of 'Cedryn' [5-45].

The valley floor ahead of you largely consists of an extensive area of reeds, reclaimed water-meadow and some rubble-strewn ground while the shrunken Llyn Eigiau reservoir which presumably once filled this trench is left hugging the base of the Craig Eigiau cliffs [5-46]. A ladder stile, perched on awkwardly-angled rocks, allows you passage left of a gate [5-47]. Your path then continues past the farm of 'Hafod-y-Rhiw' on your right and crosses another flat wooden bridge (over a leat that runs alongside the farm-track) [5-48 looking back].

In the grassland to your left stand the patched-up remains of part of the dam wall. Unlike your everyday dam, this one seems to have spent more time running along the length of the reservoir than across it [5-49] – although it is hard to imagine how it must have once appeared when there was a substantial body of water behind it. As you pass the nearest concrete barrage on your left, with the leat running close by [5-50], you will notice the service road crossing what was at one time the face of the main dam below and to your left [5-51]. Ignore a minor track exiting right – this follows the Southern banks of what is now the Afon Porth-llwyd. Instead keep to the main gravelled track, turning left, crossing the bridge where there now exists a massive gap between the two concrete walls, and then turning right to follow the service road.

Signs close by dissuade one from investigating the boulder-strewn bed of the Afon Porth-llwyd following heavy rain – flash floods are still a danger hereabouts.

The service road now runs along the right hand side of the long dam wall that still shows signs of the breach at **723653**. The minor tributary running through this jagged gap joins the Afon Porth-llwyd a short distance away – again it is difficult to grasp the scale of the flooding that caused such devastation downstream. From here it is simply a matter of following the wide, straight track, through a series of gates and ladder stiles, back to your parking spot.

**END**

## WALK 6

### Pen yr Ole Wen [17] / Carnedd Fach [18] / Carnedd Dafydd [19]
### Carnedd Llywelyn [20] / Yr Elen [21]

| | |
|---|---|
| **18.7 Km (11.7 miles)**<br><br>**1370m (4494ft)**<br><br>**Time : 8hrs 10min** | The 'heavyweights' of the Carneddau – a challenging day but rewarded by exceptional views of this corner of North Wales. Five summits, each above 3000 ft, sounds like a test of endurance but it needn't be. |

I'm not a fair-weather rambler, far from it. Although I have tried to record every walk here under optimum conditions there have been numerous 'dry runs' that were not so successful.

Two months before my first successful traverse of these tops I was battered by Arctic winds that left my gloves, bootlaces and trekking poles plastered in ice crystals. I finally gave up my endeavours that day after reaching the summit of Carnedd Dafydd with my face contorted into a frozen grin.

A fortnight later I found myself wading crampon-less through banks of deep snow, hoping to join the skiers on the white tops before again being forced back. This time I was some way short of attaining the first summit when the accumulation of ice on rock at the first real scramble led me to put off my plans for another day.

On the 'first day of Spring', perseverance finally paid off as my attempt on one of the region's best high-level walks was completed under clear blue skies and with a warm breeze at my back. I've been back many times since it's a walk I never tire of.

**North**

**Don't forget**

map/compass
whistle/torch

suitable footwear
+ clothing

food/drink

brain

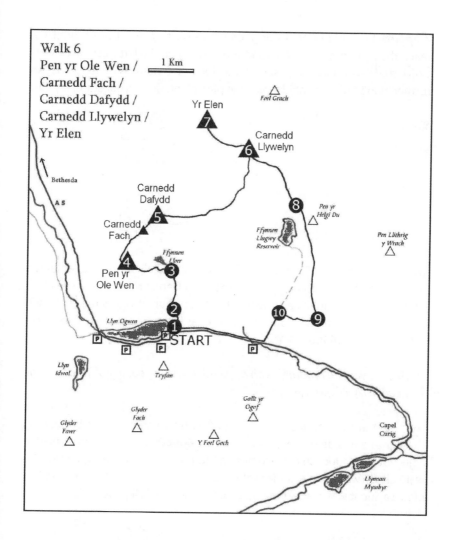

**Walk 6**
**Pen yr Ole Wen /**
**Carnedd Fach /**
**Carnedd Dafydd /**
**Carnedd Llywelyn /**
**Yr Elen**

## APPROACH

Heading from Bangor follow the A5 South through Bethesda to the end of Nant Ffrancon, turning left at Ogwen Cottage and skirting the Southern shore of Llyn Ogwen until you reach the last lay-by on the left just beyond the lake's inflow (**666605**).

If approaching from Capel Curig, continue North along the A5 until you reach the first long section of roadside parking on the left (just past Gwern Gof Uchaf farm and camp site at the foot of Tryfan). The smaller lay-by further along on the right just past the pine plantation is your starting point.

## START

1) **(666605)** →

   90° →

   360° →

Walk East along the A5 verge and almost immediately turn left to enter the private road to Glan Dena, crossing the Afon Denau river which feeds Llyn Ogwen [6-01]. Continue past the habitation on your left, cross the cattle grid and follow the farm track about 150 metres as far as the entrance to Tal y Llyn Ogwen farm at **668608** [6-02].

> *Already you are rewarded with a splendid view to your left of Y Garn at the head of Llyn Ogwen [6-03].*

Turn right at this entrance to gain a footpath that starts to climb up along the right-hand side of a dry stone wall. At **668609** a National Trust plaque adjacent to a ladder stile welcomes you to the Carneddau. As you cross the wall left by way of this ladder stile you might notice that the stile bears a plate saying it was made and presented by Holywell High School.

2) **(667609)** →

   275° →

A solid, paved track now crosses the open ground for a short distance until degenerating into a sheep track (in places signposted by a series of orange poles).

When this path approaches the Afon Lloer on your left at **667612** you are advised to ford the river as soon as feasible – the longer you put off this manoeuvre by sticking to its Eastern bank the less likely you are to find a safe crossing. There are a number of quite boggy bits along the bank that lead you close to the rock-strewn bed of the river. As the banks become rockier upstream, the ground might be drier under foot but crossing the river here is more of a challenge, particularly after a period of wet weather.

**350°**            →

This approach route, although not as excruciatingly steep as the more direct climb onto Pen yr Ole Wen from Pont Pen-y-Benglog at **649606**, still gains height fairly rapidly. But the effort this entails can be alleviated by regular pit-stops for breath – and to take in the expanding views of Tryfan [6-04] and the Ogwen valley behind you [6-05]. If you secure the Western bank at the earliest opportunity you easily regain the uphill path [6-06] which now trends left as it wends its way between a couple of craggy outcrops. The flatter bits tend to get very boggy underfoot – but the way ahead is unmistakeable.

A stone wall soon comes into view directly ahead [6-07] in the distance with a ladder stile and gate (the gate is generally locked open). Follow the path through this gateway (at **667617**).

Some of you with a tight schedule might choose to climb immediately left now directly towards the skyline and rejoin the path in the vicinity of **664619**. But the eroded path that sticks to the West bank of the stream is the more scenic option and requires less effort.

As you near the 600-metre contour there are two large, white-mottled boulders overlooking the waterfalls to your right, one upstream of the other, that make fine resting points from which to survey one's surroundings, reflect on the previous hour's exertions, and watch the Afon Lloer hurtle downstream close by.

**3)      (666619)          →**

**265°                      →**

Shortly beyond these two rocky perches the gradient eases as the path takes a swing left towards the large rock basin enclosing the small lake of Ffynnon Lloer.

The main path sticks to the floor of this corrie as it approaches the lake's shores. But to reach the first summit of the day you need to take a minor path left to gain the skyline and reach the shoulder of higher ground [6-08]. The angle quickly levels off as the broadening track threads its way between a set of rocky ramparts that guard Pen yr Ole Wen.

In places the going underfoot is wet, but there are enough knobs and knuckles of rock to hop across if you don't fancy getting your boots too muddy [6-09]. Approaching the heart of the hill [6-10], you eventually encounter a wall of ice-polished rock on your left between the 750-metre and 800-metre contours [6-11].

Pass below this to enter the corner where the wall abuts the main body of the mountain. A steep staircase ascends this corner onto a broader shelf of ground. This section of easy scrambling provides you with the day's first real burst of adrenaline and an opportunity for some hands-on experience in preparation for what follows.

Ahead of you now is the steepest section of Pen yr Ole Wen's Eastern face – dominated by an outcrop of white quartzite which acts as a geological beacon if low cloud persists. Aim for this, but keep below it by skirting its base left by the narrow track, which then leads swiftly up towards a gully of darker, often wet, rock [6-12].

> **OPTION 1**
> Some of you may be tempted to by-pass this scramble by contouring to the right beneath the outcrop of quartzite. This leads to a profusion of vague paths that criss-cross Pen yr Ole Wen's Eastern spur. They cling by their fingertips to the side wall of Cwm Lloer before gaining the main path somewhere near to the 900-metre contour.

> Whichever route you choose on this side of the mountain involves probing a maze of rocky shelves – many leading to dead-ends with exposures most of us would rather avoid. Here, more than ever, it pays to heed the advice not to clamber **UP** something you'd prefer not to have to climb **DOWN** again later.
>
> *My advice is to steer well clear of this punishing approach unless searching for the wreckage of numerous aircraft that have perished on this section of mountainside over the years.*

THIS IS THE FIRST PROPER SCRAMBLE OF THE DAY – LOOKING PARTICULARLY INTIMIDATING FROM BELOW. BUT THERE ARE AMPLE HANDHOLDS AND THE EXPOSURE IS VIRTUALLY NON-EXISTENT. FOR THOSE OF YOU INTENDING A RETURN BY THE SAME ROUTE, THANKFULLY IT IS NO MORE DIFFICULT ON DESCENT, UNLESS COVERED IN ICE.

Once you have completed this short climb, a broad protuberance of turf-capped rock on your left provides a welcome resting spot from which to take a retrospective view of the walk so far.

> *The entire route you have followed so far is conveniently laid out beneath you to the South and East. To your right stands the Mohican quiff of Tryfan [6-13] with the Bristly Ridge of Glyder Fach to its rear.*
> *Across the valley of the Afon Lloer rise the whaleback ridge of Pen yr Helgi Du, and its partner Pen Llithrig y Wrach beyond.*
> *I recall one gloriously clear day on this ridge when a dense bank of murky haze masked the hinterland of the Denbigh Moors – irrefutable evidence that breathing the air up here is preferable to that further East.*

Once you have had time to recharge, whichever method you use, a straightforward path now picks its way over two false crests as the flat, rock-strewn summit comes closer to view [6-14].

I'm no 'Roadrunner' – more of a 'Wile E Coyote' without the sticks of dynamite, so I tend to make the most of any opportunity to savour my surroundings as others career past (hence the longer than average ascent times perhaps). It's not just a case of relishing the exposure and moving on, taking in the extensive views with the click of a camera, or absorbing the sounds and scents while munching a bag of crisps. After the effort made to reach such places surely we should take time to soak up the experience – after all, it's not just about ticking off lists and improving ascent times. Or am I being naïve?

For the more curious rambler, two natural viewing platforms lie to the right of this path – perched above the deep bowl of Cwm Lloer giving dizzying views to the lake of Ffynnon Lloer below [6-15].

The cairn marking the summit of Carnedd Dafydd on the opposite side of the chasm now appears reassuringly closer. And so it is. But the steep walls of the corrie, riven by scree runnels, waterfalls and improbable paths, are reminders that in impenetrable cloud or other adverse weather conditions, this is a seriously challenging region best left to the ravens. Finally the steep, rocky track levels out [6-16] as it rapidly approaches a small cluster of stones that marks the summit of **Pen yr Ole Wen** (at **655619** – 978m/3210ft) [6-17].

> *Since the views North and West are largely hidden by the bulk of the mountain until the summit is reached, they take on an even more dramatic significance when finally revealed.*
> *In particular the skyline West is dominated by Foel-goch with Elidir Fawr towering behind [6-18]; whilst Yr Wyddfa and Crib Goch appear closer than feasible just beyond the col between Y Garn and Glyder Fawr with Llyn Idwal almost close enough to skim a pebble across [6-19].*
> *Beyond these hills, the Llŷn peninsula's stubby edge can be picked out at the sea's edge.*

**4)**     **(655619)**     →

      **300°**       →

The way ahead in daylight is obvious – a straightforward path leads North of West for a short distance before heading to the right towards a large cairn signposting the route to the next summit. But here's a tip for anyone craving more views. Take a few minutes to head slightly left (West) of the path in order to gain a clear view into Nant Ffrancon.

The almost vertical views down into the flat-floored valley of the Afon Ogwen and across to the Northern Glyderau are well-worth this detour [6-20 to 6-22] and are missed by most peak-baggers.

20°                    →

Once you regain the main path it follows the skyline, barely dropping below the 950-metre contour as it crosses a shallow, waterlogged saddle [6-23], clinging all the while to the rim of Cwm Lloer. It's up to you how close you venture to the edge – but be aware that under snow this lip of ground is notorious for harbouring cornices (in which case you might be perched on a fragile eave of snow with fresh air a metre or so beneath it rather than solid rock).

The huge cairn-cum-windbreak identifying **Carnedd Fach** (at **657627** – 965m/3165ft) is more an obstacle than a real summit [6-24], which is why it is generally classed as part of Pen yr Ole Wen. The path is forced to clamber over it – and you are unlikely to make use of the limited shelter it provides unless the wind is particularly hostile. It does provide a moment perhaps for you to reflect on the route from your first summit of the day [6-25] to your next [6-26].

The ground remains rocky as it by-passes a smaller cairn on the left (at **661629**) before scrambling the last few metres to the block-strewn summit of **Carnedd Dafydd** (at **662631** – 1044m/3425ft) [6-27]. This summit is less impressive than that of Pen yr Ole Wen, and the jagged rocks underfoot should deter anyone from lingering here for too long.

---

**OPTION 2**

If you are restricted by time or weather conditions to spending only half a day on the hills, this is the point at which to suspend proceedings with a straightforward retracing of your steps downhill.

***Time saved – a massive 4 ½ hrs.***

---

NOW YOU HAVE REACHED THE ROOF OF THE CARNEDDAU IT IS WORTH NOTING THAT FROM HERE ON (PARTICULARLY IF YOU INTEND TRAVELLING THE 'CLASSIC' ROUTE TO THE DISTANT SUMMIT OF DRUM FOR EXAMPLE) THERE ARE NOT MANY SMALL-SCALE FEATURES TO AID NAVIGATION. IN MIST, FOLLOWING THE WRONG RIDGE LINE BY FAILING TO CHECK WITH YOUR COMPASS BEFORE MOVING ON CAN LEAD YOU MILES FROM YOUR DESIRED DESTINATION.

**5)** **(662631)** →

**90°** →

The 2½ Km ridge walk along Cefn Ysgolion Duon and Bwlch Cyfryw Drum (more accurately Bwlch Cyfrwy Drum) to the base of Carnedd Llywelyn is one of the finest in the country – largely due to the sense it imparts of your being perched at the edge of the world.

*Stunning views North into the Llafar valley [6-28 and 6-29] cannot fail to draw the inquisitive away from the well-trodden path steering South of the ridge-line across wet, springy turf. The turrets of grey/black rock that form protective battlements along the cliff edge at the central section of this ridge [6-30 and 6-31] provide ample opportunity for you to adopt Fido mode and go scampering off (and perhaps even sniffing) in various directions for more exhilarating perspectives of the jaw-dropping cliffs of Ysgolion Duon and the Grib Lem spur [6-32 and 6-33] emanating from Carnedd Dafydd's Northern slopes.*
*To the North lies a swarm of B's – Bethesda, Bangor, Beaumaris and Benllech Bay laid out on your left.*
*Ahead of you stands Carnedd Llywelyn's Western face, and craning towards the sea the monster's head of Yr Elen extends from the slender neck of ridge linking it to the main summit.*
*Cwm Pen-llafar lies empty below – from here another possible route to Yr Elen can be mapped out from your raven's-eye view for another day.*

Beyond the rockier section, the ridge grows smoother and more rounded as the chasm of Cwm Lloer to your right and the intervening lumps of Creigiau Malwod and Clogwyn Mawr are replaced by Cwm Llugwy and the Ffynnon Llugwy reservoir beneath the flanks of Pen yr Helgi Du [6-34].

From the 933-metre 'low-point' of this ridge at **681636**, it takes little ingenuity to locate the path of white stones as it trails through a broad patch of wet ground before heading almost directly uphill to the fourth summit of the day. Although a dry-stone wall approaches the skyline from the right on a collision course with Carnedd Llywelyn's top, the better path steers clear of it, zig-zagging left before levelling out beneath one of the large wind-breaks marking the sprawling summit [6-35].

Unfortunately **Carnedd Llywelyn** (at **683644** – 1064m/3491ft), the third highest peak in Wales (subsidiary only to Yr Wyddfa and its neighbour Carnedd Ugain) is hardly memorable despite declarations by certain individuals that it is one of Britain's most spiritually significant summits. The shambles of walkers' cairns, wind-shelters and frost-shattered outcrops of rock will deter the more secular among us from lingering here too long.

> There is a large burial cairn located between this summit and Foel Grach (particularly noticeable from the lower slopes to the North East [6-36 and 6-37 from **Walk 5**]. This cairn is said to contain the grave of Tristran (one of the legendary Knights of the Round Table.)

**6)**     **(683644)**     →

      **350°**        →

---

**OPTION 3**

Yr Elen can be left for another day if time is at a premium, especially as linking it to this walk entails ascending Carnedd Llywelyn twice.
If you do decide to by-pass it, continue as at **point 6** (revisited).
Logistically, however, from the summit of Carnedd Llywelyn you are presented with the best opportunity you may ever have of reaching its remote outlier and any effort involved is amply repaid.

***The time saved amounts to about 1hr 15min***

---

Initially, the temptation is to pick your way between the tors goose-bumping Carnedd Llywelyn's Northern slopes in the direction of Yr Elen on the horizon directly ahead [6-38]. However, if you bear right towards the steeper slopes above Cwm Caseg you are more likely to locate the easiest path which leads down across a band of black, vertical slate to a col at the 900-metre contour [6-39]. This route avoids the drudgery of negotiating the sheep tracks criss-crossing Carnedd Llywelyn's Western slopes and your having to admit eventually that none of them are any help in making progress towards the path that becomes visible in the distance.

**270°**    →

From the col to the summit the path is clear – an eroded track surmounting two craggy shoulders before reaching the hump-backed crown of **Yr Elen** (at **673651** – 962m/3156ft) [6-40 from above the col].

The rocks outcropping here are cunningly arranged in vertical slices [6-41 and 6-42] that form a protective collar circling the tiny corrie of Cwm Caseg [6-43 and 6-44] and its shrunken lake Ffynnon Caseg. Time spent on this lofty perch quickly confirms that any approach other than the one followed from Carnedd Llywelyn would be a more difficult undertaking; yet alternative paths do lead here from Foel-ganol further North, and even from the depths of Cwm Caseg itself.

**7)**    **(673651)**    →

**175°**    →

The next section involves nothing more taxing than retracing your steps onto Carnedd Llywelyn's summit. This return leg is easier because the path beyond the col at the 900-metre contour is easily identifiable as a zig-zag cut into the grey wall of rock directly ahead of you [6-45].

**6)**    **(683644)**    →

**165°**    →

Carnedd Llywelyn looks no better when approached from the North, so it will not take you long to head for the stone wall straddling its summit. Take the path that breaches it (marked by a small cairn close by) before clattering its way downhill through a jumble of blocks and boulders then levelling onto the softer contours of Penywaen Wen. A second cairn at **689642** confirms that you are on the right track, and below you now the ridge [6-46 and 6-47] forming the Western wall of Cwm Eigiau can be conveniently studied in preparation for the challenges ahead.

**100°**        →

The route from the broad base of Carnedd Llywelyn, crossing the rocky sections of Craig yr Ysfa to the col of Bwlch Eryl Farchog, is straightforward and involves little scrambling until the very end. In dry and ice-free conditions it will provide no difficulties to the competent or experienced hill-walker.

A pair of craggy protrusions is easily bisected (or by-passed to the right) before the angle of descent starts to grow steeper. At this stage there are two options available – to keep to the edge of the cliffs above Cwm Eigiau's basin on your left, or to steer right and avoid the exposure. A combination of the two is preferable.

*The view left into the dark crucible of Cwm Eigiau with the cliffs of Craig yr Ysfa above (a favourite with climbers) is deterrent enough not to wander too near to the edge. Further along the path this danger is reinforced by a narrow gap between two columns where you are left peering vertically into the corrie below [6-48].*

Beyond this point the less intrepid will steer right of the corrie rim in order to escape the drop. But this sheltered path is not without its challenges, in particular a tricky line of descent right at the end across polished slabs where the seat of the pants comes in useful to control your downhill progress [6-49 facing back uphill]. From the base of these rock slabs a clear path clings securely to the twisting ridge [6-50] leading you easily to the floor of the col (Bwlch Eryl Farchog) near the 750-metre contour with the reservoir of Ffynnon Llugwy hopefully glinting in the sunlight at your feet on your right [6-51].

8)　　(694633)　　→

　　　170°　　　→

Facing you now the prow of Pen yr Helgi Du [6-52] appears daunting from this angle – but it is in truth a rambler-friendly hill. On my first ever attempt at this walk I spent 20 minutes hunting for a safe passage through the crags before I opted for the wimp's route as per map – bypassing a possible sixth summit by way of a narrow path that follows the Western flanks of Pen yr Helgi Du.

---

### OPTION 4

The least wearying option from the col is to actually climb Pen yr Helgi Du's Western ridge – a ten minute ascent if you know what you are doing. **See the next walk – Walk 7 – if you intend climbing Pen Yr Helgi Du on this route.**
From its summit, the remainder of the route is easy.

### OPTION 5

An alternative and more direct escape route from **694633** sees a minor track plunging to the right from the main path into the valley where it joins the service road for the Ffynnon Llugwy reservoir. From the shore the service road can then be followed to **point 10**.

---

As the path starts to rise from the floor of the col, a short gravelled section ascends a steep ramp as it begins its scramble to the summit. Immediately to its right a twisting path follows the Western side of Y Braich (Pen yr Helgi Du's whaleback ridge) – clearly visible as it trends slightly uphill, clinging doggedly all the way to the slope.

Although route finding is straightforward, the path can be particularly tiring at the end of such a long trek. It takes a tightrope route where ground falls steeply to your right (into Cwm Llugwy) and rises just as steeply to your left (the slopes of Pen yr Helgi Du) – so you are constantly trying to keep your balance to avoid stumbling into the heather bordering the path. The solution is to abandon the path by heading for the skyline on your left as soon as that prospect appears feasible, even though it involves advancing some way uphill when the aim is to get downhill as rapidly as possible.

Once you breast the skyline to your left a clear path will soon be located heading downhill. Progress is now a simple matter of an equation involving angle of slope and energy reserves.

**9)**  **(699608)**  →

     **265°**  →

Where a low wall crosses the path ahead of you step through the obvious gap in it, and bear right across tussocky grass [6-53]. A barely discernible cart track leads to a damp corner of ground at **695609** where another wall bars the way ahead. Turn left to follow this wall a short distance downhill to where it adjoins the leat drawing water from the Llugwy reservoir towards Llyn Cowlyd.

Climb the gate in front of you, cross the footbridge and climb the concrete stile to gain the footpath following the Southern embankment of the waterway. Turn right to follow this path as far as the next concrete stile. Once you cross this you join the tarmac road servicing the reservoir.

**10)**  **(690610)**  →

     **200°**  →

Turn left here and follow this service road swiftly downhill (at an excruciating angle I have to admit). The only respite from pounding the tarmac is provided by the three ladder stiles you also have to cross before finally being dumped at the A5 roadside [6-54].

Turn right out of the gateway, preferably crossing the road to its wider South verge, and follow the A5 in the direction of Llyn Ogwen.

Within less than 30 minutes you should reach your vehicle at **666605** where you left it earlier that day – unless you really are 'Roadrunner' in which case you got back to it 15 or so pages earlier and your vehicle's long gone.


**END**

# Pen yr Helgi Du [22] / Pen Llithrig y Wrach [23]

| 13.7 Km (8.6 miles) | |
|---|---|
| 890m (2919ft) | **Two interesting summits that often tend to get left on the shelf when it comes to peak-bagging.** |
| Time : 5hrs 30min | |

I had walked this pair some six months earlier when both were covered by a fresh fall of snow. A brilliant blue sky and pristine views made the day memorable enough without need for any further diversions. All it took that day was one brief look across Bwlch Eryl Farchog to deter any inherent desire I might have harboured to proceed further in that direction.

But if you have already read the previous section (Walk 6) you will realise I had unfinished business with Pen yr Helgi Du. On my first ever traverse of the Bwlch Eryl Farchog ridge (linking Carnedd Llywelyn to Pen yr Helgi Du) I had given up any hope of locating a safe scrambling route up to the latter's summit – which is why I have included a short detour in this walk. The steep path down to the col is easier to reconnoitre from above – although whether or not you actually end up following it may depend on conditions underfoot as much as on your confidence.

I would have no hesitation in recommending it to anyone looking to spice up their day. This scramble could well turn out to be the highlight of the walk. But if you have a different agenda, don't be dissuaded from making the most of what these two summits have to offer. They are worth a visit.

**North**

**Don't forget**

**map/compass
whistle/torch**

**suitable footwear
+ clothing**

**food/drink**

**brain**

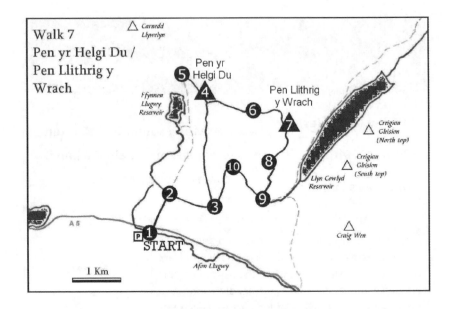

**Walk 7**

**Pen yr Helgi Du /**
**Pen Llithrig y**
**Wrach**

## APPROACH

Heading from Bangor, follow the A5 South out of Bethesda to the end of Nant Ffrancon, turning left at Ogwen Cottage and skirting the Southern shore of Llyn Ogwen. Pass a pine plantation on your left and cross the bridge over the main river. Less than 1 Km further on, on the right, is a campsite adjacent to Gwern Gof Isaf farm at **685602** (not to be confused with Gwern Gof Uchaf farm which you have already passed). Parking is available at the farm entrance for a nominal fee – drive up to the farm-house, pay your dues then park in the spaces provided back near the entrance.

Heading from Capel Curig, follow the A5 North West along the broad valley. Gwern Gof Isaf farm **(685602)** is the first habitation on the left.

Exit the farm car park across the cattle-grid onto the main A5 – turn right and walk for ¼ Km to the reservoir service road entrance on the opposite side of the A5 at **688603**. Limited free parking is available at this entrance to the Waterworks road serving Ffynnon Llugwy reservoir. There is room for about four cars, but take care not to block the gateway. If the gate is closed leave enough space for it to open fully onto the right-hand wall. And if the gate is open leave room for it to be swung shut. No matter how tempting it may appear when the gate is open, do not drive up this road in order to save some legwork by parking as high as possible above the A5 [7-01 from further up the service road] because you might end up finding your car is trapped behind a locked gate at the end of the day. If in doubt – park at the farm.

**START**

**1)     (688602)     →**

         20°          →

Follow this service road uphill after crossing the first ladder stile (or using the main gate if that is open). This long, straight tarmac strip is a gruelling climb [7-02] – in fact it is probably the most painful part of the entire walk! Continue uphill, crossing two more ladder stiles as the gradient increases unrelentingly before finally levelling off where a man-made watercourse or leat runs left to right under the road ahead of you (at **690610**).

**2)     (690610)     →**

         130°         →

Rather than sticking with the road and crossing this waterway, turn right over a concrete step stile to gain the path following the Southern embankment [7-03]. Keep to this level path, clambering over two more sets of step stiles alongside a pair of neighbouring footbridges.

A brief word here about these irritating concrete step stiles – obviously erected to deter walkers. A number along this section are wobbly, narrow, entangled by adjacent wire fencing and always at just the wrong height for graceful advance. You have been warned. (More recently some have been replaced by proper wooden stiles – presumably to cater for the growing legion of cyclists who frequent this embankment route) [7-04].

---

**OPTION 1**
The second of these two footbridges does give direct access onto the hillside – but locating a decent path uphill is awkward from here.

---

As the path trends increasingly left and the main Nant y Benglog valley opens up ahead of you, you encounter a third foot-bridge. Cross the final concrete step stile and turn immediately left to cross the leat by way of this bridge [7-05]. Ahead of you on your left is a metal ladder stile giving access onto the hillside.

**3)     (699607)     →**

**350°        →**

Cross this ladder stile. The most direct and foolproof route is to head directly uphill now, but bypassing all crags to the left rather than right [7-06 looking back down]. Once you overcome the first section of steep ground the gradient relents slightly as you eventually meet a T-junction of paths (identified by a diminutive cairn). Take the right-hand path [7-07], climbing gently to another area of flatter terrain crossed by a low wall [7-08]. Pass through the conveniently placed gap. The ground on the other side of this wall can be quite wet underfoot. Trend left before continuing onto the next set of grassy crags. The ascending path becomes more evident now until another outcrop of rock hijacks the way ahead [7-09]. Pass to the left of these crags, following the main path which now leads unerringly onto the broad ridge of Y Braich (Pen yr Helgi Du's Southern extension).

Eventually the main swell of summit fills the skyline ahead, with an intervening hummock to its right. The ground is pleasantly turfed, relatively dry (apart from one level section with a pool on your left) and not particularly steep [7-10].

> *There are fine views all along this climb, in particular the classic vista West of the Ogwen valley – Llyn Ogwen, framed by Pen yr Ole Wen, the backdrop of Y Garn and a foreshortened Tryfan immediately across valley.*
> *To the South, Moel Siabod dominates the distant skyline [7-11], whilst to its right you can cast your eyes on the more imposing side of those two minor Glyderau, Gallt yr Ogof and Y Foel Goch [7-12].*
> *Directly East, as the walk gains height, the bulk of Pen Llithrig y Wrach appears reassuringly close, with the slopes of Llethr Gwyn and Craig Wen to its right separated from Crimpiau further right by a trench beyond which nestles the Llyn Crafnant reservoir.*

There are still a number of false summits before you reach the last final push. But eventually you are given a choice of two paths to reach the top [7-13]. The left-hand path is the wider, and more direct of the two. But the right-hand one has better views to offer as it runs along the rim of Cwm Bychan, the cirque cut into the Eastern flanks of the hill [7-14 and 7-15].

Ahead on the skyline you should finally be able to pick out the solitary cairn that means there is very little 'up' left to go [7-16]. Whichever path you follow, you emerge on a level platform with a large pool beneath the final slopes leading to the top [7-17 looking back downslope]. Beyond here the fairly luxuriant turf is often replaced by anaemic stubble following dry weather through which poke upright shards of frost-shattered rock. It's a sobering thought that, if by some ecological disaster, the coarse grass covering most of Snowdonia's tops were to fail due to a change in climate or air quality, much of the landscape would resemble this gaunt, grey, balding bulge. It would not take long for soil erosion, brought about by the loss of this vegetation and its substantial root system, to change the nature of the landscape irrevocably.

This rock-strewn summit complete with cairn close to the 800-metre contour (at **699628**) is actually a false summit [7-18]. The true top is some 150 metres to the North West. Cross a small dip and follow a distinct path cut into the turf [7-19] that leads to a small pile of stones identifying **Pen yr Helgi Du** [7-20] (at **697630** – 833m/2733ft).

Perched on this narrow platform, the summit is open to all the elements borne South off the main Carneddau, but it is still worth spending time here if only to study the deep basin of Cwm Eigiau to the North East [7-21] and the last leg of **Walk 5**.

*The bulk of Carnedd Llywelyn towers above the immediate skyline to the North [7-22], together with the intervening ridge and shoulder of Bwlch Eryl Farchog [7-23].*
*Below and to your left lies the Ffynnon Llugwy reservoir [7-24] draining South into the Ogwen valley.*

The Ffynnon Llugwy reservoir supplies much of the water for the leat which feeds into the massive Llyn Cowlyd reservoir to the East. Surplus water enters the Afon Llugwy – the river which runs along the floor of Nant y Benglog, through Capel Curig, feeds the Swallow Falls above Betws-y-Coed, and eventually joins the Afon Conwy.

The name of the famous Swallow Falls is incidentally a mistranslation from the Welsh word for the falls – 'ewynnol' which means foaming. Another similar-sounding word is 'wennol' – the Welsh for 'swallow' – a simple mistake for a Saxon

---

### OPTION 2

It is from this vantage point that you have an opportunity to study the lie of the land and pick a way down to Bwlch Eryl Farchog. Bear in mind that you will also need to negotiate this same scramble back up to where you now stand [7-25 and 7-26].

Obviously, you can avoid this scramble altogether by omitting the section from **point 4** to **point 5** and back to **point 4** (since the scramble has no bearing on the completion of the main walk). But if you are in the mood for a challenge, or if it is your intention one day to complete the traverse across Bwlch Eryl Farchog from Carnedd Llywelyn to Pen yr Helgi Du then read on.

*Time for the scramble – down and back up – 25 mins max.*

---

4)      (697630)        →

   315°              →

If you are ready to allow a little drama into an otherwise relatively tame walk, this is where Act I begins. Be assured that although the path approaches the exposed, right-hand edge of the crest numerous times, it always twists left again away from any danger. Just be sure to keep your eyes peeled for useful markers that you can locate again on the return climb – the distinctive shapes of boulders or rock outcrops, scratch marks on the ground, or the nature of the sparse vegetation.

The saddle at **694634** is reached without too much difficulty, although a cover of ice or strong cross-winds would make certain situations that much more precarious. I can vouch for the winds that sweep up Cwm Eigiau, having once been blown clear off my feet while descending the relatively easy path down into Bwlch y Tri Marchog.

OPTION 3
If you intend tackling Carnedd Llywelyn from here, there is a straightforward path that follows the ridge line directly to its summit. The first section of ridge demands care; the approach from the left involving a tricky manoeuvre up polished slabs. That from the right has better hand-holds, but more exposure.

Once you reach the base of Pen yr Helgi Du's North-facing muzzle at least you now have the experience to tackle a simple scramble that looks intimidating from below but is actually just a cuddly bit of crag.

5)      (694634)      →

        135°      →

Facing this rocky snout once again you will note the obvious path of steep gravel heading up to the right. That way lies failure. Instead, you need to climb up the wall of tilting shale on the left. From beneath this obstacle you have no way of knowing what lies above – and the uncomfortable prospect of ending up in an impossible corner will cross your mind unless, of course, you have just clambered down that very same bit of rock. But after two or three easy moves you reach a narrow platform with a clear path beyond. This bears left to the edge of the cliff then almost immediately turns easily right into a shallow gully. Two large slabs of rock jammed in the floor of the gully provide no hindrance to gaining height. Above this section the path veers left again to the overhang before edging off right to less exposed, and easily scaled rock [7-27]. Before you have time to realise how breathless you have become, all scrambling is done for the day and your feet are planted firmly on the summit once more. But at least something has finally given the day an edge.

Incidentally, if the descent of this steep path has put you off a return ascent, there are numerous escape routes (just see **Walk 6**).

4)    (697630)    →

      110    →

From the main summit of Pen yr Helgi Du once more your next target is Pen Llithrig y Wrach. Descend across the small dip between the summit's two tops. A path to your left by-passes the rock-strewn false summit visited earlier should you wish to miss it out [7-28], but I always prefer to stick to the highest points of any ridge walk whenever practicable [7-29]. Beyond the false top a smaller cairn marks the beginnings of a clear path downhill to the East [7-30]. In places it is quite steep, and there are some wet patches where the muddy path threads a way between the crags. As you reach lower ground you pass the twisted remnants of a rusted wire fence before the ground levels out at the col of Bwlch y Tri Marchog at **709626** [7-31].

*This high gap gives one of the finest views (left) into Cwm Eigiau [7-32].*

Just beyond the lowest point of this col, if the wind is howling from the North out of the more desolate corners of Cwm Eigiau, a jumble of crags and boulders on the left-hand side of the path will provide you with some welcome protection perhaps as you lunch and contemplate your next move [7-33].

*Before moving on take the opportunity to study the more rugged side of Pen yr Helgi Du now you have reached its Eastern end [7-34 looking back].*

---

OPTION 4

If deteriorating weather makes an ascent of the second summit impractical, the leat you followed earlier in the walk can be rejoined by heading directly downhill into Cwm Tal-y-Braich on a bearing of 200°. This dumps you at **point 10** where the leat coils into the valley of the Bedol (close to the blue shed [7-35 and 7-36]).
I would caution you, however, that the terrain you have to cross to get there is wet and boggy and I cannot recommend this route except under the most desperate of circumstances.

***Time saved approx 1 hr 15mins***

---

**(709627)** →

**90°** →

Continuing along the path beyond this rocky windbreak you encounter a fence running along the base of the hillside ahead of you. Cross this fence by way of the ladder stile [7-37 and 7-38 from further along the path], turn right and pick your way across a small patch of wet ground onto the path that weaves its way up the Western ridge of Pen Llithrig y Wrach.

The path climbs quite steadily, presenting no difficulties as it trends first right [7-39] then increasingly left towards the edge of the cliffs overlooking Gallt Cedryn above Cwm Eigiau.

*Throughout the entire ascent there are fine views back to Pen yr Helgi Du and its higher neighbours [7-40], as well as the Glyderau across the main Ogwen valley to the South [7-41]. You might also be able to identify the long ridge of Cnicht with Moelwyn Mawr far to the South if conditions allow [7-42].*

Close to the 730-metre contour your path begins to trend right again as it reaches more level ground [7-43]. Suddenly, when you think there must be more to this mountain than the easy staircase you have just followed, there on the spiky skyline directly ahead of you is its summit cairn [7-44]. Regardless of the approach route you take, easy access across flat, rock-strewn ground leads you effortlessly to the small cairn marking the summit of **Pen Llithrig y Wrach** (at **716622** – 799m/2622ft).

This hill is probably better-known by sight than many of the other, more celebrated, members of the Carneddau range – even though most of those who have seen it are unaware of its almost unpronounceable (even to some Welsh speakers) name. It is one of the most visibly-arresting mountains facing the Northern seaboard of Wales. The block of Pen Llithrig y Wrach is clearly visible from most houses in the higher parts of Llandudno Junction above the Conwy estuary, from the A55 as you approach the Conwy tunnel, and from the Llanrwst road as you head down the Vale of Conwy [7-45]. It stands there like an enormous, old-fashioned cheese-dish plonked upon an otherwise vaguely anonymous skyline.

*To the East of you now lies the impressive Llyn Cowlyd reservoir, with the sheer slopes crested by Creigiau Gleision plunging from skyline to water's edge in an unbroken line [7-46 to 7-49].*

**7)** **(716622)** →

180° →

From the summit a clear path leads South to a series of rocky mounds (overlooking Llyn Cowlyd). The path gradually trends right as it rounds the Southern spur of the hill. Near the cliff edge you will soon come across a long line of angular slabs that appear at first glance to have been laid out in preparation for some path-building project [7-50]. Judging by the degree of weathering these slabs have suffered, the project was abandoned years ago.

Continue following this line of slabs and you slowly descend the Southern end of the mountain [7-51 looking back towards the summit]. Look out for a low, grass-covered hump (little more than a squashed pyramid) ahead and downslope to your right beneath the main mass of Gallt yr Ogof [7-52]. By picking a path that runs to the right of this mound you avoid dropping left into the main valley close to the inflow of Llyn Cowlyd. Detouring that way adds a lot of unnecessary distance to the walk (although if you do end up there you will find a perfectly adequate footpath that leads back to the A5 – but a lot closer to Capel Curig than where you are parked – see **Walk 8**).

Beyond these slabs the path can be clearly picked out as it crosses the turf-covered flanks of the hill. This is easy-going at first until it drops down a couple of craggy sections that may force you to take your hands out of your pockets. Beyond here the path maintains its distinct line; the lower slopes to your left inviting you to head towards the reservoir but the path itself continuing towards your grassy mound. Once you reach a hollow with long grass and a steep, unattractive escape route left, continue ahead instead up the opposite side of the hollow to gain access onto the mound. A short way past a patch of damp and you are faced with the main valley of Nant y Benglog below you.

From this vantage point you should be able to pick out enough details to figure out a more direct route back to the leat that you followed during the early stages of the walk. A few clues perhaps – first find the leat itself running left to right across the terrain beneath you, then a fence running directly to it that marks the transition from heather to grass, and finally a footbridge that can be seen crossing the leat where it meets the fence, and another wider bridge further right [7-53, and 7-54 from further up the hillside].

Even if visibility to the South is limited, the next stage of the walk is straightforward and relies on choosing the most direct line of descent rather than precise route-finding. The quickest way involves picking a zig-zag route down the boulder-strewn slopes ahead of you; slopes which look daunting from below [7-55] but which can be painlessly negotiated by way of the numerous sheep trods that criss-cross this hillside. Quite quickly you emerge onto a grass-covered ramp that slopes away to your left with a wire fence running parallel to it (close to **712616**) [7-56].

---

### OPTION 5

If you are in a mad rush to get back to your vehicle, there is a short-cut. But I cannot recommend that route during wet weather due to the nature of the ground you have to cross. Scan the valley to your right for the blue shed and concreted area close to **704615** (in the corner where the leat takes a pronounced bend beneath the Eastern slopes of Pen yr Helgi Du). That is your goal – **point 10**.

Cross the fence using one of the many boulders alongside it, set your internal compass on that shed, then duck your head down and go for it. It's not pretty – in fact it's downright ugly. The gradient is gentle, but the tussocks of grass and underlying bog make progress painful.

Eventually you reach a narrow creek (narrow enough to vault across with a trekking pole) that cuts through the peat just as you reach a gateway. The gate itself, of course, has been climb-proofed by heavy-gauge wire netting. If you stick to its left side, a wooden fence inside the gateway provides useful footholds. Beyond this gate cross the wide footbridge (with seemingly more water on top than underneath) leading you onto the path on the South bank of the leat.

***Time saved – approximately 20mins.***

---

**8)    (712616)    →**

**140°    →**

For a slightly more sedate return to civilisation, turn left and follow this fence line dropping slowly as it contours the slopes until it meets a crossroads of sorts; a junction of fence and collapsed wall [7-57]. Turn 90° right at this junction, crossing the fence and following another which heads directly towards the main valley floor [7-58]. The path running parallel to this second fence is very wet and muddy, but nothing like as bad as the ground you have to cross in **Option 5**.

As it reaches lower ground the fence takes a sharp turn left. You can either keep following it as it dog-legs downhill or continue ahead along slightly drier ground to pass between a couple of small hummocks. Behind these lies a patch of scrubby ground, with clumps of heather and coarse grass; the leat is now directly ahead of you and the only bridge a short distance to your left [7-59].

Also to your left you get a chance to reacquaint yourself with the fence. Cross it where it abuts against the banks of the leat, then head along a short grassy path, picking your way past a couple of puddles, to reach the bridge. Cross the leat by way of this bridge and turn right, having made use of a proper stile to rejoin the embanked path.

**9)    (711608)    →**

**275°    →**

Now it's a case of following this level path back to the reservoir service road at **point 2**. En route you pass a disused sluice gate which presumably once acted as a release valve for the leat during times of excessive rainfall [7-60]. But as you approach a distinct bend in the leat ahead of you there is evidence that some work is still being carried out on the maintenance of the waterway.

**10**     **(704615)**     →

    **210°**            →

This marks the point where both **Options 4** and **5** rejoin the main route [7-61]. It is tarnished somewhat by an untidy arrangement of wooden barriers and concrete weirs that cross the Afon Bedol where it emerges from Cwm Bychan and enters the leat. A ramshackle blue shed, tethered to its concrete plinth by guy-ropes, is the only other feature worthy of note. Perhaps it's best to pass this industrial blemish as swiftly as possible. Continue along the embankment path as before, and the loop of leat twists round to the right again as it enters the final straight.

> *Fortunately, you are immediately confronted by the classic view of Tryfan and the Bristly Ridge of Glyder Fach [7-62]. From here on a clear day it is possible to vicariously pick your way crag by crag, shelf by shelf, to either summit without having to set foot on their rocks [7-63 and 7-64].*

But unfortunately, you are required to clamber over yet more concrete step-stiles before you eventually pass **point 3** and reach **point 2** again,

Here is where this particular guidebook proves its true worth. Don't make the mistake of turning right at **point 2** and heading into the depths of Cwm Llugwy [7-65]. Likewise, don't cross the tarmac and continue along the leat in search of more stiles (prominent signs warn that there is no access to the A5 in that direction). Instead, turn left and head downhill, crossing the three ladder stiles en route until you hit the A5. From there Gwern Gof Isaf lies ¼ Km West on the opposite side of the road.

**END**

# Craiglwyn [24] / Creigiau Gleision
# (South [25] and North [26] tops)

| 16.5 Km (10.3 miles) 830m (2722ft) Time : 5hrs 45min | A complex and compelling ridge walk high above Llyn Cowlyd followed by a lakeside stroll back to civilisation |
| --- | --- |

When I was a kid I always wished I could have lived during those times when explorers embarked on journeys into uncharted territories. I longed to do the same, to be the first person to set foot on some newly-discovered island – or mountain top.

I used to play out these fantasies in the hills and valleys that surrounded the cottage in which I was raised. More often than not I ended up giving up – well and truly ensnared in a thorny bit of woodland or up to my knees in mud. Of course, the scratches quickly healed and the mud washed off. So I never got into much bother, except when I dragged the son of some 'posh' visitors on one of my hairy expeditions into the woods – all dressed up in his Sunday best.

Nowadays few of us get the opportunity to step into unmapped territory – I suppose this is one of the walks that comes closest to that. The Explorer map chooses to keep the more obvious tracks well-hidden. I can never figure out why Tourist/Leisure maps, ostensibly designed for walkers and the like, can be frustratingly fuzzy where footpaths are concerned yet painstakingly record every piffling regional boundary.

Anyway, in the case of the Creigiau Gleision ridge the map's shortcomings add a bit of a buzz to the day. This walk is one you will grow to enjoy, and one in which you are unlikely to meet many natives, restless or otherwise.

**North**

**Don't forget**

**map/compass
whistle/torch**

**suitable footwear
+ clothing**

**food/drink**

**brain**

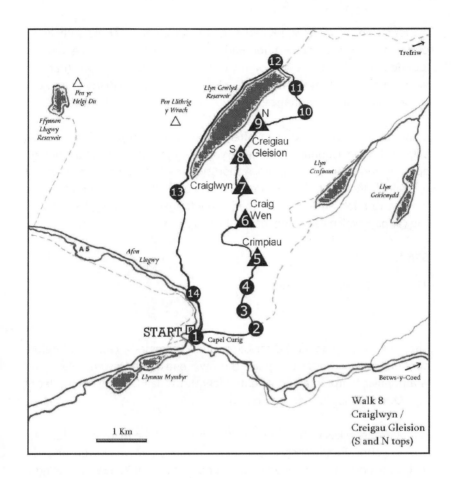

Walk 8
Craiglwyn /
Creigau Gleision
(S and N tops)

## APPROACH

This walk starts in the village of Capel Curig.

If approaching from Bangor, follow the A5 past Llyn Ogwen. As you enter the village of Capel Curig and the road swings to the left look out for the junction right signposted Llanberis and Beddgelert. Turn right here and immediately right again along the front of the shops ('Pinnacle Outdoor Shop and Café'). A car park is signposted to your left at the rear of these shops – free at the time of writing, with telephone kiosk, toilets and ample space for thirty vehicles or more.

If approaching from Betws-y-Coed along the A5 as you enter the outer limits of the village, the exit left for Beddgelert is a short distance beyond 'Cobden's Hotel' and the 'Clogwyn Outdoor Shop and Café' (which are on your right). Exit left at the Beddgelert junction, and immediately turn right to locate the car park entrance alongside the shops as described above.

If approaching from Beddgelert, after passing Llynnau Mymbyr and the Plas y Brenin National Mountain Centre on your right you come to a T-junction on approaching Capel Curig village. A short side-road left along the frontage of a small cluster of shops provides a short-cut to the A5 heading towards Bangor. Turn left onto this side-road and left again, following the signs for the car park which lies at the rear of the shops.

**START**

1)      (720583)          →

         160°              →

The minor road passing the car park entrance crosses a cattle grid before continuing along Nant y Benglog – the lower end of the Ogwen valley – and is a popular footpath along its entire length to Glan Dena at the outlet of Llyn Ogwen (and the starting point for **Walk 6**).

But our route takes us back towards the shops and the roadside – cross the busy A5 opposite the shops, heading left towards Dyffryn Ogwen, and you will see a footpath signposted on the opposite verge at **721582** to the right of the small chapel.

         70°          →

A ladder stile beside a metal gate gives access to a grassy hillside crossed by a clear path which gains height quite quickly as it approaches more rocky terrain [8-01 looking back to the start]. The path skirts the foot of the crags on your right, the 'Pinnacles', which are used as a rock-climbing playground. It then crosses a meadow before a paved section cuts through patches of reed

[8-02]. Beyond this section it leads through deciduous woodland to emerge on more level ground.

*On your right the shapely peak of Carnedd Moel Siabod juts proudly above the forested banks of the Llugwy valley [8-03].*

The path cuts a broad track through bracken, running alongside a fence on the right and shortly meeting a ladder stile in the fence. Continue past this stile and immediately ahead of you is another ladder stile at the left side of a wooden gate at **728581**. Cross this stile to rejoin the path (look out for the marker post) [8-04], partly paved with blocks of stone where it climbs to a slight rise [8-05].

Beyond this incline a stream drains the relatively level ground from left to right and is crossed by a substantial wooden footbridge at **732581** [8-06 looking back]. At the other side of the footbridge three paths set off towards higher ground [8-07].

The path on the right starts off crossing muddy ground before entering the forested slopes bordering the valley of the Afon Llugwy. The middle path, and perhaps the most obvious of the three, heads uphill between a series of grass- and tree-covered knolls. But the path you need to follow is the minor one bearing left as it skirts the knolls and drops onto the broad, flat valley floor of Nant y Geuallt.

*Directly across the valley from where you are standing are the craggy foothills of Creigiau Gleision. Beyond a small hummock of rocky ground tight against the farthest bank of the stream rises a grassy ramp, dotted with trees at its base. To its right are more substantial rock falls beneath the towering rocky turrets of Clogwyn Cigfran.*
*Your route involves negotiating this grassy ramp, crossing a dry-stone wall three-quarters of the way up, then trending right towards the skyline [8-08].*

2)      (733584)        →

        310°            →

First of all there's the stream below to cross – easy enough thanks to a slab of rock bridging the point where a faint path meets the water's edge. The river is narrow enough to step across anyway.

You now cross a flat expanse of grass with a wire fence to your right and low, rocky slopes to your left. Closer to the fence the ground can be particularly wet, although this is the most direct line to the steeper slopes straight ahead of you [8-09]. It is quite easy to avoid the boggiest bits by trending left – but aim for the right-hand base of the slope ahead of you where a ladder stile on the right allows one to cross the fence (at **731585**).

You don't have to cross the stile – it is debatable whether following the left or right side of the fence as it climbs this unrelentingly steep slope is best. I chose the left side and ended up battling through new growth of bracken as a path of sorts scaled the hillside tight against rocks on my left [8-10]. Across the fence there are no rocks until further up, but the vegetation there is more profuse.

Whichever side you decide upon, the way ahead is strenuously uphill, keeping close to the line of the fence. As the fence begins to veer off to the left it pays to climb over to its right side anyway, sticking close to it until it runs alongside a slightly rocky hump which is easily passed by heading further right.

The ground levels out at last where a partly-collapsed dry-stone wall runs across the face of the hillside. Walk through the gap to a ladder stile which crosses a fence running parallel to the wall [8-11].

**3)**     **(730586)**     →

         **20°**        →

Cross the ladder stile and turn right. The wall continues until it abuts against the dark craggy face of Clogwyn Cigfran. The fence however soon takes a more logical route, heading further left as it approaches the most difficult ground to top out on a high saddle. Following the fence as far as here is again a gruelling haul but at least it's a quick way of gaining much-needed height.

To your left you will see a pleasing little grassy trod dropping gently down-slope towards Nant y Benglog (the Eastern end of the Ogwen valley). It is possible that the source of this particular path lies not too far from where you started the walk. The map gives few clues.

Continue uphill to your right where the path soon reaches another ladder stile [8-12] which allows you to cross the wire fence again to access the rocky summit of Clogwyn Cigfran if you so wish.

*Given the unrelenting steepness of the slopes leading up to this point there's no doubt that you have already rested for a moment or two and gazed behind you at the view. If anything, Carnedd Moel Siabod is more photogenic from the valley floor than from 100 metres higher.*

Drop back down to the side of the fence and follow it through a small gap. Beyond it you ascend yet another steep, grassy slope that tops out at a rounded summit consisting of half-buried boulders [8-13].

*From here you should now be able to pick out the bulky shoulder of Migneint left of Moel Siabod. As you turn back to stare across the fence to your left you will see two valleys heading towards even higher peaks. A twist of road snakes through Dyffryn Mymbyr beneath the Snowdon horseshoe on the left. The A5 begins its run up Dyffryn Ogwen towards the meeting point of the Glyderau and Carneddau on your right. Be patient – these magnificent panoramas improve as the walk continues.*

Return to the path alongside the fence and follow it as it emerges in an open area with the dark waters of Llyn y Coryn on your left walled in on one side by pale crags [8-14, and 8-15 from higher ground]. The path along its Eastern shore can be quite wet as you are walking on what was once undoubtedly the floor of a slightly larger body of water.

4)     (731591)     →

    15°          →

**OPTION 1**
If you are impatient to get onto the Creigiau Gleision ridge proper, you can miss out the next top.
Traverse this area of flat ground and drop down to the broad valley North of here. Then continue right along the valley (East) until you meet **point 5**.

*Time saved – about ½ an hour.*

There is a pleasant diversion to your right – a barely detectable path picks its way through the heather up onto a bare little summit, **Crimpiau** (at **732595** – 475m/1558ft).

*No great altitude, but your first clear view of Creigiau Gleision directly North (or more accurately, the hummocky crags of Craig Wen and Clogwyn yr Eryr first, on the extreme left, followed by Craiglwyn and the highest point of the ridge further West) [8-16].*

*The beauty of this spot is that it allows you to compare what you see on the map with what lies in front of you; a complex stew of contours and black lines suddenly transformed into walls and paths that hopefully give you ideas of how best to approach the next stage of the walk.*

*There is also your first glimpse to the North East of the beautiful, wooded valley of the Afon Crafnant high above the village of Trefriw, together with its arrow-head, blue lake [8-17]*

**5)**     **(732595)**     →

       330°           →

It does not take much ingenuity to find a route down the North side of Crimpiau to gain the floor of the valley separating it from the rising slopes of Craig Wen. A collapsed wall keeps you company for part of this descent, And as you approach the flat floor of this valley you will see a number of footpaths trailing towards the right. You can trend right as you contour the final section of descent to avoid dropping all the way to the valley floor. Shortly you meet a clear path heading to the right, climbing gently to a gap in the dry-stone wall ahead. Pass through this gap and follow the path ahead and downhill as it aims for the valley floor again.

You are now in a high col, a dry passage connecting the Afon Llewesig flowing Westwards towards the Llugwy close to Capel Curig and the more substantial headwaters of the Afon Crafnant flowing East through the lake towards Trefriw and the main Conwy valley beyond. A footpath links the two valleys and it is likely it saw more foot traffic in the distant past than it does today. Your immediate goal is the highest point on the Northern skyline, still some distance away [8-18]. As you exit this col left there are initially no signs of a clear path. But as you skirt the left hand side of the slopes you will come across a footpath. And as you round the corner of this low spur you emerge on more level ground where a broken wall to your right heads across the gap to another, even more derelict wall on the lowest shoulder of Craig Wen [8-19].

Aim for this wrecked wall, pass through it and follow the path running left around the foot of Craig Wen's base [8-20]. This path rises onto a broad platform beneath the steep wall of Craig Wen then splits in two. The left fork keeps to low ground, circuiting the lower edge of the platform, but the right fork slowly gains height, getting closer to the rocky ramparts of Craig Wen as you circle this massive rock tower clockwise. Standing beneath its Western face, the climb to the summit looks impossible, but once you turn the corner the slopes to your right are suddenly less pronounced and it is a simple matter of zig-zagging up the intermittent fragments of path that meander between the rocky outcrops to gain the superlative summit of **Craig Wen** (at **728602** – 548m/1797ft) [8-21].

I have a soft spot for Craig Wen – it's definitely a place I know I shall revisit, perhaps when there's snow on the ground, to gaze spellbound at its wonderful surroundings.

*It is easy from this vantage point to believe that the scene laid out before you has been created just for you. Where else can you see Moel Siabod, Llynnau Mymbyr, the Snowdon Horseshoe, Dyffryn Ogwen, Glyder Fawr and Fach, Tryfan, Y Garn and Pen yr Ole Wen with barely a turn of the head? [8-22 and 8-23]?*

**6)**     **(728602)**     →

        270°         →

It is possible to head slightly West of North to regain the footpath heading towards the main ridge, but by far the easier option is to retrace your steps to the base of Craig Wen's ramparts and rejoin the path there. Once you regain the path turn right and cross a broad saddle of coarse grassland that can be wet in places. A grey rock-face on your right, Clogwyn yr Eryr, is easily by-passed left by a path which climbs quite steeply, passing left of a noticeable erosion scar of sandy soil on the heather-clad hillside [8-24].

For a while all you can see ahead of you are convex, grassy slopes. Eventually a broader skyline opens up, with the shaven face of Pen Llithrig y Wrach to your left, a distant rocky pyramid nearer centre (the main top of Creigiau Gleision) and a low pavement of grey rock closer at hand to your right. This is the minor top of **Craiglwyn** (at **730608** – 623m/2043ft).

> *Spend time to sit amongst the boulders laid out on its fairly flat summit [8-25]. You get a superb retrospective view of Craig Wen as well as the featureless plateau of Moel Defaid concealing the crags of Clogwyn yr Eryr below.*

**7)**     **(730608)**     →

        305°         →

A fairly straightforward path, gravelled in places, cuts through the heather as it approaches the Western slopes of Creigiau Gleision's main summit. After crossing the broad shoulder separating it from Craiglwyn the path takes a fairly direct assault at the steeply-dipping, fractured grey slabs [8-26] that terminate at the exposed summit of **Creigiau Gleision (South top)** (at **728615** – 678m/2224ft) – the highest point of the day.

*The serrated top of Tryfan can be picked out standing proud of the remaining Glyderau [8-27]. Llyn Ogwen is hidden by the two spurs of Y Braich (leading onto Pen yr Helgi Du) and the Southern ramparts of Pen Llithrig y Wrach with the headwaters of Llyn Cowlyd nestling below.*

*You should be able to pick out the stream entering the reservoir (fed by leat from Ffynnon Llugwy deep in the recesses of the corrie formed by Carnedd Llywelyn and Pen yr Helgi Du). There is also a view of the remainder of the ridge to the North East [8-28]. But dominating the entire scene are the scree slopes descending Pen Llithrig y Wrach's Eastern flanks into the deep waters of the reservoir [8-29].*

Llyn Cowlyd is the largest of the Conwy lakes and the deepest lake in North Wales with a mean depth of slightly over 109ft and a maximum depth of 222ft – compared to Llyn Ogwen's maximum depth of a measly 10ft.

8)      (728615)      →

      40°      →

It is pretty much a straight line to the next top. On the lower section beneath this main summit you will see a couple of pools – these are easily avoided by keeping left of them.

A small hump of rocky ground gives another vantage point before you begin the day's final ascent. It was here that I came across the day's only other walker in this secluded corner (or so I thought) – someone walking from Trefriw to Betws-y-Coed by the more scenic route. He warned me that the climb from the dam at the North Eastern end of the reservoir onto the ridge was pretty unpleasant. Ho-hum!

As you drop to a small col close to **733622** your path crosses a sizeable outcrop of white quartz cut into the grey mountainside [8-30]. This is clearly visible from far below on the opposite lake shore, like a crumbling ripple of rotten marble running through the ridge, the tumbled blocks resembling prised teeth in the scree beneath it [8-31].

A short distance ahead is the relatively unimpressive peak of **Creigiau Gleision (North top)** (at **733622** – 634m/2080ft) [8-32 from below the South top].

> At least it gives a superb view of the opposite ends of Llyn Cowlyd. To your left is an elegant stretch of blue water hemmed in by the sheer wall of Pen Llithrig Y Wrach and the Glyderau [8-33]. Check out Tryfan from here! And to your right more open water with its dam wall and the network of service roads and pipeline than run North East towards more civilised parts [8-34]. The way ahead across heather-clad hummocks looks less than promising however [8-35].

Before moving on I took one final look back at the ridge line extending away to the South. There were three figures perched on the nearest summit – getting crowded, time to skedaddle.

**9)**      **(733622)**      →

         **70°**         →

THIS IS THE POINT AT WHICH GOOD VISIBILITY PLAYS A KEY FACTOR IN REACHING THE DAM AT THE NORTH EASTERN CORNER OF THE RESERVOIR WITHOUT TOO MUCH SUFFERING. IN POOR LIGHT THERE IS AMPLE OPPORTUNITY TO LOSE THE WAY UNLESS YOUR MAP- AND COMPASS-READING SKILLS ARE ADEQUATE.

Continue towards lower ground, a mix of bare rock, dense heather and rough grass. You will see an elongated pool on your right (at **735623**) [8-36], with two tiny islands of rock at either end. Keep to the right side of this and aim for the slightly raised ground above its North Eastern end (topped by a fence) [8-37]. Once you reach this fence on its rocky pedestal turn right and follow the fence-line downhill (crossing over to its left-hand side as you do so).

---

OPTION 3

A path veers off to your left in front of this fence, and should in theory meet up with the path encountered later at **point 12** [8-38]. However, there is no indication on the map as to the path's existence. It's up to you whether you set off left and find your own route down. Good luck!

---

As the path descends the blunt end of the Creigiau Gleision ridge it is little more than a rut cut into the heather. But at least it does make progress relatively easy. On the day I first followed this walk, whenever I brushed against a clump of heather the vegetation released clouds of small brown butterflies (the 'small heath' variety I believe). This path follows the left-hand side of the fence, sometimes at quite a distance. As long as you keep an eye on the fence then you can see where you are heading [8-39]. A path can be picked out ascending the low hill on the skyline ahead (the high point of Cefn Cyfarwydd at **752631**) but we will escape the ridge before then.

The path bottoms out in a grassy basin, with heather-clad slopes each side, the occasional, incongruous fir tree, and little else [8-40 looking back uphill]. Some five minutes after climbing out of this hollow the ground closest to the fence becomes exceedingly wet as a large, vivid green patch of sphagnum moss replaces heather [8-41]. To its left is an expanding bay of reeds and tall grass, evidence that there is ample moisture not far beneath the surface of the soil.

10)     (743626)         →

        330°             →

Faced by this vivid green quagmire directly ahead, you are advised to take a

90° turn left in search of a more direct route down to the hidden valley bottom. At first all that can be seen ahead of you is the top of a little hill, covered in lush pasture and sparsely dotted with white boulders [8-42]. Aim for this and you should avoid the wetter ground to your right. Continue on this heading and you quickly encounter gentle, green slopes by-passing to the left of this hill. Further ahead on your right is another, lower green hillock with a clear path of white gravel extending uphill from its left side. Drop down easy slopes to join this path [8-43]. In hindsight, not as difficult as anticipated, but not an ascent route I would recommend unless you know exactly where you are going.

**11)**     **(740630)**     →

       0°     →

To the left this path (not marked on the Explorer map) heads upslope – perhaps even as far as that fence perched on the rocky platform beneath Creigiau Gleision. What **is** certain is that if you follow the path downhill it bears to the right as it leads down easily to the vicinity of the dam [8-44]. A low, concrete barrier meets your path a short distance from the actual dam. Cross this barrier where it abuts against an outcrop of slate surmounted by a well-constructed wall and climb over the ladder stile to the right. Beyond are grassy banks dropping down to the service track running up-valley from your right to the base of the dam then across the outflow to the reservoir's Northern shore [8-45]. A faint path continues across the lower face of the dam, crossing a series of footbridges with metal barriers giving direct access to the track (then path) following the lake shore Westwards.

---

OPTION 4

In theory you could follow the service road down-valley for 1Km to the head of a minor road.

This in turn leads to the village of Trefriw a further 4.75 Km away – involving some very steep bits of road.

There is a bus service (via Llanrwst) from Trefriw back to Capel Curig.

---

**12)    (737635)    →**

**240°    →**

A collection of rundown buildings loiters around the end of the service road beyond which a broad gravel track heads left, South West along the lake shore [8-46]. A fence drops down from the hillside at **729630** (from the ruined remains up on your right of the smallholding of Cwm Cowlyd). This fence can be crossed by a ladder stile alongside an open gate [8-47].

*As you walk the length of Llyn Cowlyd reservoir you only need look to your left to be reminded of the sheer scale of the Creigiau Gleision ridge. Behind you the dammed end of the lake resembles an 'infinity pool' with nothing but sky beyond it since its hinterland consists of much lower ground. The upper end is closed off by a wall of grass-covered rock with at its left edge a noticeable bulky outcrop of rock studding the slope beneath Llethr Gwyn.*

Certain parts of the path are quite wet, and getting past the worst bits can be tricky, but eventually your escape route from the confines of this flooded valley carries you upslope with the river feeding the reservoir on your left cut into the rock headwall. As you climb higher still towards the craggy base of Pen Llithrig Y Wrach on your right you will eventually see level ground appear ahead of you and to your left where a ramshackle footbridge crosses the river. Skirt a wet patch of ground by keeping right and the path soon circles back left towards a more modern, galvanised bridge that ejects you close to the path crossing the featureless slopes above Nant Benglog [8-48 from Walk 7].

**13)    (717610)    →**

**140°    →**

Once you cross the galvanised bridge, turn right to cross a smaller footbridge that feeds the main path. This wet path has little to commend itself. It is a fairly direct route downhill to the A5 – that's the best that can be said. The path links a number of footbridges (little more than flat sheets of

145

reinforced plastic set over the waterways draining this peaty hillside) and if you keep your eyes peeled you should be able to pick your way to the ladder stile set in the fence above Tal-y-Waun farm at **717594**.

Beyond here the path broadens to a farm track behind the farm buildings (do not follow this to the front of the farm – that is the private access road strictly for the farmer's use). Continue straight ahead along an uneven path, following an irregular line of telegraph poles to the roadside where a ladder stile adjacent to a metal gate deposits you on the side of the A5.

**14)** **(719590)** →

**95°** →

The A5 can be busy – not the best of roads to hobble alongside on tired legs. The wider of its two pavements is on the opposite side. Cross over and head off left back towards Capel Curig (behind you lie Llyn Ogwen and Ogwen Cottage at the foot of the Glyderau). The shops and your starting point are less than 1Km away.

**END**

# GLYDERAU

*This compact group of hills is justifiably popular amongst most hill-walkers and rock climbers, due not only to the obvious challenges presented by the likes of the Bristly Ridge or Tryfan's steep flanks but also due to the feeling that here you really have arrived at some vast, natural playground. And if you want to play, you need a modicum of experience as well as the correct equipment. However, despite this proviso, it's fair to say that this exhilarating landscape does have something to offer everyone.*

## TASTER 9

*Dyffryn Mymbyr is a popular spot for passing drivers and coach parties to pause and snap a few photographs of the twin lakes, and of the Snowdon Horseshoe at the valley's Western end. There are a number of large lay-bys at the Capel Curig end (just past Plas y Brenin as you drive towards Beddgelert) that allow you to park beside the lakes.*

*However, if you don't fancy the idea of a stroll next to a constant stream of traffic, it is possible to access the easy slopes on the right hand side of the road opposite the lakeside. Leaving the car park in Capel Curig village (the start point of* **Walk 8***), go through the gateway (crossing a cattle grid) and follow this track uphill. After crossing a disused drainage channel the track splits in two – take the left fork which contours the blunt base of Cefn y Capel. How far you wander along this gentle path is up to you.*

*Alternatively, take the right fork and follow the track into Nant y Benglog, the Southern end of Dyffryn Ogwen.*

*Both walks give excellent views of the adjacent mountains without the need to cross too many contours.*

**Allow a couple of hours for either walk**

## TASTER 10

*There's no competition really if you want to explore the Northern arm of the Glyderau.*

*Heading down the A5 from Bethesda, take the first turning right some 2 Km*

South of the town. Continue along this narrow road which crosses the Afon Ogwen then turns sharp left to run the length of the valley as far as Ogwen Cottage. You can park anywhere along this road in one of the large lay-bys and take a stroll along the minor road that heads all the way to Ogwen Cottage. The scenery is stupendous, yet the walk is sedate for much of its length. How far you go is entirely up to you.

Not only do you get a worm's-eye view of the peaks towering above this side of the valley, you also get to survey the sheer walls of Pen yr Ole Wen on the opposite valley side. And as the walk advances towards the Ogwen Falls the panorama of Glyder Fawr, Glyder Fach and Tryfan is displayed directly ahead.

If you want to lengthen the walk by starting closer to the Bethesda end, park in the long lay-by beside the entrance to Ogwen Bank camp site (on the right just after you leave Bethesda). From here you can access a track running along the opposite river bank by first entering the camp site approach road and crossing the foot-bridge on your left. Once on the opposite side of the river turn left onto a sinuous track which eventually meets the minor road (described above) – track and road are both favourites with cyclists.

If you do walk as far as the cluster of buildings at Ogwen Cottage (refreshments and toilet block) the wisest option is to return along the same route. The alternative stroll along the A5 is not recommended due to the volume of traffic.

**The entire loop should take no more than 2 ½ hours.**


# TASTER 11

For a close-up look at the famous slopes of the Southern Glyderau, much loved by the rock climbing fraternity, a leisurely walk up to Llyn Idwal takes some beating. Starting from the car park at Ogwen Cottage follow the early stages of the route for **Walk 10** and you will soon reach the lake shore.

If the ground is not too wet underfoot there's another excellent walk up to Llyn Bochlwyd, (go left at **point 2** in **Walk 10**). The steep, stepped path along the Western banks of the Nant Bochlwyd river is relatively easy to follow if dry. But if heading for Llyn Idwal, don't turn left for Bochlwyd. Instead keep to the main path and within a quarter of an hour you are deep in the heart of Cwm Idwal with the lake's waters lapping inches away from your feet.

The walk up to Llyn Idwal takes no longer than 20 minutes. How much longer you spend along the shore before returning to the car park is up to you.

*If you attempt any of the above tasters it will be difficult to resist the temptation to explore higher ground. Read on for further details.....*

## WALK 9

# Y Foel Goch [27] / Gallt yr Ogof [28]

| | |
|---|---|
| **9.75 Km (6.1 miles)**<br><br>**790m (2591ft)**<br><br>**Time : 4hrs 30min** | **The two Eastern outliers of the Glyderau – written off by most walkers because of the allure of their loftier neighbours.** |

My earliest, hazy memories of this pair hark back to the time I first began taking a practical interest in walking these particular hills (in the early '70's). Three student friends and I spent an agreeable afternoon climbing Gallt yr Ogof from the roadside in Dyffryn Mymbyr. Having only ventured into the Welsh mountains on one previous occasion (a wintry excursion into the Afon Llafar valley for a close-up view of Ysgolion Duon) we felt justifiably proud of our achievements in reaching the summit with minimal effort.

There was nothing to this hill-walking lark. No need to consult map or compass when conditions were so sunny and clear. There was ample time to linger, grab a bite to eat while admiring the view to the twin lakes of Llynnau Mymbyr far below. We even brought out the camera to commemorate the conquest.

A few weeks later when the photographs were returned from the chemist's, and I relived our exploits by way of the snaps and a map, it slowly dawned on me that we had missed our target by about 1000 feet and a couple of kilometres or so. We had mistaken the barely significant bump of Cefn y Capel for its much loftier neighbour. A lesson was learnt – don't rely on recall alone (having briefly scanned the map it lay discarded back at the car). A map and compass are never surplus to requirements on any hill walk; and more significantly if your walk does turn out to be unexpectedly easy you've probably gone wrong somewhere or other.

**North**

**Don't forget**

**map/compass**
**whistle/torch**

**suitable footwear**
**+ clothing**

**food/drink**

**brain**

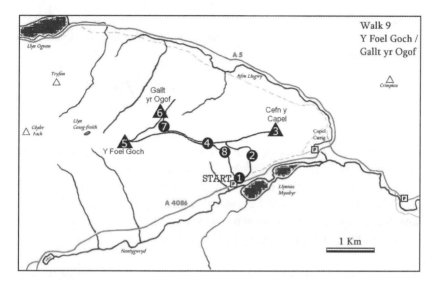

## APPROACH

Heading West along the A4086 (from Capel Curig towards Llanberis/ Beddgelert), pass the Plas y Brenin National Mountain Centre on your left followed by the twin lakes of Llynnau Mymbyr. At the far end of the second lake locate the lay-by on the right hand side of the road at **701574**. If you reach the entry road to the camp site on the left you have gone too far.

If travelling South along the Llanberis Pass, at the junction alongside the Pen-y-Gwryd Hotel turn left onto the A4086 and before you draw level with the first of the two lakes on your right (Llynnau Mymbyr) park in the second lay-by on your left at **701574**.

Following the A4086 from Beddgelert heading East, the lay-by is the second of two on your left (at **701574**) a few metres beyond the entrance road to the camp site on the right perched above the river flowing into the Westernmost lake of the two Llynnau Mymbyr.

## START

| 1) | (701574) | → |
| | 340° | → |

The path starts at the ladder stile in the stone wall that leads onto the hillside directly from the road verge (sign-posted 'Dyffryn Mymbyr' complete with the Snowdonia National Park emblem).

**25°**        →

Once over this wall bear right to cross a small footbridge and begin to contour up the grass- and bracken-covered slopes. Here and there marker posts identify the disjointed path that runs along the floor of the valley but at sufficient height to reward the walker with magnificent views. There are also ladder stiles lower down allowing walkers to follow a low-level track parallel to the main road all the way to Capel Curig.

Ahead of you a stone-enclosed paddock appears to divert this path uphill which is where our twin targets lie. Scraggly trees and tree stumps occupy the grassy spaces between the swathes of bracken. Head up the slope even more directly now, aiming for a large dry-stone wall that crosses the skyline ahead of you (ascending from the valley floor to the crags high on the left). Beyond this wall a more rugged series of crags dominates this side of the valley – the 'Ricks and Racks'. As you approach the wall you will reach a stream, complete with plunge pools, on your side of the wall.

Cross the stream to reach the far bank (a damp, grassy embankment in the lee of the wall). The easiest way now is to follow this embankment steeply uphill onto the skyline. Ease of progress depends on the level of water-logging – after heavy rainfall this section can be particularly wet.

**2)    (704579)    →**
    **10°          →**

As you gain the level ground at the headwaters of the stream (covered in knee-deep grass that cunningly hides the bog beneath) a muddy path approaches from the direction of Capel Curig to the East (crossing the wire fence on your right by way of a ladder stile). On your side of this fence the path strikes a fairly direct line uphill to your left. The going is not easy to follow in places, but the basic idea is to gain height as quickly as possible in order to reach the saddle of flatter ground further away to your left close to the 450-metre contour.

---

OPTION 1

For those of you able to resist this opportunity to detour East in order to visit Cefn y Capel, continue bearing left to the flat, boggy depression then proceed as if at **point 4**

*Time saved – 45 mins*

---

If you elect to take a closer look at the Southern end of Dyffryn Ogwen, once you reach level ground you will see to the right of this saddle, in a significant dip, a stone wall with a ladder stile. Cross this and follow a path leading East towards the minor ridge occupying the spur between Nant y Benglog (containing the Afon Llugwy) and Nant Gwryd or Dyffryn Mymbyr. The path skirts to the right hand side of the ridge's highest point but it is a simple matter to reach the top of **Cefn y Capel** (at **708583** – 460m/1509ft).

The view to the East improves if you continue a short distance further along the path, dropping slightly to reach the lower tops perched some 430 metres above Capel Curig.

**3)**    **(709584)**    →

     **255°**    →

From this perch simply reverse your steps along the knobbly ridge, passing through the stone wall by way of the ladder stile and continue West across the flat expanse of wet, boggy ground. There is a clear path here, but that is no guarantee that you can cross the entire gap with dry feet.

**4)**    **(698581)**    →

     **250°**    →

The lowest section (Bwlch Goleuni – at 441 metres) is water-logged for much of the year, although I have successfully crossed it in trainers during a summer heat-wave when the only problem was the midge population (approaching Scottish proportions).

As you cross this saddle, the slopes of Gallt yr Ogof bar the way ahead and to your right. To reach these slopes involves trending left, maintaining close contact with this extensive damp patch.

Once across it, the path turns stony underfoot and begins to climb more steeply to a wall (complete with small ladder stile). Beyond the stile, a steeper, shale path zig-zags uphill towards the next level section. For much of the way the track is clear, and even under low cloud one would be hard pressed to go astray. As the angle of ascent eventually relents the path crosses the lower slopes of a natural amphitheatre (with crags circling to your right) before climbing steeply once again. Small outcrops of shaley strata dipping at 45° into the slope make progress relatively easy.

Finally the saddle of level ground separating Gallt yr Ogof and Y Foel Goch is reached at **683583** close to the 700-metre contour. With Gallt yr Ogof playing a waiting game over your right shoulder [9-01] continue to strike ahead, uphill towards the skyline. Keep the small outcrop of crags on your right and almost immediately you emerge onto the summit of **Y Foel Goch**, marked by a cairn on your right (at **677581** – 805m/2641ft) [9-02].

The name is obviously a popular one in Snowdonia, as there are two other peaks with a similar title – Foel Goch41 (West of Snowdon close to Moel Eilio) and Foel-goch34 (Northern Glyderau – overlooking Nant Ffrancon).

A small boulder field and a couple of half-hearted wind breaks are all that embellish the remainder of this top. But when you advance West, or slightly to the left towards the rock-littered slopes overlooking the upper reaches of Dyffryn Mymbyr, this summit's charms are revealed.

*Across Cwm Gwern Gof to the North West – Tryfan's Eastern face stares back at you with the bulk of Glyder Fach to its left – in the foreground are the ribbed shoulders of Braich y Ddeugwm [9-03].*

*To the North East Pen Llithrig y Wrach towers over the broad valley containing the Llyn Cowlyd reservoir.*

*To the South lies Dyffryn Mymbyr with Llynnau Mymbyr to the left (originally a single post-glacial lake produced by melt-water before partial silting converted it into a conjoined pair) [9-04].*

*Far to the right Y Lliwedd forms the backdrop with the rest of the Snowdon Horseshoe to its right, while to its left lie Nantgwynant and Llyn Gwynant. Closer at hand as you trace the line of the Nant Gwryd river West you will easily make out the plantation beside the junction of the A498 and A4086 above Nantgwynant at the site of the Pen-y-Gwryd Hotel [9-05]. Llyn Lockwood stands across the road from the hotel.*

Llyn Lockwood was formerly know as Llyn Gwryd – its name presumably changed sometime after Arthur Lockwood, who bought the Pen-y-Gwryd hotel in the 1920's, built a dam across the lake's outflow to keep its waters in check.

The Pen-y-Gwryd hotel was used as a training base by the Everest expedition prior to Sir Edmund Hilary's successful ascent in 1953. Memorabilia are exhibited in the bar relating to this significant period in mountaineering history, and one of the ceilings in the hotel bears the signatures of the successful Everest team.

Land adjacent to the shores of Llyn Lockwood was once the site of a Roman marching camp. Suetonius Paulinus was the first Roman general to reach the shores of the Menai Strait in 60 AD. It proved too much of a struggle to conquer the local Ordovices – this marching camp being all that remains of his campaign.

Roman marching camps are a relic of these early campaigns when every night the soldiers would dig themselves in behind a makeshift defence of ditch and turf wall topped by a wooden palisade (each soldier carried stakes and a pick as part of his standard equipment). Once this temporary barrier was completed at the end of each day's march they would pitch their tents inside it.

One clammy morning, perched on this breezy summit, I took the opportunity to change into a dry T-shirt and socks. It's surprising how invigorating clean, dry kit can be half way through a walk. Nearby, crouched in one of the wind shelters, a group of ramblers consulted their maps before continuing East ahead of me onto Gallt yr Ogof. The day was overcast but warm – yet many of them wore heavy-duty water-proof coats, over-trousers and gaiters, and carried extra-large day-sacks. No wonder they gave me sly looks as I asked their 'leader' how far they had come. Perhaps they'd been up before dawn and had already topped the remainder of the Southern Glyderau? Or were at the end of a 2-day excursion taking in the entire range? Not quite – just a 2 hour ascent of this top from the Ogwen valley by way of Llyn Caseg-fraith and Cwm Gwern Gof en route to Plas y Brenin.

I'm all for coming equipped against everything the elements have to offer – but even the vaguest weather forecast for the day suggested that the light-weight, water-proof jacket in my pack was sufficient. There is such a thing as over-kill. I wonder what enjoyment any of them found in having laboured up 500+ metres of steep hillside in full winter gear. Probably as much as the Roman soldiers, burdened for battle, who first set eyes on such an inhospitable landscape?

**5)** **(677581)** →

   60°       →

Retrace your steps to the shallow col containing two small lakes surrounded pretty much by peat and the ever-present bog [9-06]. Although the map shows a path to the left of the Northernmost of these two bodies of water, the drier route is to the right of the larger, Southernmost one. The path then trails slightly left before picking its way between grey, crumbly outcrops to reach the cairned rocky summit of **Gallt yr Ogof** (at **684585** – 763m/2503ft).

**6)** **(684585)** →

   40        →

Ahead of you are two slight depressions separating further crags beyond [9-07]. The furthest one of course, complete with cairn, at **686587** (757m/2483ft) gives a better view of Nant y Benglog and the Carneddau to the North. My over-dressed fellow-ramblers did not share my curiosity; having stood on

Gallt yr Ogof's summit [9-08] for a few seconds they elected to continue East towards Capel Curig.

*From here Tryfan commands the view behind you [9-09], but it is Pen Llithrig y Wrach which dominates the opposite side of Dyffryn Ogwen – the Llyn Cowlyd reservoir to its right [9-10].*

*To its left the smooth slopes of Y Braich rise up to the flat top of Pen yr Helgi Du, with the ruler-straight service road to the Ffynnon Llugwy reservoir a mark of man's ruthless insistence on disturbing the natural harmony of an area.*

*And behind you a view of Y Foel Goch, which despite its modest position among loftier neighbours is after all the walk's highest point [9-11].*

Once you have enjoyed the views on offer it's time to retrace your steps.

220°        →

Continue along the summit crags almost as far as the lake you skirted previously. But before you reach that, drop left slightly towards the 730-metre spot height at **685584** and look out for the faint path on your left upslope of the main craggy outcrops [9-12].

7)        **(685584)**        →

110°        →

As you descend grassy slopes you will eventually come across the eroded path you followed on the ascent. Follow this East, crossing the dry-stone wall by way of the ladder stile

Dropping down onto more level ground, the broad saddle of Bwlch Goleuni, look out for the faintest of paths leading away to your right. This is marked on the Explorer map but the only indication on the ground is a slight flattening of the knee-high grass. If you are unable to locate this path don't continue East for too long. Start bearing right as soon as feasible in order to reach the top of the escarpment overlooking Dyffryn Mymbyr.

These slopes provide a fine vantage point; a final opportunity perhaps to study the Easternmost of the twin lakes occupying Dyffryn Mymbyr before you approach the hidden slopes below [9-13]. As you begin to contour these slopes you will cross the occasional wet patch between the grassy bits, but these are no worse than those already encountered on the saddle behind you.

Crossing the shelf of lower ground before you now is a wire fence with hopefully a step stile visible from where you stand (a length of blue plastic tubing covers the topmost strand of barbed wire – visible from quite some distance). Slither down the grass-covered slopes to this stile and cross the fence ahead of you.

8)     (699580)     →

       140°          →

Almost immediately you cross a deep, stone-lined ditch. Head on the same bearing to the next escarpment overlooking Dyffryn Mymbyr. Once you reach the lip of the valley side you should take the opportunity to study the layout of the land below.

Although the road is not very far below you, and the slopes are quite gentle, the easiest route involves successfully locating the ladder stile crossing the wire fence that separates the bracken-covered hillside from the grassy scrub beyond [9-14]. If you are unable to spot the stile, look out for the short section of stone wall (the shorter side of the wall-enclosed paddock you skirted on your ascent). This wall runs uphill from close to the point where the river flows into the West end of Llynnau Mymbyr. The ladder stile is slightly to the right of the line of this stone wall (where it forms a corner before turning left) [9-15].

Descending these slopes is not particularly difficult. There are a few rocky crags which are easily side-stepped before you are forced to wade through bracken in order to reach the lower slopes. En route you will come across a sizeable stone enclosure on your left marking the site of an abandoned homestead.

*Take one final look along the valley below you– Llynnau Mymbyr to your left and the Snowdon Horseshoe to your right [9-16]. There are enough details you can ponder over in the valley below to delay the return to your car a bit longer [9-17 and 9-18].*

**120°**  →

Where the bracken ends locate the ladder stile in the wire fence and cross to the rough pasture beyond. Trend right now, aiming for the slopes above the lay-by where the trees below are spaced furthest apart.

Marker posts identify the 'Dyffryn Mymbyr' path you followed earlier in the day. From here it's a matter of bearing left towards the stone-walled paddock then turning right to meet the path leading back to the final ladder-stile and the roadside at **701574** where this hill-walk began [9-19 – x marks the spot].

**END**

# Glyder Fawr [29] /Glyder Fach [30] / Tryfan (far South Peak [31] and main top [32])

| | |
|---|---|
| **9.2 Km (5.75 miles)** | **Part of the second-best horseshoe in** |
| **1065m (3493ft)** | **North Wales – a heavy-duty walk that** |
| **Time : 5hrs 30min** | **promises a feast of treats, with** |
| | **something to suit every taste.** |

Perhaps I should admit right at the start that I find this 'horseshoe' (when the ascent of Y Garn is included – see Walk 11 for directions) just as enjoyable as the classic 'Snowdon Horseshoe' – probably because the views into the Ogwen Valley are far superior to those overlooking Cwm Dyli. There are, of course, many who favour the latter – each to his/her own. I've tramped up these hills chased by Arctic wind as well as under Tropical heat and I never fail to secure that thrill and sense of achievement as I snack out on Glyder Fawr and cast my eyes West.

Here is the perfect combination of leisurely ridge-walk and adrenaline-sapping scramble. With three summits topping 3000ft (four if you follow the Y Garn option), the formidable Bristly Ridge and Castell y Gwynt thrown in for good measure, anyone completing this walk can justly hold their heads high – unless they happen to come across someone doing the 'Welsh 3000ers'….. in which case, same hills, different agenda.

**North**

**Don't forget**

**map/compass
whistle/torch**

**suitable footwear
+ clothing**

**food/drink**

**brain**

## APPROACH

From Bethesda follow the A5 South through Nant Ffrancon until you reach the Ogwen Cottage Outdoor Pursuits Centre (on your right after the road has taken a marked turn left as it begins to skirt the shore of Llyn Ogwen).

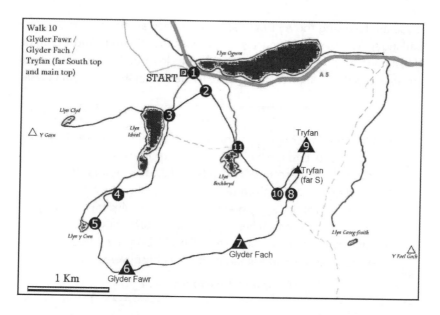

Walk 10
Glyder Fawr /
Glyder Fach /
Tryfan (far South top
and main top)

START

Llyn Ogwen

A 5

Llyn Clyd

Y Garn

Llyn
Idwal

Tryfan

Llyn
Bochlwyd

Tryfan
(far S)

Llyn y Cwn

Llyn Caseg-fraith

Y Foel Goch

Glyder Fach

1 Km

Glyder Fawr

There is ample parking in the pay-and-display car park (on your right just before you reach Ogwen Cottage – signposted Parking and Toilets). The walk starts from this location so if you have money to spare and there are spaces available look no further.

There are also a number of long lay-bys flanking the right-hand side of the road beyond. Parking here is free. There was a proposal in the late 1990's to make all roads in this part of Snowdonia clearways – thus restricting parking to designated park-and-ride or park-and-walk sites. Fortunately, the scheme was never adopted, since the notion of a National Park has always been to provide access for open air recreation – not an extra source of revenue for local authorities.

The earlier in the day you arrive here, the greater the likelihood of your obtaining a spot not too distant from the start of the walk. Be warned, however. On busy summer days many motorists choose to park on the pavement anywhere between the Ogwen Waterfall at the Western end of Llyn Ogwen and the lake's Eastern end. Legally you could be given a fixed-penalty fine if you park on the kerb. And if you think I'm being paranoid, well I'm not. I write from bitter experience (May 2003 and a zealous warden with nothing better to do one miserably wet Sunday afternoon).

If you are following the A5 from Capel Curig, keep an eye out for likely car parking spaces on your left once you approach the Milestone Buttress at the Northern foot of Tryfan. Bear in mind that the closer to Ogwen Cottage you are able to park, the shorter the distance to the start of this demanding walk.

---

### OPTION 1

Even before the walk begins, you might wish to consider the alternative route into the high col containing Llyn y Cwn.

This involves the ascent of Y Garn (see **Walk 11 – points 1 to 4**) followed by a drop Southwards from its summit to the col below. Personally this would be my preferred route onto Glyder Fawr every time. But the Devil's Kitchen is a popular feature of Cwm Idwal, cherished by many hill-walkers – and like a McDonald's burger, to be experienced once in a lifetime but probably never repeated.

*Additional time taken – 1 hr*

---

THERE ARE MANY PARTS OF THIS WALK THAT REQUIRE PARTICULAR CARE – BUT AS WITH ANY VISIT ONTO THE MOUNTAINS, WEATHER CONDITIONS AND INDIVIDUAL EXPERIENCE SHOULD DICTATE WHAT YOU DECIDE TO ATTEMPT, OR AVOID AS THE CASE MAY BE.

BEAR IN MIND THAT DURING WINTER THE OGWEN VALLEY ITSELF CAN BE FROST-FREE WHILE THE TOPS ARE THICK WITH VERGLAS (A COATING OF ALMOST UNDETECTABLE ICE). SIMILARLY, SINCE MUCH OF CWM IDWAL LIES IN SHADE FOR MOST OF THE WINTER, MANY OF THE ASCENT AND DESCENT PATHS UTILISING ITS HEADWALL CAN BE ICED UP EVEN WHEN THE TOPS ARE SUNLIT AND ICE-FREE.

THE ASCENTS OF CASTELL Y GWYNT AND TRYFAN, AND IN PARTICULAR THE DESCENTS OF BRISTLY RIDGE OR Y GRIBIN NEED EXTRA CARE UNDER WINTER CONDITIONS AND SHOULD BE AVOIDED UNLESS YOU ARE EXPERIENCED IN THE USE OF CRAMPONS.

HAVING SAID THAT, I HAVE SUCCESSFULLY COMPLETED THIS WALK IN MID-SUMMER IN JUST T-SHIRT, SHORTS AND A PAIR OF TRAINERS.

## START

1)  (649604)  →

    180°  →

Take the minor road crossing the river adjacent to the Ogwen Cottage Outdoor Pursuits Centre – signposted 'Parking and Toilets'.

Almost immediately turn left uphill following the stone path between the river and a block of buildings (Information Centre/Snack Bar). A sign on the building identifies this as the path to Llyn Idwal. Continue along this through a small metal gate and immediately across a footbridge crossing the stream exiting Llyn Idwal further up-valley.

The path ahead is well-constructed from large slabs [10-01], almost a stroll in the park during the summer but during any winter morning the ground can be slippery in places where groundwater has frozen.

**120°**            →

As the angle of gentle ascent eases and you get a clearer view ahead towards the ridge between Glyder Fach and Tryfan, the path splits in two [10-02]. To the left a minor track crosses rough ground towards the high rock basin enclosing Llyn Bochlwyd (still hidden).

THIS TRACK IS THE RETURN LEG OF THE WALK SO TAKE NOTE.

2)        (652601)        →

          240°            →

The main path bears right at this junction to continue towards Cwm Idwal where the terrain is much more rugged and immensely impressive [10-03]. The track ahead is still fairly level as it trends slightly left in search of a route through the natural dam holding back the waters of Llyn Idwal.

This natural dam is more correctly classed a 'terminal moraine'. During the death throes of the last Ice Age, the ice sheets that once buried the British Isles became reduced to smaller, localised glaciers. One small glacier filled what is now the basin of Llyn Idwal, and that glacier itself became reduced in size as global temperatures gradually rose.

The rocks and mud that the glacier managed to grind from the floor and back-walls of this basin were repeatedly dumped at its decaying snout following its unsuccessful attempts to advance down-valley. One look at the scale of the basin Llyn Idwal now occupies suggests that a significant amount of rock must have been excavated and carried elsewhere during the Ice Age. Much in fact was transported a substantial distance by the glaciers when they were at their most active. Another portion was probably carried downstream by floodwaters when the ice finally melted for good. So only a small remainder has been left to this day where it was dumped.

Charles Darwin was the first scientist to visualise the glacial genesis of Cwm Idwal when he visited the area in 1842. He in fact identified a number of moraines, marking the retreat and advance of the glacier as the climate fluctuated between Arctic and Temperate – the final retreat being some 12,500 years ago (an early case from the files of "C. S. I. Cwm Idwal" perhaps). Realising the time scale of such events Darwin was able to set the template for his Theory of Evolution.

Llyn Idwal itself now occupies the floor of the basin that once held this glacier. The lake's maximum depth is 36-feet but for the most part it is less than 10-feet deep. Llyn Bochlwyd tells a similar tale, but that lake is much shallower, now half-filled with debris from the smaller glacier once occupying its basin.

Between these two rock basins or 'cirques', Cwm Cneifion which is perched directly below Glyder Fawr also had its own glacier which overflowed into Cwm Idwal far below. There are no signs of any lake having ever occupied this highest of the three basins, but a fairly sizeable stream pours out at its exit point and plunges downslope alongside the Idwal Slabs.

According to Welsh mythology, the largest moraine below Llyn Idwal was supposedly the burial mound of the legendary giant Idwal – hence the lake's name.

Once you reach the lake, ignore the gate leading across the outflow to your right by way of a footbridge. That is an alternative route to the foot of Y Garn if you are still undecided whether to pursue **Option 1** or not. To reach the Devil's Kitchen, however, keep to the constructed path that continues along the lake's left-hand shore. Ahead of you now you should be able to pick out the route to follow [10-04].

**3)      (647598)      →**

    **195°           →**

The next section of path clings closely to the lake shore, passing through a gate in a short section of wall before slowly gaining height.

> *High above this gate the small basin of Cwm Cneifion or 'The Nameless Cwm' lies cupped beneath the skyline [10-05 seen from Y Gribin]. The huge wall of grey rock to its left, sweeping directly down to the lake side comprises the Idwal Slabs, a popular testing ground for rock climbers.*
> *Scan your eyes further right past the sizeable waterfall plunging from the Northern Upper Cliff of Glyder Fawr and they cannot fail to be drawn with some trepidation towards the black cleft in the cliffs ahead – Twll Du [10-06]. Fortunately, the path threading through the Devil's Kitchen steers clear of here, skirting uphill to the left before reaching the foot of this dark chasm although it is difficult to discern its exact route from this distance.*

The path is easy-going as it crawls beneath the grey wall of the Idwal Slabs before crossing a stream by way of a ford at **643589**. However, during periods of hard frost this section of path can often become iced up. Under such conditions it might be advisable to head left for a short distance and follow the water-filled gulley upstream towards the waterfalls. Within a short distance you should be able to locate a less hazardous crossing-point after which you can return downstream to rejoin the paved path [10-07 facing back towards the river crossing].

The path maintains its steady climb along the headwall of the rock basin, passing below a fan of scree before skirting past a large angular fragment of dark rock [10-08]. Such is its size that it can easily be picked out even from the most distant of vantage points [10-09].

    **255°           →**

Beyond here the path stubs its toe against a substantial rock-fall ahead. Although it is possible to cross this by manoeuvring upslope, this particular section again is frequently iced up in winter and is best crossed by dropping downslope. If you go down too far you may be tempted to follow the narrow path creeping some way beneath the gaping jaws of Twll Du before edging beneath the headwall of Cwm Idwal. Don't, unless your intention is merely to circle the lake back to its outflow.

**4)**    **(641589)**    →

    **240°**    →

Your route now involves climbing more steeply left, initially across coarse grass and large boulders, aiming for the base of the nearest set of black cliffs high on your left. Beyond this point you are forced to find a route through the rock-fall above [10-10, and 10-11 from **Walk 11**].

A large, boulder-strewn amphitheatre soon opens up above you on the left, a scrap-yard of large angular blocks setting traps for the unwary walker. This area and the passage onto the lower slopes of Glyder Fawr are generally known as the Devil's Kitchen.

The Devil's Kitchen is apparently so-named because of the holes worn into its rock walls – called 'the devil's cooking pots'.

The accumulation of weathered strata at the upper section of the Devil's Kitchen, close to where it emerges alongside Llyn y Cwn, is composed of rocks called 'pillow lavas'. These were formed some 350 million years ago by submarine volcanic eruptions – lava escaping from volcanic vents on the sea floor, rather like bubbles of gas erupting from a pan of boiling soup. The outer surface of this escaping lava became immediately cooled by the surrounding sea water, but the centre of these lava 'bubbles' remained molten. So when the blobs of half-solidified/half-molten rock escaping from deep beneath the Earth's crust began to accumulate on the sea floor they were still pliable enough to become squashed – ending up like pillows rather than the perfect tube shapes they would have originally had when they emerged from the volcanic vents.

The summit rocks of Tryfan and Carnedd Dafydd are composed of volcanic rocks dating from the same period but formed of lavas extruded onto land rather than under the sea so these cooled more slowly.

On many maps (and in some guidebooks) the Devil's Kitchen and Twll Du ('Black Hole') are confusingly identified as one and the same feature. Twll Du is actually the dark, vertical cleft cut into the cliffs of Clogwyn y Geifr – the back-wall of Cwm Idwal. If you wish to examine this sinister feature do so now – but be advised that there is no access onto the saddle above it containing Llyn y Cwn.

Twll Du and the adjoining cliffs are home to many rare Alpine plants. Indeed, the wall of wet rock beneath Clogwyn y Geifr is also known as the 'Hanging Gardens'.

**195°**          →

To continue into the Devil's Kitchen locate the faint path twisting its way steeply uphill to your left before reaching the base of Twll Du. This path is quickly transformed into a staircase climbing in a painfully direct line towards the skyline [10-12].

CARE IS NEEDED ONCE THE PAVED STAIRCASE DEGENERATES INTO COARSE SCREE AS ANY DISLODGED ROCKS ARE LIKELY TO TRAVEL SOME DISTANCE DOWNHILL BEFORE COMING TO A STOP GIVEN THE STEEP NATURE OF THE TERRAIN.

This section of ascent is unfortunately a depressing trudge up a largely uneven pile of loose rock. The only consolation is that height is rapidly gained, and whenever you can break away from the confines of the gully, the views behind you into Cwm Idwal are stunning [10-13]. Eventually the relentless gradient takes pity on you as the deluge of loose rock washes up against a low retaining wall on your left (close to **639587**), perched above Cwm Idwal. From here the path takes a leisurely swing to your right in search of the immediate skyline [10-14 and 10-15].

This search is soon rewarded as the flood of paler rocks subsides onto a low saddle (the uppermost section of Cwm Cneifio – not to be confused with Cwm Cneifion) between the cliffs of Glyder Fawr to your left and the grassy slopes of Y Garn to your right. At the low point of this saddle lies the small lake of Llyn y Cwn [10-16, and 10-17 from the lower slopes of Y Garn – **Option 1**].

> Llyn y Cwn's claim to fame is that in the distant past it was recorded as the habitat of monocular (one-eyed) trout and eels.
> The high saddle this lake occupies (over 710 metres above sea level) is believed to be an overflow channel created by an ice sheet spilling from the Pass of Llanberis into the adjacent Ogwen valley during a more active period of the Ice Age.

**5)**   **(638585)**   →

   180°   →

Pick your way through damp ground and bare rock towards the lake shore, keeping an eye on the steep hillside to your left.

There are two obvious paths scaling this rocky face. The right-hand path shows signs of extreme erosion and in my opinion the leftmost of the two is the better option – more of a river bed than a path at times – but relatively painless.

   135°   →

The way ahead becomes abruptly steeper for a brief section before levelling again, trending right as it crosses what looks like an almost artificial gravel embankment [10-18]. Beyond here the path grows quite a bit steeper and becomes less stable under foot as it joins the other path from Cwm Cneifio and the coarse gravel is replaced by bare soil [10-19 looking back downhill]. But the steepest section is already behind you now, and soon you reach a barren wasteland of rock fragments leading onto Glyder Fawr's summit.

**85°**  →

Bear left to head in the general direction of the highest point of the skyline – the main summit [10-20]. If visibility is limited there are plenty of cairns to guide your way [10-21] but the key is to head left and keep climbing gradually.

*If visibility is unlimited then take a look behind you and watch the panorama unfold – Nant Ffrancon [10-22], Y Garn [10-23], the Pass of Llanberis and the village itself at the junction of Llyn Peris and Llyn Padarn [10-24] – and Mynydd Mawr guarding the entrance to Dyffryn Nantlle [10-25].*

The final approach to the summit is a stroll across a rock-strewn landscape that bears remarkable witness to the power frost has to shatter rock into fragments of all shapes and sizes [10-26].

*In mist or clinging cloud the summit can be a creepy place, particularly as the crowds tend to view the lower of the two Glyderau as their playground-cum-snack area while this one provides less photo-friendly opportunities [10-27 and 10-28]. The bleached, grey-white rock and the angular protrusions that abound here present an image more akin to a primeval bone-yard, particularly when coated in hoar frost.*
*However, in clear conditions it is one of Snowdonia's prime vantage points. The views West to the Snowdon 'horse-shoe' and Nantlle beyond, and North towards Y Garn flanked by the Pass of Llanberis on one side and Nant Ffrancon on the other are supreme. I actually believe it is possible to become intoxicated by stunning views, and I find this spot is always a difficult one to leave behind even when there's a lot of walking still to be done [10-29 to 10-32].*

The top itself, promoted to +1000m status following a recent resurvey, is the larger collection of fractured rocks on the crest marking the highest of this magnificent mountain group – **Glyder Fawr** (at **642579** – 1001m/3283ft) [10-33].

**6)**     **(642579)**     →

      85°          →

Descending the broad shoulder that separates the two Glyderau, the jumble of rock fragments is eventually replaced by a fine path dropping gradually towards Bwlch y Ddwy-Glyder (919 metres at **653581**).

THE NORTH-FACING CLIFFS HERE HOLD SNOW AND BEAR CORNICES (OVER-HANGING SNOW LEDGES) ALONG THEIR UPPER EDGES LONG AFTER MOST OTHER SIGNS OF WINTER HAVE DISAPPEARED. SINCE THESE CORNICES CAN EXTEND OUT OVER THE EDGE BY AS MUCH AS A COUPLE OF METRES OR MORE ONE SHOULD AVOID WALKING ON THEM AT ALL COSTS IN CASE YOU PLUNGE THROUGH INTO THE FRESH AIR BELOW [10-34].

From this high spot one can appreciate the massive bite-marks left by the miniature glaciers occupying Cwm Cneifion and Cwm Bochlwyd at the end of the last Ice Age. Freeze-thaw action and the grinding of rock-studded ice against the bedrock at their bases gradually pulverised even the most resilient rock to dust. Only the knife-edge ridge of Y Gribin [10-35 viewed from the East] survived to separate these two amphitheatres.

---

### OPTION 2

An escape route back to the Ogwen valley makes use of Y Gribin, although care is needed in poor visibility. This is actually an easier ascent route than a descent, and it should be avoided at all costs under snow or ice unless you possess the requisite skills.

Cross this large grassy shoulder [10-36] as it heads directly North then pick a way along the crumbly path descending almost vertically North towards the saddle between Llyn Idwal and Llyn Bochlwyd.

There are quite a few steep sections initially where care is needed in selecting a line of ascent you are most comfortable with [10-37 and 10-38]. Exposure should not be under-estimated, but it is not a major factor and merely enhances the views – down into Cwm Idwal [10-39] and across to Cwm Bochlwyd and Tryfan [10-40].

---

As you drop, trend to the right and you will see some distance below you a sizeable grassy hump crossed by a clear path [10-41].
Beyond here the path descends more steeply again, but this is an easy stroll along a twisting track [10-42 looking back uphill] that eventually deposits you at the shores of Llyn Bochlwyd. This is a superb spot at which to grab a bite to eat before locating the descent path at **point 11**.

**It is worth noting that in misty conditions, and without checking your compass, it is all to easy to be misled further right onto the 'False Gribin' – a much more rugged ridge that descends steeply to the SouthWestern shore of Llyn Bochlwyd.**

*Time saved – 3hrs 15min*

As the path between the two main tops drops into Bwlch y Ddwy-Glyder you are confronted by the crumbling edifice of Glyder Fach, resembling a derelict Mayan Pyramid with sheer sides, a flat summit and small cone of boulders on its top [10-43]. Adding to the apparent dilapidation is Castell y Gwynt – a bastion of jagged rock that seems to have slid West, downhill from the summit to the very edge of the plateau without quite completing its collapse to the col below [10-44].

Intimidating from this angle, the clutter of jagged boulders and crags beneath Castell y Gwynt is easily negotiated as long as you keep a healthy distance between yourself and the cliff edge to your left. There is a by-pass path further right that avoids most difficulties, but part of the enjoyment of this route is the opportunity to tackle Castell y Gwynt head-on.

The scrambling is relatively undemanding until you reach the final section where rock runs out and you are suddenly faced with what lies beyond the serrated crest. The less foolhardy option is to reverse your ascent by a metre or two and skirt the outcrop's left hand side. Although the sheer drop into Cwm Bochlwyd is uncomfortably close, there is a solid path climbing between two vertical slabs (rather like a thread's progress through a needle's eye) that leads you safely onto the more stable ground of this subsidiary top (at **654581** – 955m/3132ft).

From here pick your way between the large boulders for another 250 metres or so to the obvious mound of rocks ahead marking the loftier summit of **Glyder Fach** (at **656582** – 994m/3262ft) [10-45].

A short distance East from the summit is the Cantilever Stone – a huge flat slab of rock balanced horizontally like a gigantic see saw upon the boulders beneath. Multitudes of climbers have abused its delicate balance in order to coax some kind of movement from it – but all have failed. This is a popular spot, not just for the opportunity to hop amongst the boulders but also to grab a bite to eat and drink in the superlative views. I have avoided including a photograph of this iconic landmark on the enclosed CD – you will have already seen it prominently featured in every other guidebook to the region.

*One of the best viewpoints of the entire walk is close to the summit of Castell y Gwynt, but Glyder Fach is perhaps a more stable vantage point from which to admire the scenery. On older OS maps its summit is also given the appropriate name of 'Y Gwyliwr' – 'The Viewer' or 'The Watcher'.*

*To the South, upper Dyffryn Mymbyr backed by the lower slopes of Moel Siabod. The road passes the Pen-y-Gwryd Hotel, flanked by woods at the shore of Llyn Lockwood, before veering off into Nantgwynant. Llyn Cwmffynnon above Pen y Pass lies closer by to the right [10-46].*

*In favourable conditions this spot provides a fine view of the Snowdon group – the undulating hump of Y Lliwedd dropping down then rising to the main summit of Yr Wyddfa, with Crib Goch in the foreground as it climbs to the right towards Carnedd Ugain [10-47].*

*Moel Hebog's smooth slopes peep above Bwlch y Ciliau, the dip between Y Lliwedd and Yr Wyddfa, while the merest glimpse of Yr Aran's summit fools you into believing it is part of the arête descending Y Lliwedd's North West ridge.*

*From hereabouts the top of Glyder Fawr takes on a more shapely form, a serrated group of four small cones arranged upon the curving plateau like an afterthought [10-48 from Castell y Gwynt].*

*To the North – Nant Ffrancon, Pen yr Ole Wen, Llyn Ogwen, and the attractive form of Llyn Bochlwyd looking like a reversed image of Australia from this angle [10-49].*

*Tryfan close-up to the North East allows you ample time to hand-pick your preferred route to its flaking top [10-50].*

**7)    (656582)    →**

**70°         →**

After such a welcome respite the path now leads very directly downhill to Bwlch Tryfan, the low point between Glyder Fach and Tryfan. Those with the ability and inclination to further their scrambling exploits will clamber over the towering rocks that mark the start of the Bristly Ridge and pick their way down the crumbling fin of black crag. But most will choose the more straightforward track that by-passes these to the right and sets off on the helter-skelter drop to the col below.

Since most people choose to walk up Tryfan first in order to end up on Glyder Fawr, you will no doubt meet many red-faced, breathless souls as they force their way up this crumbling treadmill to the invisible heights far above. The path is unrelentingly steep and is by no means an easier option on descent than the adjoining ridge. Trekking poles are recommended to aid stability where safe progress might be compromised by the state of the path underfoot (seriously eroded in places).

It is possible to avoid the ascending masses three quarters of the way down by dropping further right to a low path that runs parallel to the main route then joining it again at the col of Bwlch Tryfan (close to the 730-metre contour at **662588**) where a choice of two ladder stiles enables you to cross the dry-stone wall on your left.

---

### OPTION 3

For those of you with enough time on your hands to delay the attempt on Tryfan's summit for half an hour or so, you could do worse than take a closer look at its Northern aspect.

Keep to the East side of the stone wall and descend the slopes towards the Heather Terrace. From this vantage point you may well admit that Tryfan's most 'interesting' ascent route lies on this side (from the vicinity of the Milestone Buttress alongside the A5 below you).

OR

---

## OPTION 4
If time or weather conditions make a return to the car a wiser choice at this point, this final peak can be left for another day – from Bwlch Tryfan follow the path into Cwm Bochlwyd by way of **point 10**.
*Time saved – 1 ½ hrs*

**8)**     **(662589)**     →

        **20°**          →

You cannot have failed to notice that several paths scratch their way across the Southern wall of Tryfan. Despite this wide choice, there is not a single one that avoids a certain amount of scrambling. From Bwlch Tryfan whichever route you take to gain the crumbling summit is immaterial as long as you are prepared to use your hands when the intermittent track decides to desert you. The more popular approach follows the lee of the dry-stone wall for the first few metres until you emerge onto a more open aspect that invites you to head left. If in doubt, follow the white trails of crushed gravel where boots have reduced the grey rock to rubble Elsewhere wear and tear have given the outcrops a slightly rusty tinge.

As you gain height quite rapidly, make sure you keep a look out for the first signs of Tryfan's subsidiary summit which stands some distance South of the main top, quite prominent on the skyline to your right. **Tryfan's Far South Peak** (at **663591** – 826m/2709ft) is a noteworthy component of this fascinating mountain and should not be by-passed. Grey crags rising well to the right of your ascent path lead easily up onto the rocky bulge overlooking Cwm Tryfan to the East.

From this outlying top, descend slightly right of the way you ascended and you should notice the wall that has hauled its way up from the Heather Terrace almost 100 metres below (with a walkers' path alongside) before running head-first into the tower-block of the main summit. The most direct path is to the left of where this wall hits the hill. The fact that a path exists hereabouts is never absolute proof that following it is the wisest choice. But there are so many options that one way or another you will quickly reach the final steep section of the summit. Any vestige of a path at this stage is replaced by a clutter of boulders and slabs that lead to the central stump of rock, **Tryfan** (at **663593** – 917m/3010ft).

Some believe, probably erroneously, that the name 'Tryfan' is derived from the Welsh 'tri faen' (three stones) – its main summit actually squeezes three separate tops into an extremely limited space – this triptych is best seen from the South East. However, the more accepted explanation is that it comes from the older Welsh term 'tra fan' (sharp or pointed peak).

The twin blocks of 'Adam + Eve' [10-51 close-up, and 10-52 from Y Gribin] that stand guard on the main summit supposedly bestow the freedom of Tryfan on anyone capable of taking the decidedly risky step from the one to the other.

Tryfan is an exhilarating spot on which to spend time, despite the crowds that tend to congregate there when the sun is out. And even those who climb onto its summit merely to sit and stare should still be applauded for getting here under their own steam (unlike the pseudo-summiteers that pose on Yr Wyddfa's trig point having trekked there from an adjacent railway carriage).

9)      (663593)       →

        220°            →

A cursory scan of the Ogwen Valley Rescue Team's web-site – **www.ogwen-rescue.org.uk/incidents** – reveals just how many call-outs each month are made to this single mountain (and how many injuries are sustained walking DOWN from here – mostly to walkers' ankles).

When your batteries are sufficiently recharged, the return to Bwlch Tryfan provides the most straightforward descent route (the word 'straightforward' of course being only a relative term where Tryfan is concerned). Indeed, I managed to get myself stuck the last time I did this particular walk, scrambling down into a narrow cleft between two vertical slabs. Suddenly I was trapped between the face of the mountain and two 3-metre slabs.

Neither slab had any handholds allowing me to climb back up out of their jaws – and the gap between the pair was too narrow for me to pass through it. Eventually, by removing my rucksack and turning to face the mountain, I managed to squirm through the tiny cleft onto the next ledge below even though it was impossible to see how far below me that ledge lay. Fortunately the drop was less than a couple of metres and I was still able to reach back up to retrieve my sack!

THERE IS AN ALTERNATIVE DESCENT ROUTE DIRECTLY TO THE FLOOR OF THE OGWEN VALLEY BY WAY OF THE MOUNTAIN'S NORTHERN RIDGE, AND THE PATH IS CLEARLY MARKED ON THE EXPLORER MAP [10-53 LOOKING DOWNSLOPE FROM THE LOWER SECTION OF THIS ROUTE AND 10-54 FROM THE WESTERN END OF LLYN OGWEN]. BUT I WOULD DISSUADE ANY CASUAL HILL WALKER FROM TAKING THIS WAY DOWN UNLESS THEY HAVE ALREADY CLIMBED THE SUMMIT BY THIS ROUTE AND ARE RELATIVELY FAMILIAR WITH THE LIE OF THE LAND. THERE ARE SOME TRICKY SECTIONS, PARTICULARLY ON DESCENT WHEN ONE IS NOT ALWAYS ABLE TO SEE WHAT LIES IMMEDIATELY BELOW DUE TO THE ANGLE OF THE SLOPE.

There was a much-publicised incident recently (2007) where a pair of walkers, faced with deteriorating light, decided to follow this shorter route back to their car (safely parked on the A5 directly below Tryfan). The pair ended up having to be rescued from a ledge half way down the Northern ridge after one of them fell and sustained serious injuries. But rather than count their blessings and speculate on the wisdom of following such an obviously exposed route in poor conditions, this pair cast outrage upon a recently-purchased hill-walking guide to this area which described the existence of the direct descent route. Strangers to the area, and to hill walking by the sound of it, they claim that this loathsome publication enticed them onto the dangerous descent route – and the book ended up being removed from the shelves. Although the pair have my sympathies, it's rather like an inept driver claiming that he got stuck in a farmer's field purely because his Sat-Nav directed him to drive his HGV along the impossibly narrow farm track; preferring to rely on a third party's remote guidance than the evidence there right before his eyes.

Even keeping to the 'safer' side of the hill, there is ample opportunity for fun to be had. And if you find your sense of adventure deserting you, a path is never far away. The easier routes down keep slightly more to the West of the dry-stone wall than those followed on the ascent, but whichever way you choose you will quickly reach the col again where the return leg now turns right into Cwm Bochlwyd.

**10)**   **(661589)**   →

     **300°**   →

There is an obvious path dropping down gradually to the Eastern shore of Llyn Bochlwyd. This is a beautifully situated lake with the huge backdrop of Glyder Fach and Glyder Fawr's lower slopes – worth a moment or two's contemplation before moving on [10-55].

Once this path reaches the Northern point of the lake, cross the outflow by use of the numerous boulders there, and then bear left to climb a slight grassy rise between more rocks. As you approach the low skyline ahead opening up to the main Ogwen valley you will locate the start of the descent path that closely follows the Western banks of the Nant Bochlwyd river [10-56 looking back upstream].

**11)**   **(655594)**   →

     **345°**   →

A solid blocked path descends this final section quite steeply – eroded to bare rock or bald turf in places.

DURING WET WEATHER CERTAIN PARTS OF THIS ROUTE REVERT TO RIVER – AND UNDER FREEZING CONDITIONS, GIVEN ITS NORTH-FACING ASPECT, LARGE SECTIONS OF THE PATH CAN BE SERIOUSLY ICED UP EVEN WHEN THE HIGHER PATHS ARE ICE-FREE.

By the time it meets the 420-metre contour the gradient eases as the path emerges onto open ground. Much of this section can be very wet underfoot so it pays to stick close to the path. Although the track features stepping stones and gravelled patches in places, its upkeep is very arbitrary compared to that of the main Llyn Idwal path which this disjointed path joins close to the small set of crags ahead of you and to your right (**point 2** on the ascent route).

The way from here on is impossible to miss as stone steps descend gently to the pay-and-display car park at **649604**.

Near its end the path crosses the river (whose source lies in Llyn Idwal) by way of a wooden bridge then passes through a spring gate in a wall. Beyond these it drops down along a paved track onto the tarmac where you started your day.

**END**

# Y Garn [33] / Foel-goch [34] / Elidir Fawr [35] / Elidir Fach [36]/ Mynydd Perfedd [37] / Carnedd y Filiast [38]

**16.25 Km (10.2 miles)**

**1380m (4526ft)**

**Time : 7hrs 50mins**

**A ridge walk above Nant Ffrancon with a substantial dog-leg West to visit the neighbouring peaks overlooking Nant Peris**

The Northern Glyderau ridge has always presented walkers with a particularly frustrating problem if their line of attack begins in the Ogwen valley or Nant Ffrancon. Once on the skyline you will enjoy a superlative walk with exhilarating views, and a variety of situations to satisfy the most demanding hill-walker. But the snag is – how do you get up there in the first place? …..or back down for that matter?

Over the years I have traversed the ridge from both ends, testing every feasible combination. Unless you are happy with trespassing (?) in the abandoned corners of the Penrhyn quarries South of Bethesda, any ascent or descent of the Northern end is doomed.

Similarly, unless your ambitions stretch no further than an uninspiring trudge up onto Elidir Fawr (and retracing your steps back at the end of the day, possibly by way of the reservoir service road to Deiniolen) the Llanberis side has little to commend it.

But if you want a challenge, coupling inventive route-finding with some minor scrambling, then this is the walk for you. It will provide you with a ridge equally as good as the Nantlle Ridge – check out the lie of the land from Pen yr Ole Wen's summit if you don't believe me [11-01 panorama from Walk 6].

**North**

**Don't forget**

**map/compass whistle/torch**

**suitable footwear + clothing**

**food/drink**

**brain**

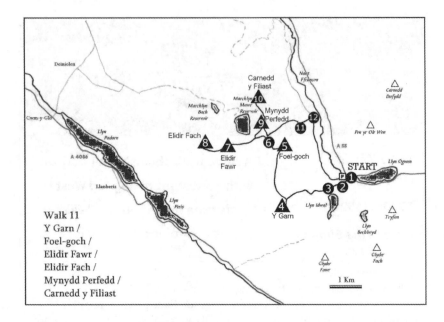

Walk 11
Y Garn /
Foel-goch /
Elidir Fawr /
Elidir Fach /
Mynydd Perfedd /
Carnedd y Filiast

## APPROACH

Heading from Bangor, follow the A5 South through Bethesda and take the first turning right some 2 Km South of the town. Continue along this narrow road which crosses the Afon Ogwen then turns sharp left to run the length of the valley as far as Ogwen Cottage. You can decide for yourself where you park along this road. There are a number of suitable lay-bys – but bear in mind that the descent from the ridge meets the road close to **638623** so there is not much point leaving your car North of here since the walk itself starts some 2½ Km South.

If travelling from Betws-y-Coed or Llanberis, head for Capel Curig and take the A5 as far as Ogwen Cottage at the far end of Llyn Ogwen. Here turn left as if heading for the main car park and Youth Hostel but continue past both along what becomes the minor road running the length of Nant Ffrancon directly at the base of the Northern Glyderau ridge.

Where you choose to park along this road is up to you, but it is pointless going further than the conspicuous outcrop of rock that dominates the field on your right close to **638623** [11-02]. In practice I have always preferred to

180

park as close to Ogwen Cottage as possible since the return walk along this minor road is an added delight at the end of a rewarding day's hill-walking.

**START**

1)     **(649604)**     →

       **180°**          →

Wherever you park, the walk itself starts alongside Ogwen Cottage Outdoor Pursuits Centre in the 'Parking and Toilets' area (same as **Walk 10**). Head along the stone path that runs uphill between the river and a block of buildings (Information Centre/Snack Bar). A sign on the building identifies this as the path to Llyn Idwal.

Immediately ahead of you is a dark cleft splitting a massive rock buttress. Rather than following the main path left, detour along the narrow track threading through this needle's eye [11-03, and 11-04 looking back down].
    The easiest path runs alongside the left hand wall of this passageway, climbing a short ladder stile then bearing right as it drops briefly. From this slate-floored chasm climb rapidly right onto a shoulder of bare ground beyond the defile at **648602** [11-05]. Having reached open ground you are immediately confronted by the Eastern face of Y Garn [11-06].

2)     **(647602)**     →

       **230°**          →

A clear path ahead of you crosses grass-covered slopes in the direction of the ridge. The path is damp in patches as it keeps to the left of the knobbly crags of Pen y Benglog but progress is easy and rapid.

Two wire fences and a dry-stone wall bar the way ahead before you reach the foot of Y Garn. The first fence runs beneath a series of rocky outcrops – cross it by way of the ladder stile [already visible in 11-06, and 11-07] and either clamber directly ahead or circuit these rocks easily to the left. The second fence crosses a flat section of open ground as Llyn Idwal comes into view on your left [11-08] – cross this one by way of the step stile. A walker-friendly touch is provided by the short length of blue plastic piping shrouding the top strand of barbed wire.

A second path forks left beyond this fence to follow the North shore of Llyn Idwal but your route trends right towards the lower slopes of Y Garn [11-09]. On your left lies a small fenced-off area where the natural vegetation is being encouraged to flourish without intervention from the indigenous goats and sheep. Just beyond here you reach a dry-stone wall with swing-gate giving access onto a steeper path [11-10].

*Before the real exertions begin take some time to study the surrounding landscape. Behind your right shoulder Pen yr Ole Wen [11-11] has dominated the scene since you reached the shoulder of high ground above the Ogwen valley. And now you are perched on higher ground the magnificent flat-floored Nant Ffrancon valley stretches North below your feet towards the Menai Strait [11-12].*

This broad valley is followed by the Afon Ogwen and two roads. Thomas Telford's A5 which replaced an ancient horse-track clings to its Eastern wall, and Lord Penrhyn's toll road between Bethesda and Capel Curig (the older of the two by 30 years – 1791-92) winds along its Western side. The return leg of the walk follows this minor road.

*Y Garn (often described as a huge armchair) fills the space in front of you [11-13 from the shores of Llyn Ogwen with Cwm Cywion and Foel-goch to its right], with the dark, forbidding crucible of Cwm Idwal to your left enclosing the cold waters of Llyn Idwal.*

Legend has it that no bird dare fly over Llyn Idwal – possibly more believable when the lake is spied in the dire heart of winter with hanging mists and grim shadows adding to the desolate feel of this location.

**3)    (644601)    →**

**270°    →**

Beyond the swing-gate the grass path is replaced by an eroded section liberally scattered with gravel as it starts to climb to the right. In places it is very steep, but large stone blocks and steps make progress relatively painless if rather direct. Stone-lined runoff drains have been positioned across the path in places to avoid erosion following heavy rain.

The angle eases as the first grass-covered saddle is reached. Beyond this the path becomes noticeably gravelly again. Another very steep section is followed by another level stretch, all the while following the right hand edge of the mountain [11-14 facing back downhill].

By now the main summit is clearly visible ahead and to the left of a false peak marking the end of the steepest ascent [11-15]. From this point you are rewarded with a fine ridge walk with only one more steep pull before reaching the 910-metre contour.

This approach follows the rim of the arête circling Cwm Clyd to the South [11-16] and Cwm Cywion [11-17] to the North. Although it is a strenuous climb, merciless on the thigh muscles, the rapid height gain and expanding views are ample compensation.

*As height is gained you get an almost aerial view of the two small lakes which occupy Cwm Clyd, as well as Llyn Idwal and Llyn Ogwen lower down the staircase [11-18 and 11-19]. The Southern face of Elidir Fawr can also be seen above the ridge separating Y Garn from Foel-goch [11-20].*

The summit itself is marked by numerous cairns and a scatter of boulders centred on **Y Garn** (at **630595** – 947m/3107ft).

*Llyn Ogwen could not have picked itself a better spot, framed by the Carneddau to the North (Pen yr Ole Wen) and the Glyderau to the South (Tryfan in particular) [11-21].*

*From this vantage point, the terrain (composed of glacial deposits) separating Llyn Idwal from Llyn Ogwen reveals the approach path in minute detail unless of course you pick a cloudy day [11-22] – even then a masterpiece in shades of grey might still await you [11-23].*

*Directly South lies the broad col containing Llyn y Cwn backed by the dark mass of Glyder Fawr [11-24], the slice of grey rock comprising Castell y Geifr perched above Cwm Idwal looking particularly imposing [11-25].*

*To the North, Foel-goch with its red scree fan dropping from Y Llymllwyd into a rock-cut cleft above Cwm Cywion [11-26].*

*Beyond the summit a fresh view West reveals Llanberis, the ruins of Dolbadarn Castle, Llyn Peris, the Clogwyn Mawr cliff face, and the slate tips below Elidir Fawr.*

**4)**     **(630595)**      →

         **345°**         →

A faint path drops down the loose slate littering the top of Y Garn onto the grass-covered ridge connecting it to the next link in the chain of summits overlooking Nant Ffrancon. Eventually the path levels out close to the 750-metre contour, but first it crosses another section of loose shale as it by-passes a pair of tilted spurs jutting East into Cwm Cywion [11-27].

Cwm Cywion and neighbouring Cwm Clyd are typical 'cirques' or 'corries' – rock basins formed by small glaciers which formed towards the end of the last Ice Age when the highest tops were ice free but the main valley floor was still occupied by a substantial glacier. Small accumulations of ice and snow on the two more shaded sides of Y Garn were allowed to grow over many hundreds of winters into mountain glaciers feeding the larger river of ice in the main valley.

When the large ice sheets began to recede North with the raising of global temperatures these small, vestigal glaciers were the last to disappear. They survived long enough to gouge deep basins into the hillsides, backed by sheer walls of rock.Their sides and back walls often owe their steepness to rockfalls caused by freeze-thaw attack at the junction of rock and ice. Meanwhile the floors of these basins, sculpted by the 'pestle-and-mortar' action of rock-laden ice, were hollowed out to such an extent that when all the ice eventually melted the resulting mass of water became trapped in the form of a lake or 'tarn'.

Interestingly, the floors of the Cwm Cywion basin and the Cwm Clyd basin lie at almost exactly the same altitude above the main valley, suggesting they share an identical history. However, Cwm Cywion is the less spectacular of the two today and its 'tarn' has almost been completed infilled over time by fallen rock and scree.

Before you begin the ascent onto the next top you get a chance to stand as close to the edge as you want to peer down into the cauldron of Cwm Cywion [11-28 and 11-29]. There are actually two lakes occupying this basin but both are fairly insignificant features, and will ultimately become completely filled by detritus from the surrounding slopes. This is also a good spot from which to survey the Northern face of Y Garn that you've just skipped down [11-30].

---

### OPTION 1
If you are inclined to miss out Foel-goch altogether, keep to the main path along its lower slopes and continue towards **point 6**.

***Time saved – less than 30mins.***

---

A fence trails along the right-hand side of the main path, inhibiting the more unwary walker from veering too close to the abyss. However, there are a number of faint paths running along the drop-side of the fence should you fancy a degree more of exposure [11-31].

All too soon the main path heads off to the left skirting the grassy flanks of Foel-goch (at **627602**). The existence of such a clear path here would suggest that the summit of Foel-goch does not merit a visit – that richer pickings lie ahead – but nothing could be further from the truth. 20 minutes spent following the gentle path that keeps abreast of the fence is time well-utilised when it gains you a summit so easily.

Often during a walk I have found myself on the wrong side of a fence and cursed the decision made earlier to cross it, or not cross as the case may be. No such predicament is posed by this particular fence – for much of its course it is quite flimsy and can easily be stepped over, and it even boasts its own ladder stile at one point.

Once you reach the truncated summit I dare anyone not to stare with disbelief at the green wedge of Yr Esgair [11-32 from Nant Ffrancon] protruding into Nant Ffrancon from the cloven face of **Foel-goch** (at **628611** – 831m/2726ft).

Yr Esgair is in fact one of three spurs extending into the main valley from the slopes adjacent to the summit, arranged like the tines of a fork. The lowest of the three, and farthest North is the grassy hump of Y Galan [11-33]. This is separated from Mynydd Perfedd by the tributary valley of Cwm Perfedd. In turn, Y Galan is separated from the main mass of Foel-goch by Cwm Bual [11-34]. The central spur, the grass-covered knife-edge of Yr Esgair [11-35], is separated from the next by the steeply hanging, tributary valley of Cwm-coch [11-36].

The final prong of the three, the naked spine of Y Llymllwyd [11-37], is probably the most impressive since its North-facing edge is a wall of sheer rock; Creigiau Gleision which is best left to rock climbers.

Y Llymllwyd comprises one of the few outcrops of intrusive igneous rock found in Snowdonia – rock formed by molten lava solidifying deep underground after forcing its way into the original bedrock. This particular rock is granite (the Bwlch y Cywion granite to be precise).

This marvel of mountain architecture goes unnoticed, of course, by those walkers who have set their sites on Elidir Fawr or Mynydd Perfedd, and dismissed Foel-goch as unworthy of their time. Indeed, even when viewed head-on from the floor of Nant Ffrancon, the beauty of Foel-goch's design remains a well-kept secret [11-38].

**5)**    **(628611)**    →

**300°**        →

From the tiny summit perch, cross to the left-hand side of the wire fence and pick your way down the steep, rock-strewn face of Foel-goch to meet the gravel path running left to right [11-39] in the direction of Mynydd Perfedd. The slopes below this path drop away into the wide valley of Cwm Dudodyn [11-40] which under desperate circumstances provides an escape route to lower ground (bottoming out in the Pass of Llanberis close to Nant Peris). The right-hand wall of this wide valley is formed by the steep flanks of Elidir Fawr [11-41].

Fortunately, your route steers well clear of these brutal slopes, and once you reach the gravel path and turn right very little altitude is lost before you rejoin the wire fence as it runs along the upper rim of Cwm Perfedd [11-42] towards Bwlch y Brecan at **625615**.

This is the lowest point of the ridge that separates Foel-goch from Mynydd Perfedd (close to the 710-metre contour). The main path here shows increasing signs of erosion before eventually splitting in two.

---

**OPTION 2**

For someone whose only agenda is to have a quick look at the ridge before retiring, this is where you retrace your steps onto Y Garn. From that summit return along your ascent path to Idwal Cottage.

*Time saved 3hrs*

**OPTION 3**

Another escape route if the weather turns nasty is to cross the ladder-stile in the fence on the right at the floor of this col and gain the minor road at the valley bottom by continuing through **points 11 and 12**.

*Time saved 3hrs 15mins*

**OPTION 4**

Depending on your energy levels, the two Elidirs can be re-scheduled for another day if time or stamina be in short supply. If that is the case keep to the right hand fork heading directly onto Mynydd Perfedd.

*Time saved about 1hr 45min.*

---

**6)    (625615)    →**

**280°    →**

Keep to the main path and follow it as it bears left, contouring the rim of Cwm Dudodyn. After passing a minor landslip on your right the path becomes narrower and significantly steeper for one particular section as it rises above Bwlch y Marchlyn.

> *Looking back at the path just taken you will be rewarded with a view of Foel-goch that underlines the steep nature of its Northern face [11-43].*
> *As you follow the Northern rim of Elidir Fawr's Eastern flanks you are also presented with a bird's eye view of the Western slopes of Mynydd Perfedd and Carnedd y Filiast [11-44], and the reservoir of Marchlyn Mawr [11-45].*

After negotiating the final steep section of crag above Craig Cwrwgl [11-46] the path emerges onto a high shelf at **616614**, a grass-covered shoulder beyond which stands the main summit [11-47]. A straightforward path climbing turf then loose shale culminates in a boulder-field, leading across almost level ground to what surprisingly turns out to be the second highest point of the day – **Elidir Fawr (612612** – 924m/3031ft) [11-48].

On closer inspection, the summit is not the point of a pyramid but a serrated ridge extending West towards Nant Peris, and the best views are obtained by following the line of crags to where they finally peter out above Bwlch Melynwyn at **609612**.

> *To the East you can clearly see the gentler flanks of Foel-goch and Y Garn and the route that brought you here from the col.*
> *Ahead to the South beyond the deep trench of Nant Peris stand Crib Goch and Snowdon (Yr Wyddfa).*
> *Easily identifiable to the South West are Llyn Dwythwch enclosed by Moel Eilio and Foel Goch, and the paved track leading down from Bwlch Maesgwm (a significant feature of **Walk 12** and **Walk 13**).*
> *In the distance Cardigan Bay glints gold between the high ground of the Llŷn peninsula and the hills of the Harlech Dome.*

Elidir Fawr itself is a notable outcrop of Cambrian rock – the same rock that is quarried at Bethesda and Llanberis for its high-quality slate.

This differs from the much younger (in geological terms) Ordovician slates that were quarried in the Nantlle Vale and continue to be mined at Blaenau Ffestiniog.

**7)      (612612)      →**

**250°            →**

Since Elidir Fach is so close it seems churlish to overlook its isolated cairn. Besides, it's unfeasible that anyone would come this far just to tackle that minor summit on its own.

---

**OPTION 5**

If you do decide to ignore this lower top despite my hard sell, retrace your steps towards **points 6 or 9.**

*Time saved – almost 1 hr*

---

A short scree slide alongside a dilapidated fence leads the way down from the main top to a flat expanse close to the 780-metre contour. **Elidir Fach** barely makes its mark on the surrounding landscape (at **603613** – 795m/2608ft) but it provides a unique opportunity to study the full length of Llyn Padarn as it floods the valley to your left. It also gives you a useful vantage point from which to study the lie of the land to the East and to decide on your next move.

---

**OPTION 6**

It is possible to head NorthEast from the cairn of Elidir Fach into the broad valley separating you from the Western wall of Carnedd y Filiast. If you head in the general direction of the buildings standing at the Western end of the reservoir you will eventually stumble across the rusty traces of a winding path heading towards lower ground. This leads to a reservoir service road (near **614625**) which occupies

---

the valley draining from the main reservoir into the smaller Marchlyn Bach reservoir [11-49]. Follow this vehicle track downhill and to your left, making sure to continue straight ahead after you have passed the outflow of the smaller reservoir. After by-passing a landscape of slate waste and disused workings on your left you reach a minor road which leads past a series of small, enclosed fields to the village of Deiniolen still some 150m above the main valley. This is a small, scattered settlement, perched high on a hillside above Llyn Padarn, with a history steeped in slate quarrying.

Few buses run from here to Llanberis so it's a case of walking down to the A4086 – the main road from Cwm y Glo to Llanberis. This end of the Llanberis Pass is a long way from where you presumably left your car. The only practical solution is the Sherpa bus back to Ogwen Cottage.

I only mention this option because it is a feasible escape route West in the event of deteriorating weather. It avoids the ridge walk back to Bwlch y Brecan, the difficult route finding down into Nant Ffrancon, and follows relatively low ground which could put you safely beneath any dense cloud cover that might suddenly obliterate the surrounding tops.

***Time saved – about 1hr (not counting the bus journey)***

There is another option which takes one from the path beneath the dam containing Marchlyn Mawr, along the foot of Carnedd y Filiast, to the disused Penrhyn Slate Quarries – but having already taken that route once I would urge anyone who considers walking a pleasure to avoid it at all costs, even though you do eventually emerge in Nant Ffrancon.

***Time saved – negligible given the arduous terrain***

Marchlyn Mawr reservoir is regularly topped up with water using a pumping system (operated by the Dinorwig Power Station in Nant Peris to replenish its fluctuating water supply during periods of heavy energy consumption). Much of Elidir Fawr has been hollowed out to accommodate the massive pipe-work used to channel this water (it's even possible to study this close up from the inside by paying a visit to 'Electric Mountain' in Llanberis). Consequently the lake level can rise rapidly regardless of rainfall (or a lack of it) so be sure to steer clear of its Southern shoreline where easy escape is not always possible.

**8)**     **(603613)**     →

      110°              →

Return onto Elidir Fawr, following pretty much the same route you took on descent. There is nothing to be gained in trying to circumvent the summit ridge by contouring East along its Northern flanks because sooner or later you will be forced to climb increasingly unstable, steep slopes above the spur of rock plunging into the lake below [11-50 from the Northern slopes of Carnedd y Filiast].

**7)**     **(612612)**     →

      80°              →

Linger as long as you like at the top, but bear in mind that there's still a good deal of ground to cover yet. Once you have recovered your breath from the painful re-ascent, retrace your steps across the shelf below the summit, along the steep path following the rim of Bwlch y Marchlyn, and down towards lower ground. As you follow the fairly level track now, look out for a minor path climbing slightly steeper ground to your left (before you reach the landslip you crossed earlier in the day). This path follows a fence as it crosses a couple of small, rocky protuberances then heads uphill across gentle slopes to the next summit.

---

**OPTION 7**
You can of course continue along the entire length of the ascent path to Bwlch y Brecan and continue back to the start via **points 11 and 12.**
*Missing out the last two summits of the day saves you some 45mins*

---

Time for another look at Elidir Fawr before you reach the flat expanse of Mynydd Perfedd [11-51]. From these slopes you can see the true nature of the hill you've just climbed (twice?) and pat yourself on the back for keeping well clear of those treacherous cliffs beneath its pyramidal top. In total contrast,

**Mynydd Perfedd** (at **622619** – 812m/2664ft) is probably the least impressive summit of the lot [11-52].

Mynydd Perfedd's name translates from Welsh to English in one variant as 'Mountain of Entrails' – not a pretty thought, but perhaps a fitting name when you are perched on the side of the A5 looking up at the mountain's haggard face with its skeletal strata exposed for all to see [11-53].

*Behind you to the South, the gentler Western slopes of Foel-goch and Y Garn contrast remarkably with their scooped-out Eastern cliffs over-hanging Nant Ffrancon. Facing the Ogwen valley almost head-on, Llyn Ogwen seems much closer, as do Llyn Idwal higher up on the right and the backdrop of the Glyderau. And still dominating the Eastern aspect stands the bulk of Pen yr Ole Wen, looking almost Torridonian in the way its walls rear up from the floor of the main valley.*
*Across the Llanberis Pass to the right stand Crib Goch and Snowdon (Yr Wyddfa) – with Moel Siabod beyond in the distance.*

**9)**   **(622619)**   →

   10°   →

A simple path leads across this rock-littered platform, first towards the edge of the cliffs overlooking Nant Ffrancon on your right then trending left to reach the boulder-strewn summit of Carnedd y Filiast [11-54]. Cross the ladder stile in the wall ahead of you then continue straight ahead to the main summit of **Carnedd y Filiast**, topped by a cairn (at **621627** – 821m/2694ft).

*Seawards to the North, Anglesey is suspended in a sheet of blue, with Puffin Island an apostrophe at its Eastern tip. Closer at hand lies Bangor; the golden walls of Penrhyn Castle standing out in the winter sunshine (built with a fortune gained from the slave trade; enhanced later by earnings from the slate beneath your feet).*
*To the West Caernarfon Castle can also be picked out; its heritage much older, perhaps bloodier, but certainly not less honourable.*

## OPTION 8

If you are determined to follow an alternative route down into Nant Ffrancon other than the one described later in the main body of this walk (involving the return across Mynydd Perfedd to Bwlch y Brecan), this is where the only tried and tested alternative begins. However, I cannot recommend it with the same conviction as I might have done a few years ago since access through the disused corner of the Penrhyn Slate Quarries seems no longer to be a recognized right of way despite its advertisement in several guide-books as the correct line of ascent or descent onto this ridge. This route also adds a significant amount of time to what is already a long walk.

Continue North, picking your way down a rough, boulder-strewn slope onto a damp shoulder of ground [11-55 from above, and 11-56 looking back towards the summit]. As you pass the shallow pools on this saddle you should be able to make out a distinct path. This clear-cut path leads directly to Carnedd y Filiast's Northern outlier at **618632** (721m/2365ft) [11-57].

From here the path (not marked on the Explorer map) continues slightly East of North along the gentle ridge of Fronllwydd. At its Northern extremity this becomes a craggy outcrop with a short, steep drop to a path alongside a section of stone wall [11-58 and 11-59]. Bear left as you pass this outcrop then follow the right-hand side of the wall as it careers downslope towards the quarries beyond [11-60] but keep a look out for the obvious gap in the wall a short distance along its length at **621641**. Turn left once you reach it and follow the path running right to left through the gap (close to the 460-metre contour) towards a short section of rough ground falling away ahead of you, littered with angular boulders and deep heather.

There was once a tumbled-down wall at the base of this hillside which gave easy access to a series of tracks serving the old quarry and still in use today – but the last time I attempted a return by this route I was thwarted by a substantial length of fencing. I would never suggest that you use one of the angular blocks to gain a leg up to enable you to cross over to the track since access to walkers is no longer encouraged [11-61]. Furthermore, once you emerge on the track below, the gate on your left adjacent to a water-filled trench (at **618643**) now warns

'Danger – Keep Out'. This gives you no option but to head in the opposite direction (right) downhill along the convoluted service road, following numerous zigzags through enormous cuttings and past a number of old dry-stone buildings towards the disused exit on the valley floor.

The quantity and scale of the waste heaps testify to the industry, which once dominated this corner of North Wales. The main quarry nearby is still excavating slate from the bowels of the hillsides West of Bethesda, and heavy traffic still uses this section of track at times (something worth bearing in mind from a safety point of view). Tempting as it may be to seek a short-cut to avoid the more convoluted loops and thus lose height more rapidly, many of the off-shoots lead to dead-ends. And with one pile of slate looking much like another it is easy to lose your bearings. Nor is there a direct route over the adjacent slate heaps North onto the main valley floor. But eventually you do escape the confines of this almost lunar landscape, reaching a gate [11-62].at **627652** where the track emerges at the side of a metalled road – a short distance from the bridge crossing the river to enter the Ogwen Bank Caravan Park (and join the A5 a few metres beyond).

*To relieve the monotony of such depressing surroundings, take the opportunity whenever possible to survey the views ahead of you. To the North lies Bethesda (and the open wound of the slate quarries to its left) with the city of Bangor beyond [11-63].*

*Above Bethesda the moorland rises in whipped-cream-like peaks firstly to Moel Faban, Gyrn and Drosgl, then closer at hand to Gyrn Wigau, Foel Ganol and the bulk of Yr Elen with the flat block of Carnedd Llywelyn behind. Directly across valley, the Braich Ty Du spur of Pen yr Ole Wen and Carnedd Dafydd dominates the scene.*

*And directly ahead Mynydd Llandegai looks as if a patch of crofting country has been transplanted there from the remoter corners of Scotland [11-64].*

Turn right as you squeeze past one of the gateposts then follow the straightforward (and perfectly legal) path-cum-cycle-track as it runs South alongside the Afon Ogwen towards Ogwen Cottage.

For part of its length this path crawls beneath yet more steep hills of slate waste [11-65] before eventually entering open valley [11-66]. It passes through a gate at **630638** to join the minor road running along the valley's Western side. From here it's a pleasant stroll along a fairly flat, country lane back to wherever you parked your vehicle [11-67].

### *Additional time – an uncomfortable 2hrs*

Lord Penrhyn (Richard Pennant to his mum and dad) was encouraged to take control of the slate quarries here in 1782 – the workings at Cae Braich y Cafn eventually became the vast Penrhyn Quarry.

Despite the visual desecration caused to the environment by the vast excavations hereabouts, Lord Penrhyn saw a need to tame the wilderness he inherited and make it profitable for farming as well as quarrying. He built Pen-Isa'r-Nant (at 631651) as a dairy and poultry farm close to his quarry. He also established a quarryman's settlement of smallholdings at Mynydd Llandegai – each cottage was provided with about ½ a hectare of pasture, sufficient to graze a cow or provide other means of sustenance when quarry work was slack.

Following the 1800 Act of Union uniting Ireland with Great Britain, there was suddenly a requirement for better transport links between Dublin and London. The existing road (built by Lord Penrhyn) between the outskirts of Bangor and Capel Curig was regularly shut in winter due to snow, and the deteriorating state of the road had recently led to the withdrawal of the mail coach to Holyhead. So in 1810 Thomas Telford was approached to suggest improvements that would facilitate the passage to Westminster of the Irish MP's.

As a result of consulting Telford, the A5 was built through Nant Ffrancon – saving 20 miles on the coastal route via Conwy and Chester. Once this road was completed, many quarrymen who lived in Mynydd Llandegai built themselves new houses along the A5 in order to be closer to work (locating most of their homes close to their chapel). Many non-Conformist chapels adopted Biblical names (e.g. Seion, Bethel or in this case Bethesda). The village thus adopted the name of the local chapel.

Interestingly, when Queen Victoria visited the quarry in 1842, on her immediate arrival 1300 explosions were set off from all parts of the quarry. Beats a bunch of flowers I suppose.

**10)**   **(621627)**   →

**150°**   →

Assuming that you have chosen to steer clear of the quarry-scarred Northern edge of this ridge, you might still be tempted to make a more express descent to Nant Ffrancon from Carnedd y Filiast. Don't. Exhaustive personal research on foot looking for alternative ways up from the valley floor or down from the summit plateau has proven that there is no easy escape that way. Take a look down into Cwm Graianog if you need further convincing [11-68].

Most of the side valleys feeding Nant Ffrancon are termed 'hanging valleys'; suspended tributary valleys with their lower reaches left perched above a much deeper main valley that was subject to greater erosion during the late stages of the last Ice Age. Consequently there is some degree of risk in descending these in poor visibility since the downslope gradient, relatively gentle at first, suddenly becomes perilously steeper before bottoming out at the main valley floor.

Geologically speaking, Cwm Graianog is considered to be a perfect example of a hanging valley – one which generated a smaller glacier of its own during the Ice Age. The floor of this hanging valley was deeply cleft by the glacier, but the resultant gash has since been filled with debris following the glacier's retreat. Consequently the valley has been left with a saucer-like floor and a pronounced rim built up of moraine material (debris left behind after ice melt).

The stream rising in this high valley actually follows the original rock channel beneath the loose stones and gravel, gushing out far below the lip of the moraine. This shapely moraine was at one time given a local Welsh name meaning 'the Maiden's Arms'.

The main valley of the Afon Ogwen below these tributary valleys once held a large lake some 30 metres deep. The lake filling Nant Ffrancon was, however, only a temporary feature, held back by the Irish Sea ice sheet. When the Irish Sea ice melted this temporary lake drained away completely into the sea close to the Northern end of the trough– giving a dramatic display I should imagine of one of the naturally-occurring catastrophes that have shaped this entire landscape.

The crags in the cwm below Carnedd y Filiast include one called the 'Atlantic Slab' – a massive sweep of rock of gigantic proportions, rippled by waves of blackened shale. For the rock-climbers among you, a good number of routes crossing this outcrop are classified as 'V diff' or less, but are considered 'alpine' in seriousness due to the scale of the climbs.

For those of you restricted, like me, to mere walking, from the summit point of Carnedd y Filiast make a straightforward retreat back to Mynydd Perfedd by way of the ascent path, and down to Bwlch y Brecan by way of an intermittent path that keeps closer to the left-hand edge of the ridge. This begins to drop down quite steeply to the main Foel-goch/Elidir Fawr path you followed earlier in the day. It also keeps in close proximity to a fence until you reach more level ground at Bwlch y Brecan itself (at **625615**).

6)    (625615)       →

      60°            →

Keeping close to the fence line now, cross the second ladder stile and pick out a fairly steep path dropping down the grassy upper reaches of Cwm Perfedd to your left [11-69 facing downslope, and 11-70 from further down looking back uphill].

ALMOST EVERY SLOPE DESCENDING EAST INTO NANT FFRANCON CROSSES STEEPLY DESCENDING, CONVEX SLOPES. THAT MEANS THAT YOU ARE OFTEN UNABLE TO SEE WHAT LIES BELOW UNTIL YOU FIND YOURSELF PERCHED ABOVE A STEEP DROP WITH THE ONLY ESCAPE BEING UPHILL RETREAT. HOWEVER, THIS DESCENT ROUTE HAS BEEN TRIED AND TESTED AND FOUND TO BE MANAGEABLE UNDER MOST CONDITIONS.

The path drops down quite gently at first as it leads you into the upper reaches of a broad valley, bound on its right by a vast hummock of ground [11-71]. The idea is to keep trending further right as you drop down these grassy slopes, avoiding at all costs a fruitless descent to the floor of the minor valley to your left. Eventually this path, in places just a faint line of discoloured grass, creeps round the snout of this hummock on your right (Y Galan) allowing you to find a safer place to descend to the main valley floor of Nant Ffrancon.

197

As you reach lower ground, with the bulk of Y Galan still blocking any escape to your right, the Afon Ogwen and flat valley floor appear beneath you and reassuringly close [11-72]. However, do not be fooled. From this altitude the more treacherous sections of the descent are still hidden below the convex slopes ahead. Take the obvious line across the slope to your right, in places following a set of widely-spaced, white rocks sunk into the turf.

Eventually the grass grows longer and coarser [11-73]. The less lush vegetation marks a change in the terrain; where the lie of the land allows you to cut across further right until you are heading along the line of the main valley [11-74]. Look out for the grey bulge of rock on the valley floor [11-75, and 11-76 from further along the walk] – this is your prime target so try to keep it in your sights.

Ahead of you a faint path can be picked out crossing the grassy slopes [11-77], not taking you any closer to the valley floor for the time being but that's not a problem. And as you continue along this line, the view directly below you opens up more clearly. A sunken fence runs parallel to the path at some distance down the hillside where coarse grass invades the pasture again [11-78]. There is no point trying to drop down just yet, however.

The section of slope that you are about to traverse becomes increasingly steep – indeed under wet or frosty conditions this section can be almost impossible to cross without at least a pair of trekking poles. Aim for a line that will keep you above the white rocks scattered below you [11-79] – and wherever possible keep to the path which at least gives you a miniscule ledge to perch upon [11-80].

The path keeps you upslope of these rocks [11-81] before fading to little more than a scuff mark in the grass again as you are finally free to start crossing contours. Unfortunately, the speed at which you are able to plunge down this particular section can become quite scary unless you have some means of slowing down. I have literally sledded down this hillside on the seat of my pants, unable to stay on my feet due to the severe angle of slope!

Fortunately there are a number of spots where you can arrest your rate of descent, and grab your bearings.

Ahead of you still, and some way downslope, an outcrop of vertical crags provides a particular feature worth aiming for [11-82] – somewhere to gain handholds and clamber downslope more elegantly. Just beyond these crags the grassy slopes finally wash up against a dry-stone wall (with a rusted fence accompanying it) behind a large patch of bracken [11-83]. Head for the right-hand end of this wall where it abuts against the cleft valley of Cwm Bual (at **635620**) close to the 350-metre contour.

**11)**   **(635620)**   →

   **45°**   →

Heading for that point where the triangular patch of bracken and wall meet up leads you to the banks of a sizeable stream tumbling down from the headwall of Cwm Bual below the crest of Foel-goch [11-84]. All rivers follow the line of least resistance down a slope – pretty much the same way as I did when I last did this walk.

Some of you may wonder why I recommend this particular route to reach the valley floor. One reason is that there are very few other points along Nant Ffrancon where you are unlikely to become crag-fast at some point or other (i.e. perched on crags below a cwm with no obvious way down). The other reason, perhaps as important, is that much of the valley floor and the gentler slopes above it are enclosed farmland. This particular route avoids all but the most open pasture. It seems to me that walkers can sometimes do themselves a greater disservice in tramping uninvited across a farmer's meadow than in picking their way carefully through a disused slate quarry. The collapsed wall and dilapidated fence can be safely crossed to gain the lower slopes [11-85 obviously looking upslope].

A faint path is now visible running through the bracken-covered slopes below you towards a grassy bump, still some way above the valley bottom. Follow this path, keeping the stream on your right and a dry-stone wall on your left. When you reach the top of this grassy bump it appears at first glance as if the ground ahead of you still has a long way to drop [11-86] and that there is no obvious way to get down comfortably. However, if you climb down a short distance you will be able to trend left towards the wall (topped by a fence) that takes a restrained roller-coaster ride down to the road [11-87, and 11-88 looking up from further downhill].

Follow the line of this wall, crossing a couple of damp, reedy patches, and before you know it you emerge unscathed onto a large area of bare grass and gravel where the stream meets the road [11-89]. This large patch of grass, completely open to the road, is a popular picnic spot – often packed with cars during the summer holiday season. I have even watched a game of cricket played on it (hardly County standard though, given the unevenness of the pitch).

In the field directly across the road from where your path emerges, and accessible by footbridge, is the grey hump of rock referred to earlier in the walk. This marks one point where a particularly resistant bit of bedrock was able to withstand the relentless grinding processes as ice sheets passed down this valley. The rock was too hard to be worn away completely, but it was sculpted nevertheless by the constant rub of grit- and stone-laden ice. Striations and furrows on its ice-polished surface clearly identify the direction of ice flow (South to North).

These rock features are called 'roches moutonées' (an Alpine term – loosely translated as 'rock sheep' since vast collections of these common to certain Swiss valleys look like flocks of grazing sheep from a distance).

This feature in Nant Ffrancon is one of a number in the immediate vicinity. A much larger one is poised above Ogwen Cottage. Indeed, most of the valleys surrounding the glaciated highlands display the same features on a larger or smaller scale.

12)    (638623)       →

       170°            →

The compass direction is given here purely to ensure that you turn right once you meet the road. Assuming you are parked somewhere between this point and Ogwen Cottage, follow the road at your leisure back to the start point. This minor road, despite some steep ups and downs at its Southern end) is a perfect end to a brilliant ridge walk – as well as an ideal introduction to the magnificent scenery of the area for anyone wary of venturing into the hills but sufficiently spellbound by their beauty to consider a closer inspection.

*One of the finest viewpoints along the road is close to* **641611** *where a farm track leads down to the left to Blaen-y-Nant farm. At this spot you face Tryfan head-on; its craggy outline poised above the narrow point where Llyn Ogwen spills into Nant Ffrancon over the Rhaeadr Ogwen waterfalls [11-90].*

*A view like this should be more than enough inspiration for anyone to put on their boots and hit them hills!*

**END**

# SNOWDON

This is the one most visitors to the area aspire to conquer. It is a startling fact that 400,000 visitors reach the summit of Snowdon each year (though not all under their own steam). Startling when you consider that only 100,000 more each year visit the ruins of Macchu Pichu in South America – undoubtedly one of the 'wonders' of the world. But do not despair if your ambitions do not match your ability to reach the summit itself. There are as many fulfilling experiences awaiting you on lower ground if you are prepared to seek them out.

## TASTER 12

Most people who are cautious of setting foot in such a classic climbing area but who still want to get to the top of Snowdon's summit settle for the train. There's nothing wrong with that, but it's hardly a rewarding exercise.

There is much more to be gained in setting off on foot along the Miners' Track as far as the old crushing mill at the end of Llyn Llydaw (**Walk 14**) – even perhaps pulling out all the stops and going up to the shores of Glaslyn. No place will give you a better feel for the immensity of the 'Snowdon Horseshoe'. And you get a worm's-eye view of the path to the summit – perhaps something to motivate you to aim further next time you visit. Just don't attempt any ascent unless you are suitably equipped.

And however far you intend walking, make sure you get to the car park early – unless you bus in by 'Sherpa' from Llanberis or Nant Peris.

**Allow yourself 2 hrs to make the most of a wonderful experience – add an hour for the extra bit to Glaslyn**

## TASTER 13

Another pleasant walk into this neck of the woods, rarely taken by the crowds, follows the easy track into Bwlch Maesgwm. Follow the same route as **Walk 13**. Once you reach the high col between Foel Goch and Moel Cynghorion, make sure you ascend the slopes of Foel Goch on your right for a short distance in order to obtain the best view towards the Nantlle Ridge. Then just head back down to the car.

*This is an easy walk under all but the wintriest conditions.*

**Should take 2 ½ hrs max**

# TASTER 14

*For a glimpse of the Western face of Snowdon, a walk along the 'Rhyd-Ddu' path* (**Walk 16**) *as far as the workings beneath the slopes of Yr Aran should not be beyond the capabilities of most fair-weather walkers – but preferably on a dry, sunny day.*
*Follow the route taken by* **Walk 16** *as far as* **point 3**. *Reaching the ridge that joins Yr Aran to Yr Wyddfa (with the drop ahead into Cwm y Llan) is certain to whet the appetite of any reluctant rambler to spend more time on the quieter side of Snowdon.*

**Again, 2 ½ hrs should cover it, but you are likely to want to spend more time exploring the landscape.**

# TASTER 15

*Follow the 'Watkin Path' as described during the first section of* **Walk 15**. *This easy track presents no difficulties until it starts its climb from the site of the old quarry workings in upper Cwm y Llan. If you get that far then you could do a lot worse than picnicking on the grassy slopes alongside before heading back down-valley.*
*Even if you decide on a shorter stroll, the Gladstone Rock is easily reached without too much effort, and on your return it is well-worth seeking out the waterfalls at* **623517** *(see* **Walk 15***) – an even greater spot to have a picnic.*

**A couple of hours well spent – whatever the season.**

*Anyone who makes the effort to explore any of these short excursions will hopefully be tempted to spend more time in the surrounding hills. Each of the four tasters described here only gives one viewpoint of Snowdon's multitude of charms. The next step is to tackle one of the real walks.....*

# Moel Eilio [39] / Foel Gron [40] / Foel Goch [41]

| 10.4 Km (6.5 miles) 680m (2230ft) Time : 4hrs 30min | An easy and rewarding ridge walk in the North Western foothills of Snowdon (Yr Wyddfa) |
|---|---|

Walking these hills in the depths of winter is not everybody's cup of tea, but on the three occasions I've done this walk off-season, conditions have been near perfect.

Llanberis may look less than enticing early morning with the Pass filled by a congealing broth of grey cloud below about 500 metres. But in such conditions the surrounding summits often poke up into a clear blue sky. I have been fortunate enough to witness brilliant cloud inversions in these hills, complete with 'Brocken Spectre' and 'glories' while appraising the scenery from the summit of Moel Eilio.

On another occasion snow covered everything above 600 metres making the view towards Yr Wyddfa particularly impressive.

Winter or summer, this straightforward route will provide most walkers with a fresh perspective on a corner of Snowdonia that is criminally overlooked by most of the region's visitors.

**North**

**Don't forget**

**map/compass**
**whistle/torch**

**suitable footwear + clothing**

**food/drink**

**brain**

## APPROACH

From Bangor or Caernarfon, bear right to enter Llanberis village from the North and turn right by the Padarn Stores into Ffordd Capel-Coch.

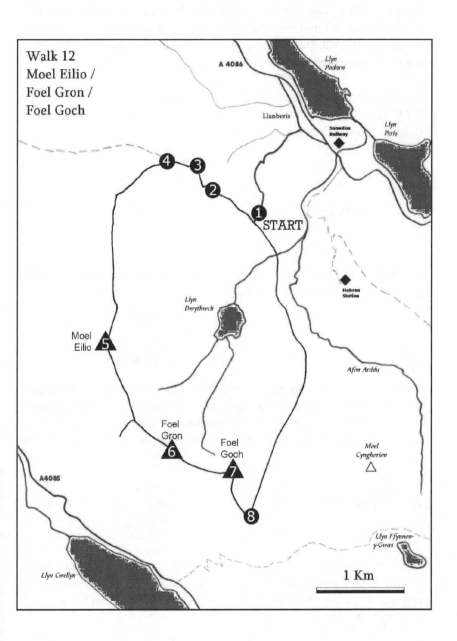

Walk 12
Moel Eilio /
Foel Gron /
Foel Goch

A 4086

Llyn Padarn

Llanberis

Llyn Peris

Snowdon Railway

START

Hebron Station

Llyn Dwythwch

Afon Arddu

Moel Eilio

Foel Gron

Foel Goch

Moel Cynghorion

A4085

Llyn Ffynnon-y-Gwas

Llyn Cwellyn

1 Km

From the Capel Curig direction, follow the Llanberis Pass and as you reach Llanberis, turn left into the village then left again at the Padarn Stores into Ffordd Capel Coch. This minor road soon narrows with passing places and the occasional closed gate.

Continue uphill past the Youth Hostel on the left to the 220-metre contour (**573592**) not far from the road end where the right-hand verge has ample space for parking between the rubble and boulders.

## START

**1)**     **(573592)**     →

        **195°**          →

Continue on foot up to the road end – cross the ladder stile to the left of the gate (assuming the gate is closed).

        **320°**          →

Immediately turn right onto a cart track that follows the line of a stone wall. This track narrows and drops gently to cross the river issuing noisily from the bowl of upland on your left [12-01]. Pass through a rusty gate ahead of you and as the path climbs again it eventually emerges onto a part-metalled road.

**2)**     **(568595)**     →

        **255°**          →

Turn left onto this road to approach the ruins of Maen-llwyd-isaf [12-02] then as soon as you draw level with it immediately turn right to continue a short way uphill to a rusty farm gate set in the dry-stone wall ahead of you.

**3)**     **(566597)**     →

         280°          →

Once you have passed through the gate turn left, following the grassy track running in the lee of the wall with a line of telegraph poles parallel to it [12-03]. On your right are the waste heaps marking the abandoned slate mines of Chwarel Fawr and Chwarel Cefn-du.

Eventually you reach another gate in the wall which crosses your path ahead [12-04]. A recent sign has been erected beyond this gate which prohibits the use of any unauthorised mechanically propelled vehicles; an environmentally responsible measure given the amount of hillside scarring such activities can cause.

**4)**     **(563598)**     →

         220°          →

Pass through this gate then immediately locate a faint scuff mark climbing left from the track's verge, passing under the telegraph lines before approaching the skyline.

         180°          →

This gives you easy access onto Bryn Mawr, the ridge leading directly to the first summit of the day (Moel Eilio) [12-05].

*North Eastwards beyond Llanberis lies Llyn Padarn backed by the slate-quarry-scarred Southern face of Elidir Fach (an excuse, if ever one was needed, to flood this part of the Llanberis Pass with impenetrable cloud).*
*West of North lie Caernarfon, the Menai Strait and Anglesey.*
*South West dipping its toes into Caernarfon Bay stands the headland comprising Trwyn y Gorlech and Yr Eifl.*

*But if light conditions are flattering, it's the bulk of Snowdon itself to the South East which is most likely to catch the eye [12-06].*

A broad, grassy track now follows the crest of this low ridge, joined by other tracks from the West, and bounded on its left by an embankment [12-07 and 12-08]. These other tracks once provided a short-cut for the communities South and East of Caernarfon to access the slate quarries on either side of the Llanberis Pass.

The boundary bank which runs alongside the main track actually dates from the 12th century and can be traced from 558595 to 557582.
The stony bank, with a slight ditch on its Western side, had a significant agricultural function in medieval times as it marked the division between the upland summer grazing lands and the main estate on lower ground. Due to the bank's extensive size, it is likely that these grazing lands once belonged to the princes of Gwynedd.

As you continue to head South you will pass a small stone enclosure (at **557595**) and a pool where the ground levels (at **557586**). Ahead of you now rises the Western face of Moel Eilio scarred by an ascent path which, from below, looks like a set of vehicle tracks. The ground here can be quite wet underfoot but there are several opportunities to avoid the muddier bits [12-09 looking back from further along the path].

A fence drops down from the summit along the right hand side of the path, and it takes a sharp turn right close to the mountain's base where a ladder stile allows one to cross it [12-10]. Don't bother. Follow the path up onto the shoulder of high ground, keeping the fence as a handrail close to your right if visibility is poor.

The ascent becomes relentlessly steep for a while but the path is wide enough for you to zig-zag along where the angle is particularly bothersome. ¾ of the way up another ladder stile crosses a flimsier fence running across the hillside [12-11]. Climb over this stile and continue up gentler slopes to another ladder stile crossing yet another fence [12-12]. On the opposite side of this fence a substantial cairn-cum-wind-shelter marks the top of **Moel Eilio** (at **555577** – 727m/2383ft).

Any torment suffered during the ascent of the mountain's steep slopes will have been wiped clear of your hard drive once you explore the scenery available from this broad summit (unless engulfed by cloud as I was when the accompanying photographs were taken).

**5)**   **(555577)**   →

  **150°**   →

To get the most favourable views you would do well to wait until you have made your way down the slopes that drop swiftly South and East from the summit. With the fence now on your left you soon reach a ladder stile ahead of you where a dry-stone wall meets the fence. Cross this stile and bear right; all the while absorbing the views ahead and studiously surveying the lay-out of ground yet to be covered [12-13].

Just beyond this stile marks the spot from which I saw my first ever 'Brocken Spectre'. Not as sinister as you might imagine. The term comes from the Alps where such features are perhaps more common. They are only ever seen during calm weather in winter when low ground (particularly deep, steep-sided valleys) are flooded with cold, damp air in the form of mist whilst the surrounding higher ground is cloud-free. This is known as a temperature inversion, where the heavier, colder, damper air has slid down hill under gravity, leaving clear (often warmer) sky above.

If the layer of mist is sufficiently thick (in my case it lay only 100 metres or so below the tops) anyone standing on a high ridge or summit looking down into a mist-flooded valley with the sun at their back will have their shadow cast onto the surface of the mist. The closer the upper surface of this mist layer is to the summit, the larger and more pronounced your shadow will be – looking rather like a giant, dark phantom or 'Spectre' super-imposed onto the cloud below. If you wave your arms you will, of course, see this large ghostly shape perform the exact same action.

In the correct atmospheric conditions, you may also see a dazzling, bright aura (or 'glory') surrounding your shadow – an even stranger phenomenon. Incidentally, if a group of you happens to be on the same ridge looking down at your 'Brocken Spectres' each individual only sees a 'glory' surrounding his own shadow.

*East (on your left) the cliff forms a rim above Cwm Dwythwch with its lake (beyond which lies the path leading back to the start of the walk) [12-14 from below the cloud!].*

*A less glorious phenomenon lies across the main valley – the carnage of slate workings at the base of Elidir Fawr.*

*West (on your right) above Llyn Cwellyn stand the forested flanks of Mynydd Mawr with the serrated bulk of the Nantlle Ridge to its left – Mynydd Drws-y-Coed looking particularly imposing, and further South, Moel Hebog in superior isolation.*

*Ahead (South East) is the North Western face of Yr Wyddfa (Snowdon), with the Glyderau and Tryfan on the skyline to its left.*

The path becomes steadily steeper as it descends to the col [12-15 – lookng back up to Moel Eilio]. Incised into the cliff edge on your left is the dark cleft of Bwlch Gwyn with a dizzying view into the depths of Cwm Dwythwch. The main col of Bwlch Cwm Cesig (**559571** – 598 metres) separates Moel Eilio from Foel Gron. This grass-covered saddle bears similarities to the gentler sections of the Nantlle Ridge.

After crossing the damp floor of Bwlch Cwm Cesig the ground begins to rise again, diverting increasingly right away from the fence and the edge of the cliffs. As the angle of ascent eases another fence crosses the slopes ahead of you with a ladder stile giving access to its opposite side [12-16].

*If visibility permits, it is worth making a slight diversion right, following the line of the fence you have just crossed until you reach the edge of the slopes overlooking Llyn Cwellyn [12-17 taken from* **Walk 20** *reveals the lake's opposite shore and these shapely slopes to best effect]. The views West towards the lake and the forested slopes of Mynydd Mawr are unbeatable and repay the 10 minutes or so spent reaching there [12-18].*

Following this diversion, return to this ladder stile, continuing along the fence-line to the cliff edge [12-19 looking back] beyond which the ground plunges almost vertically into Cwm Cesig. As you trace the line of cliffs Eastwards you should hopefully be able to pick out the highest point, the almost anonymous, subsidiary top of **Foel Gron** (at **560568** – 629m/2063ft) [12-20] some 150 metres ahead.

Approaching the summit, a broad notch on your left provides one of the finest vantage points from which to study Llyn Dwythwch and the broad basin in which it lies [12-21]. From the grass-covered mound descend for a short distance before climbing easily to a turf-covered shelf with a small heap of rocks marking Foel Gron's main (but lower) peak (at **564565** – 593m/1946ft) [12-22]. On the OS map this is the top actually identified as the summit of Foel Gron – the higher point at **560568** does not even warrant a name (so I have identified that as a subsidiary top in photo 12-17).

**6)    (564565)    →**

     **130°**    →

From here the path drops down to another broad col (at **566564** – 520 metres) [12-23]. If you turn back for a retrospective view of Foel Gron you can perhaps appreciate how it got its name. From here its profile is distinctly 'rounded' [12-24 looking back along the ridge]. A gentle climb across grassy slopes leads towards a ladder stile in a fence close to the final summit [12-25, and 12-26 looking back]. Ignore the stile. Instead, cross the next stile in the fence running left to right along the hilltop [12-27]. There are two stiles there – the one on the right leads onto the slopes above Llyn Cwellyn, the other straight ahead leads onto the flattened summit of **Foel Goch** (**570563** – 605m/1985ft) a short distance to your left. The slopes directly below and ahead of you now are the flanks of Moel Cynghorion [12-28 and 12-29 from Foel Goch's summit] climbing above the intervening col of Bwlch Maesgwm.

**7)    (570563)    →**

     **180°**    →

To reach the col at Bwlch Maesgwm (at 467 metres) if visibility is poor the easiest option is to rejoin the fence on your right and follow it downhill [12-30 looking back uphill]. Otherwise, a clear and straightforward path runs diagonally across the descending slopes from the summit itself to the 'crossroads' where a paved path heads left along the Maesgwm valley back to the start of the walk.

8)      (572559)        →

30°            →

At the foot of the col head left and keep to the paved track as it descends the Western side of the Maesgwm valley. In good light you would already have seen this paved path threading its way along the pass below as you traversed the lower slopes of Foel Goch.

*The bulk of Moel Cynghorion on your right with numerous landslips scarring its flanks [12-32 and 12-33] is an impressive sight.*

*And straight ahead of you, across the main valley of the Afon Arddu, it is possible on a clear day to make out the line of the Snowdon Mountain Railway as it climbs towards Clogwyn Station and beyond. Indeed, at the height of summer a procession of trains can be seen and heard trucking the less adventurous to the summit of Yr Wyddfa [12-34].*

As the valley broadens you pass through a gate at **578572** [12-35]. Beyond here the quality of the path improves as it eventually becomes paved [12-36]. The desolate valley that opens out to your right has little agricultural value today. The ruined cottages that can be found along most valley edges [12-37 and 12-38] are no longer considered habitable, although the isolated Ty'n-yr-Aelgerth (again on your right at **577580**) demonstrates what is possible with a little TLC.

Transhumance was a common practice in North West Wales until the end of the 18th century when the enclosure movement reached here. The stock farmer would leave his main, lowland farm ('hendre') during the summer to live in a smaller, seasonal dwelling ('hafod') in the mountains in order to oversee the cattle put out to graze on these higher pastures. Once sheep replaced cattle, towards the end of the 18th century again, there was less need to supervise the flocks in the summer as sheep need less husbandry. At the same time, cottage industries of spinning and weaving developed at the expense of raising cattle. Mountain grazing nowadays tends to be used pretty much throughout the year, almost exclusively by sheep.

Beyond this cottage the path suddenly transforms into a metalled track. Follow this, passing through a gate at **575587** where the road crosses the Afon Hwch (the river exiting Llyn Dwythwch).

This broad valley on your left is the site of a number of pre-historic Hut Circles, as well as a feature at 573589 dating back to the Bronze Age known as a Burnt Mound. Burnt Mounds are common throughout upland Wales – a number, for example, can be found on the slopes adjoining Walk 20. The purpose of such features is unclear and may vary from example to example. But they are easily recognisable – occurring beside streams and composed entirely of burnt stones (often dolerite a particular type of volcanic rock which could be reheated many times without deterioration). These rocks were used sometime in the past to heat water in a trough or large container. The mounds themselves are often horseshoe shaped, the trough having been located in the centre. Hot water produced in this way may have been part of an industrial process, or been utilised purely for something as mundane as cooking.

On your left on the raised levels of the riverbank stands a concrete monstrosity of more recent ancestry (presumably some type of radio transmitter dating back to World War II) [12-39]. ½ Km beyond this you reach the ladder stile on your right at the road head with the walk's starting point just a few more steps downhill.

**END**

# Moel Cynghorion [42] / Snowdon (Yr Wyddfa) [43] / Llechog [44]

17.3 Km
(10.8 miles)

1275m (4182ft)

Time : 7hrs 30min

**Not just a case of there and back – a neat circuit taking advantage of the 'Snowdon Ranger' and 'Llanberis' paths**

The word 'tourist' when used to describe an ascent route is often enough to deter most seasoned hill-walkers from setting boot anywhere near it. I have been just as much at fault – associating the 'Snowdon Ranger' path with Youth Hostellers, and the 'Llanberis' path with the train trundling up and down Yr Wyddfa.

Neither, of course, should give me adequate cause to disparage two of the more popular ascent routes. After all, I am not ashamed to say that I have frequently taken the 'tourist path' onto Ben Nevis's top before continuing along the stupendous Carn Mor Dearg arête. So where's the harm in choosing the 'easy' option to get you to the heart of the action that bit more quickly?

The 'Llanberis path' in particular suffers bad press because as far as most serious summiteers are concerned taking this route is just not the done thing. What tosh! When combined with the 'Snowdon Ranger' these two paths form an unconventional but beguiling 'Horseshoe' – worthy of more respect than either receives.

**North**

**Don't forget**

**map/compass
whistle/torch**

**suitable footwear
+ clothing**

**food/drink**

**brain**

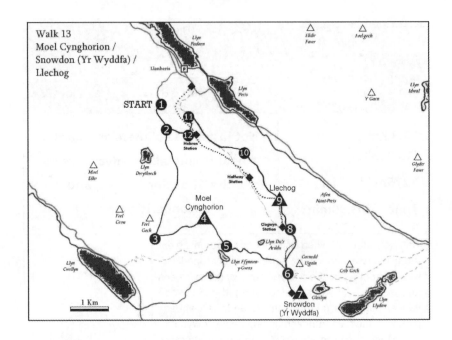

## APPROACH

Approaching Llanberis from the South (along the Llanberis Pass), follow the signs left for the village centre. As you reach the Padarn Stores on your left, take the road left adjacent to the shop (Ffordd Capel-Coch).

From the North, bear right to enter the village and turn right again just before the Padarn Stores into Ffordd Capel-Coch. This soon becomes a narrow road with passing places and the occasional closed gate.

Continue uphill past the Youth Hostel on the left to the 220-metre contour (**573592**) not far from the road end where the right-hand verge has ample space for parking.

**START**

1)       **(573592)**       →

         **195°**                →

Continue on foot up to the road end – cross the ladder stile to the left of the gate.

         **140°**                →

A fine roadway runs to the left from this gateway [13-01] – tarmac in places and driveable as far as the small-holding of Ty'n-yr-Aelgerth (at **576582**) as long as you are willing to risk your vehicle's suspension.

Continue along this road, walled on its left and fern-banked on its right. Pass a galvanised gate and ladder stile on your left [13-02] just before the road drops slightly to cross the Afon Hwch. There is what appears to be an antiquated radio transmitter – a monstrous concrete plinth topped by aerials – perched above the river banks on your right. Not an attractive prospect but a valuable landmark for later in the walk [13-03]. Pass through the rusted gate guarding the bridge and look out for a second gate and ladder stile a short distance further along the road on your left [13-04]. A sign prohibits cycling on the other side of the gate.

This ladder stile marks the spot where your escape route from the 'Llanberis Path' emerges close to the end of the walk [13-05]. If conditions are clear you can pick out the return leg on your left [13-06].

**2)     (575587)        →**

     **175°           →**

Continue along the metalled road [13-07], passing a ruined building on your left alongside a couple of trees (the remains of Brithdir at **576583**). If you have driven this far, the best place to park is on the right hand side of the road opposite these ruins. Once you reach the small cottage of Ty'n-yr-Aelgerth, 400 metres further along on the left, the roadway deteriorates into a shaley path; in excellent condition for walking or mountain-biking, but impossible to drive along [13-08].

This track adheres to the right-hand side of the Maesgwm pass, continuing to Bwlch Maesgwm at 467 metres before descending to the shores of Llyn Cwellyn. No doubt this was a significant route in the past; the only link between Llanberis and remoter regions adjacent to Dyffryn Nantlle and Beddgelert.

*The views along this entire stretch are tantalising as more and more detail emerges. The line of the Snowdon Mountain Railway can be clearly seen on your left beyond the scrubby fields forming the floor of the Arddu valley [13-09]. Then as your path swings right and gains height you are confronted by the majestic slopes of Moel Cynghorion on your left across the Maesgwm valley.*

The path continues to climb in a straight line, passing through a small gate at **578572**. Beyond here it becomes narrower [13-10] clinging to the steep slopes on your right, the base-line of Foel Goch and the ridge extending NorthWest to Moel Eilio. Despite the easy gradient, be prepared to encounter a substantial draught as this valley acts as an enormous wind-tunnel.

**3)      (572559)      →**

       **75°           →**

*As the path eventually emerges at the high col it is worthwhile pausing for breath and finding a vantage point upslope to your right from which to study the scenery to the South West. On a clear day Llyn Cwellyn, Mynydd Mawr, the Nantlle Ridge and Moel Hebog form an impressive backdrop even from this modest altitude.*

At the highest point of the pass a fence runs across the path with a ladder stile on your right. This stile gives access to the flanks of Foel Goch. Another stile (and gate) in the wall on your left [13-11] lead you onto a faint, grassy path. This path follows the line of a fence that initially clings to the wall before heading off at right angles to easily gain the Southern slopes of Moel Cynghorion [13-12 from **Walk 12**].

---

**OPTION 3**
To join the 'Snowdon Ranger' path without setting foot on Moel Cynghorion's summit, continue straight ahead at the highest point of the pass and follow the muddy path downhill until you pass through a gap in a section of dry-stone wall.
A smaller path branches off to the left beyond this wall and continues downhill through thick, coarse grassland. As you cross the 360-metre contour the 'Snowdon Ranger' path approaches from the right. Join this main route and turn left to follow it gradually uphill towards Llyn Ffynnon Y Gwas and **point 5**.
*Time saved – about 30 mins*

---

After some initial steepness the angle of ascent eases [13-13]. Another slightly steeper section follows, passing large stone blocks laid out to your right [13-14 looking across to the Moel Hebog group] before the angle of ascent relents again as the mountain levels above Bwlch Carreg y Gigfran. Beyond the fence on your left the ground falls away steeply; in places it has collapsed forming landslips slumping into the Maesgwm valley below [13-15 looking back from further along the path].

A gentle stroll across fairly level ground, which can become wet under foot, eventually leads you onto the summit which is tucked away at the extreme North Eastern end of the ridge. To reach the actual summit, first cross the fence by way of a step stile on your left [13-16]. As you follow the fence-line to the right, by-passing a rather forlorn pool [13-17] on the summit's flat surface, you finally stumble across the top of **Moel Cynghorion** (at **586563** – 674m/2211ft).

**4)**     **(586563)**     →

         **175°**          →

To get maximum benefit from the day's exertions it pays to spend some time here studying more closely the view ahead to the NorthWestern flanks of Yr Wyddfa and to the other surrounding hills.

*Directly ahead of you the rock walls of Clogwyn Du'r Arddu and Clogwyn Coch appear insurmountable beneath the main ridge of Yr Wyddfa (Snowdon) [13-18]. Hardened rock climbers will tell you that both can be tackled given the right expertise and equipment – and a decent head for heights.*

Clogwyn Du'r Arddu [13-19], the cliff directly ahead as you face Snowdon, is where Sir Edmund Hillary trained for his Everest expedition.

*Below to the left is the broad expanse of the Arddu valley, which swings Westwards towards Llanberis. From your vantage point the thought of picking a way through that uninhabited corner of Snowdonia in search of a path back to civilisation is not particularly inviting [13-20 and 13-21].*

This empty region below you would have looked quite different in the 14th century when it was considered prized summer pasture, owned by the Welsh princes of the time. The only indications of this now are the ruins of a group of structures at Cwm Brwynog Hir (594568) – a collection of hafodau or summer dwellings. These seasonal abodes were normally found in isolation, but here they comprised a group of eight or nine signifying the strategic importance of this grazing ground at the time.

*Below to the right lies the lake of Llyn Ffynnon y Gwas, an elliptical blob with a narrower waistline across its middle, and the more attractive option of the Snowdon Ranger path [13-22 and 13-23].*
*There are also fine views behind you towards Nantlle, the Moel Hebog group and the Glaslyn estuary [13-24 and 13-25].*

I have often had my sanity questioned when setting out into the hills under less than ideal conditions. Why bother heading for the tops on days when there's no scenery visible, and no company worth talking about except impenetrable cloud and torrential rain? Well, on days such as these I was lucky enough to get a set of photographs that would have lost much of their impact had the weather been clear and sunny [13-24, 13-25, 13-34, 13-41 and 13-42]. "Every cloud..... and all that".

For the record, Snowdon averages 165.5 rainy days per year; with an annual rainfall total of 1433mm, and annual sunshine total of just under 1360 hours.
Based on the above criteria, you should manage one dry, sunny day every two visits you make to the summit – unless you confine your trips to the winter months, or are just unlucky of course.

The section of path exiting East from the summit sticks like Velcro to the edge of the precipice; set far enough from oblivion for you to experience exposure on a truly grand scale without jeopardising your safety. As it descends the slopes of Clogwyn Llechwedd Llo the sheer scale of the cliffs provides clear evidence of Yr Wyddfa's status as the highest peak in Wales. Soon a point is reached where the only options are to turn back or cross the fence and ladder stile ahead and to your right [13-26] (unless a hang glider or parachute are available).

Proof of how treacherous even the gentler terrain of Moel Cynghorion can be in foul weather is given in a cautionary tale concerning the death of the Reverend Henry Wellington Starr of Northampton. In September 1846 he left the 'Snowdon Guide' hotel beside Llyn Cwellyn (now the site of the 'Snowdon Ranger' hostel) in order to climb Snowdon. He set off late in the day despite being advised to put off his journey due to thick mist on the summit. He was met by some farm labourers on the ascent path close to Llyn Ffynnon-Y-Gwas – then never seen alive again.

Despite a concerted effort by the locals to search for him over the ensuing weeks, his remains were not discovered until June of the following year beneath the cliffs adjacent to Moel Cynghorion. The tragedy of his demise was overshadowed by the momentary misappropriation of his valuable watch – later 'found' in a nearby stream by one of the local guides who first came across the body.

If walking this section in misty or windy conditions you will not need much convincing as to why the path leading from Moel Cynghorion's summit to the fence needs extra care and concentration (check the sheer drop on your left for confirmation!).

The narrow path continues quite steeply downslope to the col of Bwlch Cwm Brwynog [13-27] close to the 520-metre contour between Clogwyn Llechwedd Llo and Clogwyn Du'r Arddu. The ladder stile in the fence on your left provides an escape route into the upper Arddu valley, but this line of retreat cannot really be recommended.

Ignore this stile – instead continue along the faint path that runs parallel to the more prominent track below you close to the lake shore. That path is the 'Snowdon Ranger' that runs from the shore of Llyn Cwellyn to Snowdon's summit. From this col it can be seen traipsing its way Westwards across lower ground, skirting the base of Moel Cynghorion [13-28 looking West along its route].

Eventually you reach the lowest point of Bwlch Cwm Brwynog – still a few metres above the main path and lake.

The Snowdon Ranger path was once one of the more popular routes to Yr Wyddfa, taking visitors from the 'Snowdon Guide Hotel' in Nant y Betws on the Northern shores of Llyn Cwellyn to the summit. During the nineteenth century the building now housing the Youth Hostel was the home of one Evan Roberts who acted as guide and escort to anyone wishing to ascend Yr Wyddfa (he was the one who modestly described himself as the "Snowdon Ranger"). When local guides led travellers up onto Snowdon using this route, their horses were usually left at Bwlch Cwm Brwynog and remounted on return.

A few months after completing this walk I discovered that I was not the first to complete this 'unorthodox' horseshoe. As early as the 1770's when Thomas Pennant was brought up to Snowdon by local guide Hugh Shone, they came up from Cwm Brwynog through Bwlch Maesgwm and descended by the Llanberis Path.

5)  (591557)  →

125°  →

Once you reach the lowest point of the col keep left, and by continuing along the faint path that brought you down Moel Cynghorion's flanks in a short time you meet the main path as it begins its determined climb to higher ground [13-29 looking back along the route].

Llyn Ffynnon y Gwas (*The Lake of the Servant's Well*) that lies below you to your right is allegedly named after the luckless shepherd (whilst in the employ of a local farmer) who drowned here as he was busy washing sheep.

Like many small lakes in Snowdonia, its waters in the recent past were harnessed by the local quarrying industry – but all that remains of the dam now are small earthworks at the lake's South Eastern end.

In places this path is badly eroded and rutted, but even the steepest sections of ascent (employing a series of graded zig-zags) are leisurely enough to pose no substantial problems to anyone except the infirm.

A number of large cairns have been deposited at strategic points – wherever the path doubles back on itself, or where it skirts closer to the sheer drop above Clogwyn Du'r Arddu. However, as long as the path itself is not obscured by snow you are unlikely to stray from it even in densest cloud cover. I have followed this path in howling wind, torrential rain and impenetrable fog (all on the same morning) and was able to reach its junction with the 'Llanberis Path' some 500 metres higher without any difficulty.

There follows a series of steep stone steps, badly eroded in places. Other than these the path has few distractions to take one's mind from the physical exertion of gaining height. Perhaps that is not a bad thing because you soon reach more open terrain where the angle of ascent eases (convex slopes leading to the high pass of Bwlch Glas – the col where the Crib Goch/Carnedd Ugain path, Pyg track, Llanberis path and Snowdon Ranger path meet up).

From here the mass of Snowdon looms to your right with the steep face of Llechog directly across the huge amphitheatre further right (that's the 'Rhyd-Ddu' Llechog – not the 'Llanberis' Llechog – confusing I admit). The Rhyd-Ddu path approaches the summit along that ridge – and would provide a perfectly adequate return route were transport back to the walk's starting point not a problem.

Given the moderate nature of this path it makes one wonder why guides were needed at all to provide assistance to those intending reaching Snowdon's summit.

However, it is worth noting that during their heyday most guides were employed for their knowledge of where various plants could be found, rather than for their leadership skills. Indeed, the first 'recorded ascent' of Snowdon was made by a botanist searching for specimens – apothecary Thomas Johnson on August 3rd 1639. There is absolutely no doubt that locals had reached the summit before this date – but Johnson receives the accolade even though he employed a local guide to help him reach the summit.

**6)** **(608550)** →

   **120°** →

The railway track is an incongruous intrusion as it suddenly appears from the sunken skyline to your left and crosses directly across your path. Beyond the track, which you should cross with some care, is a slightly raised path heading left to right (the Llanberis Path). A large marker stone identifies this significant junction to assist those intending descending by the 'Snowdon Ranger' path – a spot on the ground easily missed in low cloud.

You join the embanked path and continue to the right, following a broad track which in places is wet and eroded, and in others crosses solid ramps of rock as it climbs steadily towards the main summit. Although the path runs roughly parallel to the railway line, there is now sufficient distance separating the two to allow you to feel you are out in the wilds. Until, that is, the station roof puts in a distracting appearance below you on the right. On the left an eroded series of paths climb the short distance to the stone pillar that marks the summit of **Snowdon (Yr Wyddfa)** (at **609544** – 1085m/3561ft).

The summit is marked by two spiral sets of steps that climb to the pillar itself where countless walkers (and rail travellers) have posed over the years. Some swear there are only 19 steps from the base of the plinth to the top, whilst others maintain there are 20. One early winter morning in total solitude I was allowed an unhindered ascent of the spiral staircase from the North East side (20 steps up) and descent of its South Western flight (19 steps down). Something tells me that these 39 steps are not the ones made famous by John Buchan – or Alfred Hitchcock for that matter.

Snowdonia began catering for tourists in earnest around 1800 with the opening of Beddgelert's 'Goat Hotel'. The 'Royal Victoria Hotel' opened in Llanberis in 1832 – followed by the 'Capel Curig Inn' at Capel Curig, and the 'Prince Llywelyn Hotel' in Beddgelert.

Many guides lived in the villages nearby and it became a tradition for visitors to Snowdonia to employ a local guide for the day.

However, refreshment on the summit of Snowdon was not generally available until a wooden hut was built by Morris Williams of Amlwch in 1837. He later set up in partnership with William Williams (the 'boot boy' at the hotel in Llanberis) who attired himself completely in goatskin to give the appearance of a mountain savage. John Roberts of Llanberis set up a refreshment tent in competition on the Llanberis side of the peak. William Williams ('Wil Boots' as he was known locally) became a celebrated guide due to his unrivalled knowledge of local plant life (particularly the much-sought-after ferns). It was rumoured that many guides transplanted rare ferns from the hillsides and placed them in more inaccessible spots in order to make their services indispensable.

Having said that, Wil Boots was concerned enough about the dwindling flora of the region to set up a small reserve close to Llanberis village where the scarcer ferns could be grown and preserved in their natural habitat. This nature reserve now lies buried beneath the Llanberis by-pass! Wil met just as tragic an end. He died on 13th June 1861 while searching for ferns on cliffs beneath Clogwyn y Garnedd (high above Glaslyn) – the rope he used to lower himself broke.

By the end of the nineteenth century guides on the streets of Llanberis were such a common sight, pestering visitors with the offer of their services, that the local police were required to intervene. Many of the more unscrupulous ones would take their customers' money, lead them at speed into the hills, and abandon them on the slopes and return downhill in search of fresh prey.

In contrast to the wooden huts and tents that first adorned the summit approaches, the café building familiar to most visitors was designed by renowned architect Sir Clough Williams-Ellis and erected in 1935. Despite numerous refurbishment the building became an eyesore and its long overdue demolition began in 2006. It was replaced by a magnificent natural stone edifice ('Hafod Eryri') comprising information centre, refreshment facilities, toilets and washrooms, station platform, shop and staff accommodation which opened to the public on 12th June 2009.

7)    (609544)    →

      340°         →

Before leaving Snowdon's summit, there is no doubt you will want to make the most of the views at hand.

*Although the highest point of England and Wales is a wonderful viewpoint (particularly as you gaze on the sweep of ridge South towards Yr Aran) the outlook is better from below the summit as you retrace your steps to the high col of Bwlch Glas.*

*From here you can look back at Snowdon's peak, with the serrated edge of Y Lliwedd beyond [13-30]. Below lie the lakes of Glaslyn and its larger neighbour Llyn Llydaw in the lower basin [13-31] with the upper zigzags of the Pyg Track almost beneath your feet [13-32]. To their left the path-scarred lower slopes of Carnedd Ugain lead the eye upward to the lofty massif of Crib Goch.*

*Westwards the sea sparkles at the horizon [13-33], with the intervening hills of the Moel Hebog group [13-34] and the Nantlle Ridge as well as the Nantlle Vale [13-35]. Closer at hand the lakes of Llyn y Gader, Llyn y Dywarchen and Llyn Cwellyn occupy the floor of the main valley below you.*

Eventually you must head back downhill, and most likely on foot since the train rarely has empty seats for the return to Llanberis.

Many visitors are under the false notion that they can walk up Snowdon, and if overcome with fatigue or foul weather hitch a ride back by rail. Unfortunately, the train generally leaves Llanberis with a full quota of passengers, and since most have return tickets and choose to use them there are rarely vacant seats on the descent.

Retrace your steps along the low embankment above the line of the railway to Bwlch Glas. A prominent marker stone marks the exit route to the right for those descending towards Pen y Pass (via the Pyg Track or the Miners' Track).

Continue a short distance further, with the railway line now plainly in sight on your left) and you encounter a second marker stone which identifies the junction of the 'Snowdon Ranger' path – to your left – and the Llanberis path – straight on.

**6)**   **(608550)**   →

   **0°**   →

The Llanberis path is a straightforward track dropping gently at first along the broad, North Western shoulder of Carnedd Ugain. The railway follows its own route although heading off in the same general direction [13-37].

Your path veers further right, crossing loose, eroded slopes. With the cliffs above Cwm Glas dropping sheer away to the immediate right, the path then takes a sharp left away from any danger. From here to where your path sneaks under the railway line the path is particularly unstable and badly eroded [13-38].

THIS HILLSIDE IS ONE OF THOSE NOTORIOUS BLACK SPOTS WHERE PEOPLE MISJUDGE THE TERRAIN AND FREQUENTLY END UP INJURING THEMSELVES – OFTEN DUE TO HAVING ON INAPPROPRIATE FOOTWEAR WITH WHICH TO TACKLE THE DEMANDING SLOPES.
THE RAILWAY LINE AND CLOGWYN STATION ARE CLEARLY VISIBLE BELOW TO YOUR RIGHT, BUT THEIR PROXIMITY DOESN'T PREVENT YOU COMING A CROPPER UNLESS YOU KEEP YOUR EYES FIXED ON THE CRUMBLING PATH.
THE AREA IS NICKNAMED "KILLER CONVEX" BY THE LOCAL MOUNTAIN RESCUE TEAM!

As you cross the 830-metre contour the angle of descent relents and your path meets the railway line itself. Scattered along its edges you are quite likely to find lumps of coal shed by the engine – the scorched turf in places ample testament to the fact that many of the fallen cinders were still red-hot [13-39].

*The spot where your path merges with the railway line provides an excellent viewpoint into the large corrie beneath Clogwyn Coch containing Llyn Du'r Arddu. The lake was once much larger in size; its floor now buried under fallen scree and its waters shrinking even more as it slowly silts up [13-40 and 13-41].*

The path soon slips down the slopes on your right and sneaks beneath the railway by way of an underpass [13-42 from higher up]. The main Llanberis Path now continues ahead and downhill once it emerges from this short tunnel, but in order to reach the final summit of the day you need to bear right and follow the left-hand side of the railway track to Clogwyn Station itself. If there is a train in the station, it is quite likely that it is parked here while the more intrepid passengers disembark to take photographs of the dramatic scenery. Ignore any funny looks they might give you – most 'walkers' rarely set foot this close to the station so they will assume you are lost.

It was on the 6th April 1896 that the Snowdon Railway carried its first passengers to the summit. Regrettably there was a fatal accident on the descent when the braking system failed to control the speed of the engine which was fixed to the rear of the passenger carriages. The two engineers were able to leap clear before the engine derailed and plunged off the mountainside near to Clogwyn station. As it happens, the passengers inside the carriages were at no time in any danger, but the commotion caused one, Ellis Griffiths Roberts (landlord of the 'Padarn Villa Hotel' in Llanberis), to attempt to jump to safety. He was killed – the line was closed for a year subsequently for modification, and has maintained an excellent safety record ever since.

The railway pretty much follows the line of the old pony track to the summit.

**8)**     **(607561)**     →

325°     →

As you approach the station (it's actually little more than a platform and outbuilding), carefully cross over to the right-hand side of the railway track.

> OPTION 6
> You can always continue along the Llanberis Path from here on down to **point 11** – missing out Llechog but that also means missing out on some stunning scenery.

Continue following the right-hand side of the track across a gently descending shelf before bearing right onto the rocky promontory overlooking the Pass of Llanberis. Cross the short section of grey slabs onto the exposed outcrop and you are there – the summit of **Llechog** (at **605567** – 718m/2355ft). This is probably the least technically-demanding summit in the book because there is virtually no actual ascent necessary to reach it. Once you are walking along the nearby path it's simply a case of a short sidestep or two.

*The summit area gives an impressive view of the upper reaches of the Pass of Llanberis; the crest of Glyder Fawr immediately ahead, and the distinctive outline of Moel Siabod in the distance beyond the valley head [13-43 and 13-44]. There is also the unusual perspective of Crib Goch's three pinnacles as viewed from the NorthWest perched above Cwm Uchaf.*
*Down the length of the Pass the two lakes of Peris and Padarn extend long fingers towards the lowlands adjacent to Caernarfon and the Menai Strait (although their view is partly obscured by Tryfan (not the more celebrated member of the Glyderau but a lesser-known top further along the ridge forming the South Western wall of the Pass) [13-45].*

**9)**     **(605567)**     →

230°     →

Retrace your steps, but trending to the right in order to keep closer to the line of cliffs overlooking Llyn Peris. From Llechog there are another five rocky promontories forming the crenulated cliff-edge of the Pass's South Western walls. Some of these are less clearly defined than Llechog itself, but continuing along the skyline of this ridge is a worthwhile exercise before dropping left to the tourist path.

There are no difficult sections, and even in poor visibility one would need to be extremely foolhardy to find oneself falling off the steep Northern face of this ridgeline.

*But the view into the Pass below can certainly induce dizziness as you seem to hover over the tiny slate-roofed cottages and green fields of Nant Peris below [13-46].*
*Directly across the valley, the better-known Tryfan's bristly crest peeps over the saddle between Glyder Fawr and Y Garn [13-47]. While behind you to the South the spectacular cliffs of Clogwyn Du'r Arddu cut a deep gouge into the North Western face of Snowdon [13-48].*
*This ridge also provides a wonderful vantage point for the Eastern snout of the Nantlle Ridge [13-49] and the elegant corries sculpted into the sides of Moel Eilio and Foel Gron [13-50].*

As you continue along the ridgeline you meet up with a fence which takes quite a precarious line in places as it runs along the crest of the cliffs. The best route keeps as close to this fence as you can stand, and as you continue this tightrope walk above the Llanberis Pass the views never let up.

*Most impressive is the steep Cwm Padrig with the cataracts of the Afon Las (the stream draining Llyn y Cwn in the col between Glyder Fawr and Y Garn) [13-51 and 13-52]. Elidir Fawr with its slate-strewn base is less photogenic, but still striking in the sheer scale of its destruction [13-53]. Across to the West you are also able to contemplate the route you followed earlier in the day along Cwm Maesgwm [13-54].*

As you reach the final top of the helter-skelter ridge before it trundles away to Llanberis and the lowlands between Llyn Peris and Llyn Padarn [13-55] take the opportunity to study the land to the SouthWest.

In clear conditions the railway and the Llanberis Path can be easily picked out on the slopes below (the path now having crossed to the right-hand side of the railway track) [13-56]. You will also see the grey roof of Hebron station further right, a ruined building to its left (all that remains of Hebron chapel) and a faint track running ahead and slightly right to cross a minor incised stream before bearing right again towards the incised valley of the Afon Hwch and the cluster of aerials stuck on their concrete plinth [13-57]. The path between Hebron chapel and this concrete plinth is your eventual route back to the start point.

**10)**   **(596581)**   →

        270°   →

Once you find the view North dominated by the slate heaps desecrating Elidir Fawr there is not much left to occupy the discerning eye. Pick a way carefully left downslope and you soon meet up with the well-constructed Llanberis Path as it heads to your right downhill towards civilisation.

The point along the ridgeline from which you select your escape is not of vital importance. The slopes descending towards the Llanberis Path are nowhere particularly steep; the rockier parts can be circumvented as can the wetter patches of ground. Once you reach the path – and perhaps meet up with other walkers who are puzzled as to where you appeared from – head right, gently downslope.

        **310°**   →

There is one gate and ladder stile to cross at **586584** [13-58]. Then eventually the path takes a wide turn left and drops down slightly more steeply before bearing further left to meet a kissing-gate at **582589**. Beyond this gate is a minor road – heading left towards a couple of isolated farms located in the upper reaches of the Arddu valley, and right towards Llanberis where it emerges close to Victoria Terrace at the Southern end of the village. From here you should be able to spot the aerial cluster on its tall concrete plinth now directly across the valley as you pass through this kissing gate [13-59].

**11)**     **(582589)**     →

          **180°**          →

99% of the foot traffic heads right from here along the track to Llanberis and the teashops beside Llyn Padarn. Our route heads left (just to be different).

Llyn Padarn is the starting point of the annual 'Snowdon Race' – usually held on the fourth Saturday in July. The record for the fastest time to the summit is 1 hour 2 minutes and 29 seconds (on foot, of course).

Follow the track left and eventually downhill, around an S-bend that passes beneath the railway through a large arch before climbing quite steeply to track level with the inauspicious buildings of Hebron station now on your left.

**12)**     **(582584)**     →

          **195°**          →

A ladder stile on your right gives access to a wet paddock alongside the ruins of Hebron chapel – a sorry stone building; its slate-clad gable-end wall and three main windows much the worse for wear. Another ladder stile to the right of these ruins leads to a muddy path crossing scrubby pasture [13-60 looking back towards Hebron chapel]. This ground was bizarrely strewn with the abandoned top sections of beheaded telegraph poles last time I crossed it. Beyond the next ladder stile (in a fence ahead and to your left) a clearer track continues ahead, crossing the incised bed of Afon Arddu by way of a footbridge.

Follow the path on the opposite bank and this easily leads you to the ladder stile giving access to the road you followed earlier in the walk (adjacent to where it crosses the Afon Hwch).

**2)**     **(575587)**     →

**325°**     →

Climb over the stile, turn right onto the metalled road, pass through the rusted metal gate and follow the road back to the start of your walk.

**END**

# WALK 14

## Snowdon (Yr Wyddfa) [43] / Carnedd Ugain [45] / Crib Goch (West [46] and East [47] tops) / The Cwm Dyli Horns [48]

| | |
|---|---|
| 11.8 Km (7.38 miles)<br><br>1100m (3608ft)<br><br>Time : 6hrs | An epic ridge walk; considered one of the most exhilarating in all of Snowdonia – the more stimulating half of the classic 'Snowdon Horseshoe' |

Early starts – I can take them or leave them. But the opportunity to have the summit of Snowdon all to myself (if only for a precious fifteen minutes) made getting out of bed before five-o'clock worth it this once. Also, with the last weekend of October a mere week away, the chance to spend long hours in the hills would rapidly diminish with the light of day.

Just a full moon for company on a virtually empty road all the way to the car park at Pen-y-Pass. Then a struggle in the pitch black to find the pay-and-display contraption (£4.00 – dawn 'til dusk). Ouch!

The Miners' Path is scorned by many hill-walkers – considered only fit for families with toddlers in tow, the elderly or frail. But I think it's a cracking path – one easy enough to negotiate with the sun still an hour from rising. 2¼ hours later I had that stone pillar and its slab steps spiralling up to it all to myself. Quite a strange feeling as every other time I've been here the trig point has resembled Bass Rock with its share of human gannets.

Of course, there were ulterior motives to my early start: priority one, nabbing a parking spot – and priority two, true artists always do their best work in solitude (or in my case, if I ended up making a complete ass of myself on the Crib Goch ridge then the smaller the audience the better!).

**North**

**Don't forget**

**map/compass whistle/torch**

**suitable footwear + clothing**

**food/drink**

**brain**

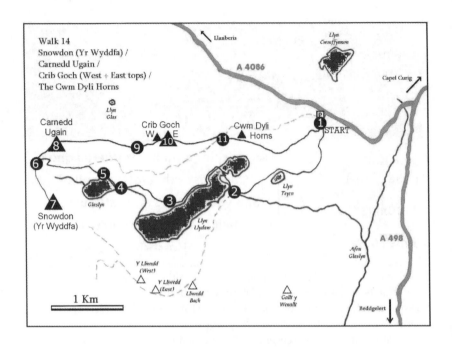

Walk 14
Snowdon (Yr Wyddfa) /
Carnedd Ugain /
Crib Goch (West + East tops) /
The Cwm Dyli Horns

## APPROACH

From the village of Llanberis proceed down the Pass of Llanberis along the A4086 as far as the Gorphwysfa/Pen-y-Pass Youth Hostel on the left (at **647556**). There is a double car park opposite on the right-hand side of the road (pay-and-display) as well as a toilet block, but any arrival after 09.00 at the weekend or during the holiday season is unlikely to be rewarded by a parking space due to its popularity.

From the village of Capel Curig take the A4086 Westbound. After passing through Dyffryn Mymbyr (past the twin lakes) with the view of the 'Snowdon Horseshoe' directly ahead [14-01] you reach the Pen-y-Gwryd hotel on your right. Turn right at the junction just after the hotel. The aforementioned car parks are less than 2 Km on your left.

From the village of Beddgelert take the A498 Eastbound through Nantgwynant. Once you reach the top section of this steep pass you will see the junction left signposted for Llanberis. Take this turning and the aforementioned car parks are less than 2 Km on your left.

There are few alternative parking spaces close by (or at least close enough to justify walking the tarmac to the start of the Miners' Track). A hand-full of pull-ins lie along the main Llanberis Pass, but are better utilised by those of you wishing to explore the crags on either side of the road. Some elect to park on the verge of the A498 close to the A4086 junction, but they are then faced with an arduous trek to and from the start of the walk.

For those of you who prefer not to gamble on finding an appropriate parking spot, the best option is to leave your car in Llanberis itself (ideally at the Southern end of Llyn Padarn rather than in the village itself), or in the park-and-ride car park in Nant Peris village from which local bus services (Sherpa) run regularly to Pen-y-Pass and back (for timetables consult www.traveline.org.uk).

## START

1) **(647556)** →

   **180°** →

Wherever you choose to leave your car and however you make your way to the car park opposite the Gorphwysfa/Pen-y-Pass Youth Hostel, this is where your walk begins. The Miners' Track path exits this car park almost directly opposite the main car park entrance.

The Youth Hostel occupies what was once a set of Welsh stone cottages. These merged into the 'Gorphwysfa' inn when the road was constructed in the early nineteenth century. In turn the 'Gorphwysfa' was converted to a Youth Hostel in 1967 by which time the hotel's clientele had diminished.

The road running along the Pass of Llanberis was first constructed in the early 1830's by local copper miners, allowing them to transport ore along the Miners' Track to Pen-y-Pass then along the main valley through Nant Peris to Caernarfon. Until the road was built Nant Peris could only be reached from Cwm-y-Glo (at the NorthWestern end of Llyn Padarn) by water. So ore produced by the Nant Peris copper mine was transported to Cwm-y-Glo by boat.

237

For the record the Pyg Track exits the adjoining car park from its South-Western corner (on your right as you face the hills).

As you exit the car park left you will see a large information board describing the Miners' Track to Snowdon. The path itself is sound underfoot; comprising a combination of fine gravel almost as smooth as fresh tarmac, and solid slabs. The width of the track barely changes all the way to the opposite end of the causeway crossing Llyn Llydaw.

After about 40 metres the track crosses the first of several streams running down into the upper end of Nantgwynant. The gradient is hardly taxing over the next 3½ Km – the path barely climbs at all (and indeed drops slightly at numerous points).

For now ignore the side-track exiting right at **647554** – a steeper path that runs parallel to the Pyg track, crossing the grassy hummocks of the Horns (which form a spur of crags above the North-Eastern end of Llyn Llydaw) before eventually joining the Pyg track at the upper end of Bwlch y Moch. This is your dessert once the main course has been successfully ingested.

*Below you on your left the pipeline taking water from Llyn Llydaw to the power station lower down in the valley next comes into view.*

Opened in 1906, the power station is now only used as a reserve power source. Despite that, it is capable of reaching its full 6 MegaWatt capacity in approximately 4 minutes.

*Shortly after Llyn Teyrn is seen on the left with the cliffs of Cwm Dyli behind (part of Snowdon's 'Horseshoe'). This vast amphitheatre is formed by Y Lliwedd to the left, Snowdon straight ahead and Crib y Ddysgl/Crib Goch to the right.*

Unlike the section circling Llyn Llydaw, the path here maintains a respectable height above Llyn Teyrn's shoreline. Leaving this first lake in its wake the path bears right again as it approaches the shores of Llyn Llydaw [14-02 from **Walk 15**].

In winter, when frost or a light scatter of snow coats the flanks of Yr Wyddfa, it is often possible to make out the stratification of the rocks that make up Wales's highest summit. Snowdon is composed of layers of volcanic debris (mainly ash and rock fragments) folded into a massive trough (a gigantic synclinal trench in the older Cambrian rocks which today lie some 17,000ft below the present sea-level).

It might seem illogical that the summit of Wales's highest peak coincides with the base of a major geological down-fold. But since rock is inelastic, it becomes fractured when distorted– where the rock is folded into a trough or syncline the cracks in the rock are bunched up tightly, greatly strengthening the fabric of the surrounding rock.

But where the rock is folded into an arch or anticline the cracks in the rock open up, greatly weakening the surrounding rock and allowing a multitude of natural forces to erode and eventually wear them away. Neighbouring up-folds of rock many thousands of metres above Snowdon's summit were worn away over time – but Snowdon itself survived due to the more resistant nature of its geology.

2)      (635545)        →

    320°             →

Now you should be able to make out a small building on the left close to where a path exits left. This building is the valve house controlling the water supply. The path it stands beside is the direct route onto Y Lliwedd and eventually the Snowdon summit (Yr Wyddfa) – the return leg of the classic anti-clockwise circuit of the complete 'Horseshoe'. Your path continues right along the Northern shore of Llyn Llydaw by way of the broad causeway beheading the lake's North Eastern-most bay from the main body [14-03 from **Walk 15**]. From the Northern end of the causeway the path swings to the left, clinging to the lake's shoreline as it approaches the Gothic ruins of the old Britannia copper mine's crushing mill [14-04 from **Walk 15**].

The main Miners' track was constructed by Thomas Telford; this causeway being added in 1853 to allow traffic to reach the mines up-valley without the long circuit of the right-hand end of the lake.

It was built by the Cwm Dyli Rock and Green Lake Copper Mining Company under the direction of the mining captain, one Thomas Colliver. The level of the lake was lowered by 12 feet and some 6,000 cubic yards of waste rock from the mines were used to construct the embankment, which was crossed for the first time on 13th October 1853.

It is perhaps difficult today to imagine that this area was once a hub of industrial activity due to the mineral-bearing rocks in the surrounding slopes. Within living memory high grade ores of zinc, and more especially copper were mined here (lower grade ores still lie unexploited close by). An aerial ropeway brought rock cut from high up on the mountain sides down to the crushing shed at Llyn Llydaw's shore. Working conditions were deplorable – both underground where the minerals were extracted and in the sheds where the rocks were crushed and pulverised. This ore was finally sluiced down water channels into the settling ponds beside the lake where the copper salts were allowed to separate from the mother rock.

When mining first started here the processed ore had to be carried in sacks on men's backs to the summit ridge (1000 feet higher at Bwlch Glas) then taken by horse-drawn sleds to a spot on the Beddgelert-Caernarfon road close to what is now the youth hostel (formerly the 'Saracen's Head') using the 'Snowdon Ranger' path. When the road along the Llanberis Pass was constructed the present Miners' Track replaced the route over Bwlch Glas, eliminating the gruelling journey over Snowdon's Northern ridge.

Most workers were put up in barracks during the week (being 'allowed' home at weekends). The ruins of one set can be seen close to Llyn Teyrn – another can be seen above Glaslyn. Many of the miners lived in Bethesda but were billeted beside Glaslyn and faced the 12-mile trek across the Glyderau at the start and end of every working week! Puts most of today's commutes into perspective.

The crushing plant, built in 1850, has obviously fallen into disrepair since operations ceased here soon after the First World War. However, there are signs that it is currently being restored to its former glory. Some would say that the landscape has suffered enough scarring and any signs of its industrial past should be allowed to disintegrate gracefully.

However, those who worked these rocks should be considered just as significant a part of the region as the surrounding ridges and peaks. The superhuman efforts of men (and young boys) in such an inhospitable landscape deserve a fitting tribute; to be treated with respect rather than scorn.

**3)** **(628544)** →

270° →

A short distance beyond the ruins of the crushing plant the path begins its steady climb from the 440-metre contour (a mere 80 metres higher than the walk's starting point) to the shores of Glaslyn some 160 metres higher. Below, to the left of this path, the Afon Glaslyn can be seen cascading in falls into Llyn Llydaw, hampered by a large delta of debris the river has constructed over the years [14-05 from **Walk 15**].

For a short section the path splits up with an older footpath contouring left across the slopes beneath before rejoining the main path just short of the lake – but the better constructed path keeps to the right, clinging to the steep slopes and crossing a stream by way of a short stone causeway.

**4)** **(620546)** →

300° →

The stream issuing from Glaslyn tumbles away on your left as the path skirts the Northern shore of the lake. Steep slopes ahead, directly beneath Snowdon, broadcast the inescapable fact that the honeymoon period has finally come to an end. Following my early start, it was at this point that dawn gradually cracked with a pink blush on the rocks followed by sheets of strawberry and vanilla on the lake surface [14-06 and 14-07 looking back across Glaslyn]. But surprisingly someone had already beaten me onto the summit. Somewhere high on the ridge above [14-08] there was a sudden flash of light.

Neither a shooting star gone to ground nor a distress call – just some early birds commemorating their visit with a Kodak moment.

A small bay comes into view ahead of you as the path swings to the right – backed by steep, dark, water soaked slopes which are often iced up in winter. The path bears left to skirt the bay and away to your right a line of rubble, just beyond a small scar of quarrying, marks the start of the climb up towards the skyline [14-09 and 14-10 from Walk 15]. High to your left, the vast precipice beneath the summit point of Snowdon is Clogwyn y Garnedd.

The original name of Glaslyn was 'Llyn Ffynnon Las' – 'Lake of the blue well' or 'Lake of the green well'.
Welsh ponies were once used to carry tourists up this steeper zig-zag section of path from the shoreline of Glaslyn to Crib y Ddysgl.

**5)**    **(617547)**    →

　　　　 310°    →

The sudden change from wide, level track to narrow, eroded path is a shock to the system, but there are ample assists along the way to steer the inexperienced. Keep your eyes open and you should be able to spot the bits of constructed pathway among the rubble (basically short, stepped sections) – first left of the ascent line, then right as you gain height relatively easily. It is worth noting that during wet weather much of the 'path' hereabouts is crossed by cascading streams descending the valley walls into Glaslyn. And in winter it can often be coated in ice for much of the day.

One level section leads left to a gap overlooking Glaslyn; a gap closed off by a pile of loose boulders. Erosion and deteriorating mine workings beyond this point have rendered an old path that once ran that way impractical. Instead climb to the right and follow the more obvious route. Eventually this scramble meets a well-constructed, level path running left to right (a spur of the Pyg track). Turn left to follow this track and after another short section of steep ascent you reach a second stretch of well-tended path (the main Pyg track).

Perhaps now would be an appropriate point at which to discuss the derivation of the Pyg track's name.

The general consensus today is that the 'Pyg track' is so named because it once ran from Pen-y-Gwryd to the summit. That is the spelling I have used throughout – but the acronym is probably pure delusion.

Many claim that 'Pig track' is the correct spelling. It is certainly the spelling that was used up until the beginning of the 20th century. The track was either called 'Pig track' because it goes through Bwlch y Moch (one meaning of the Welsh word 'moch' is 'pigs') or more probably because 'pig' is the Welsh word for 'peak'. 'Peak track' makes more sense as this route leads to the summit. On earlier maps, the last zig-zag section of path is named 'Llwybr y Mul' (The Mule's Path).

Bear left to continue along this broad track, which ascends less strenuously now towards the headwall of the saddle between Snowdon and Carnedd Ugain. Ahead of you progress is eventually blocked by a construction of boulders enclosed within wire-net cages. These have been built into an erosion-proof wall which runs up the mountain slope to your right. Your path turns sharp right here and continues uphill in the lee of this wall. Although plainly artificial, as you reach higher ground you will notice how the upper section of the barrier has become naturalised by a thin cover of scree, lichen and other vegetation. At the top end of this wall the path takes a sharp left turn and maintains a relatively straightforward line directly to the skyline at Bwlch Glas where a vertical marker stone identifies the end of the climb.

THIS SECTION OF ZIG-ZAGS THAT CLIMBS STEEPLY TO THE MARKER STONE ON THE SKYLINE ABOVE IS NO GREAT CHALLENGE, BUT IS NOTORIOUSLY ICY ON WINTER MORNINGS AS IT IS NORTH-FACING AND SEES LITTLE WINTER SUNLIGHT.

Once you emerge onto the broad saddle between Crib y Ddysgl (the cliff wall of Carnedd Ugain) and Snowdon, the broadening view ahead and the prospect of the route to the summit never fails to add a spring to the step and reduce the weight of your rucksack significantly.

**6)    (608549)    →**

**190°    →**

*After facing a wall of rock for so long, the skyline to the West provides an exhilarating array of ridge-tops, valleys and lakes. Who cannot fail to be stirred by the graceful contours of the Nantlle ridge, book-ended by Moel Hebog on the one side and Mynydd Mawr on the other?*

The summit of Snowdon now stands less than 100 metres higher to the South along a clear, easy path on a slight rise above the railway track on your right. This final section is shared by the two other paths ascending Snowdon from the North West – the 'Snowdon Ranger', and the Llanberis path.

As the unsightly railway station buildings appear ahead of you, the path climbs slightly left before reaching the spiral plinth bearing a tiny stone column. This significant edifice marks the highest point in England and Wales, the summit of **Snowdon (Yr Wyddfa)** (at **609544** – 1085m/3561ft) [14-11 facing West].

**7)    (609544)    →**

**330°    →**

As you would expect from such a height, the views are spectacular given the right weather conditions.

*Y Lliwedd's crucible on one side [14-12] – the blue-green folds of Nantlle the other. The serrated ridge from Bwlch Main and Clogwyn Du helter-skeltering towards Yr Aran immediately South [14-13] and the remainder of your walk mapped out for you to the North.*

On a clear day this summit is a great place to stand and ponder – but today there's too much walking still to do. And I can hear the train huffing its way nearer (carrying a group of orange-vested workmen rather than tourists – it's still too early in the day for that lot just yet).

*Carnedd Ugain [14-14] and Crib Goch [14-15] with the tightrope ridge stretched between them [14-16] are laid out before you as you peer North-East from the summit. From here the gentle curving slope onto Crib y Ddysgl's flat, plateau-like top is as inviting as the crags beyond it are intimidating.*

## OPTION 1

From this point it is feasible to retrace your steps to Bwlch Glas and follow the Pyg track back to Pen-y-Pass.

If weather conditions or confidence make crossing the Crib Goch ridge unwise then this is by far the more prudent choice.

The direct return from the summit of Snowdon steers clear of Carnedd Ugain altogether, but rather than return to Pen-y-Pass immediately it is worth the short diversion onto this second summit since reaching there is relatively undemanding.

***Time saved – approximately 1hr 15min***

Retrace your steps to Bwlch Glas but ignore the first marker stone identifying the exit right onto the Pyg track. Instead continue a short distance along the clear path to where a second marker stone identifies the parting of the ways – left across the railway and down the 'Snowdon Ranger', straight on to Llanberis, or right along an easy track onto the summit of **Carnedd Ugain** (at **610551** – 1065m/3493ft).

This summit is such a contrast to Snowdon's elegant pyramid – a tabletop strewn with angular fragments of rock, its trig point marked by a small stone pillar.

## OPTION 2

Having reached the two highest summits in Wales, there's no shame in making a cautionary retreat now – either by a straightforward reversal of your route down the Miners' track, or opting for a Pyg track descent that rejoins the main walk at **point 11**.

From there you can take in the Horns or follow Option 3 back to the car park.

CAUTION IS ESSENTIAL FOR THE NEXT BIT AS ANY SLIP COULD HAVE SERIOUS CONSEQUENCES. PERHAPS YOU COULD TAKE NOTE OF SOME COMMENTS PICKED AT RANDOM FROM A VARIETY OF PUBLICATIONS REGARDING THE RIDGE AHEAD OF YOU:

*"A wolf in wolf's clothing….."*
*"…..this has to be one of Britain's all-time greatest scrambles….."*
*"…..with enough exposure to turn your stomach inside out."*
*"Bring a head for heights….,"*
*"…..it's not technical, but you will need nerves of steel."*

Reading the above will either have you chomping at the bit to continue, or spin you on your heels as you retreat to Bwlch Glas. Spare a thought for the father and son who had to be assisted off the main ridge [14-17 from **Walk 15**] by the local Mountain Rescue barely a fortnight after my traverse. They had taken their dog with them (!) and got into difficulties due to the fact that they were inadequately equipped.

IN WINTER CONDITIONS, OR IF THERE ARE STRONG CROSS-WINDS, EVEN EXPERIENCED WALKERS ARE BEST AVOIDING THE NEXT SECTION OF THE WALK. THE LOCAL MOUNTAIN RESCUE ESCORTS BETWEEN 5 AND 10 PEOPLE OFF THE RIDGE EACH YEAR, AND 2 OR 3 HAVE TO BE BROUGHT DOWN BY STRETCHER. ON AVERAGE 1 PERSON A YEAR PERISHES WHILE ATTEMPTING THE CROSSING – NOT NECESSARILY SOMEONE UNACCUSTOMED TO SCRAMBLING IN THESE HILLS.

8)     (610551)     →

       80°          →

The continuation East along the ridge from Carnedd Ugain's summit starts easily enough. But the path soon becomes steeper before reaching the first section of exposure; a razor-edged ridge of small pinnacles followed by a very blocky, airy path marking the Eastern limb of Carnedd Ugain [14-18 looking back].

This Eastern limb is also named Crib y Ddysgl – literally "the rim of the dish". Although the exposure is not as pronounced as the Crib Goch section, the irregular surface and the gradient are enough of a trial if the ridge is buffeted by winds.

A path of sorts follows the same line slightly South (right) of the crest, but it is too-often swept away down-slope by the scree chutes that corrugate Crib y Ddysgl's Southern face. The most reliable route is that which crests the ridge all the way to the 1001-metre pinnacle (close to **615553**) at the junction of Carnedd Ugain and Clogwyn y Person [14-19].

The latter ridge presents a cliff-face best left to the roped-up brigade approaching from Cwm Glas or Cwm Uchaf to the North [14-20].

*Take this opportunity to study the ridge ahead of you beyond the obvious dip in the escarpment (Bwlch Coch) [14-21] as well as the stunning view back towards Snowdon itself [14-22].*

*You will also get a close-up of the Llanberis Pass from here with Llyn Peris and Llyn Padarn stretching North towards the lowlands adjacent to the Menai Straits. And closer at hand [14-23 from Crib Goch summit], nestling on the rock shelf below, is Llyn Glas – a tiny lake with an island close to its outflow. This island is colonised by a mature pair of Scots pines – a species not native to Snowdonia. For many years their presence provided botanists with hours of conjecture until local students admitted they had been planted there as a prank. The little tinkers!*

Although the drop from this ridge into Bwlch Coch looks impossibly craggy and steep from the top, a clear path meanders between the rocks and boulders. This path emerges onto a broad, grassy saddle, eroded in places to reveal the red rocks that give the ridge its name.

9)      (622551)        →

        70°             →

Bwlch Coch at 858 metres marks the starting point of a 70 metre ascent that looks five times higher given the foreshortened view of Crib Goch's pinnacles you get from down here.

The Crib Goch ridge could be a mirror image of Carnedd Ugain's, but with 3 pinnacles rather than one – and an airy ridge at the end leading to a relatively accessible summit. But exposure is what this part of the walk is about – and there's plenty of that in store.

So on to the pinnacles. The first involves tackling the rock face head-on. The most direct route is up a wide gully, steep enough to require both hands but no great challenge. A jumble of rocks chokes the top of this gully but is easily bypassed. Much of the fun involves picking a route that you are comfortable with through this chaos.

The second pinnacle requires less effort because you start higher, but it then descends to an almost vertical wall dropping onto a narrow, sloping slab that separates it from the third. There is an intermittent path lower down to the right of the crest but it's no help because it will not lead you onto the third pinnacle. Instead scree and treacherously loose ground fall away steeply to the Pyg track some distance below.

It is best to keep as close to the top of the crest as possible before descending left and contouring this final corner of crag as you approach the hiatus. In order to gain the narrow exposed ledge that crosses this notch in the ridge use the secure handholds to your right to lower yourself delicately onto the sloping ground below. Once there, instinct will haul you easily onto the third pinnacle.

This is the bulkiest of the three but also the least exposed once you gain height. Then with the pinnacles behind you [14-24], all that remains is the relatively level path onto the twin summits of Crib Goch [14-25 from the final section of ridge]. So much has been written about the ridge itself that many forget there is higher ground still to reach.

The summit crag can be gained by first passing to the right then approaching from the South East if you are unable to find a sound line directly off the ridge. But whichever line you take, the first top is soon under your feet, the main summit of **Crib Goch** (**West top**) (at **625552** – 923m/3027ft). It's a fairly small perch, so despite the amazing views and the huge sense of relief in having reached there safely this is not a spot you are likely to pose on for long. Besides, there's still a bit more work to do yet.

You now have a short, rocky tightrope to contend with before reaching the second top [14-26]. Exposure is greater along this section than on the Crib y Ddysgl ridge (steep slopes plunging to the left of that crossing are here replaced by a vertical drop into Cwm Uchaf). But the path along this crest is easier on the feet – the rock is certainly stable and the gradient is level for much of the way.

If balancing is not your forte it is possible to follow a line slightly to the right of the skyline, using the ridge itself as a handrail. Most walkers will no doubt use a combination of the two. As long as you keep your eyes focussed on the next step you are unlikely to go wrong.

All too soon the exposure decreases as the ridge begins to climb through well-jointed crags onto the slightly lower of the twin summits, **Crib Goch (East top)** (at **625553** – 921m/3021ft).

| | | | |
|---|---|---|---|
| **10)** | **(625553)** | → | |
| | **100°** | → | |

As expected, I seemed to be the only person attempting a clockwise passage of the tops that morning. By virtue of the early start I met barely a hand-full of walkers along the ridge – all heading West. But now that I took a few moments on this wider summit to gather my thoughts and enjoy the views North towards Glyder Fawr more and more walkers kept emerging from the slopes below, desperate for information on the conditions that they were likely to encounter along the ridge itself. Some also hinted that anyone choosing to descend the hill-face they had just hauled themselves up might need his head examining some time soon!

Initially I did have second thoughts about my route-planning. The descent path from the summit area is very steep, with the real predicament before long of how to avoid a scary slide down a wall of bare, crumbling rock. It's a matter of wedging boots into cracks, searching out miniscule hand-holds and using the seat of one's pants wherever possible to slow down the rate of slide from one mini-ledge to the next. Great fun.

Once the ground levels again trekking poles are a definite boon, and they certainly aid a speedy descent until the final section of the Easternmost ridge above Bwlch y Moch. This exposed section is nothing major, but it often presents enough of a challenge on ascent to deter many apprehensive walkers from progressing any further.

One rocky outcrop is almost impossible to overcome without turning your back on the drop for part of the way. I'm no great shakes at climbing blindfold, but that's what it feels like half way down. The best approach is to keep to the centre of the obvious groove for the first few metres (while facing outwards) before grabbing sound handholds on your right and twisting your body over to the right in order to swing yourself out and downwards in one smooth, effortless movement onto footholds below (at which point you end up facing inwards). It sounds tricky (especially if wearing a rucksack) but the rock is secure, and as long as you are confident that you know where at least one of your feet is going to finish up you will reach the base of the traverse without too much effort. A walker I met coming up from beneath this section of crag told me he had his heart in his mouth as he watched me squirm down the final bit of rock. Oh he of little faith.

From here onwards the path is much easier underfoot as it crosses Bwlch y Moch and heads in the direction of the Pyg track's Northern variant. Shortly before joining the track you reach a set of rounded boulders that are easy to stumble across with heavy legs and tired feet. One easy option is to keep to the left and step over two strands of wire to gain level ground without the hassle of picking your way through more rock. But you will soon discover that you are now on the wrong side of a wire fence running parallel to the path as it eventually reaches the Pyg track. Fortunately the wire is slack and barb-free, so stepping over it presents no problem.

A short stagger downslope [14-27 looking back towards Crib Goch] and you reach the Bwlch y Moch crossroads (where the Pyg track, running left to right, is quite possibly as busy as many a High Street on a Saturday afternoon by now) [14-28 from the lower slopes of the Horns].

If you are in a rush to get back to the car park, turn left and follow the Pyg track downhill [14-29]. It can be muddy in sections and not as walker-friendly as the Miners' track. There is a steep, stepped descent quite early on [14-30], closed in by a wall on its right, but the path is well-constructed and where the bedrock is exposed it is fairly slip-proof (unless iced-up – when extra care is needed).

Eventually the path levels off [14-31 facing back towards Bwlch y Moch] and is quite an easy stroll. Near the end of the walk the path actually has a nervous breakdown and you are cast adrift to pick safe passage between a jumble of large boulders.

But then it swiftly regains its composure [14-32] before dropping down a staircase of slabs towards the end of the path beside the white buildings ahead and on the left. You emerge at the Westernmost of the twin car parks at the side of the A4086.

***Time saved – approx 15 mins***

To your right the Pyg track crosses a ladder stile [14-33] and continues up the valley towards Snowdon's summit.

**11)     (633552)        →**

**35°              →**

There's still time for a bit more ridge-hopping if you are up for it. Cross over to the other side of this track and follow the skimpy path running alongside a fence on your right [14-34] before heading off towards the set of crags on the skyline ahead.

Follow this path a short distance upslope then cross a step stile in the fence to continue skirting the rocks on their right-hand side (while the fence turns left and runs beneath the line of crags) [14-35]. Far down to your right now lies Llyn Llydaw with the Miners' track crossing left to right [14-36]. Further right the upper leg of the Pyg track is visible squirming along the flanks of Crib Goch.

Climb a few more metres and on the immediate skyline to your left is a massive block of bedrock at **635553** [14-37]. Presumably this is the first of the Horns – the humpy outcrops of rock and turf that form the sinuous ridge separating the Eastern corner of Cwm Dyli from the pass of Llanberis. The next Horn, the highest of the set lies a short distance East across a low shelf of waterlogged ground [14-38]. Nowhere near as impressive as the Horns of Alligin in Glen Torridon, even the highest of the **Cwm Dyli Horns** [14-39] is unable to scrape above 2000-ft (at **634552** – 609metres/1998ft) but this neck of high ground still deserves greater accolade than it gets.

Beyond this summit the ridge can be seen clearly twisting first right then sharply left to reach a steep headland of dark cliffs overlooking Pen y Pass [14-40]. Your route follows the same line as far as the lowest indentation in the left-hand spur – then drops down over the shoulder of the ridge to cross easier ground to the East. Ahead a faint path leads you across bare rock and some wet ground, dropping then climbing again but barely crossing any contours as it keeps to the highest rim of the basin enclosing the Northern 'head' of Llyn Llydaw [14-41]. It's a splendid viewpoint down to the lake, but it's unlikely any walker toiling towards the summit will cast a glance in the direction of this ridge. Most of them are oblivious to its existence.

The fence puts in another appearance now, joining your path from the left. In order to avoid increasing exposure to the right, cross the step stile [14-42] in the fence and continue along the path using the fence as your handrail. To descend the next dip, keep the fence close to your right-hand side because you might need its support as the path follows a plunging line down steep slopes [14-43 looking back from the next rise].

The path is crammed so tightly into the gap between the hillside on your left and the fence on your right that at first it's like walking in a narrow trench.

*The floor of this final substantial dip is as good a spot as any to take a final glance South towards the shoreline of Llyn Llydaw and the base of Snowdon [14-44], or North towards the Pass of Llanberis and the lower section of the Pyg track [14-45].*

The next dip [14-46 looking back from the next rise] is quite waterlogged, but there are one or two strategically placed stones allowing a dry crossing. The slopes above rise more gently; a collapsed wall to the left heading off in the direction of the headland perched above the pass of Llanberis. But your path still runs close to the fence to crest a grassy hump with a broad depression beyond. This depression has two prominent grassy mounds [14-47]. A path runs across the low ground beneath the smaller, right-hand one (the mound with a single rocky outcrop). But you need to follow the fence as it runs along slightly higher ground to the right of this mound, and cross the fence as it emerges from behind it (X marks the spot).

The broad valley on the opposite side of the fence descends in the general direction of the upper Afon Trawsnant (just East of Pen y Pass) [14-48]. You should hopefully be able to pick out the faint path etched in the coarse grass and follow it directly downhill.

50°          →

Keep on this bearing for the short distance it takes you to reach flatter ground where the going is substantially wetter underfoot (the dampest parts are identified by a large reed bed).

100°          →

Head further right to skirt the dampest bits, and the slopes suddenly open out ahead and below, revealing hummocky terrain, a fenced-off rectangle of natural heath-land, and the distinctive strip of the Miners' track (reassuringly closer than you would expect) [14-49]. Take a fairly direct line downslope now, trying to avoid the wettest parts but at the same time aiming to edge past the left-hand side of the fenced-off area [14-50]. You quickly emerge onto the main Miners' track near to where a small stream is diverted beneath it – at **647554** or close by.

Turn left along the track and within minutes you will see the Gorphwysfa Youth Hostel buildings directly ahead of you, and a car park now probably filled to bursting [14-51].This is a tacky return to 'reality', and possibly an ignominious end to an epic walk. But as you remove your soggy boots, stow away your rucksack and eventually escape onto the A4086, ask yourself "How many of the 400,000 visitors a year to Snowdon's summit are able to savour similar experiences at the end of their journey?"

**END**

# Y Lliwedd (West [49] and East [50] tops) / Lliwedd Bach [51] / Gallt y Wenallt [52]

| | |
|---|---|
| **13.8 Km** <br> **(8.63 miles)** <br><br> **1035m (3395ft)** <br><br> **Time : 6hrs** | **The final 'nail' in the classic 'Snowdon Horseshoe' – encompassing the serrated Southern rim of the vast corrie enclosing Llyn Llydaw** |

Another early start, it always pays dividends – you can pick your own parking spot, avoid rambler-gridlock on the narrower bits and escape the worst of the summer heat (that's the theory anyway).

In reality, on a Sunday morning in July at the height of a rare heat-wave, crowds and traffic were unavoidable, and the motionless air was already uncomfortably tepid by 08.00 a.m.. Still, on the novel side of 07.00 a.m. I did get to see a mangy old fox crossing the road a car's length in front of me as I cruised South along the Conwy valley.

This promised to be the kind of day when many walkers, no doubt, set off with the intention of completing the 'Snowdon Horseshoe' only for dehydration and near-tropical heat to get the better of them. Under such conditions even gaining the summit of Yr Wyddfa is an achievement.

So when I reached Bwlch y Ciliau I nearly gave up, quite aware that the 'interesting' ridge of Y Lliwedd had been my goal all along. But, being a glutton for punishment, I felt my feet being pulled towards Bwlch y Saethau by some invisible force. Yr Wyddfa's summit was so close, and the conditions so perfect.....

**North**

**Don't forget**

**map/compass**
**whistle/torch**

**suitable footwear**
**+ clothing**

**food/drink**

**brain**

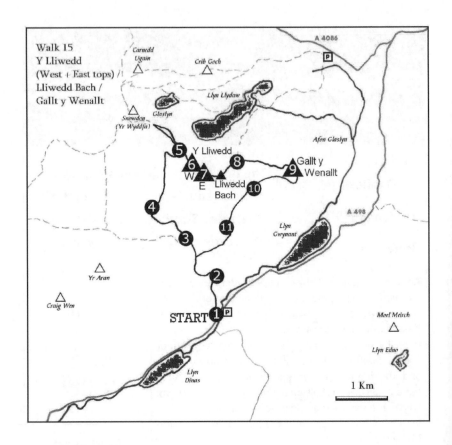

Walk 15
Y Lliwedd
(West + East tops) /
Lliwedd Bach /
Gallt y Wenallt

Carnedd Ugain
Crib Goch
Llyn Llydaw
Snowdon (Yr Wyddfa)
Glaslyn
Afon Glaslyn
Y Lliwedd
Gallt y Wenallt
Lliwedd Bach
Llyn Gwynant
Yr Aran
Craig Wen
START
Moel Meirch
Llyn Edno
Llyn Dinas
A 4086
A 498

1 Km

## APPROACH

From Capel Curig take the A4086 (signposted Llanberis and Caernarfon). Continue straight ahead as you pass the right-hand exit into the Llanberis Pass, and descend into the steep-sided valley of Nantgwynant. Llyn Gwynant laps the roadside on your right and woodland masks the steep slopes on your left. The valley opens out as it approaches the village of Bethania. The car park on the left (with toilet facilities) is signposted well in advance, occupying a stretch of tarmac running parallel to the main road (Pont Bethania car park – at **628507**).

From Beddgelert take the A4086 (signposted Capel Curig and Betws-y-Coed). Shortly after skirting Llyn Dinas on your right and steep, wooded slopes on your left you pass through the tiny village of Bethania – chapel, PO/shop and a house or two. Just before this road crosses the Afon Glaslyn, look out for the signpost for parking on your right where a disused tarmac section of road makes use of an older stone bridge leading you into Pont Bethania car park (at **628507**).

## START

1)   (**628507**)   →

    310°    →

Exit the car park left to join the A4086, crossing the main road where it bridges the Afon Glaslyn. There is a wooden farm gate on your left in the wall on the Bethania side of the river. Opposite on the right is a tarred road crossing a cattle grid before running along the banks of the Glaslyn river. As recently as 2005 the access route followed this tarred road, but since then much of the Watkin Path has been upgraded.

The start of the Watkin Path now lies between the two (a set of steps leading through the wall) [15-01 looking back towards the road]. In 1998 the National Trust asked for donations so that it could purchase most of the land occupied by Snowdon. Since then much of the funds have been spent on improving access – amongst other things completing the Watkin Path 111 years after it was started.

The original Watkin Path was constructed by Sir Edward William Watkin to run from the South Snowdon slate quarries (where the cart track ended) to the West of Y Lliwedd and on through Bwlch y Saethau to join the 'Beddgelert Path'). It was Watkin, incidentally, who first ran trains from Manchester to Dover and set to work on a Channel Tunnel (aborted by the unadventurous government of the time after reaching a mile underground). He also set in motion the erection of a tower to rival the Eiffel Tower at the site of what was later Wembley Stadium. The Watkin Tower was opened to the public in 1896 when its first stage was finished.

However, it was never completed due to lack of funds and was demolished six years after Watkins' death.

This is one of the more popular routes to Yr Wyddfa (Snowdon) – but unfortunately, it also boasts the lowest starting point of any of the approach paths to the summit.

The Afon Glaslyn is the same river that empties from Glaslyn lake at the foot of Yr Wyddfa – exiting this rocky basin by way of a set of steep falls and a sizeable delta to enter Llyn Llydaw, passing through Cwm Dyli and thereby practically circling the Snowdon massif before entering Nantgwynant, Llyn Gwynant, then Llyn Dinas and beyond to finally enter the sea in the vicinity of Porthmadog. If we had the wings of eagles, what a flight it would be to trace the course of this river from summit to sea. But here in the realm of boots and trekking poles, we are forced to keep to the path that goes through the wooden gate at the top of the stone staircase, past an Information board then following a series of rock steps and flat bits that climb gently through deciduous woodland into the valley of Cwm Llan.

Two wooden footbridges set close together cross one of the many tributary streams that cascade down the wooded slopes on your left [15-02]. Beyond these go through another wooden gate and continue under the welcome shade of branches as you pass a ruined building on your left. A National Trust notice-board gives an insight into the present-day workings of 'Hafod y Llan' farm – purchased by the Trust in order that the estate be maintained using traditional, sustainable methods for the benefit of local wildlife and people.

**2)     (626513)     →**

      5°     →

Continue along the path through the metal gate ahead of you (ignoring the farm track doubling back to your right [15-03]). That track indirectly leads to 'Hafod y Llan' farm on the main valley floor and the tarred road giving access to the Bethania bridge.

The gradient remains remarkably genteel as the path now skirts a series of bracken- and tree-covered crags on your left (marked Castell on the OS map – the site of an Iron Age hill fort) before entering the wider, upper reaches of Cwm Llan.

*The landscape now opens up dramatically on either side [15-04].*
*Ahead, and to your right, you should now be able to see up into the valley of the Afon Cwm Llan. The waterfalls crossing a large outcrop of rock are particularly eye-catching [15-05], as is the dark bulk of Craig Ddu encroaching on the valley from the right.*

Evidence of an old tramway can be seen dropping towards the path from a distinctive notch in the skyline on your left. Choked with ferns and other damp-loving vegetation this incline runs steeply down the hillside ahead of you, crossing the line of the path and continuing across lower ground to your right past a stone ruin. Much of this area bears testimony to the quarrying and mining that once thrived hereabouts (although exploitation of this particular valley was restricted to a short period between 1840 and 1882).

As the path swings in a leisurely sweep to the right again you reach the aforementioned incline [15-06]. Although one could conceivably scramble up this rocky corridor to reach the approach path to Yr Aran, it is not advisable since there is an easier alternative ahead.

New signage has also been placed along the Watkin Path recently (since 2006), and a small metal plaque at the foot of this section of old tramway now points South West along a cutting through the bracken-covered slopes to Craflwyn. This is an area of botanical interest beneath Yr Aran's Southern flanks, owned by the National Trust – part of which has restricted access.

The main path now begins to gain height gradually as it runs along a sturdier base of huge rock slabs [15-07]. Two gates (the larger one locked) lead through a dry-stone wall. Beyond this the valley narrows again; the river on your right confined to a rock-cut gorge with numerous waterfalls.

As you continue to climb you will notice a small footbridge (at **623516**) below you to the right perched above one particularly impressive plunge pool [15-08 looking back from higher up the path]. The return leg of this walk from Gallt y Wenallt rejoins the Watkin Path by way of this bridge (actually, it's a slab of slate – narrow but stable, and good practice for your sense of balance). A fairly straightforward path also heads upstream on the opposite bank of the river leading up from Nantgwynant to the ruined quarry buildings at **620522** [15-09].

**3)    (621520)    →**

**340°    →**

Continue uphill from the fern-shrouded slopes of this gorge and soon the path levels out again. On the opposite bank of the Afon Cwm Llan stand the ruins of the aforementioned quarry buildings – and ahead of you the river plunges over the first of the many rocky hurdles that propel it in a series of steep drops totalling 200 metres to the floor of Nantgwynant [15-10].

The first thing you could well notice beyond this point is the change in background sound-effects – the constant crash of the torrent has been replaced by little more than a gentle babble. Ahead the grey gravel path continues in a roughly straight line into the upper reaches of Cwm Llan, crossing the river as it does so, while to the left a red gravel path ascends the adjacent slope [15-11].

---

### OPTION 1

This side-track, tinted rust-red by iron compounds in the rocks that were hauled down-valley to be processed for various ores, leads to the opposite side of the upper Cwm Llan valley where there is still evidence of much mining.

It also leads by way of higher ground to Bwlch Cwm Llan – a high col beyond which one has the option of climbing Yr Aran to the South, Yr Wyddfa via Bwlch Main to the North, or descending West to the village of Rhyd-Ddu

---

Continue straight ahead along the grey gravel trail of the Watkin Path which eventually crosses the river by way of a solid bridge close to a set of ruins on your right. These collapsed walls, surrounded by a slate fence and standing beside a small stand of conifers, mark what was once the residence of the quarry manager, 'Plascwmllan' [15-12]. Passing this ruin you draw ever closer to the massive bulk of Craig Ddu towering above the valley floor on your right; a huge hump of bare rock with tailings of scree along its base [15-13]. At the foot of its right flank what was once a substantial ramp of scree has been incised by a tiny stream running down from the crags above.

Some 300 metres beyond the ruins of 'Plascwmllan' you come upon a massive boulder to the left of your path upon which is cemented an inscribed plaque – at **618523**, the 'Gladstone Rock'. When I was here in 2005 the inscription was clear for all to see – little more than twelve months later and it was badly faded and barely legible, presumably due to weathering.

This plaque commemorates the ceremonial opening of the Watkin Path on Monday 13th September 1892. David Lloyd-George attended and an address was given on this spot by William Ewart Gladstone (then in his 83rd year – having been elected to a fourth term as Prime Minister). His speech to 'the people of Eryri' (Snowdonia) promised them future representation in government. Reports of the ceremony record that the event was followed by communal hymn-singing.

I suppose the existence of a Welsh Assembly more than 100 years after this historic event has been well worth the wait for the local farmers and quarrymen (and their families) who could already see their livelihoods disappearing due to modern industrial technology.

From this point the path skirts to the left of a large rocky spur that stands proud of the crags of Craig Ddu to your right [15-14]. This spur presents a superb expanse of slab right at the edge of the path, tilted at about 45° and perhaps inviting one to test one's skills in reaching its tiny summit some 100 metres above.

Shortly afterwards the path meets a set of spoil heaps. Also forming the right-hand slopes enclosing this line of path is a large, grass-covered embankment with a flat top that is composed of rock waste [15-15 from higher up the path]. Abandoned quarry workings occupy much of this corner of upper Cwm Llan [15-16 from **Walk 16**]. On this side of the river the quarrymen's barracks stood, with the slate-dressing sheds located lower down on the opposite banks at the base of the slopes beneath Yr Aran.

*Across the valley the rust-tinted track you by-passed can be seen following the opposite river bank leading to the disused quarries [15-17].*
*Above this track, Yr Aran is the only feature visible to the West [15-18 from higher up].*
*To the right of this peak lies the col of Bwlch Cwm Llan; the starting point of the path leading up onto Yr Wyddfa's Southern spur – featured in* **Walk 16***.*
*To the North, the valley head (Cwm Tregalan) lies trapped beneath the sheer walls of Yr Wyddfa's South Eastern face, with the fissured grey-white rocks beneath Allt Maenderyn [15-19] appearing particularly imposing.*

**4)**   **(614525)**   →

   **50°**   →

At this point, staring up to the summit of Yr Wyddfa [15-20], the way ahead appears impenetrable despite the path's confident persistence. It is at this point that the Watkin Path sheds its sheep's clothing, cutting into the heart of the rock by way of a series of steep, narrow sections.

After climbing up a short staircase of slate steps to reach the upper levels of the waste heaps, the path turns sharp right onto the hillside. A marker post at the entrance to more extensive ruins points out the correct way to proceed [15-21].

As it continues up these slopes the path now devours contours at an unprecedented rate. However, it is not uncomfortably steep and the infrequent patches of wet ground hardly present a problem. It is worth noting that on winter mornings this can become one of the icier sections of the walk – not much sunshine penetrates here until early afternoon.

Hopefullly, as you study the imposing ramparts of Y Lliwedd on your right you should be able to make out a faint dent on the skyline ahead that is as likely as not Bwlch y Ciliau.

If visibility precludes this luxury, at least the path provides no navigational problems. Even under a cover of snow there are a number of cairns that ensure you keep on track. At **616536** close to the 590-metre contour the path makes another sharp turn to the right as it makes one final, serious attempt at reaching higher ground. Clambering across several boulders (in places no doubt embedded into the path to avoid erosion) the final 200 metres are a cruel contrast to the lower sections of the path.

*Given the unrelenting nature of this short section of path you will have ample opportunity to turn South and scrutinise Yr Aran from a loftier vantage point. To its left Traeth Bach and the extensive coastal lowlands close to Porthmadog are easily identifiable [15-22].*

*Over your right shoulder you cannot fail to notice the pyramidal top of Yr Wyddfa – no doubt already swarming with bodies eager to colonise the trig point [15-23].*

*And scarring the slopes beneath it, a plethora of scree-runs and paths invite immediate access to the highest point in the whole of England, Wales and Ireland.*

Eventually the path crests at the 744-metre-high col of Bwlch y Ciliau; an extensive saddle of wide, rocky ground between Yr Wyddfa and Y Lliwedd.

**5)    (619537)    →**

310°    →

From here the Watkin Path can be easily picked out as it cuts a rusty trail beneath and to the left of a pair of rugged protuberances [15-24]. Behind you the sheer walls of Y Lliwedd climb high into the azure sky [15-25]. But the best views are yet to come.

Turn left to head towards Snowdon, and if you share my curiosity it is worthwhile taking the short detour onto the subsidiary path climbing to the right of the main path. This gives access to the crest of the immediate skyline. Suddenly the ground ahead of you plunges over a sheer rock wall, a fall of over 300 metres to the shoreline of Llyn Llydaw [15-26].

*From this airy vantage point Yr Wyddfa's profile remains unflattering.*
*But the ridge provides an excellent spot from which to study Carnedd Ugain and Crib Goch [15-27], and to identify the paths that skirt the blue expanse of Llyn Llydaw – namely the Miners' Track that crosses the causeway at the lake's furthest end, the Pig Track contouring the slopes to its North, and the skyline route onto Crib Goch [15-28].*
*Only the merest slice of Glaslyn can be seen from here but the rocky delta formed where its outflow reaches Llyn Llydaw is clearly visible.*

The next little peak on this ridge is only a short distance ahead but the path following the crest provides a good deal of exposure – the first of the day [15-29]. A little scrambling leads onto a fairly broad top, given its miniscule size.

The final series of outcrops can be reached more easily by dropping left back onto the Watkin Path (now close by and not much lower than the ridge) [15-30]. The broad col of Bwlch y Saethau lies beyond, sprawled at the feet of Yr Wyddfa's South Eastern spur.

To the right of this higher col a cairn marks the point at which a subsidiary path from the shores of Glaslyn meets Snowdon's South-Eastern spur. The spur of Cribau, this set of crags that drop in a succession of steep, rocky steps to the outflow of Glaslyn, is sometimes used as an alternative descent route by walkers deciding to truncate the Snowdon Horseshoe. But it is better used purely as an ascent route since locating the correct line of descent (despite the cairn on the ridge) is tricky, and unless you have good scrambling abilities is best avoided. Taking the incorrect line can prove disastrous as one look below will confirm.

---

### OPTION 2
Snowdon's top is less than an hour away now – to reach it all you have to do is continue along a steep pull up the clear path to the finger post on the skyline at **609543**, then turn right to gain the café building and the summit behind it.

---

On such a perfect day I had to pop up there for a ten minute Snowdon-fix before retracing my steps to Bwlch y Saethau.
If you are similarly tempted, make sure you return to the finger-post before attempting to drop back down to the col.

## OPTION 3

Having reached Yr Wyddfa, if you intend missing out Y Lliwedd altogether retrace your steps West along the ridge-line (past the finger post) and descend Bwlch Main to Bwlch Cwm Llan at the foot of Yr Aran. From here, scramble down a scree-filled gully to join a muddy path. Follow that easily over damp ground to eventually meet the main Watkin Path at **point 3**. From here retrace your steps to Nantgwynant.

Whether you have made the long diversion to Yr Wyddfa or not, you should now return along the lower level of the Watkin Path beneath the upper lip of the basin enclosing Llyn Llydaw to reach **point 5** again [15-31].

## OPTION 4

If one look at Y Lliwedd's awesome outline or deteriorating weather make you decide you might be wiser returning to the roadside this is the point at which to do so.
Simply retrace your steps along the Watkin Path.

### Time saved – approx 2½ hrs

5)      (619537)        →

        130°            →

A path, clearly marked with cairns, continues East up the steep slopes towards the skyline ahead. But there is ample opportunity to grasp some rock and haul your way though a maze of crevices, turrets and chimneys. Handholds are excellent and much of the rock is stable – the high degree of polishing in places attesting to the number of hands and feet that have already successfully clambered up its steep slopes to gain its twin tops.

You can get as close to the edge of Y Lliwedd's airy crest as your nerve allows [15-32]; or if you err on the side of caution keep slightly South (right) of the mountain's snarling lip. Whichever option you pursue you are likely to come across a section of path again sooner or later – handholds and toeholds keeping within spitting distance of each other as you get closer to the main summit – **Y Lliwedd (West top)** (at **623533** – 898m/2947ft) [15-33].

This is the higher of the two peaks, the West Peak, and the narrower. Warm updrafts of air from the depths of the corrie below sometimes carry swarms of midges from Llyn Llydaw's shores onto the mountain top reducing any temptation to loiter there for too long. But if the insect gods are kind there are views in all directions from here worth taking the time to savour.

*Almost directly South Moelwyn Mawr can be seen beyond the long ridge of Cnicht (the latter appearing especially un-Matterhorn-like from this angle).*
*Yr Aran with Moel Hebog behind [15-34] – to its left Tremadog Bay and the fertile valley floor of the Glaslyn estuary West of Llyn Dinas before the dogleg South into the Aberglaslyn Pass – to its right Bwlch Cwm Llan with its tiny lake just visible on the floor of the col.*
*The Southern spur of Snowdon – a huge fracture scarring its sheer rock walls like the slash of a scimitar. Its pyramid summit – colourful people-shapes visible even from here as they take it in turn to pose and pout upon its trig point [15-35].*
*The neighbouring top of Carnedd Ugain – salmon pink scree fans and stone chutes adorning its flanks high above the gem of Glaslyn [15-36]. Then the gentle drop onto Bwlch Coch followed by the towering purple pinnacles that lead onto Crib Goch [15-37].*
*This ridge in turn drops down to Bwlch y Moch and the green slopes of the Cwm Dyli Horns forming the backwall of Llyn Llydaw's decapitated head – Llyn Teyrn nestling completely detached to its right [15-38].*
*On the horizon above these the teapot lid of Glyder Fach lords over everything – to its left the almost rectangular slab of Pen Llithrig y Wrach sticking its head above the lower slopes of Y Foel Goch [15-39].*
*Dyffryn Mymbyr stretches East – Llyn Lockwood at one end and its own twin lakes at the other – and further right again the unmistakable profile of Moel Siabod [15-40] bringing us almost full circle to Carnedd y Cribau then Cnicht. And if you look closer still at the detail laid out on every valley floor or on the*

*slopes adjacent with their myriad paths you could plan a lifetime of walks from up here.*

**6)**   **(623533)**   →

   115°         →

The path drops no more than 20 metres to the right before making a direct assault on the broad shoulders of the next peak. No scrambling here, just a straightforward footpath onto the broad, blocky summit of **Y Lliwedd (East top)** (at **624532** – 893m/2929ft) [15-41 from the West top, and 15-42].

---

**OPTION 5**

From this summit you can still turn around and descend back into Bwlch y Ciliau and thence return along the Watkin Path back to the car park. This is a straightforward case of retracing your steps but it makes for a rather longer walk than the one recommended here.

---

**7)**   **(624532)**   →

   110°         →

Since most people (myself included) prefer circular walks, there is a way to rejoin the Watkin Path without having to revisit Y Lliwedd's twin peaks or the upper confines of Cwm Tregalan. Maintain contact with the main ridge as you cross bare rock, almost resembling a block pavement in places and a dry river bed in others, to descend easily to a small saddle separating you from the postscript to the Lliwedd ridge [15-43 to 15-46] – **Lliwedd Bach** (at **627532** – 818m/2683ft).

*Again there are superb views as you approach this minor summit – down into the valley of the Afon Cwm Llan [15-47 and 15-48], and back towards Yr Wyddfa [15-49] (now one of a set of three with the twin tops of Y Lliwedd). The ground to the right descends in uniform green slopes to Cwm Merch [15-50] whilst that on the left falls away in a guillotine cut to the shores of Llyn Llydaw [15-51].*

*If you have yet to attempt* **Walk 14** *and want some idea of what Carnedd Ugain [15-52] and Crib Goch [15-53] look like close up this ridge provides an excellent observation point.*

---

**OPTION 6**
If by chance you have arranged for a second set of wheels to wait for you at the Pen-y-Pass car park (for directions see **Walk 14**) it is possible to descend from this final 'nail in the horseshoe' to join the Miners' Track close to the pump-house at **635545**. Alternatively a regular bus service runs from the car park back to Nantgwynant (and on through Beddgelert to Porthmadog).
But if the truth be told the descent to the lake shore from here is a painful slog.

---

Drop down the ridge to a saddle beyond which stretches a broad platform dotted with small pools [15-54]. From the ridge's lowest point a clear track drops away down loose ground to the left [15-55] – that is the escape route of Option 6 (the official return route for those completing the 'Snowdon Horseshoe').

**8)**   **(631535)**   →

    **100°**   →

Ahead of you the ridge drops down more sedately, by-passing left of these pools before making a slow swing right as it extends in waves to the outlying top of Gallt y Wenallt poised above Llyn Gwynant.

---

**OPTION 7**
There is in fact a more direct way to reach the Watkin Path without the long walk out to Gallt y Wenallt but it should be followed with caution – and not attempted in poor visibility.
As you make your way down from Lliwedd Bach, still some 20 metres or more above the floor of the saddle ahead of you, a path veers off to your right (just after the ground levels out a short way after one

---

particularly steep descent). Below you, again on your right, you will notice an extensive rock pavement of grey and black mottled stone. Cross this section of bare rock and another below it as you head for the obvious heaps of red waste littering the valley floor beyond. Ideally you should aim to reach the rightmost (Westernmost) heap first in order to pick a viable way East.

A series of disjointed paths eventually deposits you at the foot of the falls at **634530**.

The course of the Afon Merch can be seen clearly below together with a gravel stream bed that resembles a walker's track from a distance. However, the correct route skirts right, away from this river.

Aim instead for an overgrown spoil heap to your right, and beyond this a grass covered track can be seen a short distance downslope with ruined buildings almost hidden in the lee of the hillside to its left **(point 10)**

### *Time saved – approx 45mins*

It is perhaps an oversight on the part of the OS map that the upper reaches of Cwm Merch are not identified as a DANGER AREA. I would warn prospective visitors to steer well clear of the Option 7 section of the walk in anything less than adequate visibility.

The entire slopes are perforated by a series of open clefts in the ground, cut deep into the bedrock by miners over a century ago and now left unguarded to the elements and to any unwary rambler. Many are little more than a metre in width, extending for tens of metres from end to end, and descending to who knows what depths? Only the steady drip of groundwater and a distant echoing splash confirms that these pits are not bottomless – but gazing into their depths the darkness is only occasionally broken by shafts of sunlight illuminating the motes of red dust that still hang in the air.

Many of these clefts are treacherously masked by small clumps of shrubbery or bracken, and it does not take much imagination to start wondering who or what may already lie rotting in their depths.

The lowest point of this saddle is quite wet [15-56] but a faint path can be seen running to its right, skirting quite a sizeable pool [15-57 and 15-58] as it approaches the crags overhanging Cwm Dyli. Surprisingly the slopes plunging down to your left remain unremittingly steep. Despite that you might encounter the pair of billy goats (complete with long curved horns) that were making the most of the shade offered by the crest of the ridge when I passed by [15-59].

*This ridge gives a bird's eye view of Cwm Dyli and the two rocky portals of Clogwyn Pen Llechen and Craig Aderyn bisected by the pipeline carrying water from Llyn Llydaw to the turbines on the floor of Nantgwynant [15-60].*

To reach the outlying top of Gallt y Wenallt keep as close as you can to this ridge-line as it bears further and further right. It's a bit of a helter-skelter path – three damp saddles separating grassy tops with the occasional rocky outcrop [15-61]. The Southern flanks of Y Lliwedd to the right, littered with vast scree slopes of orange waste from the mining hereabouts [15-62], maintain an overbearing presence as you head to the lip of rock overlooking Nantgwynant.

And finally there is nowhere else for the crest to go once it has reached the final summit of **Gallt y Wenallt** (at **642532** – 620m/2032ft) before plunging almost vertically to Llyn Gwynant in a series of grass-covered slopes and small boulder-fields angling more and more steeply to the valley floor.

*The slopes on the opposite valley side are a complete contrast to those plunging South from this ridge. They are mostly green, dappled with deciduous wood-land above the narrow strip of cultivated fields on the valley floor. And above all this stands the rocky bulk of Carnedd y Cribau with Moel Siabod beyond [15-63]. Further to the right the broad saddle of Bwlch y Rhediad is clearly visible [15-64].*

**9)**      **(642532)**      →

          **180°**          →

It is worthwhile descending a short way down the slopes above Nantgwynant as you begin the clockwise circuit of Gallt y Wenallt's summit. This gives expanding views of the valley to your left. Where the Northern corner of Llyn Gwynant comes into view there is a circular patch of white slabs laid out on the hillside beneath your feet [15-65]. This then gives way to steep grass-covered slopes with a conspicuous promontory of turf-capped rock. This is a good spot to spend a few minutes watching the canoeists on the lake below.

There follows a bit of a steep pull up to the immediate skyline on your right – keeping well above the large scree fan to reach a small, grass-covered ridge heading in the direction of Yr Aran and the return path [15-66]. Unfortunately there is the large valley of Cwm Merch between you and the Watkin Path – as well as more goats (three kids and a nanny last time I checked). To your right the gentler slopes of Y Lliwedd's Southern aspect appear as high as Snowdon's from this low viewpoint [15-67].

Grey crags and grassy patches are disrupted by dark, sinuous clefts cut into the hillside, bordered by bright rust-coloured detritus [15-68 and 15-69]. These are the old workings of Cwm-erdd copper mine – the excavation was restricted to a narrow portion of the valley headwall. Old ruins can be seen at the lower end of these workings [15-70]. Without losing more height than necessary it is quite a simple matter to contour the valley sides to your right, crossing a couple of boggy bits, to reach these ruined buildings.

230°        →

A collapsing dry-stone wall and a fence make a more direct descent to the valley floor but the easiest route keeps well to the right of these [15-71 and 15-72]. Eventually the wall cuts across the valley floor almost running right up into the set of crags on your right that appear to separate you from the ruins [15-73]. But the faintest of paths threads a way between wall and crag to the banks of a tiny stream (almost masked by the massive fan of waste rock alongside) that descends in spectacular fashion from steeper rock on your right to the main valley below on your left [15-74].

Stepping stones close to the foot of the falls (or a second set slightly further downstream) give easy access to the opposite banks [15-75]. Here ruined buildings occupy a shelf of land at the foot of the workings with a sizeable heap of rust-covered waste extending uphill.

**10)** **(633530)** →

   **220°** →

There are more ruined buildings below the shelf – as well as rusted machinery and the remains of an enormous pulley wheel [15-76]. A couple more goats also put on a show – scampering along the top of the dry-stone wall like a pair of tight-rope artistes.

A clear grass-covered track runs across the front of the main set of ruins and climbs onto a fairly level terrace [15-77]. As you proceed along this track you may well be able to pick out much smaller excavations in the hillside on your right; little more than splits in the fabric of the mountain's skin where narrow, ore-rich seams were extracted.

Follow the track South West, quite high above the valley of the Afon Merch [15-78] and on the uphill side of the dry-stone wall. This section of walk is a pleasant finale to a fairly strenuous trek. For a short time the track climbs, but then it soon drops at a gentle gradient as it contours the steep hillside. The wall on your left splits in two then rejoins again like a braided stream and the gap between path and wall also increases for a time before they almost reunite again as they head towards the immediate skyline beyond [15-79].

Once the main valley floor appears ahead of you with the A498 meandering through the trees you should be able to pick out a fence approaching the wall on your left from its left. The two meet at a gate and just to the right of this junction is a wide gap in the wall [15-80]. Soon after, the track you are following makes a sudden loop to the left and drops a little more steeply to pass through this gap.

**11)** **(628522)** →

   **220°** →

As soon as you pass through the gap in the wall bear right, ignoring the clear track running almost ahead but increasingly steeply downslope. After crossing some damp ground the track progresses downhill quite rapidly itself, passing through a broad space between two rocky spurs before becoming stony underfoot. It then passes through a gate in a dry-stone wall beyond which it drops down through dense woodland, encountering a ladder-stile en route.

The ground at the other side of the stile is very wet but ahead is a clear path running down through the trees to eventually approach the Eastern bank of the Afon Cwm Llan.

Close by the waterfalls at **623517** the path crosses the river to reach a series of rocky outcrops, bounded by a wooden fence on their right-hand side. The river crossing consists of a slab of solid slate, some 18 inches wide but sturdy enough to erase any feelings of instability even if you are lacking goat genes. A short, steep trudge up a narrow path through bracken and over a short rock step leads to **622516** where you can reacquaint yourself with the Watkin Path. Turn left onto this broad track and retrace your steps downhill to the woodland and the roadside beyond (at **628507**)

**END**

# Yr Aran [53] / Craig Wen [54] / Clogwyn Du [55] / Snowdon (Yr Wyddfa) [43]

16 Km (10 miles)

1265m (4149ft)

Time : 7hrs 15min

**Snowdon's magnificent Southern ridge is worthy of a full day to itself. This route, incorporating the Rhyd-Ddu path plus a detour onto the Southern outlier of Yr Aran ranks with the finest in Snowdonia.**

The Rhyd-Ddu path onto Snowdon has the honour of being the one I followed on my first-ever ascent of Snowdon back in my long-haired student days. Over the years I have followed it in fair weather and the foulest – alone and with human or canine company – looking for variations to add a bit of pizzazz to a relatively easy, sometimes dreary stroll.

So despite starting and ending on the less popular side of the summit, this diversion via Yr Aran, culminating in the traverse of the magnificent Southern ridge of Snowdon should be sampled by anyone who professes to love Snowdonia.

It is a walk of contrasts. The dark, deserted slate quarries to the West of Bwlch Cwm Llan possess a hopeless sense of neglected abandonment not shared with the ruined workings in Cwm Llan itself. And the rugged, narrow spine of rock either side of Clogwyn Du is a vastly different prospect to the gentle Western spur of Llechog. For those keen to experience both sides of the highest point in England and Wales, an optional descent of the Miners Track or Pyg Track to Pen y Pass is a fitting end to an exhilarating walk (with regular bus links via Beddgelert back to the station car park at Rhyd-Ddu). Although parts of this walk are as crowded as any, there are other corners where you will have the hillside to yourself.

**North**

**Don't forget**

**map/compass
whistle/torch**

**suitable footwear
+ clothing**

**food/drink**

**brain**

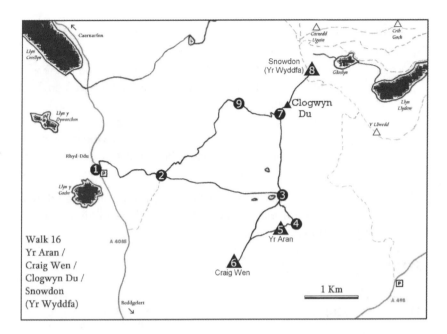

## APPROACH

From the direction of Caernarfon, take the Beddgelert road (A4085) through Caeathro and Waunfawr, passing the NorthEastern shore of Llyn Cwellyn. 1 Km beyond the inflow of this lake you enter the village of Rhyd-Ddu. The main pay-and-display car park is at the Southern end of the village on the left hand side of the road (at **571526**)

From Beddgelert, take the Caernarfon road (A4085) North along Nant Colwyn. As the Nantlle Ridge becomes increasingly prominent on your left and the forested area recedes from the roadside you will be able to pick out Llyn y Gader, again on your left. Rhyd-Ddu is less than ½ Km beyond and the main pay-and-display car park lies on your right before you enter the village.

This car park has always been busy during the summer; it being the starting point of the popular Rhyd-Ddu path up Snowdon. In recent years, following the renovation and continued extension South-Eastwards of the 'Welsh Highland Light Railway' from Waunfawr to Porthmadog (eventually), this car park now also serves passengers using the stop created at Rhyd-Ddu so it gets even busier.

It was August 1877 when the North Wales Narrow Gauge Railway first carried passengers between Cwellyn and Dinas junctions (where it met the main line to Caernarfon). The service was extended to the Snowdon Ranger station on 13th June 1878 and to Rhyd-Ddu on 14th May 1881. (Rhyd-Ddu station changed its name to 'South Snowdon' to attract more travellers).
However, the service eventually became bankrupt, carrying its final passenger in 1916 – until its rebirth in 2005.

Like all popular walks in Snowdonia, an early start is recommended during the summer months (particularly at weekends) since there is little alternative parking available close by [16-01].

**START**

1) **(571526)** →

   **325°** →

Walk Northwards through the car park passing the pay-and-display ticket machine (having paid your £3 for a full day) and the toilet block on your left. Steps on your right lead to the platform serving the light railway [16-02]. The platform and the new system of gates are recent additions; improvements for rail passengers and hill-walkers alike. Ignore the first gate on your right (for vehicles), and use the second set to cross the railway line then continue along the broad track leading Eastwards.

   **125°** →

This track shortly forks left to Ffridd-Isaf farm (marked 'private road') [16-03], but your route forks right beyond the vehicle barrier guarding the track ahead. Continue uphill along the clear track between the waste heaps and a series of old quarry workings, including a large, pit-like shaft fenced off on the right hand side of the path at **574526** [16-04]. Beyond these desolate remains of the area's industrial past stands a slightly more up-to-date galvanised metal building on your left [16-05]. The main track-way continues through a wide gateway on its right by way of a new, walker-friendly gate at **578526**.

Any walkers who have not used this path since 2007 will be pleasantly surprised by the commendable efforts made by the National Park Authority to upgrade this route. Almost all the old ladder stiles and rusty kissing-gates have been replaced by sturdy wooden gates that are easy to operate. The dry-stone walls in which these gates are fitted have also had a make-over, possibly in anticipation of the opening of the new café on the summit sometime in mid-2009.

A short distance uphill from here you reach another pair of gates giving easy access to the other side of the wall. Beyond it the path levels out – a slate-covered track crossing open ground with the twin targets ahead of you on the Eastern skyline.

The path takes its time climbing towards a series of massive, rounded outcrops of rock, some fringing the edge of the path as you pass them by [16-06 and 16-07 looking back]. Pass through another renovated gateway [16-08] and beyond a smaller set of crags on your left, tucked in a corner behind a rocky outcrop on your left is a low wall topped by a fence (at **583524**) [16-09]. A new gate here gives access to a relatively easy, direct ascent of Snowdon [16-10] – the 'Rhyd-Ddu path'. Here is where the return leg of the walk rejoins your ascent route. On older maps the 'Rhyd-Ddu path' is called the 'Beddgelert Path'.

2)      (583524)        →

        100°            →

---

OPTION 1
For an immediate route up Snowdon continue along the 'Rhyd-Ddu path' – reversing the descent route from **point 7**.

---

Hopefully you have resisted the temptation to head left here directly onto the main summit. This 'tourist path' has little to commend it except as an easy descent route. Instead continue a short distance East towards another brand new, galvanised gate set in a wall alongside a rusted gate [16-11 before upgrade and 16-12 after].

*Since the views ahead along the early stages of this walk are fairly uninteresting you will undoubtedly have turned to look behind you time and time again for inspiration.*
*To the SouthWest lies the Moel Hebog triptych [16-13].*
*The Nantlle Ridge and Mynydd Mawr with Llyn Cwellyn at its foot dominate the West; the cliffs of Craig y Bera often at their most attractive from this viewpoint just after dawn.*

The path beyond this gateway used to be quite wet underfoot to start with as it cuts directly through bunches of reeds obscuring an extensive, flat valley floor. But recent path improvements seem to have cured the problem utilising crushed aggregate as a more resilient surface. Ahead you should be able to pick out this straightforward path as it climbs in a series of gradual zig-zags to the skyline col separating Yr Aran on your right from the rather unimpressive Southern spur of Snowdon on the left. Have no fear – appearances can be deceptive because it doesn't stay unimpressive for long.

The path is in no particular hurry to gain height, crossing a couple of streams – one by way of a set of slabs [16-14]. After crossing a ladder stile (one of the few yet to be replaced – mid-2008) alongside a rickety, rusty gate [16-15] the path crosses an impressive construction of natural stone and cement bridging a third stream incised quite deeply into the surrounding terrain [16-16].

Beyond this the path becomes narrower as it approaches the first set of ruined buildings and scarred remains of extensive quarrying [16-17].

*On the left hand side of the path the first of a pair of large, deep excavations bears witness to the valley's industrial past [16-18]. This could be considered an eyesore when viewed from up close despite the waterfall cascading into its far corner.*

*Much of the rock was removed from these pits by hand, but it would take a good deal of ingenuity now to clamber unaided out of either of the pair given the almost sheer drop and the smoothness of their enclosing walls.*

Better to keep on the path and continue towards the waste heaps. You actually have a choice since there are two embanked, overgrown tracks heading uphill [16-19]. Whichever you take does not matter since they soon join up again (my choice would be the left one since the track on the right degenerates into wet ground higher up).

As the main path levels out again it runs alongside a series of slate waste tips, keeping close to a large retaining wall on your right [16-20]. After narrowing, the path eventually emerges in the heart of the old quarry workings [16-21]. You are confronted by a steep embankment ahead of you topped by a ruined building – an old winding shed that once pulled laden carts up the incline. Your ascent path veers left of this embankment [16-22] and contours steep slopes that drop to an overgrown dip separating the workings from the main mass of the hillside on your left. After gaining a fair bit of height in a relatively short distance, the path broadens out as it emerges between the waste tips at the top of the incline close to the ruined winding shed. Ahead and to your left is a third enormous pit cut into the surrounding rocks; steep-sided and choked with slate waste [16-23].

A ladder stile on your right gives access to damp ground close to the base of Yr Aran [16-24], but our route continues ahead and upwards towards the next ruined winding shed [16-25 and 16-26]. This one stands atop a slightly lower incline and the direct route to the top is the quickest solution if not the easiest. The slate is loose underfoot in places, and can be greasy after heavy rain, but in no time at all you pass between the two walls [16-27] at **600522** (all that remain of the winding-house). Once you reach this level most of the initial climbing is over and done with. Time for a quick retrospective peep at your route so far [16-28]. The path broadens out, acquiring a rusty wire fence along its right hand side. Beyond the flattened heaps of slate on your right lies a small, dark reservoir once used for the quarrying operation.

After a short section of paved path [16-29] followed by some hummocky, wet ground the twisting path reaches the crest of the skyline immediately ahead of you at Bwlch Cwm Llan. The Cwm Llan valley lies far below, and on your left is the main ascent route up Snowdon (following the opposite side of the valley to that taken by the Watkin Path).

*This is the best spot from which to study the contrast between the shaded, scarred valley you have just emerged from and the sunlit, verdant, almost manicured terrain of Cwm Llan [16-30 and 16-31] beyond.*
*Both were extensively quarried, but the tidy slate heaps, level terraces and ruined buildings that cling to the lower slopes of Y Lliwedd add a certain charm to the wild landscape. One can almost imagine the valley teeming with activity beneath your feet, the air ringing with the sounds of chisels on rock.*

**3)**     **(605522)**     →

        **175°**          →

A dry-stone wall runs the length of the skyline (now at your feet) but there is no need to cross it just yet. To your left a clear path of red shale trends steeply up towards Snowdon's Southern spur [16-32]. But to gain Yr Aran's summit involves a detour right and some tricky route finding.

> ## OPTION 2
> To shorten this walk significantly it is possible to avoid setting foot on Yr Aran. Climb left instead and follow the track towards Snowdon's summit.
> ### *Time saved – 2hrs 15min*

To your right a low dry-stone wall leads towards the base of the day's first summit [16-33]. As you follow the line of this wall across grassy slopes the ground soon descends quite steeply and you face a series of rounded crags ahead of you with another dry-stone wall to their right. A short section of scrambling follows a path left which eventually drops you down to the low col between you and the main body of crag ahead. From here the best option is to trend right to get around the pronounced hummock blocking the way ahead. Keeping to the left-hand side of the wall the path climbs quite steeply, in places crossing wet slabs of rock where there are enough handholds to make it a relatively easy scramble.

*As the ground levels out you pass a body of water on your right (with the slate tips and the Nantlle Ridge beyond). There is also a worm's-eye view behind you of Snowdon's summit and the main South ridge.*

There are numerous ways to reach the lower slopes of Yr Aran but the most straightforward involves remaining on the left-hand side of the dry-stone wall and following the eroded path – climbing grass-covered slopes and rounding the corner of the main mass of crag on your left as you go [16-34 and 16-35]. Once the path begins to level off (before climbing between a fresh set of crags) cross the ladder stile in the wall to reach grassland to the right of the wall [16-36]. A faint path can be picked out crossing this shallow col, parallel to the wall you have just crossed but maintaining an increasing distance from it as it scales the rocky hummocks to your left [16-37].

As you gradually bear left, you eventually enter a broad depression [16-38] where the dry-stone wall takes a sudden turn to escape the line of crags. In the lee of these crags and on the opposite side of the dry-stone wall lies very boggy ground containing a small pool (at **606519**) [16-39, and 16-40 looking back from much higher up the slope]. Had you not crossed the wall earlier, the path threading through the crags would have led you to this extremely damp corner. Your only escape would then have been to by-pass the small body of water and head for yet another ladder stile crossing the wire fence just beyond the corner in the dry stone wall on your left [16-41 from higher up].

From the floor of this saddle aim for the dilapidated stone wall that struggles to climb from the wire fence onto the slopes. Ahead and to your right you should be able to pick out an eroded path scaling those same slopes [16-42]. Follow this path which sticks close to the wall as it gains height quite quickly until eventually you reach a fairly level platform of grass-covered ground. Beyond here the collapsed wall decides it has had enough climbing for a bit and heads off to the left.

---

### OPTION 3
For those who relish a bit of a scramble it is possible to continue directly uphill from here to the top of Yr Aran. Keep to the left of the prominent rocky outcrop forming the summit ahead of you.
Follow the rubble-choked neck of the scree chute [16-43 and 16-44] that

---

fans down to meet you. Beyond these scree-covered slopes,
a steep, rocky channel climbs left onto the shoulders of the summit.
Be warned that in icy conditions this North-facing slope is
notoriously unstable.

Head left in the same direction as the wall and look for a ladder stile on the skyline above and to the left where the Eastern spur of Yr Aran falls away into Cwm Llan [16-45]. The path follows the upslope side of the dry-stone wall, climbing gradually through a litter of large, flat slabs of rock. This wall eventually dissolves into the rock-covered ground, but a clear path emerges, contouring the slopes before climbing steeply to the ladder-stile already spotted earlier. You pass an outcrop of smooth, grey rock on your right [16-46] just before the path levels out at the ladder stile with a dilapidated wire fence alongside [16-47].

**4)**     **(608517)**     →

       **250°**        →

Ignore the stile and bear right to climb a zig-zagging staircase path leading easily towards the summit [16-48]. You are unlikely to miss your way from here on, even under snow, as there are also a number of rusted fence posts way-marking the ascent route. Once you reach the flat, grassy top, you pass another rusted fence post a short distance from the small cairn capping the summit area of **Yr Aran** (at **604515** – 747m/2450ft) [16-49 and 16-50].

The summit of Yr Aran is a fine, airy spot from which to survey the surrounding countryside. Its broad, level, turf-capped ridge extends 200 metres or so East to West, decorated here and there by tilted outcrops of slatey rock and with its Westernmost end marked by a rusting fence-pole.

*At this height on Yr Aran's summit ridge, it is relatively easy to pick out the summit of Snowdon with its café adding a surreal touch to the skyline (or not, if obscured by cloud [16-51]). Then in a clockwise direction, your eyes follow the sweep of the ridge down to Bwlch y Ciliau then back up to the crags of Y Lliwedd (with Crib Goch's pinnacled heights peering over the saddle) [16-52 and 16-53].*

*Further right the isolated outlier of Moel Siabod [16-54] gives way to the lower peaks beyond Nantgwynant before the ground descends further to the Glaslyn Estuary.*

*Blocking out a broader view of the seaboard is the Moel Hebog group [16-55], the Nantlle Ridge [16-56] and Mynydd Mawr [16-57].*

*Caernarfon, complete with castle besides the Menai Straits, can be picked out just above Llyn Cwellyn with the gentle green slopes to the lake's East marking the start of the Snowdon Ranger path as it begins the traverse to that café again.*

---

**OPTION 4**
If you wish to give Craig Wen a miss, retrace your steps to the col of
Bwlch Cwm Llan and continue as from **point 3** (revisited) as below.
***Time saved – approx 45 mins***

---

**5)**  **(604515)**  →

  **230°**  →

The South Western flanks of Yr Aran are in stark contrast to its Northern and NorthEastern exposures, and show all the signs of offering easier going for those seeking to escape its summit. But it is a long haul South if you intend continuing to Beddgelert. Similarly, heading West towards Rhyd-Ddu involves crossing a vast expanse of featureless ground before meeting the A4085 some distance South of the village.

However, a short detour in this direction onto the lowly summit of Craig Wen is worth a little time and minimum effort [16-58].

Yr Aran's South Western slopes provide a relatively steep but easy drop to the 600-metre contour where the angle of descent begins to level slightly (in the general vicinity of **599514**). From this broad, grassy col a faint path sunk into the turf can be seen heading towards the flat-topped hill ahead. A tiny cairn picks out the left-most hummock of the set as the actual summit of **Craig Wen** (at **597509** – 608m/1994ft) [16-59] which resembles a gun-emplacement when viewed from the North.

*Views from Craig Wen are restricted to the panorama of the Nantlle hills to the West. Everything to the South is masked by the angle of slope, but facing North rewards you with a close-up view of Yr Aran's elegant form as well as a widescreen glimpse of Yr Wyddfa [16-60].*

**6)**   **(597509)**   →

      **50°**        →

Retrace your steps to the broad col at the base of Yr Aran and then pick your way to the left, skirting the mountain's slopes and dropping down gradually as you do so. There are a number of faint paths trending off in this direction, steering well clear of the steep rock face and the bulky scree cascading along its base [16-61].

As you circuit the Western flanks of Yr Aran you will hopefully be able to pick out the path you followed earlier in the day on your ascent from Rhyd-Ddu. Look out for the lake adjacent to the waste slate tips West of Bwlch Cwm Llan (at **601521**). Aim in the general direction of its right-hand shore, but do not drop too low just yet as your ultimate objective is the section of dry-stone wall that runs 50 metres or so to its right [16-62]. As you get closer you will notice a wire fence running left to right from the lake's furthest shoreline to the wall, and a ladder stile where the two meet [16-63]. Head for this ladder stile and climb over it to join the obvious path climbing up to the rocky crags immediately South of Bwlch Cwm Llan.

---

**OPTION 5**
This is the point at which you can make a hasty exit to Rhyd-Ddu by following the path West back through the derelict quarry workings.

***Time saved – approx 1 hr 30 mins***

---

**3)    (605522)    →**

**0°    →**

A grassy bank in the lee of the tumbledown wall that straddles this col is as good a place as any to sit and prepare for the next stage of the walk – to take time to study the valley of Cwm Llan perhaps and the amazing slopes above it. There are few better vantage points from which to watch the world go by – or stand still even.

*On one memorable visit here I found the time to sit and contemplate the grass beside my feet where a mass of dew prisms slowly formed from the melting frost. Then just as enthralling – I could only gawp in wonder as a Chinook helicopter on a practice flight buzzed the adjacent corrie walls before hovering less than a metre above Yr Aran's summit. Half an hour earlier and I could have hitched a lift.*

But there's something else worth contemplation close by – the track leading onto Snowdon's Southern ridge [16-64]. It forms the uppermost section of a path that detours West from the Watkin path, scaling the Southern valley wall of Cwm Llan to this hiatus.

From this point North the route along the ridgeline is direct and invigorating – not least due to the sense of exposure (never as much of a problem as it can be on Crib Goch) as the ground drops sheer away to the right.

Initially the path consists of block steps that allow you to gain height relatively rapidly [16-65]. Then as it rounds a corner trending to the right the path begins to level off, passing a conspicuous outcrop of red rock on your left striated by veins of white quartz [16-66 looking back downslope].

Ahead of you now is the day's first section of hands-on scrambling. This involves clambering up a low wall of tilted rocky outcrops that form an enclosed corner. The most direct route is to climb up the thick vein of quartz threading through the darker rocks on either side [16-67]. This bit of a scramble is easy enough and you quickly regain level ground where a path continues in the required direction [16-68].

*While you let your adrenaline levels return to normal take a look back at the route you supposedly followed earlier in the day en route to and from Yr Aran [16-69 looking back]. It looks suitably massive from here.*

The path now climbs in gentle undulations towards the 704-metre top of Allt Maenderyn a short distance ahead and to your right. As you begin to ascend the ridge to this inconspicuous summit you will see a small body of water below to your left [16-70] – presumably this once supplied water to the quarry workings West of Bwlch Cwm Llan. From Allt Maenderyn the path drops gently to a high saddle, Bwlch Maenderyn [16-71 from the top, and 16-72 looking back from the saddle]. All too shortly after this lull you are presented with the next major obstacle, the rearing snout of Clogwyn Du.

As you approach the base of this steep ground you will notice ahead of you to your left a ladder stile crossing over a fence [16-73] to the next section of ascent.

Beyond this fence an eroded path of red rubble crosses increasingly steep ground [16-74 looking back to the stile] before running abruptly into a wall of angular, tilted bedrock [16-75]. This scramble is a sheer delight under dry conditions. It involves pulling yourself onto a large outcrop of tilted slab, rough enough to provide good grip, and not sloping too much to deter one from walking upright across it rather than on all fours [16-76 looking back downslope]. If the rock is iced-up or greasy, keep left and use the corner wall of crag for support.

Once that bit of fun is over with, rejoin the path as it takes a wide sweep right (with a low stone wall on your left) [16-77 looking back down] to gain another small shelf of more level ground. A number of sizeable cairns point you in the right direction – ahead, and up, onto the next steep section [16-78 and 16-79]. Another slight descent, then the broad, clear path drags itself up in the general direction of a prominent grassy hump to the left of the Snowdon summit [16-80 and 16-81].

Soon your path by-passes a jumble of large, grey boulders on your right perched high above the basin of Cwm Tregalan.

*This is a good spot to look back and figure out the true nature of the ridge you have been following for the last half hour [16-82 looking back].*

The smooth, but arduous slope ahead crosses a convex top beyond which a short section of crags finally plonks you on the summit of **Clogwyn D**u (at **605546** – 931m/3054ft) [16-83, and 16-84 looking back from further along the ridge].

Although Clogwyn Du tops 3000ft, it is not considered one of the official Welsh 3000-footers due to its proximity to Snowdon (insufficient loss of height between the two adjacent summits relegates this magnificent spot to the status of 'subsidiary top').

*Needless to say, a spot this close to the highest point in Snowdonia yields stupendous views – not least the close-ups of Crib Goch [16-85], Glyder Fawr [16-86], Y Lliwedd, and in total contrast the low-lying, Glaslyn estuary and coastal town of Caernarfon [16-87].*
*There is also an excellent opportunity to study the line of the 'Snowdon Ranger' path from above [16-88] where it drops into Cwm Brwynog, and the return leg of the 'Rhyd Ddu' path along the ridge of Llechog [16-89] once you have played tag with the day's highest summit.*

The path from here to Snowdon's summit (crossing Bwlch Main) follows the ridge North, but a few metres below Clogwyn Du's spiny top a path hairpins back South on your left [16-90, and 16-91 looking back].

TAKE NOTE OF THIS POINT WHERE THE PATHS SPLIT AS THIS IS WHERE YOU WILL JOIN THE ROUTE BACK TOWARDS RHYD-DDU ONCE THE LAST PEAK OF THE DAY HAS BEEN BAGGED.

7)       (604546)       →

         35°             →

---

OPTION 6
Having come so far it would be unforgiveable to miss out on the highlight of the day – a trip onto Snowdon's summit. But if time is short

or weather conditions require a hasty descent, follow the 'Rhyd-Ddu'
path by taking this forked path left (continuing from **point 7** revisited).

*Time saved – less than 1 hr*

The summit trig point of Snowdon is only 800 metres or so further North
now [16-92 when the original café was there, and 16-93 during the construction of
Hafod Eryri – neither particularly appealing]. To reach it the path skirting the
Eastern rim of the Bwlch Main arête is straightforward as long as you do not
wander too close to the edge.

After a tightrope section running along the summit of the arête [16-94], the
path at times seems unable to decide which side of the ridge to follow. It
starts off on the Western side of the ridge-line then crosses over to the
Eastern side (high above Cwm Tregalan), before finally opting for the
Western side.

Suddenly most of the fun is over as you reach a broad, grassy ramp at the
foot of Snowdon's summit area [16-95]. The final slog between loose rocks
and near-vertical crags can appear steep and unrelenting [16-96] but it takes
little real effort to gain the summit – **Snowdon (Yr Wyddfa)** (at **609544** –
1085m/3561ft).

*The views are spectacular from here given the right weather conditions.*
*Llyn Llydaw far below in the heart of the Snowdon horse-shoe with the*
*Miners' Path causeway splitting it in two [16-97]. Crib Goch to one side and*
*Lliwedd's crucible [16-98] the other, framing the Glyderau.*
*Further afield one can pick out the Glaslyn estuary, Nantlle valley, and*
*Llynnau Mymbyr near to Capel Curig.*

### OPTION 7

For a more novel end to this circular walk it is possible at this stage to
continue a traverse of the entire summit of Snowdon by descending
Eastwards using either the 'Pyg Track' or 'Miners' Track' to the car park at
Pen –y-Pass (see **Walk 14** for more detail).
There is a regular bus service back to Rhyd-Ddu via Beddgelert (where it

**8)**     **(609544)**     →

      215°         →

Once you have hugged the pillar, eaten your sandwiches, sipped your juice and watched swarms of jubilant walkers appear from the direction of Llanberis (emerging onto Bwlch Glas from the 'Snowdon Ranger', Llanberis Path, Miners' Track or Pyg Track) you will probably feel that it is time to move on.

Face South again and pick your way through the rubble until you meet the clear path edging its way across Bwlch Main. Pass the stone pointer marking the Watkin Path exit point [16-99], making sure you continue straight ahead [16-100 and 16-101] rather than wander left into Cwm Tregalan. Within too short a time you reach the high col where one path revisits the crags of Clogwyn Du again and the other forks right across the slope to eventually reach the obvious spur pointing a steady finger Westwards towards Llyn Cwellyn [16-102 and 16-103].

**(7)**     **(604536)**     →

      220°         →

The descent to Bwlch Main is refreshingly invigorating after the duress of the final section of ascent before reaching Snowdon's summit. And the path running West across the Llechog ridge gives a more direct return route to Rhyd-Ddu; enlivened by numerous steep sections but made rather oppressive by the obvious mark of man.

This gentle ridge, the Llechog spur, should not to be confused with the neighbouring ridge of the same name forming part of the Southern wall of the Llanberis Pass. On its right is a near-vertical drop into Cwm Clogwyn which contains the triple lakes of Llyn Nadroedd, Llyn Coch and Llyn Glas [16-104] (once a single, larger lake until the last melting glaciers some 10,000 years ago dumped enough debris to separate the one into these three). Llyn Ffynnon y Gwas lies about 100 metres below these three at the foot of Moel Cynghorion. To the left of Llechog the slopes are much less severe – the ridge line almost dividing the landscape at your feet in two. The topography to your left is the result of much gentler weathering than the freeze-thaw action of snow, ice and meltwater that chiselled away at the slopes on your right where shade predominated.

The path from the slopes beneath Clogwyn Du to the North West tip of Llechog is undemanding; some zig-zagging (in tandem with a wire fence) [16-105] at the steeper bits where the spur attaches itself to Snowdon's main massif makes the angle of descent easier. Much work has also been done to preserve or repair the path where erosion and the tramp of countless feet threaten to wreak havoc. But it has to be said it looks better on the way down than on the way up.

**9)**      **(597538)**      →

       **255°**         →

Close to the 730-metre contour where the flat top of Llechog begins to plunge downhill again before taking a twist North to the floor of Cwm Clogwyn, the path turns left through a gate set in the wall ahead [16-106, and 16-107 looking back uphill] and follows another set of leisurely zig-zags down towards Rhyd-Ddu.

The flatter sections of path are often wet underfoot; indeed the first steep section above Rhos Boeth (**593533**) can feel pretty much like following a stream bed. Keeping to the fairly well-constructed path is the sensible option. There are a number of steeper, staircase descents – one dropping down to a wall with a gate installed [16-108].

*The fairly tedious going, however, is rewarded by close-up views of Dyffryn Nantlle [16-109] and Llyn Cwellyn [16-110] (something sadly lacking during this route's ascent unless you keep peering over your shoulder).*

*The view ahead to the Moel Hebog group [16-111] is also a sign that the end of this distinctly rocky track is not far away.*

There is still a fair bit of ground to cover – generally a straightforward sequence of rocky descents linking large, flat, grassy hollows. The solid path maintains a sinuous line heading further West and South. Finally, with Mynydd Drws-y-Coed directly ahead of you the narrowing track only has one last substantial section of level, terrain to cross. And soon a low outcrop of dark rock on the immediate skyline marks the point where the 'Rhyd-Ddu Path' rejoins the track you ascended earlier in the day. As you draw closer you will see the gate in the wall ahead of you, the one you by-passed earlier in the day at **point 2** [16-112 looking back the way you have just come].

**270°**     →

This descent path from Llechog was also known as the 'Beddgelert path' because having passed through the gate at **point 2** it is possible to continue straight ahead rather than turning right for Rhyd-Ddu. A rough path runs South West for just over 1Km, passing Ffridd Uchaf farm then emerging on the A4085 close to Pitts Head (at **577514**). The village of Beddgelert is still 3½ Km away but today our interests lie elsewhere.

Pitts Head was originally the name given to a massive boulder adjacent to the Beddgelert-Caernarfon road that supposedly resembled the head of Prime Minister William Pitt when viewed in profile.

More significantly, that boulder is composed of a very distinctive rock-type only found outcropping in a few locations nearby (Allt Maenderyn en route to Clogwyn Du to the East, and the summit of Moel yr Ogof and flanks of Moel Hebog to the West) The rock is a 'tuff', composed of layers of ash laid down during a blitz of volcanic activity some 450 million years ago when thousands of feet of ash and volcanic debris were deposited on top of each other and flattened due to the overlying weight of fresh ejecta.

In the case of this particular tuff the layers of ash trapped bubbles of volatile fluid rich in minerals like silica, and as these bubbles cooled relatively slowly they were able to crystallise into nodules. As they cooled these nodules grew one layer after another into spheres that ranged in size from marbles to cabbages. These spheres are massed together into layers of rock each resembling a geological 'Aero' (where bubbles of air are replaced by rock different in texture to that surrounding them). Some of these spheres later became squashed or deformed, but they are still distinctive enough to identify the rock type as unique to this corner of North Wales. This distinctive rock type is given the name Pitts Head Tuff and is a significant geological rock type of the Ordovician period.

Go through this gate, turn right and follow the track back to the car park at Rhyd-Ddu. Your feet might be throbbing after so much tramping on solid slab, but it's a small price to pay for completing such a gem of a walk.

**END**

# NANTLLE

*These hidden territories are often written-off as the haunt of those who spend days lost (orienteering) in the Beddgelert Forest or riding their mountain bikes along the numerous forest tracks that embroider the Northern flanks of Moel Hebog. But there is much more to discover in this forgotten corner of Snowdonia.*

## TASTER 16

*Any journey along Dyffryn Nantlle presents you with a perfect view of Craig y Bera (the steep cliffs along the Southern rim of Mynydd Mawr). If you park close to the shore of Llyn Cwellyn you also get a closer look at the bulk of the mountain.*

*A number of forestry paths run along the lake shore – park as if starting* **Walk 17** *– head through the gate into a paddock (which acts as a summer camp site) and keep to the forest track. Unfortunately the views tend to be restricted by the trees on this side of the valley.*

*Alternatively, a short walk along the 'Snowdon Ranger' path towards Snowdon's summit gives a superb retrospective view of Mynydd Mawr and Y Garn. The path starts 1¼ Km North of the bridge where the Afon Gwyrfai drains out of Llyn Cwellyn (the footpath is sign-posted on the right-hand side of the road as you head North towards Waunfawr, a few metres beyond the 'Snowdon Ranger' Youth Hostel – with ample parking in the car park across the road). Although this path goes all the way up to Snowdon's summit, it doesn't mean you can't have just a little nibble at it.*

## TASTER 17

*The Nantlle Ridge makes such demands and requires so much commitment from the walker that it is not the place to stroll onto if you only have an hour or so to kill.*

*But a drive (or better still a cycle ride or walk) along the road following the floor of Dyffryn Nantlle will give you a close-up view of these spectacular mountains – some of the most dramatic scenery accessible by road in Snowdonia.*

*You can also reach the foot of Y Garn from the Beddgelert Forest by following the track that runs above the Western shore of Llyn y Gader. Views from here across to Snowdon are seriously impressive.*

## TASTER 18

*The 'tourist' side of the Moel Hebog ridge is easier to gain access to than the one where* **Walk 19** *starts from– just follow the Caernarfon/Rhyd-Ddu road out of Beddgelert. Some 2Km North of Beddgelert, on the left-hand side of the road as you drive in the direction of Rhyd-Ddu, is the Beddgelert Forest which covers much of the lower slopes of Moel Hebog.*

*There is ample space for parking or picnicking, as well as a camp site, visitor information centre and shop. The Forestry Commission has constructed several paths leading onto the mountain's slopes, as well as a network of tracks that can be used for walking, cycling and orienteering.*

***Anyone visiting this area will appreciate that the best views of all must be from the surrounding ridges. For those of you tempted to explore further, why not try one of the following walks? Mynydd Mawr's ascent is one of the easiest in the book. I dare you to give it a try.***

## WALK 17

# Mynydd Mawr [56]

**6.8 Km (4.25 miles)**

**560m (1837ft)**

**Time : 3hrs 10min**

**An isolated mountain perched above Llyn Cwellyn with views into Dyffryn Nantlle**

This particular walk differs from all the others in this guide – it is the only straightforward 'there-and-back' walk included. However, the simplicity of the route in no way detracts from its qualities. Indeed, anyone looking for their 'first hill experience' in Snowdonia could not choose a better starter than this one. Mynydd Mawr's location makes it an unrivalled spot from which to study the Nantlle Ridge close by as well as the Western slopes of the Snowdon massif.

I can remember the first time I did this walk; the main bulk of Snowdonia under an extensive cover or snow, but the lowlands of Dyffryn Nantlle and the shore of Llyn Cwellyn already bearing signs of an early Spring. The demarcation line between dazzling white and fresh green looked as if it had been drawn with a set-square. Another vivid memory I carry of that particular day was watching from the rim of Craig y Bera as a pack of nine foxhounds scrabbled directly up the scree chute from Dyffryn Nantlle to gain the main summit, baying for blood all the way. The valley itself was a renowned hunting area in the past, but it is likely these hounds were merely chasing a pre-laid scent rather than a live wolf or wild boar.

**North**

**Don't forget**

**map/compass**
**whistle/torch**

**suitable footwear**
**+ clothing**

**food/drink**

**brain**

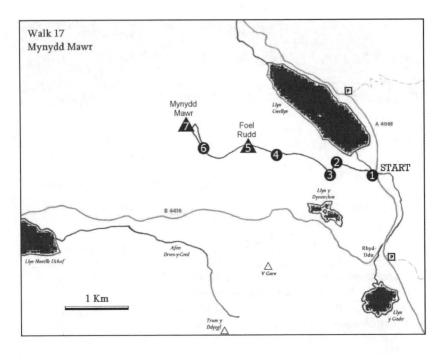

## APPROACH

Follow the A4085 South West out of Caernarfon. As you leave the village of Caeathro continue South straight across the roundabout and follow the road through Waunfawr and Betws Garmon.

Alternatively take the same road (A4085) North West out of Beddgelert passing through Rhyd-Ddu.

Park beyond the inflow of Llyn Cwellyn at the South end of the lake – one ideal spot lies on the gravelled verge outside the gated entrance to the property of Planwydd (at **568540**). But if you decide to take advantage of this convenient space, make sure you do not block access to this property or the paddock adjacent which is used as a camp-site during the summer. If in doubt, ask for permission first if the house shows signs of someone being at home.

Alternative parking can be found at Rhyd-Ddu 1 Km or so South, or anywhere beside the shore of the lake further North where the road has a number of small picnicking bays.

**START**

1)      (568540)      →

     280°           →

Pass through the smaller of the two gates in the brown wooden fence (a sign on the larger gate which leads to a popular, seasonal campsite warns against feeding the bears in the forest!) [17-01].

There is a notice-board advertising the numerous features available for the visitors to the camp-site, including the nearest pub in Rhyd-Ddu. But before you are tempted to wander off in search of refreshment, there's the slight matter of a walk to complete first. From the left-hand verge of the forest track, cross the ladder stile immediately right of the dwelling. A path heads up to the right across the grassy slope to meet the edge of the forest plantation [17-02]. A step-stile there lets you cross the fence at the forest edge [17-03 looking back towards the start of the walk].

Once you have climbed over the fence, head to your right along the clear path through thinning forest with the few surviving conifers always downslope on your right [17-04]. The path eventually levels out and for a time becomes fragmented as you pick your way through a fallen, moss-covered wall [17-05 looking back]. Head gently uphill until the path emerges onto a gravel forestry track (at **563541**).

PAY PARTICULAR ATTENTION TO YOUR SURROUNDINGS HERE; MAKING SURE YOU CAN IDENTIFY THE SPOT WHERE THE NARROWER PATH YOU HAVE JUST CLIMBED UP FROM THE FOREST EDGE JOINS THE FOREST TRACK. YOU WILL NEED TO BE ABLE TO FIND THE SAME SPOT ON YOUR RETURN.

2)      (563541)      →

     300°           →

Turn right then almost immediately left at a marker-post identifying a minor forest trail heading uphill through the recently-cleared plantation [17-06].

This footpath climbs quite steeply through scrubby undergrowth, eventually bearing left as it ascends Bwlch y Moch. As you reach the skyline a ladder stile allows you to cross the fence, which marks the boundary between the forest and the open hillside at the 250-metre contour [17-07 looking down from the flanks of Foel Rudd – x marks the spot].

**3)**     **(561540)**        →

      290°                →

Cross the stile and turn right; if necessary using the fence on your right as a handrail to cross the hummocky ground leading directly Westwards [17-08]. Another fence soon cuts across your route, running downslope to the left but a ladder stile at **559542** allows you to continue uphill.

*From just above this point there is a substantial gap in the forestry on your right now allowing you a clear view of Llyn Cwellyn and its Eastern shoreline [17-09 and 17-10].*

Press on ahead, still using the fence as a handrail if you so wish. As you approach a level section beneath the steep face of Foel Rudd, this fence bears left then takes a 90° turn right to accommodate a corner of plantation that has crept up from the shores of Llyn Cwellyn to the mountain edge at the 400-metre contour [17-11]. More recently this plantation has been harvested, leaving only bare scrubland – a warning that sometimes the map unintentionally lies. A short step beyond this point you come upon another fence, complete with ladder stile, running along the base of Foel Rudd [17-12].

**4)**     **(553543)**        →

      280°                →

Cross the ladder stile and continue ahead up quite a steep, rocky staircase leading to a small cairn at **552543**.

THIS IS THE STEEPEST SECTION [17-13 LOOKING DOWN TO THE LADDER STILE] BUT IT
SHOULD PROVIDE NO REAL DIFFICULTIES UNLESS COVERED IN SNOW OR ICE. JUST
TAKE EXTRA CARE WHEN COMING DOWN – BEARING IN MIND THAT MOST ACCIDENTS
HAPPEN WHEN DESCENDING.

The ground levels off beyond this cairn, the path passes through a gap in a
collapsed wall [17-14] and finally climbs less steeply to the cairned summit of
**Foel Rudd** (at **548544** – 570m/1870ft) [17-15].

*This is a superb vantage point, if you need an excuse to pause and regain
your breath. Below to your right stretch the waters of Llyn Cwellyn with Foel
Gron and Foel Goch's Southern flanks on the opposite valley side, together
with the lower reaches of the Snowdon Ranger path [17-16 to 17-18].*
*To the East, the South West ramparts of Yr Wyddfa (Snowdon) monopolise
the scene, with Yr Aran a solitary outlier to its right.*
*South is the broad valley in which Rhyd-Ddu lies, occupied by Llyn y Gader
and Llyn y Dywarchen with the high fortress of Moel Hebog furthest ahead,
and closer at hand the Nantllle Ridge.*

5)      (548544)      →

        240°          →

The path begins to level off again as it skirts the headwall of Cwm Planwydd
(the valley of the headwaters of the Afon Goch) on its right [17-19 and 17-20].
As you follow this path the ridge-walking here is quite similar in nature to
the easier sections of the Nantlle Ridge which lies less than 2 Km across
Dyffryn Nantlle to your left. You can choose to walk as close to the edge of
Craig y Bera as your head for heights or the weather conditions permit. This
is a spectacular cliff from whichever direction you choose to view it; from the
neighbouring Nantlle Ridge or looking back from the start of the Rhyd-Ddu
path onto Snowdon. But nothing beats being up there on the rim of the cliff
itself, looking down at the world from a bird's perspective [17-21].

*Views from the top are stunning, particularly out towards the Llŷn peninsula,
and Yr Eifl. From such an altitude Llyn Nantlle Uchaf and the tiny settlements
on the valley floor look unreal, as if they have been captured on an aerial*

*photograph [17-22]. Incidentally, for those of you planning on taking photographs during this walk, you could well be disappointed if you hoped to catch dramatic pictures of the Nantlle Ridge. For much of the day you will end up pointing your camera directly into the sun so could well end up with little more than dramatic silhouettes [17-23 shows Mynydd Tal-y-mignedd from the summit of Mynydd Mawr]. A walk taken at dawn or dusk, of course, is the obvious solution.*

Beyond the final notch of the Craig y Bera escarpment the path can be clearly seen heading to your right, away from the cliff edge, rising slightly before turning further right again onto the lower slopes of the main summit [17-24].

**6)**     **(542543)**     →

       **340°**          →

Mynydd Mawr is nowhere particularly steep, and from this Southern approach you will hopefully be able to make out the easiest line to follow [17-25]. Firstly make your way onto the broad platform half way up [17-26], then trend across the slope around to the right of the rocky summit where a tiny cairn is perched on this slope at **541545**, presumably placed there to guide you in murky weather.

From the cairn bear left, crossing loose rocks to gain the actual summit itself [17-27] – a low windbreak marking **Mynydd Mawr** (at **539546** – 698m/2290ft).

*Not for the first time today your eyes will be drawn to the views out to the South West – towards Yr Eifl and the Nantlle vale [17-28].*
*Behind you, as well as the Moel Eilio-Moel Cynghorion ridge and Snowdon [17-29], the frayed top of Tryfan can be spotted peering above the shallow gap of Cwm Cneifio alongside Glyder Fawr [17-30].*
*But from this summit you also get your first glimpse out to sea – in particular towards the South Western tip of Anglesey; the sand dunes of Newborough Warren [17-31] and the tiny 'island' of Ynys Llanddwyn complete with lighthouse [17-32] (this island is the shrine of St. Dwynwen – the Welsh version of*

*St. Valentine). The 'island' is actually attached to Anglesey by a thread of land.*

As well as admiring the natural scenery it is worth bearing in mind that the Nantlle area was once as vital to the Welsh economy as Llanberis or Blaenau Ffestiniog. Slate was mined from the nearby hillsides. The mass of slate tips above the village of Nantlle are testimony to this area's industrial past – a 180-metre deep hole was excavated as part of the Dorothea slate mine, hence the large amount of waste. There used to be a second lake in the valley – Llyn Nantlle Isaf, but as the Dorothea quarries developed it was found that the lake was flooding the workings. The river channel of the Afon Llyfni was deepened and the lower lake drained until all that remain now are water meadows.

At the time the Dorothea was not only the deepest slate mine in the UK but also the largest man-made hole in the world. More recently its flooded shafts have become a Mecca for divers (although a dozen or so lives have been claimed by its dark waters).

What amazes me is the contrast between the almost pristine elegance of Llyn Nantlle Uchaf [17-33] and the waste tips less than a mile to the North [17-34], both the indirect result of the area's geological past. Geologically, the slate of the Nantlle area is of the same age as that at Blaenau Ffestiniog (Ordovician) – considerably younger than the Cambrian slates of Llanberis and the Penrhyn Quarry.

Fortunately Mynydd Mawr has evaded such extensive excavation – it is composed of different rock – granite rather than slate.

7)   (539546)   →

  160°   →

As you may have guessed, the return is a straightforward retracing of your steps so does not require any detailed description. Just turn around and do the walk in reverse.

## OPTION 1

However, it is possible to extend the last leg of the walk by way of the upper Nantlle vale and the village of Rhyd-Ddu.

When you reach the ladder stile at **point 3**, instead of turning left to cross the fence, turn right to follow a fairly straightforward path descending Westwards.

On your left the path passes a boggy trough between the prominent crag of Clogwynygarreg and the higher slopes.

This boggy area is all that remains of the Northern extension of Llyn y Dywarchen, a reservoir tucked behind Clogwynygarreg, and nowadays used by anglers [17-35].

As it passes the Northern tip of Clogwynygarreg your path is squeezed through the gap in a concrete barrier [17-36] before following the line of an old level, crossing a couple of footbridges and emerging on the B4418.

Turn left and follow this steep road as it climbs due East then SouthEast past the access to the reservoir.

Its shoreline provides one of the finest viewpoints from which to admire the Western face of Snowdon, after which all that's left to do is continue along the minor road to Rhyd-Ddu, turn left at the junction with the A4085, and within less than 1Km you reach the start point of the walk.

*additional time – no more than 1hr 30mins*

---

Llyn y Dywarchen has an island in its centre which, as recently as the last century, was believed to float upon the surface of the lake. Local legend had it that the island changed its position depending on the currents and wind direction, often carrying unsuspecting cattle along with it.

**END**

# WALK 18

## Y Garn [57] / Mynydd Drws-y-Coed [58] / Trum y Ddysgl [59] / Mynydd Tal-y-Mignedd [60] / Craig Cwm Silyn [61] / Garnedd-goch [62] / Mynydd Graig Goch [63]

**28 Km (17.5 miles)**

**1355m (4444ft)**

**Time : 9hrs 30min**

**Seven peaks linked in a magnificent chain – the Nantlle Ridge – extending from the base of Snowdon almost to the Western seaboard.**

Prestige, the coefficient of 'cool' or 'uncool', is a strange thing that makes many of us do things by convention rather than by choice.

It's a fair bet that 95% or more of the vehicles parked at Rhyd-Ddu on any given weekend belong to walkers destined for the top of Snowdon. A mere handful will have crossed the road and tackled by far the best ridge walk in North Wales.

It's true that a complete traverse of the ridge presents logistical problems unless one is prepared to reverse the long walk out. But the sad fact is that if you tell most people you have actually walked up Snowdon they will look upon you with greater 'esteem' than if you let slip that you have walked the Nantlle Ridge end to end (unless they are fellow hill-walkers).

If these seven tops were a few miles further away from Yr Wyddfa, the ridge would undoubtedly be as popular with hill-walkers as the Glyderau. But regardless of the herd instinct to head East, I can guarantee that if you have not yet set foot on the ridge, once you do so you will be more than eager to revisit them again and again.

**North**

**Don't forget**

**map/compass
whistle/torch**

**suitable footwear
+ clothing**

**food/drink**

**brain**

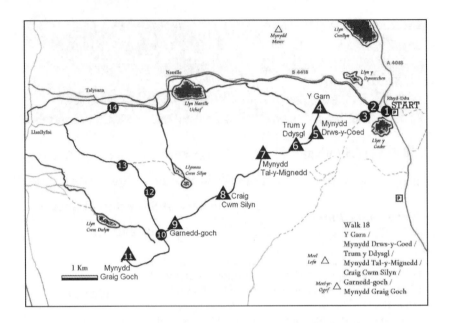

## APPROACH

Travelling from Caernarfon, follow the Beddgelert road (A4085) through Caeathro and Waunfawr, passing the NorthEastern shore of Llyn Cwellyn. 1 Km beyond the inflow of this lake you enter the village of Rhyd-Ddu. The main pay-and-display car park is at the Southern end of the village just after the last of the houses on the left hand side of the road (at **571526**)

From Beddgelert to the South, follow the Caernarfon road (A4085) along Nant Colwyn. The Nantlle Ridge becomes increasingly prominent on your left and as the forested area recedes from the roadside you will see Llyn y Gader, again on your left. Rhyd-Ddu is less than ½ Km beyond with the main pay-and-display car park on your right just before you enter the village.

This car park is busy most weekends, and throughout the summer; it being the starting point of the popular Rhyd-Ddu path up Snowdon. In recent years, following the renovation and continued extension SouthEastwards of the 'Welsh Highland Light Railway' from Waunfawr to Beddgelert (and eventually to Porthmadog), it now also serves passengers using the stop created at Rhyd-Ddu. Consequently, an early arrival is recommended (particularly as the walk is a lengthy one).

---

## OPTION 1

If you wish to avoid paying the parking fee, there is space for three or four cars at the roadside at **567526**. Starting your walk from here also cuts out the 400-metre crossing of the floodplain of the Afon Gwyrfai as it exits Llyn y Gader.

If you park here, commence the walk as from **point 2**.

### *Time saved – approx 20 mins*

## OPTION 2

Logistically, the ideal alternative to a protracted road-walk back to Rhyd-Ddu at the end of the day is to have your car waiting for you at the Western end of the ridge – close to the road-end at **496511**. This can be achieved quite easily when two car-owners tackle the walk together; the second car being used to run the walkers to Rhyd-Ddu for the start of the walk while the first is left at the road-end.*** see Option 7

To reach this parking spot by car, follow the Nantlle valley along the B4418, passing through Nantlle village itself (if travelling from Rhyd-Ddu) and crossing the Afon Llyfni bridge where the river exits Llyn Nantlle Uchaf. Some 500 metres or so after passing the Ty Mawr East slate tips on your left (now a waste storage site) take the next side road left alongside a small housing estate (a sign just beyond this turning marks the start of Talysarn village). Follow this side road for 1½ Km then take the first turning left again (easy to miss – it's just after you pass one of a pair of houses on your right – the second of which, 'Gwynfaes', is painted completely white). Follow this minor road right to its end where a rusty gate gives access to open ground with more than adequate parking space (at **496511 – point 13**).

If driving from Penygroes, take the Talysarn/Nantlle road (B4118), passing the leisure centre and bypassing any exits left into Talysarn itself. The B4118 then takes a sharp turn right to cross the Afon Llyfni, following which the housing estate appears on your right with the side road to the right again immediately afterwards. Follow this for 1½ Km before taking the minor road left and following it right to its end.

## START

**1)**    **(571526)**    →

    **260°**    →

No matter how many cars you use, the preferred starting point for the walk is at the Rhyd-Ddu end. From the pay-and-display car park, exit onto the road and pass through the metal kissing-gate directly opposite the car park entrance [18-01]. This leads onto a sunken causeway of slate slabs crossing extremely wet ground comprising the Northern shore of Llyn y Gader [18-02]. In places the slabs are submerged, but with a hop and a skip it is possible to reach the far end of this crossing with your boots dry.

On reaching the straggle of trees ahead of you, with a white cottage to its right [18-03] the path drops down left to follow the banks of the river draining out of Llyn y Gader (the Afon Gwyrfai). Here your direction-finding is ably assisted by an arrow sign affixed to one of the trees and a slightly slapdash handrail of green metal piping. Almost immediately you are led to a metal gate allowing entrance to your right onto the footbridge crossing the river [18-04].

A ladder stile with signs advising you that you are entering sheep-grazing country gives access to a broad, dishevelled footpath of slabs and wet mud, penned in on two sides by wire fencing. This quickly leads to a broad, gravelled track which is the private drive to the property on your right (Tan-y-Llyn) at **568526** [18-05].

    **280°**    →

Facing Tan-y-Llyn, you will see a narrow path crossing the opposite verge and heading off to the left onto a rise covered in reeds and gorse bushes (there is also a small 'footpath' sign adjacent) [18-06]. Follow this footpath briefly uphill then down again across a muddy section to rejoin the driveway [18-07]. Continue heading right until you reach a galvanised metal gate with a metal ladder-stile beside it [18-08].

Crossing this stile places you at the roadside (the B4118) with a bridleway sign pointing through a flimsier metal swing-gate on the left [18-09 looking back from the other side of the gate].

Up until the early 1970's walkers were barred from setting foot on the Nantlle Ridge as local landowners fiercely guarded their private property. Fortunately, the Snowdonia National Park Authority have since been able to agree access arrangements with all concerned.

The galvanised gate marking the entry to Tan-y-Llyn bears a sign instructing all walkers that the driveway is a private road, and should only be used for access to the footpath following the direction signs. Respect these instructions as it is in all walkers' interests that private landowners are not subject to situations that might make them regret allowing access to their land.

**2)      (566526)      →**

      **225°      →**

Pass through the swing-gate and follow the clear track across flat, marshy ground, keeping the dry-stone wall then wire fence to your right [18-10]. You eventually reach a wooden gate at the end of this track. Pass through the gate, ignoring the entrance gate on the right to Drws-y-Coed Uchaf farm [18-11]. Instead turn immediately left and follow the broad track which swings to your right after crossing a small makeshift bridge, reaching a ladder-stile beside another farm gate a short distance ahead of you (almost exactly on the 200-metre contour).

Beyond this stile a minor track veers away to the left, keeping to the lower ground. This crosses the Western shores of the Llyn y Gader basin, reclaimed from its quarrying past, as it heads towards the multitude of bridleways, mountain cycle tracks and footpaths that criss-cross the Beddgelert Forest. But your route involves scaling the hillside facing you [18-12 from **Walk 16**].

**3)      (564524)      →**

      **255°      →**

Once you have crossed the ladder-stile (or walked through the open gate alongside it), start heading upslope. In places the path is indistinct, crossing muddy or water-logged turf, scars of bare rock (one next to a boulder with a large white arrow painted on it pointing left) [18-13] and the occasional dry patch. But boot-prints and a line of eroded furrows reveal the way ahead [18-14]. A fence crosses the meagre grazing ground above you with another ladder stile and metal gate alongside it [18-15]. Cross the stile and continue up steeper ground onto the broad flanks of Y Garn.

Across this section much of the path is confined to the (mainly) dry courses of seasonal mountain streams; shallow ruts of varying steepness bedded by shattered shale and mud. But eventually the angle of slope relents above the 550-metre contour as the path levels out. For a while here it skims close to the cliff edge on your right [18-16], giving an awesome glimpse of the vale below, before advancing further to crest the skyline above [18-17].

*Unless you have already paused to regain breath, you will probably not have paid much regard to what's behind you. But take a moment now to study the view East before other attractions divert your attention.*

*Llyn y Gader nestles at the foot of Yr Aran [18-18] – the Southern ridge of Snowdon flexing its shoulders behind the village of Rhyd-Ddu [18-19].*

*Further left lies Llyn y Dywarchen; the smooth slopes of Moel Eilio, Foel Gron and Foel Goch forming a superb backdrop [18-20 and 18-21].*

Once you top the next shoulder of ground you are confronted by a massive wall of grey, angular boulders [18-22]. Crossing these takes a degree of care – some have lain immobile for centuries whilst others wobble with the least touch. A line of rust-tinted rocks shows the route numerous boots have trodden before you.

The ground levels off again before a dry-stone wall crosses the low skyline ahead, complete with ladder stile [18-23]. The final obstacle is a section of collapsed wall that merges into the boulder-field. Clamber above this, cross the ladder stile and you are suddenly on the flat top of the day's first summit. More boulders provide much of the same scenery, as well as two massive stone cairns, and a smaller one off to the right perched close to the precipice marking the summit point of **Y Garn** (at **551526** – 633m/2076ft).

There is a good deal of evidence on top of Y Garn that ancient burials took place here (beneath the large cairns).

The ancient practice of burying the dead beneath cairns was considered a pagan practice once Christianity took hold in Wales, with only thieves and murderers being interred in such fashion afterwards. Bwlch Gylfin, on the valley floor directly below Y Garn, supposedly holds the remains of defeated soldiers (as attested by the multitude of burnt bones found there).

*Prepare to prop open your eyelids. The view West from this summit has to be one of the most impressive in Snowdonia, largely due to the sheer drop on three sides and the sweep of the Nantlle Vale literally at your feet [18-24].*

*The pale, scree-covered walls beneath Craig y Bera merely add to the superlatives offered by this vista [18-25].*

**4)**    **(551526)**    →

      175°        →

Once you have drunk in enough of the views, turn and look South at the talon of black rock that claws at the sky. This is where you are headed next. A broad, vegetation-covered notch lies between the summit point and the Westernmost cairn adjacent to the dry-stone wall that plunges SouthWest to Clogwyn y Barcud. From the upper lip of this notch a faint path crosses the platform of tussocky grass in the direction of Mynydd Drws-y-Coed.

This mountain is a total contrast to Y Garn. A mere 100 metres above its level-headed neighbour, it presents a series of intriguing rocky obstacles; spiced with exciting exposure to your right. And from a distance it is easily picked out from neighbouring tops by the bite-mark in its summit ridge [18-26 from the South West].

The approach path follows the line of the dry-stone wall to your left before reaching a field of grey angular blocks where the easier route heads off to the right, close to the edge of the deep chasm beneath the Clogwyn y Marchnad cliffs [18-27 looking back towards Y Garn, and 18-28].

*Even at the height of summer this section of ridge can present a creepy setting when the clouds close in. Its proximity to the sea invites curtains of low cloud to scrape its highest rocks en route to Snowdon. Like an open-topped sports car with the obligatory trailing white scarf, clouds tear themselves to streamers and shreds as they pass between the jagged teeth of the ridge.*

*Sinister outcrops of grey rock overhang the corrie – one bearing the profile of a Roman-nosed head [18-29], another resembling the 'cannon' on Tryfan's North face. To reach the summit, you have to pass within an arm's reach of these weird sculptures.*

*But when the clouds clear, all sense of foreboding is removed by an exciting preview of the route ahead [18-30].*

The final challenge on the approach to the next summit is a stubborn stud of fractured rock, near-vertical as you approach it from the North A short scramble of 5 metres or so plonks you on its flat top, but despite the multitude of hand-holds it is the kind of ascent that once started cannot be reversed. An alternative approach involves dropping left to a low cleft within the mountain's fractured Eastern face and scrambling up a wide notch from which one can haul oneself onto the rocky top.

Eventually the path appears again, meandering between the final splinters of shale onto the highest point of **Mynydd Drws-y-Coed** (at **548518** – 695m/2280ft).

**5)      (548518)        →**

     **195°              →**

Exposure on the right does not relent as your path now circles the corrie headwall in search of the next summit a short distance away. But the path here is much easier to follow, with the amplitude of the helter-skelter element much dampened. Outcrops of grey, gnarled rock are easily by-passed as smoother, level ground emerges; the narrow pathway worn into the smooth turf capping for much of the way [18-31 looking back towards Mynydd Drws-y-Coed].

As you top the final rise a ladder stile stands guard on the left giving access beyond the wire fences to an expanse of gentle, green slopes above Cwm Du and the Beddgelert Forest [18-32]. But ignore this stile as the path to the summit runs off to the right and roughly parallel to this eroded path before emerging on the exposed top of **Trum y Ddysgl** (at **545516** – 709m/2326ft).

---

### OPTION 3

For a hasty exit off the ridge where weather conditions require it, cross the aforementioned ladder stile and contour South along the long spur dropping to the forested slopes blanketing Cwm Du [18-33].

Once you reach one of the numerous tracks that run through the Beddgelert Forest it's a matter of heading East towards the bridleway that leads Northwards along the foot of Y Garn and eventually to **point 4**.

***Time saved – about 6hrs 30min***

If you miss this altogether, numerous cycle tracks lead East into the forest before joining the Rhyd-Ddu road at **576509**, less than 2Km South of the car park.

---

6)      (545516)       →

230°                    →

In low cloud or limited visibility it is worth checking your compass at this point to ensure you do not inadvertently head downslope to your left onto the spur separating Cwm Du from Cwm Dwyfor. If you make this mistake, you will begin to notice a rapid increase in gradient to your left and the further downhill you stray the more gruelling a haul you face regaining the steep slopes to your right. The path from Trum y Ddysgl is barely a smudge on a smooth, broad convex slope of patchy grass [18-34 looking back up to the summit].

It leads gently down to the 590-metre contour where a slender saddle of ground links this hill and the next. From a distance, crossing this saddle to gain the slopes leading to the next top looks a stroll [18-35]. But at its lowest point the path is forced to cross three deep notches which are virtually hidden until you are upon them [18-36]. The correct line across this triple bogey presents no great difficulty and soon you regain the fairway that extends towards the ascending slopes beyond. An untidy, dry-stone wall on your left accompanies the final section of path as it advances upon a better-constructed wall crossing the skyline ahead. Pass through the gap in this wall and on your right stands the obelisk identifying the top of **Mynydd Tal-y-Mignedd** (at **535513** – 653m/2142ft) [18-37].

This obelisk was erected by local quarrymen to celebrate Queen Victoria's Jubilee in 1887.

I have mixed memories regarding the very first time I set foot on this ridge. As I picked my way across the crags of Mynydd Drws-y-Coed, two young lads from Manchester caught up with me and insisted I continue the rest of the walk in their company even though they appeared to be a good deal fitter than me. The day had little else to offer – low cloud and heavy drizzle meant there was little if any scenery to admire. By the time we reached the top of Mynydd Tal-y-Mignedd we were ready for refreshments. One of the lads decided he was going to climb to the top of the obelisk first; so up he went using just his fingers and the soles of his boots for support. Posing high above us, his brashness soon deserted him once he realised he would not be able to get down as easily.

By the time we finished our snack five more walkers had turned up, a group of young 'executive-types' from Cambridge. For some unknown reason we all decided to continue the ridge walk as a single group – the 'Cambridge Five' leading the way. Some thirty minutes or so later the cloud thinned enough to reveal the surrounding countryside for the first time that day. Llyn Nantlle Uchaf nestling in the sunlight below our feet was not what we were expecting to see! Instead of dropping down to Bwlch Dros-bern, our guides had mistakenly led us down the North West spur of Mynydd Tal-y-Mignedd. That's what comes of trusting someone who lives somewhere flat I suppose.

**7)**       **(535513)**          →

       **195°**           →

Don't make the same mistake that we did that day – a quick check of the compass takes only a few seconds, but can save a good deal of embarrassment, and perhaps avoid unexpectedly truncating a marvellous walk.

The descent of Mynydd Tal-y-Mignedd's Southern spur begins as an easy-going stroll, until you drop below the 600-metre contour. Beyond this point the smooth, gentle, grassy slopes are transformed into a rough, weathered spillway of vertical slabs and serrated rock, more perilous when made slimy by condensation [18-38 looking back to the summit from the col].

Recent reports in the outdoor press of 'hill rage' had left me bemused. Could it possibly be true that walkers were being bullied by more aggressive sorts who were on a mission to get to the next top ahead of everyone else?

The descent path from Mynydd Tal-y-Mignedd is the last place you would want to be when Whacky Races kick off. Yet suddenly I heard the tramp of running feet behind me as three male veloceraptors raced past at break-neck speed, dressed in black Lycra with day-glo logos and flimsy running shoes.

A short distance further back, two females of the species followed, lost in conversation, but still focussed on keeping up with their partners.

*"…..the weird thing is that everybody's heard of me….."*

I side-stepped onto a flimsy pedestal of rock alongside the narrow path to allow them to overtake. No gesture of acknowledgement. No slowing of pace.

*"…..but none of them have ever met me….."*

I watched as the pair practically danced down the steep track, hopping from one red-hot rock to the next, arms wide apart and raised at elbow height as if steering some imaginary bicycle.

I guess anyone could feel momentarily intimidated by such an incident if one was of a nervous disposition. Me, I just felt envious of their nimble feet and superior sense of balance. The feeling soon passed – I was out here to enjoy the day, not to set some new land speed record. Besides, I figured there was more chance of them needing rescuing than me once they twisted an ankle or two.

Eventually the angle of slope does relent as you reach the lowest point of the col (515 metres at **532508**). Bwlch Dros-bern is a broad saddle with a slight hump half way along it [18-39 and 18-40]. Clamber over this and you easily reach the ramparts of the next summit [18-41].

270°       →

A faint path, attached in places to isolated fragments of dry-stone wall, appears from nowhere high up on the Eastern face of Craig Cwm Silyn. It is possible to clamber up the crags to the right of this path to reach the skyline. But the vertical section is a tough scramble [18-42] which may prove too much for those of you whose legs are beginning to feel the pace so late into the walk.

A short detour to the right adds very little to the length of the walk and soon gives easier access onto the rocky heights. A faint track runs along the base of the mountain in the general direction of the Craig-las valley [18-43]. Look out for a sizeable slab of rock on the right-hand side of this path shaped like a miniature sugar-loaf (rounded shoulders forming its right side but a vertical wall its left) [18-44]. To the left of this rock a faint path of paler gravel exits upslope and winds through the grey outcrops onto the main hillside, rapidly gaining height as it trends increasingly Southwards [18-45]. Eventually it runs up against the dry-stone wall marking the overhang of Craig Pennant beyond which the sheer corrie wall drops into the valley of Ceunant yr Allt above the headwaters of the Afon Dwyfor in Cwm Pennant itself.

Keeping this wall on your left now, follow the indistinct path steeply onto the broad top. You are immediately confronted by a boulder-field reminiscent of that on Y Garn (although closer up you may think it bears more similarity to the one on Glyder Fawr) [18-46]. Pick your way carefully through the frost-shattered slabs until you reach a broad cairn on your right marking the summit of **Craig Cwm Silyn** (at **525502** – 734m/2408m) – the high point of the day [18-47 from Garnedd-goch].

*A final chance perhaps to study the magnificent ridge behind you [18-48] before turning Westwards again to face the next challenge; the gentler outline of Garnedd-goch with the outlying massif of Yr Eifl peering over its right-hand shoulder.*
*To the left Morfa Bychan and Morfa Harlech probe the Irish Sea, whilst to the right the lowlands between here and Caernarfon stretch to the Menai Strait. You also get an opportunity to study Llyn Nantlle Uchaf nestling in the Nantlle Vale – and the road along which you could well be walking close to the end of the day.*

**8)**    **(525502)**    →

**250°**    →

After such exertions, the following section is a welcome respite. The flat top of Craig Cwm Silyn and its neighbour, scattered with splintered boulders, extends Eastwards for more than 1½ Km. En route to Garnedd-goch you pass a substantial cairn poised above a mass of splintered grey slabs and later a square-sided cairn-cum-windbreak overlooking a collection of boulders on the right as the ground descends gradually [18-49 looking back along this section of ridge].

To the extreme right of this is a sheer drop into Cwm Silyn itself with its twin lakes hidden from view far below. The rocks above this basin are the haunt of rock climbers – the Great Slab being a particular favourite. However, the topography we are faced with is considerably less demanding. Incidentally, neither cairn already encountered marks the actual summit point of this rocky plateau.

A gap in a dry-stone wall at **518499** allows you to advance along the right-hand side of a second wall running ahead towards the main top. Where the wall forms a corner with two others [18-50], a ladder stile gives access to the flat summit plateau of **Garnedd-goch** (its triangulation pillar clearly identified at **511495** – 700m/2296ft).

> **OPTION 5**
> Should you decide that Garnedd-goch is to be your final summit of the day it is possible to bear right at the triangulation pillar now and follow the line of a wall down steep slopes to **point 12**, but this short-cut can be particularly arduous and is not recommended. If you insist on missing out the seventh top, Option 6 provides a less demanding escape route.

**9)**    **(511495)**    →

**230°**    →

From the summit continue ahead down the slopes into the col of Bwlch Cwmdulyn. These slopes are much more walker-friendly than those descending Mynydd Tal-y-Mignedd [18-51] and by keeping the dry-stone wall to your left, it is a simple matter to make your way downhill as directly or indirectly as you wish.

*As you drop further into this dauntingly deep col, there is the bonus of the expanding view below you and to your right of Llyn Cwm Dylun [18-52 and 18-53]. Another comforting compensation at this stage in such a long walk is that your route does not involve a direct descent to the floor of this deeply-incised valley.*

You only need to continue downhill until you meet the clear path running right to left directly across the heather-clad hillside (at **508492**) [18-54]. This path runs across slope, passing through one of several gaps in the wall.

---

### OPTION 6
Many hill-walkers walking the ridge ignore the seventh top – deciding it is not a valid part of the ridge-walk due to its relatively lowly height. Should you decide that this last summit is one hill too far then this is the best point at which to head for low ground.
Turn right onto this path, proceeding as if at **point 10 (revisited)**.

*Time saved – approx 1hr 15min*

---

The path's appearance is also marked by a small cairn bearing an upright slab in its centre [18-55]. Although this assemblage of rocks appears rather ephemeral compared to the colossal piles on the mountain tops, it serves an obvious purpose in identifying the main escape route off the ridge.

**10)**  **(508492)**  →

145°  →

From the aforementioned cairn turn left, crossing the wall by way of the adjacent gap, and follow the path's extension East of South across the slope.

Descending less than 10 metres, the path soon reaches the headwall of the valley entering Llyn Cwm Dulyn [18-56].

As the path crosses the headwall in a gentle loop another dry-stone wall crosses the skyline from the left. To your right the stream feeding Llyn Cwm Dulyn soaks its way between two scree terraces before plunging down more steeply over the 500-metre contour. Fortunately the path steers well East of this tricky section [18-57].

Fairly flat, featureless ground now heads gradually upslope towards steeper terrain. Greeting you en route to the main summit area is a small barrier of crags topped by a small cairn [18-58]. This is easily crossed to reach another featureless plateau beyond. From a distance this ground looks as if it should be sodden and difficult to cross, but the opposite is true. Patches of loose rock appear here and there where the turf capping has been eroded away, but any surface water is clearly visible and easy to avoid.

Eventually you are confronted by a gnarled collection of grey rocks forming a long wall spanning the summit area from South East to North West. The best approach is to join this wall at its South Eastern end (on your left) where a small dry-stone windbreak marks the start of the path to the skyline [18-59].

Scrambling through the loose rock you quickly gain a minor summit topped by a cairn [18-60]. Of course, this is not the true top. That would be too easy. Descend Westwards, carefully picking your way through the rough, angular slabs of rock that litter this vast area. Ahead of you on the skyline is a serrated crest of rock with a wall beneath it [18-61].

Head for this wall, and as you get closer turn right in order to find somewhere to cross. It soon becomes apparent that there is no crossing point – unless you follow the wall all the way right to where it makes an unsuccessful attempt to ascend a plug of rock [18-62]. The top of that plug is the actual summit. But there are still rocks and views to explore on the crest ahead of you.

As you get closer to the corner where the wall takes a right-angled turn towards the summit plug, you will find a set of three stepping stones jutting out of the wall [18-63]. These have been placed there to allow walkers to climb over to its opposite side. It's a tricky manoeuvre since the descending steps on the opposite side have for some reason been placed behind you (requiring one to perform a 180° turn once you reach the top of the wall).

There then follows a short, ascent across solid, step-like crags, following an anti-clockwise, spiral route right up onto the crest itself. Although the immediate foreground is an untidy mess of large grey slabs and frost-shattered boulders, the views to the ends of the peninsula are spectacular in all directions [18-64]. This is the Western-most top of the ridge walk, indeed the Westernmost summit of all those visited in this series of walks so drink in all you can [18-65 and 18-66].

*From here the expanse of the Llŷn peninsula is laid out ahead of you, backed by a blue sea that embraces it from all sides. And behind you the sinuous line of rock that stretches almost all the way to Snowdon's top.*
*Unfortunately, due to its proximity to the Irish Sea, haze or low cloud frequently obliterate much of what lies beyond.*

To gain the main summit, drop down easily to a patch of open ground alongside the wall you recently crossed. Take a line slightly left of where the wall runs head-on into the rock plug [18-67]. This allows you to scramble to within spitting distance of the top – but unless you are a rock climber you will need to circle left, and cross another dry-stone wall that abuts the opposite side of the rock plug. From here it's a matter of hopping up a couple of shallow steps onto the lichen-coated crag that forms the summit of **Mynydd Graig Goch** (at **497485** – 610m/2000ft).

Amusingly enough, this 'minor' top has only recently been re-measured (September 2008) and suddenly acquired official, elevated status to 'mountain' – the Ordnance Survey were able to confirm that the summit reaches 609.75m (which means it tops 2000ft by 6 inches). I have no doubt that walkers who have in the past ignored this ridge will suddenly be revisiting this corner of Snowdonia in order to reach the elusive seventh top!

**11)**     **(497485)**     →

      135°          →

Although it is possible to descend the Western flanks of the ridge in order to reach one of the minor roads far South of Llanllyfni I would strongly dissuade anyone from doing so. There is no designated footpath to the West of this end of the ridge, several dry-stone walls bar the way since you are crossing enclosed farmland, and the lower sections would certainly involve some degree of trespass. Besides that, the walk back by road to Rhyd-Ddu from this neck of the woods does not bear thinking about. Similarly, I would advise you not to attempt a more direct return to the cairn first encountered at **point 10** even though a dry-stone wall leads North Eastwards from the summit.

The Northern and Eastern slopes of Mynydd Graig Goch are unrelentingly steep as they drop to the shoreline of Cwm Dulyn. For a while it is feasible to follow the right hand side of this wall as it exits the summit. Then, when it begins to fall more steeply to low ground (where the path heading the same way passes through a small gap between the wall and a massive block of rock), veer right to contour across the hillside. You will easily reach the small cairn on the low crest ahead of you From here, bear right again across more featureless ground, reversing the ascent route as you cross the valley headwall and you soon reach that gap in the wall again and the cairn at **508492** [18-68].

**10)**     **(508492)**     →

      320°          →

Continue straight ahead now along this faint track as it contours the Western slopes of Garnedd-goch, dropping gradually as it crosses bare turf and a number of waterlogged patches. The further you follow it, the clearer it becomes. For much of its way a curious collection of tiny standing stones (almost like headstones) strategically identify the correct line of the path – an invaluable aid when snow covers the ground [18-69].

However, close to the 490-metre contour (at **505496**) the path splits in two on the map but not so clearly on the ground. After a short section of steeper descent along a stony section of path, look out for where it becomes grassy again as it runs down left across the slope in the direction of the main valley floor [18-70]. Since you need to continue well to the right, look out for traces of another path rising across the slope close to the base of the boulder outcrops scarring the hillside above [18-71]. Once you spot it, patches of trampled grass become more apparent as you weave your way gradually upslope again towards the skyline. More stone markers soon confirm the correct route. And where the path skirts the lower margins of the boulder-field on your right you will pass close to a large, grey boulder resembling the tip of an asparagus [18-72 and 18-73 looking back from further along the path]. To its left on the immediate horizon a single finger of rock points the way ahead. The path heads that way and begins to assert itself once more. Suddenly the landscape opens up ahead of you revealing easier ground and the first signs since you left the car park this morning that habitation might be near at hand [18-74].

It is advisable to study the lie of the land from here (if visibility allows) and work out your next move. For example, take note of the patch of dark forest plantation beyond the lowland directly ahead of you – keep well clear of the low ground leading towards it or anywhere left of it, no matter how much more direct that descent route may appear from these lofty slopes. Instead, the route you need to follow aims for the foot of the low hill to the right of that plantation; specifically it aims for the right-hand corner of the triangular field at the hill's base. Finding your way to that spot significantly reduces the distance you will eventually have to cover by road if you are headed back to Rhyd-Ddu. – And, of course, if you took Option 2 this is where your wheels will be waiting for you [18-75].

As the path circles the lower flanks of Garnedd-goch, heath-land is replaced by tussocky grass and two walls appear ahead of you – one descending from the high slopes to your right, the other crossing low ground ahead of you and to your left [18-76 looking back from a short distance East of the car parking area]. According to the Explorer map the path you are following crosses the wall ahead of you and on your left before it joins the second wall descending from your right. But in reality the path runs right into the corner where both walls meet. There a sturdy wooden gate leads you onto lower ground to your left [18-77]. The second wall descending from your right, incidentally, follows the direct but arduous route to the summit of Garnedd-goch (referred to in **Option 5**).

**12)**  **(504503)**  →

   **320°**  →

Pass through this gate and follow the line of descending wall (keeping to the left of it) until you reach the margins of a large stone enclosure [18-78]. The wall keeps to the right of this enclosure, but your path passes to its left. Just beyond, a small scattering of boulders leads you to a ladder stile in the wall ahead of you.

Once you have crossed the ladder stile you are inside a small paddock. In the wall ahead of you and to your left is another ladder stile (at **498508**) which the map suggests you should make for along the 'footpath' shown. Don't even attempt it. The solid ground this 'path' crosses is in fact a complex network of streams, bogs and a mass of sodden turf floating on deep black water. I suppose there are days when being a map-maker is not the best job in the universe – when it's wet and miserable, turning dark even though there are still acres of featureless terrain to study, measure and record. On days like that one can excuse someone marking a path on the map that is visible from afar – even if that person never actually set foot on it for want of time.

There is a much easier solution. Once you cross the first ladder stile into the paddock, keep going straight ahead along a muddy path running parallel to the paddock's right-hand boundary wall. As you reach a patch of grassy, wet ground where a stream emerges from the wall on your right, veer closer to the wall by crossing the stream. Follow the stream's bank to the corner of the paddock where a breach in the wall is ineffectively blocked by a rusted sheet of corrugated metal [18-79].

Cross the collapsed wall at the right-hand side of this metal barrier to enter a dry corner of tussocky grassland with a fence closing it off from the rest of the field. If you bear right here you will find that one of the fence-posts has been shortened to allow you to step over into the field beyond. Turn left after crossing that fence and head slightly upslope along a section of track.

The track bears right, but if you go left you will find a clear path running parallel to, and on the right side of, a combination of dry-stone wall and wire fence [18-80]. This path crosses a shallow dip before climbing easy ground to reach a large track running left to right (providing access to walkers and cyclists to the twin lakes of Llynnau Cwm Silyn).

On your left the track runs through an open gateway (poorly served by a rusty gate) [18-81]. Follow this track through that gateway and it shortly leads to a closed, rusty metal gate in another wall ahead of you. There is space on this side of the wall for a dozen cars or so – perhaps yours is amongst them, or could it be that they all belong to other walkers, or climbers chancing their skills on the slabs above Cwm Silyn?

**13)**     **(496511)**     →

No compass directions needed from here really. If you are returning to Rhyd-Ddu by foot, as I have on numerous occasions in the past, you have a 12½ Km road-walk ahead of you. If you are fortunate to be accompanied by fair weather then at least you will be able to make the most of an enjoyable walk through the Nantlle Vale.

---

OPTION 7
If you did leave your car here, this is where you get in it and drive off into the sunset.
*Time saved – 2hrs 45min*
***One more recently available alternative (2009) is to employ the services of a local taxi company **(Huw's Taxis – 01286 676767 or 07967 881903)** who will ferry you from **point 13** to Rhyd-Ddu either at the start or finish of a linear walk for little more than the cost of a day's parking at Rhyd-Ddu.

---

Whether you are on foot or wheels, you need to open that rusty gate in order to join the metalled lane behind it. Follow this lane downhill, passing a number of small-holdings (many in ruins), and many hopefully still thriving – including "The Railway Study Centre" at 'Tal-eithin Isaf'. Intrigued? I was. I kept imagining a converted barn full of apprentice station announcers wearing headphones, and honing their pronunciation techniques.

On your descent from the road-end you will no doubt have noticed quite a number of footpaths (marked on the OS map) heading off to the right of your route, supposedly providing a short-cut North. But most of these paths are no longer viable; the majority lose themselves in the quarry tips littering the lower slopes East of Llanllyfni.

In the 12th century any walk along the Nantlle Vale would have been far more hazardous than it is today. The entire valley was forested, probably up as high as the 600-metre contour, and wolves, foxes and wild stags were hunted. The main hunting lodge was located at Baladeulyn – of sufficient importance to be visited and stayed in by Edward I in 1284. Access to the lodge was by way of a riding trail cut through the forest from Drws-y-Coed.

It was said that the forest was so dense that daylight was only visible as one approached Rhyd-Ddu – close to the high pass called Bwlch Goleugoed (no longer identified on the map, but presumably close to the highest point of the pass at 555533).

Nantlle is reputedly named from the cry released by a strange, mythical beast discovered close to Llyn y Gader. This creature was chased by hunting dogs down the valley to Baladeulyn where it was slain, screaming as it perished. Hence "Nant y Llef" = Valley of the Cry.

However, the valley might also be named for the Celtic sun god – Lleu.

When you finally come to a T-junction, turn right and follow this road past a small collection of houses, a school and the 'Tanrallt Mountain Centre'. After passing a series of slate heaps you approach a small housing estate on your left. Just beyond here the minor road meets the B4418.

**14)    (494526)        →**

No compass directions needed again. Just make sure you turn right onto the B4418 heading towards Nantlle village. The road crosses the Afon Llyfni as it drains out of Llyn Nantlle Uchaf. There was once a Lower Nantlle Lake (Llyn Nantlle Isaf) a short distance East, but quarrying and subsequent waste tipping has obliterated much of it. 'Pont Baladeulyn' (a short distance East of Nantlle village at **514534**) testifies to there being two lakes here in the past ("Baladeulyn" means a low-lying area between two lakes).

Passing through Nantlle these days you are unlikely to come across many wolves or to get lost in the forest – there is even a pavement for a kilometre or so. And you will no doubt have noticed a bus shelter and a couple of bus-stops. Do not be tempted to linger in the hope that public transport will provide you with a painless return to Rhyd-Ddu. At the time of writing, the service from Caernarfon only runs as far as Baladeulyn school (at **516535**) before turning round and heading back towards Penygroes. In theory you could catch this bus on its roundabout run to Caernarfon, then another from there to Beddgelert by way of Rhyd-Ddu – but it is a long round trip!

*The Nantlle Ridge is visible in its entirety along the Southern side of the valley from this point onwards anyway; more than enough inspiration to re-energise the most flagging feet [18-82 and 18-83].*

*Other little features make the walk along the vale a delight. At **519535** a torrent of water crashes down the hillside from the left before passing under the road en route to Llyn Nantlle Uchaf.*

*Further along on your left, the scree slopes and rocky skyline of Craig y Bera compete with the ridge on your right for jaw-dropping views.*

*At **541535** you will come across the poignant skeleton of a small community, Drws-y-Coed village with the gable ends and chimney stacks pretty much all that remain of the quarrymen's cottages almost buried beneath the dark crags of Clogwyn y Barcud.*

*At **547534** what appears to be a massive wall of stone blocks topped by a platform of pastureland turns out to be a hand-built dam confining the dwindling waters of a reservoir. This was no doubt once used by the local mining industry. An incline runs up the opposite hillside towards the gap between the lower slopes of Mynydd Mawr and Clogwynygarreg.*

*The latter, a daunting wedge of striated rock, forms an attractive counterpoint to the summit of Snowdon poised above it [18-84].*

*And as you climb to Bwlch Gylfin and the high ground South of Llyn y Dywarchen (a reservoir now dedicated to fly-fishing) take a look across the valley on your left at the cliffs of Craig y Bera beneath the hidden summit of Mynydd Mawr.*

From the crest of Bwlch Gylfin the road descends in a tight zig-zag to Rhyd-Ddu village, but at least you have the opportunity to reacquaint yourself with the damp shortcut across the Afon Gwyrfai before reaching the A4085.The only buzz left at the end of the walk, if any is needed, is crossing over that last bit of road to reach the car park.


**END**

# Moel Lefn [64] / Moel yr Ogof [65] / Moel Hebog [66]

9.1 Km (5.7 miles)

795m (2608ft)

Time : 4hrs 30min

**The Southern outliers of the Nantlle Ridge – not as popular due to their out-of-the-way location**

Porthmadog on a late summer Bank Holiday Saturday, enjoying perfect weather – filled with traffic and tourists. Porthmadog one week later, with the same weather – now much more restrained. An ideal opportunity to spend half a day in the adjoining hills – after the obligatory pilgrimage to Cob Records, of course.

I had put off this first-ever visit to the Moel Hebog group for a number of months – largely due to the fact that I could not find a straightforward description of an appropriate approach route. I'd already visited the forests North-West of Beddgelert on many occasions – excellent for mountain-biking and orienteering. And I knew that a number of paths led from there to the top of Moel Hebog as well as from the village itself. But getting to the top of all three closely-linked summits without going astray in the network of forestry roads and old tramways that occupy this region seemed easier said than done. Even the maps did not provide a clear-cut solution, until I came across a path from the West that was sure to suit my purpose.

Follow this one and you could well have most of the route to yourself.

**North**

**Don't forget**

**map/compass
whistle/torch**

**suitable footwear
+ clothing**

**food/drink**

**brain**

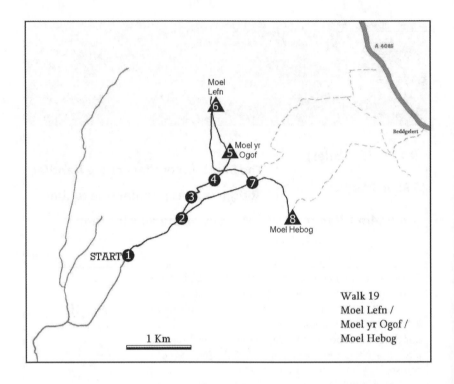

Walk 19
Moel Lefn /
Moel yr Ogof /
Moel Hebog

1 Km

## APPROACH

The Beddgelert side of the Moel Hebog group features a large forest plantation infested with a squirming mass of cycle tracks and paths that are aimed at a 'tourist-friendly' approach to a set of hills that tend to be overlooked by most hill-walkers. There are even orienteering courses laid on if you are interested. In contrast, the view to these summits from the West is far more enticing [19-01]; the only question is "How does one reach them without a trek almost as long as that from Rhyd-Ddu to the farthest end of the Nantlle Ridge?"

There is an answer, as long as you have transport to this fairly remote corner of Snowdonia. Just be warned that the network of lanes serving this region can be more confusing to follow than any mountain path.

Heading from Caernarfon towards Porthmadog along the A487, once you reach the other side of Bryncir village and have passed a road sign pointing left to Garndolbenmaen, look out for a second road sign pointing left to Dolbenmaen and Cwm Pennant. Turn left here and follow this road (increasingly narrow with passing places), ignoring a junction right (towards Cwmystradlyn). After a sharp bend to the right at **526450** (where a lane to your left accesses a bridge crossing Afon Dwyfor) you shortly come to a chapel on the left with a red telephone kiosk and post box directly ahead of you at a two-forked junction (at **531454**). Take the right fork here and follow it to its end.

If you inadvertently drive past the exit for Dolbenmaen and Cwm Pennant you come to another signpost soon after pointing left to Brynkir Woollen Mill, turn left here and follow this road until you come to Golan community centre (the old primary school) on your left. Very shortly afterwards take a junction left turning almost back on yourself. If you reach the Brynkir Woollen Mill on your left you have missed the turning left and gone too far.

This road to the left is the Cwmystradlyn to Cwm Pennant road. Continue along it, passing one junction right (to a dead end) where the road takes a sharp turn left, then crossing the Afon Dwyfor before arriving at a T-junction at **519433** where a sign points right towards Cwm Pennant. Take this right fork and follow it to the two-forked junction described above (at **531454**).

Heading from Tremadoc towards Caernarfon along the A487, follow this road for about 2½ miles as far as a sign pointing right for Brynkir Woollen Mill. Turn right and follow this road ignoring the first junction right leading to Cwmystradlyn (a favourite lake with fishermen). After passing the woollen mill on your right you go past two sets of cottages again on your right. Immediately after the second set is a narrow side road to the right. If you come to Golan community centre (the old primary school) on your right you have come too far and need to backtrack.

Take this road to the right and continue along it, passing one junction right (to a dead end) where the road takes a sharp turn left, then crossing the Afon Dwyfor before arriving at a T-junction at **519433** where a sign points right towards Cwm Pennant. Take this right fork and follow it to the two-forked junction described above (at **531454**).

Take the right fork here and follow it to its end. Once you reach the end of the road you are at the entrance of Cwrt Isaf farm [19-02].

If still in your car you will notice that there is nowhere to park. Turn around and drive back down valley for about 200 metres until you approach a section of solid grass verge on your left (almost adjacent to a gateway) with enough space for two or three vehicles without blocking access. The left grass verge is preferable to that on the right which is often wet and muddy. Closer to the farm there are spaces which have 'no-parking' signs, but there are plenty of other pull-ins which can be utilised responsibly further down-valley.

Walk back along the road towards Cwrt Isaf farm, cross the Afon Cwm-llefrith at the farm entrance, and head off right towards some out-buildings. A ladder stile to their right marks the start of this walk at **540464** with another just beyond [19-03 looking back from the second ladder stile].

**START**

1)    (**540464**)    →

      20°             →

Phew!

Now that you have finally started the walk you need to be aware that this approach path along the Northern bank of the Afon Cwm-llefrith is classed as a permissible footpath. To all intents and purposes, the farmer who owns the land it crosses graciously grants permission for walkers to use this path, but maintains the right to withdraw that permission when his agricultural activities take priority.

Some of you may question whether this arrangement should still apply following the crucial date of 28th May 2005 when the Countryside Rights of Way Act 2000 finally became law in Snowdonia permitting everyone the freedom to roam on foot on any open land above 600 metres. But of course, access to that land can still occasionally be subject to temporary restrictions. In much the same way that ramblers in Scotland respect the wishes of landowners during the deer-stalking season in September and October (or, at least responsible ramblers do), so we should also stick to the same code in Snowdonia – if only to avoid giving hill-walkers a bad name.

So, assuming access is available on the day you visit, cross the first ladder stile, pass the group of three farm buildings on your left, and then climb the second ladder stile alongside a gate to gain access to a field. Skirt this field's right-hand edge close to the river bank (the Afon Cwm-llefrith) and after a short climb towards a small collection of trees you reach a gate in the wall on your right with a ladder stile alongside it bearing small markers identifying a walkers' path [19-04]. Cross this stile and another one shortly afterwards [19-05 looking back].

**70°**      →

The path veers to the right of the pastureland in order to keep close to a wire fence as it begins to climb gradually. Ahead of you a collapsed section of dry stone wall crosses the grassland, but your path keeps to the right of this [19-06]. A small group of spindly conifers stands alongside the river bank ahead of you to your right, and directly above their tops looms the Western face of Moel Hebog. To its left is the col between its own smooth flanks and the craggier outline of Moel yr Ogof. A path of sorts heads directly to this col by way of the ladder stile visible in the line of fencing crossing the field ahead of you and to your left [19-07].

Make your way to this ladder stile and use it to cross the fence. Beyond this fence the ground is wetter, festooned with much coarse grass and expanses of reed where the ground has failed to drain completely into the river below.

---

### OPTION 1
If you intend heading directly to the col – Bwlch Meillionen at **560475** – stick to the track that leads haphazardly from this ladder stile. The path is certainly less clear on the ground than it would appear to be on the Explorer map – in places it is a footprint in mud, in others a wide cart

---

track embossed on the reeds – but it climbs in a fairly straight line to a ladder stile in a dry-stone wall – **point 7** at **560475**.

On the skyline to your left a smaller set of crags on top of a shoulder of land marks the second top of the day, Moel Lefn. From here it seems that a direct, as-the-crow-flies approach is the most feasible route without the luxury of any more ladder stiles.

But it pays to continue on along the damp path towards the col for a while. It follows a grassy terrace, some distance above the stream to your right that has incised itself a deep channel [19-08 looking back along the path]. Shortly your path passes a large block of stone on your left [19-09], and further along on the same side you should notice a solitary tree rooted to a clump of crag – hawthorn or rowan (I confess I did not investigate – but once you see it, you'll know which tree I mean). On your right, meanwhile, the river passes through a wire fence as it hurtles down-valley [19-10].

**2)      (548469)      →**

**70°                    →**

Just beyond on your left a series of large, grey-white boulders protrude from the coarse grass and run a ragged line left towards the lower slopes of Moel Yr Ogof. These mark as good a point as any to depart the floor of the valley and head for higher ground by more direct means [19-11]. The slopes on the left (now hopefully facing you) consist of scatterings of loose rock, patches of grass, very little reed, and small clumps of gorse. A succession of craggy outcrops, topped by the odd thistle, provide ample opportunity to gain height more directly as you reach the first bit of high ground of the day [19-12].

*From this vantage point you should be high enough to see the sea to the South in an almost unbroken line above the South-West flanks of Moel Hebog. Evidence of mining scars its face directly to your left.*
*A persistent stone wall runs from Moel Hebog's summit to a block of conifers ahead of you (across the valley) while on this side of the valley a partially-collapsed stone enclosure now contains a captive bed of reeds [19-13 from*

*higher up the hillside]. Most people would call this kind of landscape featureless but a trained eye can weave fabric from its many details.*

Perhaps while studying the 'featureless' terrain from the top of these crags you will have also studied what lies ahead of you next. High on the skyline to the right a dry-stone wall can be seen running downhill towards you from the horizon left of Moel Lefn. The wall barely begins its descent of the hillside in your direction before being cut off in its stride by another wall running across the slope left to right [19-14]. Reaching this T-junction of walls by the most direct route is the key to keeping this walk as short and sweet as possible.

Having abandoned the valley path you might still be tempted to continue along the same line in the general direction of Bwlch Meillionen. The crest of a series of crags in the lee of this dry-stone wall runs left to right across the slopes separating you from Moel yr Ogof and Moel Lefn. However, crossing the wall by legitimate means further up-valley could prove impossible. Most dry-stone walls are not made to be climbed over unless there are obvious step blocks inserted. A thoughtless short-cut can lead to wall collapse (which can have serious consequences for the farmer's attempt to separate his flocks from neighbouring pastureland or an amorous ram).

If, instead, you initially bear left towards where the wall heads more steeply downslope into the upper reaches of Cwm Pennant you will find a way across. For much of its length the wall is topped by a wire fence and looks impregnable. But once you reach the wall, if you then head right and head in the general direction of Moel yr Ogof you will very shortly reach a large boulder which the wall takes full advantage of [19-15]. It is possible to clamber onto this rocky stump, step over the wire fence and drop down carefully to the other side without disturbing a single stone [19-16 from the other side of the wall].

| 3) | (550473) | → | |
|---|---|---|---|
| | 80° | → | |

A relatively gentle, grassy slope now separates you from the base of Moel yr Ogof [19-17] – the first summit of the walk and from here seemingly within touching distance. However, as you crest the immediate slope you meet another set of dry stone walls [19-18]. No problems crossing this one.

The wall crossing the slopes right to left is collapsed in many places allowing easy passage [19-19], but the next wall running downhill on your right presents a new snag. The solution is to keep down slope of the collapsed wall and head further right. As you stumble across the junction of collapsed wall and solid wall (the T-junction of walls already spotted from much further down the hillside) you will notice there is a passage between the two, leading into a small sheep-pen which gives unencumbered access to the foothills of the two nearby summits.

I have been here when it was a simple matter of walking through the gap – but have also been here when the passage was shut off by a crude barrier of corrugated tin (relatively easily stepped over) [19-20]. Whatever the situation when you are here, once you reach the open slopes beyond the wall trend slightly right to reach the grassy ramp leading up onto Moel yr Ogof. There is still a substantial wall separating you from Moel Lefn further to your left [19-21], but if you gain the summit of Moel yr Ogof first then access onto its Northern neighbour is straightforward.

4)      (553475)        →

        60°              →

Sometimes during a walk in the hills we need a boost to release a fresh spurt of energy – a chocolate snack or a swig of juice. Getting to the top of the first summit of the day does it for me nine times out of ten. So to indulge yourself, rather than heading left towards Moel Lefn divert your boots directly ahead (North East) towards the grey rocky mass of Moel yr Ogof – originally scheduled as the second top. It is much closer than its neighbour, and when you finally reach the top of Moel Lefn there is no need to drag yourself onto Moel yr Ogof again a second time during the return leg en route to Moel Hebog.

The direct approach is easiest despite the lack of any clear path [19-22]. A long, steep ramp of grass leads onto a platform above which a set of crags and some scree give awkward access to the skyline ahead of you. As you approach the rockier sections the best approach is to aim for a point midway along the mountain's profile [19-23]. A path zig-zags between the crags [19-24] allowing you the opportunity to scramble if you so wish before reaching the cairn marking the top of **Moel yr Ogof** (at **556478** – 655m/2148ft) [19-25].

*North, the Nantlle ridge takes pride of place [19-26] – the cliffed face of Craig Cwm Silyn to the left of Moel Lefn [19-27], separated from the graceful curves of Mynydd Tal-y-mignedd and its summit obelisk by the broad col of Bwlch Dros-bern [19-28].*

*To the right of Moel Lefn a spur leads to the flat summit area of Trum y Ddysgl with the bite-mark separating it from Mynydd Drws-y-Coed [19-29] (Mynydd Mawr sneaking a look over the ridge between these two).*

*Llyn y Dywarchen and Llyn y Gader are just visible in the valley beyond the forested slopes to the East. Beyond this pair, across valley stands the smooth wall of Moel Eilio, Foel Gron, Foel Goch and Moel Cynghorion leading in a series of standing waves all the way right to the North-Western corner of Yr Wyddfa [19-30].*

*This is as fine a vantage-point as any towards Yr Wyddfa's Western façade – Yr Aran further right with Y Lliwedd tucked in beyond – while set back further right stands Moel Siabod which seems instantly recognisable wherever you stand in Snowdonia [19-31].*

As well as the stunning views all around you, the rocks at your feet also bear further scrutiny before leaving Moel yr Ogof's summit.

The more observant amongst you might have wondered at the origin of the coarse, white-veined rocks that form the main mass of the mountain [19-32]. Then as you begin the descent North, these are replaced by massive white boulders composed of a matrix of pebbly concretions bonded together like mortar [19-33]. And finally as you get closer to Moel Lefn those blocks are replaced by a fine-grained rock with almost a paisley-like texture of convoluted strata [19-34].

These are all volcanic rocks, dating from the period when this part of Wales was subject to cataclysmic eruptions, most occurring undersea. Some geologists suggest that the summit area of Moel Yr Ogof is the closest thing in the UK to the preserved remains of a terrestrial volcano (one that actually stood above sea-level when it erupted).

Moel yr Ogof is what I call a proper summit – a tiny pyramid of rock with slopes sweeping away in all directions giving an air of greater exposure than actually exists.

5)      (556478)      →

        335°          →

Picking your way through the wreckage of a 450 million year old eruption on the way to the col between Moel yr Ogof and Moel Lefn (a paltry 80 metre drop through a steep staircase of crags and boulders [19-35 looking back uphill]) you are given ample opportunity to study the lie of the land and identify the grassy path leading onto your next summit.

First you need to cross the ladder stile at the junction of a dry-stone wall and fence. A straightforward track crosses gentle grassy slopes (moist in sections) towards the rocky outcrops ahead marking the false summit of Moel Lefn [19-36]. Beyond this first craggy pyramid a mini-cairn can be seen perched on nearby crags to the right marking the true top of **Moel Lefn** (at **552485** – 638m/2094ft) [19-37].

Rather like the serpentine ridge of Cnicht, Moel Lefn has another mini-summit beyond [19-38], worth a stretch of the legs if only for a closer view at the Southern slopes of the Nantlle Ridge. The partially-hidden valley between Moel Lefn and the Nantlle ridge is Cwm Pennant [19-39]. Although a motoring dead-end, a narrow pass between the two mountains links it by footpath to Rhyd-Ddu by way of Bwlch y Ddwy Elor (The Pass of the Two Biers!).

In the not-too-distant past, the watershed between intervening valleys often used to mark the parish boundaries. Consequently bodies were often transported from one valley to the next in order that the deceased could be buried in the parish of his birth.

Mourners would bear the corpse on the 'parish bier' up long rough paths such as that along Bwlch y Ddwy Elor – and at the watershed they would be met by a party carrying the bier of their own church on which the body would complete its journey to the churchyard.

6)      (552485)        →

        220°            →

To avoid retracing your steps, descend the Western slopes of Moel Lefn to a distinctive path skirting the summit's flanks. Admittedly, you still finish up crossing the ladder stile again, but as soon as you reach its other side drop down steeply right to meet a path contouring some distance below Moel yr Ogof's slopes. This path crosses below a variety of scree slopes – some obviously no longer active (consisting of lichen-coated slabs); others are fresh enough to clatter downslope under your feet as you make your own contribution to the weathering process [19-40].

Eventually the bulky mass of Moel Hebog itself stands ahead of you as you round the Southern flanks of Moel yr Ogof [19-41]. A substantial dry stone wall emerges close by on your right as you negotiate the final, tricky corner of Moel yr Ogof.

Hidden among the crags high to your left (marked on maps at 559478) within the jointed Southern slopes of Moel yr Ogof is a cave which gives the mountain its name – one reputedly occupied by Owain Glyndwr during his period as a fugitive fighting a guerrilla war against the English before his capture in 1413.

The cave's legend has, however, been corrupted over time. Originally the mountain was named Moel Ogof Elen (the hill of the cave of Elen, wife of Macsen Wledig – the Roman emperor 'Maximus').

You can either stick close to the wall or clamber left across a short, grassy slope to reach a high col threading its way between rounded crags to emerge above a waterlogged depression at the mountain's snout. The small, sinewy lake occupying this rocky indentation at the floor of the col is not marked on the Explorer map [19-42].

To reach the floor of this basin you need to head left for a while away from the wall (the ground falls away very steeply otherwise). Having descended the wide staircase of grassy terraces well to the left of the wall, bear right again, keeping as close as you can to the dry-stone wall if you wish to keep your feet dry [19-43]. In parts this involves scrambling across a couple of gnarled outcrops – in others there are stepping stones.

Ahead of you next is a clear path leading towards a narrow corridor cut into the crags that appear to bar the route onto Moel Hebog. This cutting looks like it gives you a short, easy passage onto the hillside beyond, but once you enter its damp confines it delivers a surprise to jog the shortest of attention spans. Beyond, the way ahead drops steadily along a steep, eroded path to a broad col below [19-44, and 19-45].

Finally you have reached Bwlch Meillionen at the foot of the large crags close to the 540-metre contour – the final bit of low ground between you and Moel Hebog [19-46 and 19-47]. A wall on your right bearing a ladder stile identifies your eventual escape route back to Cwrt Isaf farm.

---

**OPTION 2**
If you decide to leave the third summit for another day, proceed from here as if reversing Option 1 back to **point 2**.

*Time saved – approx 1hr 15min*

---

7)      (559475)        →

        120°            →

It is now merely a case of following the line of the dry-stone wall directly up the slopes of Moel Hebog's North-Western face. If you opt for the path on the right-hand side of the wall the going is quite easy for the first 50 metres or so. But studying the way ahead it will soon become evident that a better path runs along the wall's left-hand side. A gap through the wall comes to your rescue as the angle of slope eases among a jumble of crags before the steepest section of ascent.

From here on the going is still fairly gruelling up a steep path, gravelled in places but mainly consisting of bare grass. The slope is convex and its angle is such that the summit is never visible on the skyline until you practically pop out alongside the concrete cairn itself marking **Moel Hebog** (at **564469** – 782m/2565ft) [19-48 from the Beddgelert Forest below].

The summit is a fairly broad area of rocky fragments and short grass with very little close by to grab the attention. Although I'd had the Western ascent all to myself, the summit was as crowded as any hill top in late summer. The more popular route to this summit emerges close by – a 'tourist path' picking its way up the Northern ridge, below which lie the forested slopes West of Beddgelert.

*This relatively isolated summit still yields superb views in all directions. To the North-West lie the Nantlle ridge, Moel Lefn and Moel yr Ogof. To the North East, Yr Wyddfa and its entourage. To the East, Cnicht and the Moelwynion. To the South-East, Tremadog Bay.*

8)     (564469)     →

       315°          →

The return from the summit to Bwlch Meillionen is a straightforward reversal of the ascent, much easier on the down than on the up. Keeping the dry-stone wall on your left-hand side all the way down, you encounter one section close to the bottom were the path is replaced by a steep section of polished, wet slab [19-49 looking back from the col below]. This can be easily by-passed on the right.

You then reach the floor of the col where you should easily locate the ladder stile in the wall on your left. On my very first visit here, as I headed back down to the col I was trailed by a curious group of walkers who had been vocally perplexed by my earlier emergence on the summit from an unexpected direction. Fortunately for them, I was able to direct them to a path that descends easily to the right from this col to reach the forestry below (where a path would eventually lead them back to Beddgelert village where their mini-bus was parked).

7)      (559475)        →

        240°            →

Cross the ladder stile on your left and follow the faint path downhill. In places the path is not very clear, often splitting in two.

If you lose the correct line you may find yourself having to scramble down steeper ground to regain the path. But there are no obvious difficulties, and you soon reach a clearer section where the path trends left towards the river. On its opposite banks stand the old workings of the Moel Hebog mines. In places the ground can be very wet underfoot but that is a small price to pay for unhindered progress.

A section of gentle grassland follows, the river keeping close by on your left [19-50]. Gradually the river crosses a series of rocky steps, the path running alongside giving enticing glimpses of the cataracts below. But then quite abruptly the river takes a spectacular plunge over a final set of crags to meet the flat valley floor below where it runs headlong into a dry stone wall (diverting the water left across a gravelly floodplain). An easy escape path heads off to the right, giving more controlled access to this valley floor [19-51]. Ahead of you a ladder stile crosses the dry stone wall that would otherwise bar the way. But before crossing the wall, it is worth heading left to study the river and the waterfalls directly upstream [19-52 looking from beyond the wall].

After you cross the ladder stile the path runs closer to the river again, passing through a gap in a section of collapsed wall then crossing a series of wet patches. Then suddenly you reach familiar territory again – the river passes through wire fence and on your right now you pass the solitary tree that imprinted itself on your memory banks on the ascent, followed by that isolated block of stone.

Now it's a simple case of heading back down the main valley floor along the path which quickly returns you to Cwrt Isaf farm where your walk began.

**END**

# MOELWYNION

*This discarded sector of Snowdonia rarely features in the itinerary of any tourist visiting North Wales. Yet its hills are as beguiling and awe-inspiring as any further North, and its significant role in the region's industrial past makes it worthy of more than such wanton neglect.*

**TASTER 19**

*There is no finer introduction to the area than the drive from Betws-y-Coed to Porthmadog by way of Dolwyddelan and the Crimea Pass. Follow the A5 East out of Betws-y-Coed, crossing the Waterloo Bridge, and very shortly take the exit right signposted Dolgellau and Blaenau Ffestiniog. As you follow the A470, if you really want to test your 'I-Spy' powers look out for the pair of Sequoias (or 'giant redwoods') at the roadside on the right (at **755539**) just beyond the left-hand junction for the 'Pont y Pant Hall' hotel. These towering specimens are a magnificent pair, and if you give the bark of either tree a hefty punch you might be surprised at the result.*

*The much-improved A470 passes through the tiny village of Dolwyddelan (worth a stop by the riverside) before climbing up the Crimea Pass.*

*There is a National Park lay-by on the left just before the crest of the pass. If you intend a brief exploration on foot, park here, turning left out of the car park and head towards Blaenau Ffestiniog. Very shortly you see a track on the opposite side of the road (at **700486**) which leads you along the base of Moel Dyrnogydd. From here there are impressive views East towards Moel Siabod and the upper reaches of the Lledr valley.*

*Continuing the drive South, you descend steeply towards the quarry-scarred environs of Blaenau Ffestiniog. Although it bears the mark of dereliction, the town is still a viable community with a proud heritage and indestructible spirit. You have the option of driving through the town itself (left at the roundabout) or skirting it (right at the roundabout). The latter provides the more scenic route as it takes you past the waterfalls on the Afon Goedol – truly awesome when in full spate (park on the right-hand side of the road in the lay-by at **690443** then walk a short distance down the road). A footbridge over the river gives even closer views.*

Continuing along this road (the A496) you eventually reach an awkward road junction (at **687416**) where you need to go straight ahead if heading to Porthmadog. En route you will pass through the village of Penrhyndeudraeth, passing the entrance on your left to the 'Italianate village' of Portmeirion (where cult TV series "The Prisoner" was filmed in the 1960's). Eventually you cross the 'Cob' causeway to enter Porthmadog. As you do, take a sneaky look to your right – there across the impounded estuary of the Glaslyn lies the panorama of Cnicht and the Moelwynion.

### TASTER 20

If you want to take a closer look at the hills and feel some slate under your feet, an excursion into Cwmorthin comes highly recommended. Follow the directions for **Walk 22** and try at least to walk as far as the old chapel on the shores of the lake. This is the spot which more than most epitomises what the region lost when the slate industry foundered. And if you want to cool your feet off afterwards, there's a river close to the car park just across the foot-bridge.

### TASTER 21

If returning to the Welsh Borders by car, having sampled a bit of Welsh hospitality, one of the region's finest drives takes the twisting road West of Llan Ffestiniog. Retrace the route taken for **Taster 19** as far as that awkward road junction on the A496. Instead of dropping down left for Blaenau Ffestiniog continue up the steep hill. This takes you through the small village of Llan Ffestiniog. Having climbed up to the centre of the village keep right, and as you reach its Eastern end, after just passing under a railway bridge you immediately see a junction left (the B4391).

Follow this road as it heads almost directly towards the massive grey mound of Manod Mawr. There follows a series of loops more reminiscent of roads traversing the Italian Alps. A lay-by at **734417** is worth seeking out. Park here and continue along the road on foot for a short distance to gain a gob-smacking view into Cwm Cynfal. The upper falls (Rhaeadr y Cwm) are breathtaking – particularly following a period of heavy rain, or when partly frozen.

From here continue ahead by car, crossing a cattle grid then reaching a junction on your left just before the Pont yr Afon Gam bridge (opposite what once claimed to be the highest petrol station in Wales! – now closed down). Turn left at this junction and you soon climb onto open moorland with the huge expanse of Migneint laid out on your right.

The scenery barely relents as you pass the minor side road left dropping into Cwm Penmachno. If you have plenty of time this is worth a quick detour just for a glimpse into the beautiful forested valley below. Then continue past the patch of moor-land home to Llyn Conwy, source of the Afon Conwy (hidden higher on your left) before eventually dropping down to the tiny village of Ysbyty Ifan. A few miles further along you come to a T-junction – the A5. To the left lies Betws-y-Coed, and to the right Llangollen and the border country.

## WALK 20

## Allt-Fawr [67] / Moel Druman [68] /Ysgafell Wen (named [69] and unnamed [70] tops) / Moel Meirch [71]

| 16.25 Km (10.16 miles)<br><br>930m (3050ft)<br><br>Time : 6hrs | The five highest points of the lake-studded upland plateau that extends from Nantgwynant to the Southern edge of the National Park high above Blaenau Ffestiniog |
| --- | --- |

On a 'mountains-as-celebrities' list, not many of the Moelwynion (apart from Cnicht or Moel Siabod) would warrant a single line of publicity in the tabloids.

Anyone, who has ever traipsed along the Watkin Path towards Yr Wyddfa, turned around to draw breath and scanned the skyline directly South, will have seen little across Nantgwynant to encourage further exploration. The sole feature that catches the eye is the back wall of the corrie containing the waters of Llyn Llagi. Closer inspection only serves to emphasize the fact that if this was all Snowdonia had to offer, the roads and campsites would be empty most Bank Holiday weekends.

However, under optimum conditions these five tops combine to offer an intriguing day in the hills. What this patch of high ground lacks in glamour, altitude and 'scrambleability' is more than made up for by opportunities to hone your route-finding skills, indulge your curiosity and admire outstanding views of a largely unpublicised and undiscovered corner of North Wales. Having already visited this area on numerous occasions in search of the direct path onto Moel Meirch – during the height of summer (heat haze/midges/losing the path), and early autumn (swollen rivers/bottomless bogs/losing the path again) I now offer an alternative route that should not only be foolproof but also make a day in these hills one to remember for all the right reasons. If you can, choose a frosty day with crisp ground underfoot, keep map and compass close at hand every step of the way, and if you have a pair of heavy-duty rubber gloves pack them as well just in case.....

**North**

**Don't forget**

**map/compass**
**whistle/torch**

**suitable footwear**
**+ clothing**

**food/drink**

**brain**

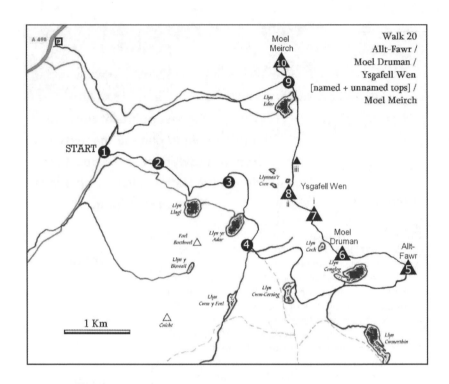

## APPROACH

Look out for the minor road that crosses the Afon Glaslyn at **626503** (just off the A498 Beddgelert-Capel Curig road) just before the river enters Llyn Dinas.

If driving West from Capel Curig, this minor road exits left some 300 metres beyond the large car park at **627507** (the start point for the Watkin Path – see **Walk 15**). You will need to keep your eyes peeled for this side-road as there is no road sign warning you of the junction up ahead, and the exit only becomes visible at the last minute. As soon as you have passed an old chapel and some stone cottages on your right look out for a five-barred gate facing you on the left – the minor road turns left just in front of that gate.

If driving from Beddgelert Eastwards, after passing Llyn Dinas on your right you will encounter the minor road a short distance ahead, again on the right. Beyond the Red Dragon Holiday Apartments and Bryn Dinas Bunkhouse on your left, as the road begins to curve left, the side-road exits on your right at

**626503**. Again, look out for a five-barred gate facing you on the right (another one) and turn right just in front of it.

The road you are on now is very narrow, hemmed in for much of the way by dry-stone walls, and passing-places are few and far between. The road also climbs more and more steeply as it abandons the valley floor some 125 metres below. But, of course, that means there are less contours you have to cross on foot to gain the skyline ahead.

Shortly after passing the smallholding of Bryn Bedd on your left (at **637495**) the road takes a sharp turn right. In the past the space just before this bend (alongside the wall on the left – at **637494**) was often used as a parking spot for a couple of cars. But now it has been designated a passing place, and in order to maintain clear access to the gateway on your left and to the farm track ahead of you it is advisable to drive on.

The start of the walk is only 500 metres further along, and there are a couple of roadside pull-ins close by into which your car can be squeezed (these are set at right-angles to the road itself, and are too small to serve as passing-places). Just watch your suspension on the rocks!

Perhaps a better option lies another 500 metres along this road, opposite a mass of old slate workings on the right (at **633485**) where there are spaces for a dozen or so sensibly parked cars.

---

### OPTION 1

Here's a novelty – you probably haven't even put your boots on yet, and it's already make-your-mind-up time.

There is an alternative approach, commencing with the direct ascent of Moel Meirch. In the past this was a popular route to Llyn Edno; used as a straight there-and-back walk to the lake, or to the summit close by. But completing the entire route in reverse is not recommended as finding the correct line onto Moel Meirch from here is notoriously frustrating, and more recently a failure to maintain the public footpaths hereabouts might well lead you to give up in despair before even reaching your first summit.

For those of you with a masochistic streak, walk back along the road to

---

the right-angle in the road at **637494**. From here you have a choice – either continue straight ahead along the footpath described near the end of the walk (Option 7) and reverse every step of the way, or turn right onto a broad, gravel track that swings behind the forest plantation now on your left. This leads to Hafodydd Brithion farm. Carry on through the farm yard and you emerge onto wet pasture where a bridge crosses a stream. Once across the stream turn right and pick your way through the trees towards the ladder stile in the wall up ahead of you. For more detail refer to the rest of this walk's write-up.

*Time saved – none obviously. But the ascent route is arduous, and becomes increasingly difficult to identify as you reach higher ground. Likewise, the return leg from point 2 to point 1 can be tricky to follow, particularly in its lower sections where you can easily become baffled if this is your first time in these hills.*

## START

1)       (635490)        →

         105°             →

A small, white house (formerly a chapel) set back from the roadside marks the point where the public footpath from Nantgwynant crosses this minor road and heads East towards Llyn Llagi [20-01 looking back to the start from much higher up along the walk]. A signpost points East through a large gateway where a hairpin of farm track serves the larger of the two houses close by the farm of Llwynyrhwch. The footpath short-cuts ahead; crossing a rough paddock to the left of the nearer, white-gabled stone cottage [20-02]. It then continues, by way of patches of crude paving, a rickety kissing gate and a plank bridge, towards the farmhouse of Llwynyrhwch directly ahead. Your path heads off to the left in front of this farmhouse then passes a small circular column set at the corner of the grounds [20-03 looking back].

A marker post alongside the column points the way forward to the ladder stile set in the wall a short distance ahead of you [20-04]. To its right a small waterfall emerges from the hillside above, an indication of the sodden ground ahead of you. On the other side of this stile (at **637490**) lies a damp, shaded cutting enclosed by the stone wall and a sparsely-wooded wall of crag directly in front of you.

A narrow staircase path leads easily through these crags [20-05 and 20-06] onto a platform of rock. From here for a short distance the path follows the banks of a small brook [20-07 and 20-08] before heading off towards the rocky hummocks directly ahead [20-09]. The route straight across this wet pasture can be squelchy, but if you choose instead to bear further left along the only visible path towards a low 'island' of sounder ground you will soon find that the going gets even wetter.

As you head towards the tree-clad crags ahead of you, if you look to your right across the brook to its opposite bank you should see a footpath sign [20-10]. It points uphill in the same general direction that you are headed so do not assume that the path you are following is the wrong one. It's just one of numerous paths criss-crossing this area – many petering out after a few yards and giving the walker no clear indication where best to head next.

Indeed, all about you the landscape is rather a jumble of sparse vegetation, mossy crags, half-hidden water-courses and scattered points of reference. Most people think that once they have got the 'entire picture' in their heads, the dots that make up the picture can be written off. But you ignore the dots at your peril because it's these that often provide your bearings or co-ordinates.

The first time I explored this region I stored as much detail as possible in my memory banks for future reference. For example, the most feasible line of ascent through the crags began where a solitary tree stood left of the path with low-slung branches that caught in the trekking-poles strapped to my rucksack. And once I reached the next level section, a half-buried boulder cleft in two provided a memorable waymark. Features like this are worth memorising in case you should ever need to escape by reversing the way you came rather than continuing the entire loop. But bear in mind that things you have already noted on the way UPHILL can appear totally different when seen again on the way back DOWNHILL.

No doubt you will focus on your own personal identifiers – items that you can easily pick out in a muddled landscape that will help you keep to the right track should you ever come here again.

Once you reach the crags ahead of you, climb up a short pull to reach a sizeable patch of flatter ground [20-11 looking back]. Beyond this grassed area, pick your way through a clutter of rocks to reach another patch of open ground with a distinctive cleft boulder directly ahead of you [20-12].

A broad grassy track continues beyond this boulder towards more crags. Head uphill through these rocks towards the obvious flat-topped outcrop of dark rock on the skyline to your left [20-13]. As you gain height your path runs alongside another small stream for a time [20-14 looking back downhill]. Then with the flat-topped outcrop now alongside you on your left, continue past it by bearing further right beneath the overhanging branches of a pair of large trees.

To their right a wet, grassy path continues in the same general direction breaching the remains of a dry-stone wall as it does. Easy ground now heads upslope [20-15, and 20-16 looking back downslope] to a broad grassy saddle. The ruins of a small building stand close by [20-17] – possibly summer shelter for a shepherd – proof that at least some rewarding human activity has been carried out here in the distant past. These ruins also provide another valuable waymark, easily visible from a distance, should you need to locate the path for a premature retreat.

To the left of these ruins a dry-stone wall runs across the slopes beneath Clogwyn Drain [20-18]. Locate the ladder stile in this wall – there's no need to climb it because there is a gap in the wall next to it. Go through this gap and turn right heading upslope [20-19].

**2)**      **(643488)**        →

   95°                    →

The ground here can be extremely wet underfoot as the path veers away to the left of the wall before eventually heading to flat, open ground [20-20].

Continue along the Eastern bank of a narrow watercourse (more of a ditch which appears to have been straightened sometime in its recent history) towards its source; Llyn Llagi. There are several large boulders to pick a way through before you reach more open grassland with the back-wall of Craig Llyn-llagi beyond. A collapsed dry-stone wall cuts across the slopes ahead of you, crossing your path close to the 350-metre contour (at **647486**) where a ruined building stands alongside the path [20-21].

---

### OPTION 2

To completely by-pass the corrie enclosing Llyn Llagi and avoid the straightforward path climbing up to the skyline (one of the few marked on the Explorer map), turn left once you pass through the collapsed wall and climb steep, grassy slopes [20-22] onto the platform at the Northern base of Y Cyrniau. En route you encounter a series of dry-stone walls on the upper slopes, but there are sufficient gaps in them to make continued progress uphill problem-free. Eventually the angle of slope eases considerably, Moel Siabod peeps over the Eastern horizon, and you encounter the first of the day's innumerable tiny lakes that adorn this upland plateau.

Although this is not the easiest escape route from the deep basin containing the lake, it rewards every effort with superb views behind you of Llyn Llagi [20-23] – far superior to the gloomier scene you are often presented with from the reservoir's shoreline.

*Time saved – approx 15 mins*

---

If you do fancy a closer look at the Llyn Llagi reservoir (even though its waters are often shrouded in shade for much of the day) cross tussocky grassland to your right until you face the backwall of Craig Llyn-llagi [20-24] and the falls. Heading further right leads to a low wall behind which the Afon Llyn-llagi exits the reservoir, but the prospect facing you from shoreline-level is hardly one of the area's most photogenic views.

*At this relatively low level the wall of rock enclosing this small reservoir dominates the Southern skyline, with the shallow notch close to its Eastern end marking the point where the stream issuing from Llyn yr Adar plunges down to Llyn Llagi.*

*During dry periods this barely contains a trickle, but following particularly wet weather I have seen a sizeable waterfall spurting through this narrow cutting (large enough to be clearly visible from the A486).*

To regain the clear path exiting the corrie floor, look out for a small bank of slate waste on the slopes to your left [20-25]. The path can be seen contouring the grassy slopes above it to reach the North Eastern corner of the corrie where it emerges at the Northern base of Y Cyrniau. Take a straight line to the bank of slate waste and clamber up easy slopes to meet this straightforward path. The path in places resembles a stream bed, but it presents no difficulty as it advances upon the high col above you [20-26, and 20-27 looking back downhill].

**3)**   **(654486)**   →

   **75°**   →

As you finally emerge onto more level ground this path trends to the right [20-28]. The skyline appears substantially closer now, but almost behind you on your left you might be intrigued by a small lake perched right on top of a low platform. A five minute stroll along a slender path [20-29] leads to this body of water at **655488**. This hidden jewel has an unusual viewpoint West to Nantlle [20-30] and North West towards the Snowdon group [20-31] that +99% of walkers in this area are likely to have missed. Another five minute stroll returns you to the path again, continuing left towards Llynnau'r Cwn (the three Dog Lakes – no relation to the US 70's group Three Dog Night).

Soon after crossing a small stream, with a set of falls on your right descending the steep slopes of Y Cyrniau [20-32] you are met by another stream running down the shallow trough towards you [20-33] (this stream exits the Northernmost of the Dog Lakes). Cross to the right-hand bank of this stream and head up steep slopes onto the rocky crags of Y Cyrniau [20-34].

**OPTION 3**

If your intention is to reach Moel Meirch without further ado, keep to
the left side of the stream. A path follows it towards these three lakes,
climbing easy ground to their left until you reach a wire fence where
your path joins a T-junction : left towards Moel Meirch or right towards
Ysgafell Wen.

Turn left, keeping to this side of the fence at all times. This next section
is actually a descent along the diminishing Northern spur of Ysgafell
Wen. The ground is extremely wet underfoot (when not frozen solid)
but the views ahead to Llyn Edno with the Snowdon skyline behind it
are compensation enough [20-35]. Once you reach the shoreline of Llyn
Edno continue as from **point 9**.

*Time saved – approximately 4 hours.*

These slopes are hardly taxing. But once you reach the wet saddle where the
path crests this low ridge before emerging onto its Southern flanks (close to
**659486**) you are entitled to pause and take what will be your final look at
this Northern skyline [20-36] until much later in the walk.

155°          →

With Cnicht and Llyn yr Adar dominating the views ahead and to your left
[20-37], drop down fairly gentle slopes in order to reach the Eastern shore of
Llyn yr Adar close to **657479**. There is a sizeable outcrop of crag to clamber
over en route [20-38]. Beyond it you encounter a small stream but this can be
quite easily hurdled as long as you are able to find a dry bit of bank for take-
off and landing.

215°          →

Climbing the gentle slopes on your left now is a faint track heading in the
direction of Cnicht [20-39]. Follow this track until it reaches an eroded notch
at the North Eastern end of the Cnicht ridge (at **658477**) where a dilapidated
cairn identifies this crossroads of paths [20-40].

**4)**      **(658477)**      →

   **135°**         →

Turn left to join a steeply descending path of loose shale and bare soil [20-41, and 20-42 looking back up the path]. In the deep cleft on your right, a tributary valley perched high above Cwm Croesor, lies the slightly shrunken reservoir of Llyn Cwm y Foel [20-43].

---

The reservoir of Llyn Cwm y Foel once supplied water to turn the turbines of a power-house serving the underground quarry at the head of Cwm Croesor. In the late 1940s the dam showed need of urgent repair if the inundation of Croesor village down-stream was to be avoided.

Getting building materials up to such a remote site posed a major headache. Mules had been used when it was constructed, but were now found to be in short supply. In the end, and at great expense, a helicopter was employed for the job. Somehow during the operation it crashed – fortunately without loss of life.

---

The path crosses a stream before following a sinuous line across a turf-capped shelf [20-44]. You then have to drop down a steep, scrambly bit of rock to reach a broad saddle [20-45] with steep ground to its left and some distance beyond. To reach the higher ground ahead of you involves crossing a boulder field then scaling some bare rock to reach a substantial rib of crag running downhill from left to right (close to **661476**) [20-46]. On older maps this outcrop is identified as an 'Old Level' so presumably some trial quarrying was carried out here at the height of the slate industry.

*As you walk the rocky tightrope uphill to your left along this crest there are spectacular views behind you that are worth a glance – Moel yr Hydd with Llyn Cwm-corsiog on this side of the valley (seemingly at its foot but with the upper reaches of Cwmorthin intervening) [20-47], Moelwyn Mawr with the Llynnau Diffwys lakes (again apparently at its foot, but separated from it by Bwlch y Rhosydd) [20-48 and 20-49], and furthest right Cnicht with Llyn Cwm y Foel tucked beneath its base [20-50].*

If you continue steadily upslope, hopping from outcrop to outcrop, you eventually reach gentler terrain, where the boulders are more rounded and marsh-mallowy [20-51] and a clearer view of Llyn Cwm-corsiog emerges behind you to your right [20-52].

Where the crags eventually fizzle out you reach a large, boggy depression South and West of Moel Druman. However, by dropping from the ridge [20-53 looking back to the skyline from the valley floor] towards the lower ground to your right you reach a broad valley floor, with a stream (draining from Llyn Coch into Llyn Cwm-corsiog).

This valley has a fence running along its entire length to the North Western shore of Llyn Cwm-corsiog. Double back and drop down to your right in order to follow the path that runs close to this fence for much of its length [20-54].There are places where it is possible to cross the fence and gain more direct access to higher ground across valley which is your next goal – but unless you really do have heavy-duty rubber gloves in your sack it is best to wait until you reach the shoreline of the lake at **664472** where a stile is available [20-55] – suitably insulated against the electric current running through the fence's wires.

Once over the fence you have to turn left and follow the lake's shore back to where the river enters the lake [20-56]. Use stepping stones to cross the river then from its opposite bank gain the immediate high ground ahead of you, eventually reaching the high point of the spur overlooking the stone dam at Llyn Cwm-corsiog's Southern end [20-57].

Many of the lakes hereabouts had their levels raised in this way during the height of the slate industry in order to ensure adequate supply of water for the quarries in the valleys below that relied on water-powered machinery.

As you round the snout of this spur, continually trending to your left, you climb a particularly wet, muddy slope of peat incised by tyre-tracks presumably worn into the turf by all-terrain bikes (increasingly used by local farmers to reach the more inaccessible parts of their land). Below you to your right the entire length of Cwmorthin suddenly opens up, revealing increasingly dramatic views as you contour the sidewall of the valley [20-58].

Continue left and you soon notice a deeply-incised gorge separating you from Allt y Ceffylau (the continuation of Cwmorthin's Northern headwall) [20-59]. This gorge carries the stream issuing from Llyn Conglog to your left. Strike up the steeper slopes on your left to reach the immediate skyline with the large lake stretched out beyond it. Facing the lake's outflow, drop down a short incline on your right to reach the stream's banks close to this outflow at **672472** where it is an easy matter to cross over to the opposite bank [20-60].

95°        →

From there it's a case of heading upslope again in the direction of the day's first summit. As you easily gain the high ground of Allt y Ceffylau there are fresh perspectives on your right to Cwmorthin [20-61] and the abandoned slate workings beneath Moelwyn Mawr [20-62] as well as Cnicht over your right shoulder [20-63].

Gently undulating slopes now climb gradually towards the skyline ahead of you. But as you approach Allt-Fawr you might notice a small, prominent cairn atop a rocky spur across the shallow dip on your right [20-64]. This edifice marks the spot along the high cliff-top of Allt y Ceffylau (at **680472**) where an old path from the Gloddfa Ganol slate mine in the valley below reaches the skyline (en route to Llyn Llagi).

0°        →

If, like me, you choose to visit this cairn you have the dubious pleasure of picking your way across a pool-studded platform in order to reach the obvious rocky shelf ahead of you [20-65]. A fence runs along the base of this shelf (looking suspiciously electrified – but inert the last time I was here). Cross the fence and ahead of you to your right, almost four hours into the walk, stands **Allt-Fawr** at **681477** (698m/2289ft), the highest point of your day and only just within the National Park boundaries [20-66 from the West after crossing the fence, and 20-67].

When the Snowdonia National Park was designated in 1951, certain areas were excluded as being too unattractive or industrialised to warrant inclusion – in particular Llanberis and Blaenau Ffestiniog.

Ironically Llanberis (with its Slate Museum, Electric Mountain exhibition, lakeside attractions and Snowdon Mountain Railway) and Blaenau Ffestiniog (with the Llechwedd Slate Caverns and Ffestiniog Railway) are both now magnets to visitors.

*To the South East lies the noble carnage of Blaenau Ffestiniog and its slate mines – from here you can see why it was not considered cute enough to be included in the National Park [20-68].*

*Aran Fawddwy pokes its head over the skyline beyond [20-69]; at 907 metres, the highest mountain in Southern Snowdonia (mightier than the more renowned Cader Idris, hidden far to the right, which reaches a mere 893 metres).*

*To the North East lies the Crimea Pass (Bwlch y Gorddinan) – the escape route to Dolwyddelan and Betws-y-Coed, and usually the first major road in North Wales to be closed whenever there is heavy snowfall [20-70]. Astride it stand Moel Dyrnogydd to its West and the higher ridge of Moel Farlwyd/Moel Penanmen to its East [20-71].*

*To the North Carnedd Ugain and Yr Wyddfa fronted by Y Lliwedd [20-72].*

*To the West, Cnicht (all three humps easily identifiable) with Moel Hebog peering over its right shoulder [20-73]. To the South West the anticlimax of Allt y Ceffylau, with Moelwyn Mawr and Moelwyn Bach towering above it [20-74].*

*Directly South, Llyn Trawsfynydd, backed by the Rhinogau, with the Vale of Ffestiniog to its left [20-75 and 20-76].*

**5)**    **(681477)**    →

       280°      →

Rather than overdose on views for the rest of the day, turn to face North and plan your next line of attack [20-77]. Retrace your steps along Allt-Fawr's ridge then drop down steep slopes, aiming for the strand of dry ground between Llyn Conglog on the left and the smaller lake on the right. Keep the non-electric fence on your left until a ladder stile allows you to safely cross it.

Spongy ground and a clear path rise gradually to the base of Moel Druman [20-78]. Steep crags ahead of you and on your right (at its Southern end) give relatively easy access onto the summit a mere 50 metres above the surrounding ground. But if you stick close to the fence and pass through the gate at **672476** [20-79] even easier slopes on your right lead you onto the summit of **Moel Druman** at **671476** (676m/2217ft) [20-80 looking back downhill towards Allt-Fawr].

> From the rocky shelf outcropping South of Moel Druman's top you get a bird's eye view of Llyn Conglog to your right with Llyn Trawsfynydd in the distance beyond [20-81].

### OPTION 4

Obviously, there is the option of by-passing Moel Druman without setting foot on its summit – just go through the gate and continue along the path to the other side of the saddle on the skyline ahead of you. But you'll never get a better opportunity to tick it off your list!

***Time saved – barely 15 mins***

**6)**     **(671476)**     →

    **320°**     →

The Northern slopes of Moel Druman are not particularly steep and you soon reach the broad saddle of boggy peat separating it from the next section of ridge [20-82]. The corner where the path abandons the fence (where the fence heads off 90° to the right) is particularly wet, often a foot or more deep in gloop. And conditions do not improve much until the path begins a gradual descent [20-83], gaining rockier terrain as it gets closer towards Llyn Coch and Llyn Terfyn.

Llyn Terfyn is easily identified among the scatter of pools mottling this boggy plateau. It is sunk into a slatey hollow with fragmented rocks forming its shoreline and steep cliffs marking its North Western boundary [20-84 looking back]. As you pass to the right-hand side of these cliffs the fence reappears on your right, a handrail to guide you towards the next summit.

A wide, badly eroded track runs along the opposite side of this fence towards the rocky bluff ahead of you, but the easier ground sticks to the left-hand side of the fence [20-85]. On your left a knuckle of rock pokes at the sky somewhere above Cnicht [20-86] but if you pass to the right of this outcrop the fence leads you to a high gap [20-87] with the unremarkable summit of **Ysgafell Wen (named top)** just across the fence on your right at **667481** (672m/2204ft).

I use the term 'unremarkable' because there is no cairn to identify the ridge's highest point – just a sharp outcrop of rock raised slightly higher than the surrounding crags [20-88]. Unless you knew it was there it could quite easily be missed. From this top, the neighbouring, unnamed summit with its little pinnacle cairn looks a long way off [20-89] but in reality it can be easily reached within less than fifteen minutes.

**7)**      **(667481)**      →

      310°      →

Sort out a way to descend the craggy bits of the summit's NorthWestern flank and you reach gentle, grass-covered slopes with a path that is relatively dry compared with what you have experienced so far. Of course, that soon changes as it meets a gateway in the fence running left to right across your route [20-90]. Paddle through the gateway and turn right to follow the fence-line downslope, ignoring the ladder stile just beyond this gateway.

The low wall of grey rock ahead of you grows rapidly closer until you are directly at its foot [20-91], ready to pick the most direct way onto its summit; **Ysgafell Wen (unnamed top)** (at **663485** – 669m/2194ft). Although this is not the main summit of Ysgafell Wen, it is clearly visible from the surrounding terrain; providing one of the finest viewpoints [20-92] as well as an opportunity to scan the route ahead.

**8)**  **(663485)** →

    **10°**        →

You can descend slightly to the right or slightly to the left as you follow the natural line of the ridge towards the next section of low ground. If you bear right you follow a steep path that joins a fence on your right, leading to the Eastern end of the Easternmost of the three Dog Lakes at **664487** [20-93 looking back towards the unnamed top]. But if you enjoy a bit of fun to liven up what will prove to be a scramble-free day, bear left instead to descend pleasant slopes to the lake's Southern shoreline. To reach the path at the Eastern end of the lake might involve you getting your feet slightly wet unless you can scrabble across the tilted slab of rock separating you from your intended destination [20-94 looking back from dry land].

There is yet another summit ahead of you, a third Ysgafell Wen as it were – only some 10 metres lower than the summit just vacated. Although this pimple does not feature as a 'top' in any guidebooks, and I have not given it separate billing here, it is still worth a quick visit since it involves little more than a five-minute detour to reach its summit [20-95 looking back]. And it adds completion to the day's efforts.

Once you have reached the end of the Ysgafell Wen ridge, there follows a helter-skelter route up and down rocky bluffs sandwiched between boggy hollows – some substantially boggier than others. Although you can choose your own line of attack across the rockier bits, it pays to keep close to the fence (running parallel to the path on your right-hand side) as you negotiate the hollows. In places the fence-posts can provide support as you are required to cross several difficult patches of quagmire.

Eventually you reach crags overlooking Llyn Edno, with the day's final summit beyond it [20-96].

*This fine viewpoint encourages one to pick off the entire panorama of Snowdonia as you scan the Northern horizon – Moel Hebog and neighbours, the Nantlle ridge, Yr Wyddfa, the Llanberis Pass and Glyderau, Pen Llithrig y*

*Wrach and Moel Siabod.*
*And of course Llyn Edno itself with one geometrically straight shoreline (no doubt tracing a geological fault-line) reminiscent of numerous lochans generally found in North-Western Scotland.*
*Moel Meirch is the highest pointy bit of the series of rocky crags that stand above the lake's North Eastern corner.*

The fence has already veered off to the right, but there is a more direct line you can follow to reach the Eastern end of this lake. Descending from these crags you first cross a small section of steep slab which can be slippery when iced up. But once you reach the peaty hollows again it is pretty much an action replay of what you have already encountered [20-97 looking back] – spongy ground where the water-table seems to be located barely below the lace-holes of your boots.

The extreme North-Eastern corner of Llyn Edno is made up of a series of finger-like embayments [20-98], and crossing the streams that drain Eastwards into more bog can prove difficult following prolonged wet weather. The surest means of getting across is to find the narrowest sections of stream closest to the lake itself. Heading further right towards the fence only presents you with the double hazard of water and mud.

I have completed this walk in mid-winter when most of the ground was frozen solid, but even then this particular bit adjacent to the fence left my boots thick with mud.

From a distance, you might already have noticed a relatively clear path weaving its way above the crags that hem in the lake beyond this point. First passing to the right of the extensive crag ahead of you [20-99], a clear path turns swiftly left behind the crag (away from the fence line low to your right). From here it climbs into the col separating the crag (now on your left) from the main body of Moel Meirch on your right. This path is the return route to the road, and a cairn marks the correct path to take from here on (in theory anyway).

**OPTION 5**
If you decide to miss out Moel Meirch, follow this path back to the end of the walk (as described following the return to **point 9**).

*Time saved – approximately 30 mins*

**9)**     **(663501)**     →

         330°              →

For the time being ignore this path heading off through the col. Instead cross a shallow, grassy trough [20-100] to reach yet another rocky shelf ahead of you. From its base a staircase path climbs steadily, skirting a series of crags until you emerge on a level platform surmounted by the naked rock of Moel Meirch. The highest point is marked by a prominent outcrop with a distinctive, miniature pyramidal shape, easily reached and with enough standing room for one – the summit of **Moel Meirch** (at **661503** – 607m/1991ft) [20-101].

**10)**     **(661503)**     →

          145°              →

From here it's a case of picking your way through the summit's rocky ramparts to regain the path. To retreat from the base of Moel Meirch to **point 9** you might as well keep close to the wire fence (now on your left-hand side) since this guarantees the most direct route.

**9)**     **(663501)**     →

         240°              →

Once you regain the path entering the col (now on your right), head right along it and beyond the highest point of the saddle locate a more intermittent path that runs down a broad valley towards the course of the Afon Llynedno [20-102 and 20-103]. In places the path that descends this valley is similar to a stream bed – in others it completely disappears. Generally, if you keep to the left-hand side of the main valley you will locate the path again as often as you misplace it.

---

### OPTION 6

Having followed this 'popular' path back to the road on several occasions, and not found the experience particularly enjoyable, I offer this alternative. It's a cop out perhaps, but one I would recommend if your sense of adventure has reached its limit.

Retrace your steps as far as the base of the third top of Ysgafell Wen, then from there head off to the right, following the faint path that runs North of the Dog Lakes before joining up with a clear track running along the Northern base of Y Cyrniau. From there it's a case of retracing your earlier steps past Llyn Llagi – no doubt reacquainting yourself with all those little features you noted during the ascent as you descend the slopes back to the roadside.

***Time saved – none, it could even take you 15 mins longer. But you should at least find your way back at the first attempt.***

---

Once the path reaches the first section of flat ground you will hopefully notice a pair of small waterfalls (little more than springs really) flowing from the cliffs set back on your left [20-104]. The two streams issuing from these waterfalls run across your route left to right and soon combine to form one watercourse. You are advised to cross both streams upstream of this confluence and head for the ruined sheepfold on the opposite bank (at **652498**) [20-105].

A grassy path weaves its way between the walls of this ruin then continues downstream, keeping a healthy distance from the river on your right. Shortly this path passes through a gap in a collapsed dry-stone wall beyond which there is a significant drop (the stream taking a similar plunge over polished slabs in a series of cataracts [20-106]). But for walkers it is an easy matter to clamber down to the right to reach the lower shelf of grassy ground close to the river edge. From there the path can be clearly seen running downstream, parallel to the river.

Unfortunately, from here on the path becomes a frustrating mixture of heather, rock and mud. In places, steeply incised tributary valleys enter the main valley from your left, and although it is usually a straightforward matter to cross these narrow gaps, choosing the right path can be a matter of trial and error. If you drop down closer towards the main river you often finish up at a dead end perched above the churning water. If instead you choose to climb out of the side-valleys, plunging through deep heather most of the time, you will find that any paths you meet bear further left, climbing higher above the main valley floor when in fact your aim is to get down-valley as quickly as possible.

However, even if you do end up on the higher crags above the main valley, by a mixture of trial and error you will locate an escape route to the right that leads you back towards the river. You often end up joining a path that has been clearly visible from a distance running along the river's grass-covered banks, and wonder how you missed such an obvious feature in the first place.

In contrast, the opposite bank of the river is impeded by massive dry-stone walls and dense vegetation. So be thankful that at least you are on the easier side of the valley. Persevere with the path (clear on the map – invisible for much of the time on the ground) and eventually, after passing through two boulder-strewn sections your patience is finally rewarded.

The river suddenly parts company with the path as it plunges straight ahead through a deep gorge. Fortunately the path takes a 90° turn left (close to **644496**) into a dark, damp corner over which tower the precarious tops of a tall, dry-stone wall.

As the wall shrinks to a less intimidating height a gap opens up on your right leading towards a collection of sheep enclosures [20-107]. The path finds its own way through this maze, then runs along the left-hand side of another dry-stone wall (on the other side of which lies green pasture and signs of civilisation). Climb the ladder stile over this wall to reach the field on your right [20-108] and if you look across the paddock stretching to your left you will notice a sunken, collapsed wall running downslope from left to right with some trees beyond.

There is a wide gap between the two main treed areas, and your route involves heading towards the first tree at the right-hand edge of this gap. As you approach this large tree, pass below it to its right, dropping down steeply at first into another paddock. A path runs off to the right, passing through an opening in a wall into more pasture beyond. However, you need to head left instead across wet ground towards a muddy patch alongside a stream.

A wooden bridge composed of railway sleepers crosses this watercourse, giving access by way of a very muddy track to the farm of Hafodau Brithion. Follow this track past the farm buildings and you meet a wide, gravelled roadway (the main driveway to the farm from the road). Follow this as it drops slightly – flanked on its left by a plantation of dense woodland. Then at an obvious bend where the trees end and the track splits in two, turn sharp right and follow the track up to the road (with another stand of dense conifers now behind the moss-covered dry-stone wall on your right).

---

### OPTION 7

To avoid passing through the busy farmyard it is possible to continue right, following the stream to where it meets a wall.

Cross a tributary stream to head left, climbing through a small set of crags beneath overhanging trees. Beyond here an unkempt path runs slightly uphill and left alongside the wall. Shortly you come up against a fenced barrier denying access to the dense woodland ahead. Turn immediately right through a collapsed wooden gate in the wall and after crossing a short ramp of grass you meet a much broader track. Follow this for a short distance left and uphill to meet the roadside at **637494**. Cross the ladder stile alongside the footpath signs and continue straight ahead along the road to the start point of the walk some 500 metres away, passing the farm track on your left.

---

This farm track emerges at the roadside at **637494**. Turn left onto the road and you are left with just a short stretch of tarmac to follow back to where you parked your car.

**END**

# Cnicht [72] / Foel Boethwel [73]

**9 Km (5.63 miles)**

**575m (1886ft)**

**Time : 3hrs 30min**

Erroneously named the 'Welsh Matterhorn' – a miniature mountain perched at the end of a relatively low-lying ridge.

Unlike most of the hills of Snowdonia, the mountain of Cnicht and the tiny village that lies at its foot share an intimate association. Croesor, nestling at Cnicht's shapely foot, is the starting point of one of the easier walks in the book. But one should not underestimate the route because Cnicht has all the character and qualities of a much loftier peak.

Its rugged appearance and secluded position can make it a mini-adventure for anyone prepared to tackle it head-on – an ideal 'first summit' for the younger hill-walker. And the final approach from the West presents a variety of easy scrambling opportunities. From its summit the expansive views make the most of Cnicht's exposure and its position relative to Snowdon and the surrounding hills as well as to the Western seaboard. There are also a number of descent options, (including this diversion to the neighbouring ridge of Foel Boethwel)

The beauty of this summit is that any walk you choose to follow can be as long or as short as you like. If time is pressing, Cnicht and back will take you less than three hours; but there are enough interesting features close at hand to keep the curious among you occupied for half a day or longer.

**North**

**Don't forget**

**map/compass whistle/torch**

**suitable footwear + clothing**

**food/drink**

**brain**

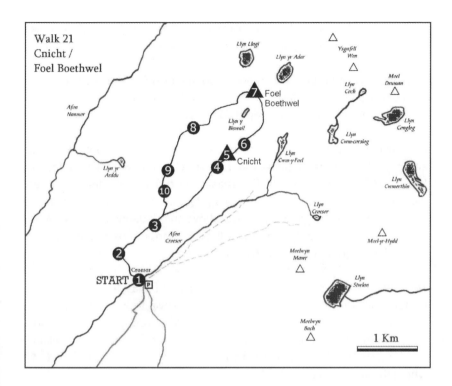

Walk 21
Cnicht /
Foel Boethwel

Llyn Llagi
Llyn yr Adar
Ysgafell Wen
Moel Druman
Llyn Coch
Afon Nanmor
Foel Boethwel
Llyn Conglog
Llyn y Biswail
Llyn Cwm-corsiog
Cnicht
Llyn Cwm-y-Foel
Llyn Cwmorthin
Llyn yr Arddu
Llyn Croesor
Moel-yr-Hydd
Afon Croesor
Moelwyn Mawr
Croesor
START
Llyn Stwlan
Moelwyn Bach
1 Km

## APPROACH

From the lowlands alongside the Afon Glaslyn close to Porthmadog, the skyline to the East and North East is dominated by the peaks of Cnicht, Moelwyn Mawr and Moelwyn Bach [21-01]. This is considered by many to be the classic view of these three tops.

The most straightforward access to Cnicht involves penetrating the hidden valley of Cwm Croesor in order to reach the village of Croesor where this walk begins.

If driving along the A498 road from Beddgelert towards Tremadog, at **594462** (Pont Aberglaslyn) take the left-hand junction onto the A4085 side road that runs to Penrhyndeudraeth. From Pont Aberglaslyn follow this road tortuously Southwards as it eventually traces the serrated line between the flat land close to sea-level (Traeth Mawr to the West) and the knobbly, rocky promontories of disintegrating high ground (the Moelwynion to the East).

1Km South West of the right-angled bend at **618428**, just as you approach the outskirts of Garreg, take the minor road left (signposted Croesor) that squeezes past an arched gateway at **614421**.

If travelling from the direction of Trawsfynydd or Porthmadog, once you enter Penrhyndeudraeth along the main street (the A487) take a side road (the A4085) that exits North. This road soon turns right, climbs a steep, narrow street and crosses the Ffestiniog Railway before swinging left and entering more open ground perched above the flatlands of Traeth Mawr. Shortly after you pass through the 'village' of Garreg look out for the side road exiting right to Croesor at **614421**.

This very narrow side road passes the walls of Plas Brondanw before climbing steadily for 3½Km, from close to sea-level to just above the 150-metre contour. As the angle of ascent eases, after you negotiate a double bend, you will reach a crossroads. Turn left here heading into Croesor village. On the right-hand side of the road is a sizeable, free car park at **631447** where the walk starts.

**START**

1)      **(631447)**       →

         305°              →

The car park alongside the Afon Croesor has an information board giving route details as well as other facts of interest about the locality.
Walk back to the road, turn right, cross the bridge over the stream and head uphill towards the chapel ahead of you on the right-hand side of this road.

The stone wall beneath this chapel has the faded word 'Cnicht' painted upon it with an arrow pointing left (signifying the correct direction to take). Continue straight ahead quite steeply uphill along the narrow road by-passing the chapel and a scattering of houses on the right-hand side.

As the road continues uphill it becomes enclosed on both sides – by a grass embankment topped by fencing on the right, and a dry-stone wall on the left [21-02 looking back downhill]. The distinct pyramid of Cnicht can be clearly seen on the right-hand skyline. Thankfully the initial steep ascent relents as the road begins to descend for a short stretch, swinging between some trees before reaching the gateway to a farm on your left at **629448**. To the right of this gateway is a metal gate and ladder stile giving access to a broad track. It is feasible to drive up to this point, but parking here is strictly inadvisable [21-03].

Cross the ladder stile and follow a clear track (composed of slate waste) gradually gaining height again as it passes through damp, scraggly woodland. Part of the way along you will pass through a new wooden gate in a wooden fence before eventually reaching level ground where the track splits in two (at **628451**).

The narrow track that continues ahead of you soon becomes at best a partially-overgrown footpath as it leads downhill across a damp saddle of ground, eventually dropping down into the Nanmor valley. The broader track passing through the gate on the right is the one you should follow to get onto Cnicht [21-04]. This and the path you follow later during this walk are clear for most of the way but you would be hard-pressed to pick them out on the OS map. Route-finding is not helped by much of Cnicht being shared by two separate sheets (OL17 and OL18).

2)      **(628451)**        →

        45°                 →

Go through the wooden gate (with a yellow route-marker on its left-hand post) onto the open, shaley track that begins to climb in a more Easterly direction. In places this path can be wet underfoot, but the going is never difficult as the rocky track leads ever closer towards the summit gracing the skyline ahead of you.

Gaining height gradually at first, the track weaves through reeds and sparse grassland before passing through an open gate. Beyond it the path degenerates into a series of ruts in the turf as it leads down towards a flat patch of wet ground [21-05]. The low walls of a collapsed building stand ahead of you, and to their right the ground clambers along what looks like a dry stream bed to reach a series of crags topped by a dry-stone wall just visible from this lower vantage point.

Bear right before you reach this tumbledown ruin (as per the small marker post pointing right) and as you approach the dry-stone wall perched on top of the crags you encounter a ladder stile allowing you to climb over it at **632454** [21-06].

| | | |
|---|---|---|
| **3)** | **(632454)** | → |
| | **40°** | → |

Once you reach the other side of the wall turn left (again as indicated by the marker post opposite the foot of the stile) [21-07]. Ahead of you now is a broad, grassy ridge leading towards the summit (although the base of Cnicht is still hidden by the rise of the land) [21-08]. Follow the faint track along this broad ridge as it climbs onto a shoulder of flatter ground. Here and there a few slabs of rock poke through the shallow turf but they are easily skirted by way of the path. The track passes through the remains of a collapsed wall and immediately beyond it stands a tiny stone enclosure [21-09] (at **635457**)

TAKE NOTE OF THE MINOR PATH HEADING OFF LEFT TOWARDS LOWER GROUND – THIS CONSTITUTES THE FINAL LEG OF YOUR RETURN ROUTE FROM FOEL BOETHWEL.

Beyond this enclosure the path leads in the direction of the summit now clearly visible on the skyline ahead. The path initially splits into two broad, grassy carriageways as it climbs the gentle slope – a set of crags diverting it to either side like a natural mini-roundabout.

*Now that you are above the 350-metre contour, the surrounding scenery opens up dramatically. Behind you the flatlands of Traeth Mawr are clearly visible – a patchwork of green fields, copses, pools and marsh-land extending to the sandy margins of the Glaslyn estuary [21-10].*

The estuary of the Afon Glaslyn was once navigable all the way up to the Aberglaslyn Bridge (at 594462) – indeed Beddgelert was a busy seaport during the Middle Ages.

But in 1811 an embankment was built across the river at Porthmadog (the 'Cob'). This was part of a cunning plan by William Madocks MP to provide an easy crossing point for traffic heading West to the Llŷn peninsula – he proposed a ferry terminal be sited on the North coast of Llŷn, thus opening up the entire area to Irish trade. The 'Cob' was also to provide access to his planned new towns of Porthmadoc and Tremadog.

The tiny village of Tremadog was built first, close to Madocks' home at Tan-yr-Allt. Porthmadog followed as the proposed site of the port needed to handle the increase in trade. However, his original intention never succeeded; Holyhead was chosen as the main port for the Irish mail. And although much of the Glaslyn estuary (some 7,000 acres) was reclaimed for grazing land, it is frequently inundated after heavy rain.

*Further right the slopes of Moel Hebog dominate the view [21-11]. And on the extreme right Yr Aran and its neighbours seem close enough to touch. Sweep your eyes left of the sea view and you are faced by the opposite wall of Cwm Croesor and the bulk of Moelwyn Mawr.*

The next level section is often wet underfoot but drier ground is close by on the right where a set of low crags are separated from the cliffs rising further to your right by a dry-stone wall topped by a fence [21-12]. Keeping close to this wall you will soon reach a ladder stile that allows you to cross over onto the boulder-strewn slopes of these cliffs [21-13]. A faint path contours beneath the steep wall of black rock on your right. The path eventually splits in two. The right-hand fork is badly eroded and gives difficult access onto the saddle of ground separating these cliffs from Cnicht's lower slopes. The better option is to follow the worn, rusty left-hand fork down at first, then easily upwards as it skirts above the worst of the coarse scree to reach that same saddle [21-14].

Gentle slopes topped by turf and an intermittent path now give easy access onto higher ground where the path eventually begins to pick its way through upended outcrops of shale [21-15, and 21-16 looking back downslope].

The angle increases in steepness, necessitating some simple scrambling for the first time today. Soon, however you reach another broad platform of level turf [21-17 looking back], with nothing but the bare summit of Cnicht now clearly ahead [21-18].

4)      **(644465)**        →

        **40°**             →

From this angle the mountain appears as a perfect triangle, but almost split in two – one half composed of slabs of bare, grey rock; the other a mix of sparse grass, scree and crag. A path can be seen climbing steeply along the line bisecting the centre of this triangle. This direct approach is the easiest route onto the summit. Begin by heading right at first across the triangle's base along the clear path cut into the turf. This path then makes a hasty ascent of the rock walls above you, climbing almost vertically at first. However, after some initial scrambling among the ribs of rock, the angle relents as you reach the spine of crag and loose boulders beneath the skyline [21-19 looking back]. The final line of attack requires a diversion left in order to approach the highest point from the North [21-20 looking back, and 21-21]. A succession of jagged, splintered slabs guards the hidden summit, but with minimum effort this awkward scramble suddenly springs the unsuspecting walker onto the knobbly ridge of **Cnicht** (at **644466** – 689m/2260ft).

> *From here the views are unmatched.*
> *The mountain's own humped ridge like some partially-buried dinosaur's spine extends further North East towards Ysgafell Wen and its lake-studded surroundings (Moel Siabod lurking in the background) [21-22].*
> *Then your eyes are drawn left to Yr Wyddfa and Y Lliwedd [21-23]; to their left the distant Nantlle Ridge giving way to the Moel Hebog group, and eventually the coastal lowlands of the lower Glaslyn [21-24].*
> *But most impressive of all is the deep trough of Cwm Croesor at your feet running parallel to the route you have already taken [21-25]. Finally, completing the circle, sweep your eyes past the backdrop of Moelwyn Mawr and Moelwyn Bach to pick out the hidden valley of Cwmorthin surrounded by evidence of the region's slate mining history [21-26].*

**5)**     **(644466)**     →

**225°**     →

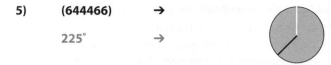

Every visitor to Cnicht should at least consider exploring the remaining two tops that form the summit ridge. They comprise a pair of rock-studded mounds, quite close together but separated from Cnicht's main summit by a lower plateau of damp ground [21-27]. To the right of the spine, scree slopes angle away towards the upper reaches of Cwm Croesor [21-28 and 21-29]. To the left untidy ground drops to the shores of one of the area's numerous lakes [21-30].

A clear path picks its way along the ridgeline and it's only as you approach the final top that you need to remove your hands from your pockets. The direct approach follows a short section of steep scrambling through angular rock – with abundant handholds and minimal exposure.

Once you reach this top you have used up your last chance to put hands onto rock for the day – unless you opt to miss out the second peak of the day and return the way you came.

---

### OPTION 1
If you have had enough for the day and if your mission is to reach the car park as directly as possible, return from this Easternmost top by the approach route….. you hardly need compass bearings to find your way back. It's a simple case of retracing your steps.
***Time saved – 1 hr plus***
***OR***
### OPTION 2
However, if you have time for a little extra scrambling, there are opportunities to sample a bit more excitement as you descend from Cnicht's main summit. As you drop to the right onto the ascent path, it is possible to exit this path further to your right and slide or scramble your way down the slabs and crags that make up Cnicht's Northern aspect. It's not particularly pretty, but it provides a diverting fifteen minutes or so and makes you thankful that you did not attempt the ascent by the same route.

---

*From the Easternmost top (at **648469**) the view beyond reveals the tracks that provide access to Ysgafell Wen and its neighbours.*

*There is also a full-frontal view into the upper corner of Cwmorthin – the quarry-scarred valley that leads onto Moelwyn Mawr's Northern slopes.*

---

### OPTION 3

Anyone wishing to forego Foel Boethwel's ascent but fancying an alternative route from the direct or indirect returns offered by Options 1 and 2 can reach Croesor village by way of Cwm Croesor.

Head for lower ground beyond the summit's Eastern top [21-31]. You eventually reach a path cut into the turf, doubling back on your right to head back down towards Cwm Croesor. The slopes it contours are quite steep, but with care you soon find yourself a short distance above the Western shores of Llyn Cwm y Foel (close to **653468**); a reservoir dammed at its Southern end.

It is not a particularly attractive body of water – strand lines a good two metres or more above the water level show how the reservoir has shrunk in recent years. The breach in the ugly, concrete wall ahead of you explains the fall in the lake's level. A path follows the shoreline as far as the dam. It is then possible to cross the river flowing through the breached dam – descend below a small cataract – then recross the river to regain its Northern bank.

Now follow the rusted and disrupted pipeline down-valley, avoiding the precipitous route taken by the river, A footpath delineates the easiest route, at times hugging the underside of a slate wall on your right in danger of collapse due to the scree slopes above.

Eventually as you reach the main valley floor you meet with the straight-forward track running past Canolfan Blaencwm.

From here a long, straight track-cum-roadway leads along the entire length of Cwm Croesor until you reach the metalled road at **636449**. Shortly you meet the crossroads with the car park to your right.

***Allow approx 1hr 30min for this return leg***

---

6)     (649469)          →

     30°                       →

However, there is one more '600-metre+' summit to be climbed – one that you are unlikely ever to consider setting foot on unless you have already wandered as far as Cnicht's Eastern outlier. Unlike any other summit in this book, it is fair to say that Foel Boethwel does not command an imposing posture above the countryside surrounding it. Indeed, even from the lofty position of Cnicht's Eastern top you would do well to pick it out even though it lies less than a kilometre away to the North.

Looking to your left towards Llyn y Biswail, more elegant and elongated from this angle despite its dubious name ('biswail' being the Welsh word for 'dung'), you will see the knobbly ridge that forms the lake's far (North Western) shore and rises gradually as it heads in the direction of Moel Meirch [21-32 from Cnicht's summit ridge]. Follow that hummocky spine with your eyes and somewhere along its line the ground just about manages to creep above the 600-metre contour.

From Cnicht's Easternmost summit an easy stroll across springy turf follows a clear track descending the ridge's gentle ramparts. Where the track splits in two, keep left heading towards Llyn yr Adar (the large body of water stretched out on the platform of peaty moorland ahead of you and slightly to your left – helpfully as far as identification is concerned, this lake also has a tiny island) [21-33].

The right fork skirts the headwall of Cwm-y-Foel – with a sharp reversal to the right as it heads back down into Cwm Croesor. This is the route to take if you are following **Option 3**. The left fork continues to descend gently towards the North East, eventually reaching the shores of Llyn yr Adar. There it mingles with the multitude of paths that run North towards the upper edge of the corrie above Llyn Llagi, and East towards Moel Druman and Allt-Fawr (see **Walk 20**).

295°          →

But there is no need to go as far as the lake's shore. Once the angle of slope reveals Llyn yr Adar's Southern shoreline ahead of you, turn left and cross easy ground to a damp saddle of boggy ground containing a small, ephemeral pool tucked away further again to your left (at **651476**) [21-34]. Moisture from this pool drains sluggishly through wet ground and between islets of grey rock before consolidating into a stream feeding Llyn yr Adar.

Descend to this low embayment, bearing slightly right to reach some rocky outcrops. Hopping onto these will ensure dry passage to the rising ground directly ahead. A short climb onto the low ridge beyond gives little clue to where the elusive summit itself lies. But if you look along the spine of hummocky ground as it trends right above Llyn yr Adar's Northern shores you should be able to pick out the tiny pile of stones marking the highest point of the ridge, **Foel Boethwel** (at **650476** – 602m/1975ft) [21-35 from Cnicht's North Eastern end].

Even an insignificant little top like Foel Boethwel owes its existence to the nature of the underlying rocks hereabouts. Much of this lake-studded upland area is composed of mudstone or siltstone – generally soft and easily worn away by the ice sheets that once blanketed the region. But some 450-470 million years ago (towards the end of the Ordovician period) when much of this part of North Wales was subject to frenzied volcanic activity, vast amounts of molten rock either escaped from volcanoes (many undersea) or were injected into the adjacent strata if unable to find a weak point to break through the overlying crust. These igneous intrusions, sandwiched between the older, original rocks, cooled relatively slowly to form sheets of dolerite – a much tougher cookie than mudstone. Over time as the overlying rocks succumbed to the elements these dolerite intrusions were exposed to the elements but did not wear away so readily.

As you might expect, Allt-Fawr, Moel Druman, Ysgafell Wen, Moel Meirch, Craig Llyn-llagi, Cnicht and Foel Boethwel all correspond to points on the ground where dolerite reaches the surface.

Dolerite is what is termed a 'basic' igneous rock – formed from molten rock low in silica or quartz (which is why they usually end up being dark in colour). When 'basic' molten rock erupts onto the surface it forms basalt (the same rock type found in the Giant's Causeway in Northern Ireland or in Fingal's Cave on Rhum).

The other main type of igneous rock is termed 'acid' because it has a high silica content. The commonest acid igneous rock is granite – which as a consequence is usually a paler grey or pink in colour. Mynydd Mawr is chiefly composed of granite which again was injected into the surrounding bedrock towards the end of the Ordovician period. Close by in Cwmorthin there are large outcrops of rock composed of rhyolite which erupted onto the surface – the 'acid' equivalent of basalt.

Further afield, the twin tops of Y Lliwedd correspond exactly to where two small 'islands' of rhyolite survive on a bed of basaltic rock. Interestingly, Snowdon's foundations are rocks composed of ash and other fragments from a rhyolite-type flow whilst much of its summit is made up of coarser volcanic debris from a basalt-type eruption.

In the simplest of terms whether molten rock beneath the earth's surface forms an acid or basic igneous rock is pretty much due to how far deep beneath the earth's crust that lava or magma originated. Magma which is mainly acidic in nature is denser and more viscous (and so flows less easily) than basic magma so the two tend to appear at quite separate levels in a region's rock strata following volcanic activity even though they may have been formed at the same period geologically (and originated from the same underlying well of molten rock).

**7)    (650476)    →**

**220°    →**

Now that the geology lesson is over you will find little else to keep you perched here for long unless it's time for a bite to eat and a refreshing drink. Once you have basked in the summit's muted glory, head West along this broad, knobbly spine of ground away from Llyn yr Adar in the general direction of Llyn y Biswail. Eventually you come across outcrops of quartz-veined rock; patches of white in the predominantly grey crags.

Llyn y Biswail fills the low ground to your left but easier progress is maintained by keeping to the modest ridgeback as you skirt the lake's Northern shore (crossing partially-buried sections of collapsed wall along the way). You eventually reach a dry-stone wall running across the valley left to right but breached here and there by substantial gaps. Turn right to follow the line of this wall as it drops over the lip of ridge and heads downhill to your right.

*Facing left you get a better idea of the length of the Cnicht ridge – the character of the mountain masked by its more familiar Western pyramid.*
*You might also take time to study the craft of the dry-stone wall builder – shown off here to good effect by a short section of lattice work (a strange headband of perforated wall cresting the ridge [21-36]).*

As you continue downslope the path becomes wet in places, but once you drop below the skyline bear left through one of the gaps in the wall. Cross the slopes beyond to enter a broad valley with a large stream feeding it from the left and threading its way downhill in a series of small cataracts [21-37 looking back]. Your path runs parallel to this stream, and eventually meets up with it before it makes its final steep descent to the flat floor of the valley [21-38].

Perched above this final set of falls you will see the river splitting and rejoining itself before passing through a gap in a dry-stone wall with a ladder stile on its opposite bank (at **641472**). Crossing this braided stream and reaching the lower ground on its opposite bank presents no difficulties. Ignore the ladder stile on the floor of the valley. Instead follow one of the faint paths that run left and parallel to the wall.

| | | | |
|---|---|---|---|
| **8)** | **(640472)** | → | |
| | **235°** | → | |

The dry-stone wall takes a slightly sinuous line before heading off in search of higher ground (the hummocky foothills of Yr Arddu) [21-39]. However, the path you need to follow bears left away from this dry-stone wall in the direction of the obvious breach in the skyline. This significant gap is Bwlch y Battel – a natural passage linking Nanmor valley in the North to Cwm Croesor in the South. Passing between the litter of angular boulders strewn at the entrance to the col the ground turns increasingly wet as you approach the boggy margins of a large, unnamed lake (at **636467**) [21-40]. Present-day maps show a submerged track bisecting the lake but you are better off following the faint path along the right-hand shoreline which gives dry passage to the far shore.

On older editions of maps for this area there is no lake shown – just a patch of marshy ground (hence the bizarre route followed by the original path, and presumably the lack of a name for the present lake).

Continue straight ahead now, keeping to the right of the prominent hillock on the immediate skyline [21-41]. There is a path of sorts through this area of wet ground – although in places what you appear to be following are wheel ruts probably left by the local farmer's all-terrain bike. Beyond the hillock you enter a damp, grassy hollow where the path swings slightly right to approach a mass of fallen rock at the base of a distinctive rocky cliff [21-42].

9)    (636465)    →

    195°          →

As you get nearer to these fallen rocks your path combines with a stream that eventually escapes through the narrow gap ahead to tumble quite steeply to the next grassy hollow beneath. Fortunately there is a clear, white gravel path on the right-hand bank of the stream that leads you easily to lower ground [21-43, and 21-44 from lower down looking back upstream].

    95°          →

This reed-covered hollow is wet but it is possible to avoid the worst by crossing the stream close to a large dry-stone enclosure on your left.

By picking a way through the loose blocks at the base of these slopes on your left you reach the dry-stone wall that can be seen crossing grassy slopes further ahead as it heads towards a set of dark crags on the hillside beyond.

10)   (634460)    →

    205°          →

A more substantial wall appears as you turn the corner of the rocky spur on your left where it meets the fern-covered banks of a stream [21-45]. Almost immediately you will come across a large gap in this wall. This leads to other fern-covered slopes across which a path climbs towards a disused quarry at the base of Cnicht. Your route heads off to the right of this path but a wire fence bars the way. However, it is possible to climb over the fence where it abuts against the wall (taking care not to become entangled in the topmost strand of barbed wire – or to dislodge any stones).

There is a second gap in the wall a short distance further along through which the stream emerges. But this gap does not provide a means of passage for walker or sheep (as it is barred by a grille of rock slabs carefully inserted by the craftsman who originally built the wall).

*On the other side of this wall you should be able to identify the large outcrop of dark crag facing you across the valley floor; the cliffs you by-passed on your approach to Cnicht's South Western end earlier in the day.*

The floor of this valley is particularly wet hereabouts and although the fence you crossed eventually meets up with a collapsed dry-stone wall heading directly across the valley on a collision course with these dark cliffs [21-46] it does not provide a recommended route of escape. From this low ground you also get a clear view of Cnicht's Western top.

Once you have passed through the first gap in the wall, and safely reached the other side of the fence, turn right to cross the stream and head upslope bearing slightly left of the wall. If you continue far enough along this low ridge and turn to look back again you will notice signs of extensive tunnelling into the mountain's basement rocks – a couple of deep clefts together with waste tips at their entrances [21-47].

Quarrying hereabouts was never carried out on the same scale as it was further East in Cwm Croesor and Cwmorthin. In many cases small-scale quarrying became a sideline utilised by local farmers to supplement their meagre income. All too often these excavations proved largely uneconomical and were soon abandoned.

As you cross the drier patches aim for lower ground further left by way of a faint path. Ahead and on the left now lie two grey heaps of waste rock. Cross to the first of these and join the clear path that traverses its upper surface. This path leads on to the second and larger of the two tips where there are sizeable ruins alongside [21-48].

Continue heading upslope of these ruins and on the low skyline to your left you should be able to pick out a small stone enclosure. Alongside it is the main ascent path to Cnicht. Turn right once you join this path and retrace your steps to the ladder stile in the wall at **632454** (**point 3**). Cross the stile and simply reverse your ascent route all the way back to the outskirts of Croesor village.

**END**

# WALK 22
## Moelwyn Mawr [74] / Moelwyn Bach [75] / Moel-yr-Hydd [76]

| 11 Km (6.9 miles)<br><br>820m (2690ft)<br><br>Time : 5hrs | **Three majestic tops – a trio of gems in the rough setting of this industrially-scarred corner of Snowdonia** |
| --- | --- |

I have no excuses for avoiding this group of summits for the best part of my walking days. I had often wondered about what reaching their tops might be like – reading the guide-books and studying plenty of maps – it's just that I could find little in their austere, craggy outlines to attract. Things were not helped much by the photographs I had seen – dark, misshapen hulks of slate, beached in an industrial wasteland, and capped in almost every view by dark, brooding cloud. After all, Blaenau Ffestiniog close by is allegedly one of the wettest towns in Wales.

I can remember being brought here on a school trip to visit the Pumped-Storage Hydro Electric Power station at Tanygrisiau, followed by an afternoon deep inside Trawsfynydd nuclear power station. What I don't recall is being inspired by the surrounding hills.

So, with myriad doubts in my mind, I finally made my way into this slate-tip-shrouded corner of the National Park. What an eye-opener. The first day I spent in these hills remains one of the most cherished mountain memories I have. And I've returned many times to rekindle the experience. Despite, or perhaps because of the profuse evidence of man's exertions in this harsh, inhospitable area, a visit here remains long in the memory for all the right reasons.

Allow yourself a full day – preferably rain-free. And yes, don't forget your head-torch!

**North**

**Don't forget**

**map/compass**
**whistle/torch**

**suitable footwear + clothing**

**food/drink**

**brain**

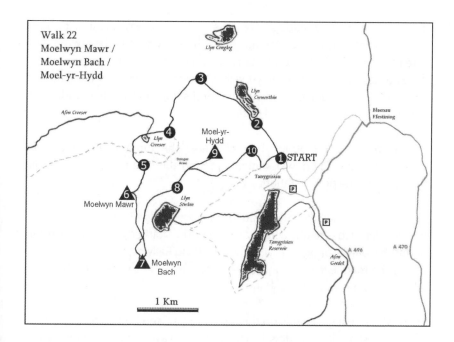

Walk 22
Moelwyn Mawr /
Moelwyn Bach /
Moel-yr-Hydd

## APPROACH

From the North follow the A470 Dolgellau road through Dolwyddelan and over the Crimea Pass. The road drops down steeply into Blaenau Ffestiniog – but at the foot of the hill at the roundabout don't turn left towards the town centre. Instead go straight ahead along the A496, following the signs for Porthmadog – the road immediately crosses the railway line, takes a sharp bend right than another left.

This road passes the large 'Rehau' factory on the left then on your right is a turn-off for Tanygrisiau and the power station. Turn right here, ignoring the first side road left that leads to the power station.

From the South, if driving from Ffestiniog along the A470 continue through the town of Blaenau Ffestiniog until you reach the roundabout. Take the A496 left here, and continue past the 'Rehau' factory on your left to the turn-off right for Tanygrisiau and the power station. Turn right here, ignoring the first side road left that leads to the power station.

If driving from Porthmadog, cross the 'Cob' causeway, passing through Minffordd and Penrhyndeudraeth. Ignore the exit right for Maentwrog then take the next left (A496) signposted Blaenau Ffestiniog. The road runs along the Southern side of the Dwyryd valley, enters a section of woodland and after crossing a bridge on a sharp bend drops downhill along a sudden exit road left (signposted Blaenau Ffestiniog).

Follow this road for about 4Km and take the turning left signposted Tanygriasiau and the power station, ignoring the side road first left again that leads to the power station.

From here, continue directly ahead to the cross-roads with the village school on your left. Go straight across along 'Ffordd Dolrhedyn', up a steep hill, under the railway bridge carrying the Ffestiniog Railway, then uphill again to where the road levels off. Ignore the next exit left at the crest of the steep hill, continuing straight ahead instead.

Then after passing a chapel on the right and terraced houses on the left the road bears sharp left and downhill towards the playground. Don't follow that road, instead continue straight ahead onto a much narrower road, 'Dolrhedyn Terrace', which is a dead-end. A short distance on the left is a gravelled area with enough space for about a dozen cars [22-01].

## START

1)      (683455)      →

        315°      →

At the far end of this improvised parking space are three gates as you face up-valley. The one on the left is a small kissing-gate allowing access to the river close by and the footbridge – this is your return route. To its left is a slate marker stone inscribed 'Y Cnicht' 'Moelwyn' and 'Cwmorthin'. The wider gate on the right, with another kissing-gate alongside it, leads onto a steep track of crushed slate heading uphill to each of these three destinations.

*Take a moment to marvel at the wall of slabs on your left where the river escapes Llyn Cwmorthin en route to the Tanygrisiau reservoir in a series of vertical falls and plunge pools [22-02 and 22-03 from beneath the falls on the return leg, and 22-04 from the path above].*

After some initial steepness the gradient eases, as does the river's descent alongside the track (its course is now channelled between slate embankments). Shortly on your left on the opposite bank of this stream you will see a strange pyramid construction of slate blocks surrounded by flagstones, and with a triangle of paler stones extending out from each of its four corners. At one time this was a 'slate garden' carefully tended by a local quarry-man [22-05].

The track splits up a short distance ahead [22-06]; the right-hand fork climbing up between heaps of slate waste. Ignore this diversion and turn left instead. Follow the level track to where the waters of Llyn Cwmorthin materialize ahead of you with a reed-covered weir at its Southern end where the river drains out of it [22-07].

**2)    (679460)    →**

**260°    →**

Walk across the two slabs of slate (an eco-friendly footbridge) that spans the river on your left to join the path following the lake's Western shore [22-08]. Set back on the left of this path is a row of ruined cottages – only a few walls and two chimney stacks left intact – perched beneath the steep crags of Foel Ddu [22-09].

These are the sorry remains of what was once known as 'Rhosydd Terrace' – six cottages that provided accommodation for the married men who worked in the nearby Cwmorthin Quarry and their families. The unmarried men were less fortunate – forced to live in squalid barracks further up the valley, closer to the working area.

Due to the quarry's remote location, most quarrymen barracked in the valley from Monday morning to Saturday afternoon as there was no train to ferry them to and from work unlike the other Ffestiniog quarries.

*On a sunny day this is a pleasant spot – pale green reeds and lily pads filling the nearer, left-hand corner of the lake close to its outflow. Behind the lake tower the sheer cliffs of Allt y Ceffylau, the Western extension of the high ground comprising Allt-Fawr.*

*Under ideal conditions the myriad reflections in the lake can be mesmerising [22-10 to 22-12].*

Follow this level track – passing through a kissing-gate next to a locked gate [22-13]. The track rounds a rock spur on the left then passes through a second kissing-gate next to another gate [22-14]. Ahead of you on your left, next to a tall pine tree, are the ruins of a chapel (at **672463**) [22-15].

Rhosydd Chapel also doubled as the schoolhouse to educate the children of the quarrymen and local farmers (although boys were expected to take up work following their ninth birthday).

One can imagine an itinerant preacher being summoned here on a dismally wet and windy Sunday to take the three services for the local congregation. There could have been few more austere settings for a place of worship – yet the chapel was the hub of the local community. And given the hardship and deprivation the average working family endured in these parts, the best salvation any preacher could hope to offer was for each man to love the Lord, obey the Bible and be satisfied with his lot in this life.

Much of Llyn Cwmorthin is silting up (although slate, not silt, is the main culprit). A good deal of waste has been washed into the lake from the tips on its Eastern shore, or from other detritus carried down by the river descending from Llyn Conglog (once an upland reservoir feeding this lower lake). Set behind a small stand of mixed conifers and deciduous trees in Llyn Cwmorthin's Westernmost corner are the ruins of 'Cwmorthin Hall' – originally the home of the Rhosydd Quarry manager. On the left-hand side of the track stands a large group of ruined buildings, once dressing sheds for the slate brought downhill from Conglog Quarry. Behind it rise conical mountains of slate waste from the much larger Rhosydd Quarry on higher ground to the West.

**3)    (670466)    →**

**270°**    →

If you have kept your eyes peeled as you followed this track you will already have seen it bearing left beyond these buildings and climbing steadily to higher slopes [22-16]. There would appear to be a short-cut leading through the slate tips on your left but that is best ignored.

> *As you gain height at last it is worth looking back at the shrunken waters of Llyn Cwmorthin – the massive slate tips at its furthest end spilling into the lake. The solitary pine tree and ruined chapel stand isolated on its South Western shore facing the headwall of Allt y Ceffylau and the higher crags of Craig Nyth-gigfran. The scene has a distinctly gothic feel about it even in bright sunshine.*
> *Below, the rectangular floor-plan of the old slate-dressing sheds has retained some integrity – although the walled enclosures now double as seasonal sheep pens [22-17 and 22-18].*

Follow the track up the valley head to where it levels out again as the slate tips encroach on both sides. On your right two rectangular structures remain half-embedded in the hillside [22-19 and 22-20]. It is likely that their function was linked to the stream channelled alongside – possibly a water-wheel was attached to one or the other in the past.

From these buildings the path rises through the waste again to finally level off at the head of the main valley. This ascent route follows Bwlch Cwmorthin, and beyond lies Bwlch y Rhosydd which leads down over the high saddle into the upper reaches of Cwm Croesor. Set on this level plateau between the two passes are the surface ruins of Rhosydd Quarry. Close by is where the barracks were located – 'Cwmorthin Cottages' as they were called [22-21].

Despite appalling living conditions, the quarrymen led a full social life in the evenings. As well as the chapel down in the valley bottom (where they attended mid-week sessions of the 'Band of Hope' to reinforce temperance, and the 'Seiat' to ponder over other religious and philosophical matters) they also spent a great deal of time in the 'Caban'.

The 'Caban' was a building used as a canteen and social club where nights were spent debating working conditions, composing intricate lines of Welsh poetry ('cynghaneddion') perhaps in competition at a local Eisteddfod, singing hymns and no doubt putting the world to rights. Despite often having only a basic education, most of the quarrymen could pick out familiar verses in the Bible, and could argue for their rights if pushed. Sadly the only signs that remain here now of sophisticated rhetoric are the words 'English Out' scrawled in white paint on one of the walls. This is almost certainly a contemporary addition.

Pick your way carefully across the waste-strewn ground. In places it shows sign of subterranean collapse, but not on a catastrophic scale. There is a multitude of tunnels perforating these hills since all the mining was carried out underground. Some of the surviving entrances can still be seen, but their slate lintels and arches are almost level with the ground now due to subsidence. Directly South is a tall, conical heap of slate waste with a walled ramp leading up its left-hand side from these disused workings (think of 'Macchu-Pichu' and you get the picture). Closer to the bottom of this ramp is a tunnel entrance cut into the rock on the left [22-22 and 22-23].

Rhosydd and the neighbouring Croesor quarries lie deep within the bowels of Moelwyn Mawr. Rhosydd was the larger of the pair with 170 chambers arranged over 14 floors.

In the later stages of their development the two mines slowly approached each other's extremities until each accused the other of poaching its slate. To settle the matter, and enable more accurate surveying of each mine's margins, a short tunnel was cut to connect the two mines. This tunnel was also used to improve ventilation – and could be used as an escape route in the event of an accident. However, the Rhosydd manager eventually had a wall built across it to deter his own miners absconding from work before their shift was due to finish by escaping into the adjacent workings.

The tunnel at the bottom of this ramp is the No. 9 adit, one of the main entrances into the underground quarry. It was a horizontal transport and drainage tunnel, extending over 2200ft into the hill on a gradient of 1 in 86. Wagons were hauled in and out using a continuous belt or rope which was winched by a water-driven wheel.

All levels below No. 9 adit are now flooded, and sometime around August 1998 a substantial collapse resulted in the chamber at the end of this opening being totally destroyed

YOU CAN GET CLOSE ENOUGH TO PEER INTO ITS BLACK, DRIPPING MOUTH, BUT KEEP YOUR HEAD-TORCH FOR LATER. THIS IS NOT A PLACE TO INVESTIGATE TOO CLOSELY.

Follow the ramp uphill – it continues onto another short path climbing across the lower slopes of the waste tips [22-24]. At the top it passes between two short sections of wall – probably once the site of a winching-tower [22-25]. Flat ground lies beyond with your first glimpse of Moelwyn Mawr on the skyline directly ahead.

> To the right are the upper reaches of Cwm Croesor with the long ridge of Cnicht, topped at its Western extremity by its rocky summit. The word 'Matterhorn' hardly springs to mind, does it?
> A track can be picked out clinging to the lower slopes of the mountain not far beneath the defunct reservoir of Llyn Cwm y Foel.
> The serrated crest of Moelwyn Mawr stretches across the Southern skyline, grassy slopes on the left, scree covering much of its middle, and steep cliffs on the right. A small hillock of grey crags also occupies the foreground in front of its Eastern end.

Finished slate from the Rhosydd Quarry was originally taken down past Llyn Cwmorthin to the Cwmorthin tramway on pack-horses – and thence by rail from Tanygrisiau to Porthmadog. But the tramway was owned by Cwmorthin Quarry and there was fierce rivalry between the two quarries since Rhosydd Quarry and Cwmorthin Quarry were owned by two different companies.

In 1864 the owners of Rhosydd Quarry constructed the Croesor tramway which carried the finished product directly from their dressing sheds down Cwm Croesor to Porthmadog. From there, of course, it was exported worldwide.

4)　　(665458)　　→

　　255°　　→

OPTION 1

The more direct route from here bears left towards the grassy ramp ascending the left-hand shoulder of Moelwyn Mawr.

Keep to the left-hand side of the last set of ruins you pass on the uppermost shelf of the quarry workings [22-26] and there is a path cut into the turf heading in the direction of the higher ground just below Moelwyn Mawr's summit ridge. This path emerges on a flat area of grassland [22-27] with more heaps of slate waste in the distance on your left. As you get nearer to these heaps there is a ladder stile giving access to a fenced area [22-28]. A red warning sign to its left [22-29] warns about the dangerous condition of the path which runs perilously close to the crumbling edge of the collapsed workings close by. However, across this stile a perfectly safe path continues uphill [22-30 looking back] towards the lower slopes of Moelwyn Mawr. An arrow sign alongside this path confirms that you are on the right track [22-31]. It is now an easy jaunt up gentle, grassy slopes forming the saddle separating the higher tops from Moel-yr-Hydd [22-32 looking back] and you quickly reach the ladder stile close to **point 5** [22-33].

*Time saved about 40mins*

On my first visit here I was too enthralled by my surroundings to think about any short-cuts just yet. Llyn Croesor looked worth visiting – at least on the map it looks a potentially idyllic spot for a picnic.

As you face Moelwyn Mawr you will notice a small, square roofed building still in a fairly good state of repair set away to the right-hand side of the ruins [22-34]. Behind it to the left is a ladder stile crossing a wire fence. Climb over the stile onto wet, spongy turf that continues by way of hummocky ground along the Northern shore of Llyn Croesor. A prominent pyramid of crags stands on the right-hand side of the stone barrier holding back what unfortunately turns out to be a sorry excuse for a lake.

Llyn Croesor has all but dried up, or leaked away. All that remains apart from a shallow pool is a patchwork of vegetation, mud, slate and the occasional sheep carcass. And the stone barrier or dam holding back the flood is actually a pair of walls built onto a causeway [22-35]. A track crosses this from one side to the other before heading to the right, downslope towards Croesor Quarry.

There are hardly any signs of the Croesor mine visible at ground level. After almost 100 years of slate production, the Croesor and Rhosydd quarries both closed in the 1930's. At the peak of production over 500 men were employed here, turning out over 11,000 tons of finished slate annually.

*The grey walls of Moelwyn Mawr tower above the green slopes ahead of you. Below, to the right, are the remains of Croesor Quarry – little more than a platform of crushed slate waste with the ruined foundations of a few buildings and a hidden ramp leading to a track winding down the valley side [22-36]. Again much of the quarrying here was carried out underground. Since the quarrymen lived in Croesor village or on the neighbouring small-holdings the site was much smaller than many others nearby.*

Follow this track as it descends quite steeply to the right towards the site of the old quarry. But in order to avoid losing too much height, aim towards the right-hand end of Moelwyn Mawr's skyline. If you look directly uphill from the track you will notice a small grass-covered knob of white rock at the top of the slopes immediately flanking the path [22-37]. Head up the slopes towards this bulge of white rock.

As you gain height and the ground levels off you will see a fenced-off square of grass, and looking back towards Cnicht a small pool lies just to its left

[22-38]. Between the fence and the pool is the faint path that exits Cwm Croesor onto these slopes.

From this relatively low vantage point the Northern face of Moelwyn Mawr looks impregnable [22-39], but the col well to the left of its scree-covered slopes is easily attainable. As you turn left now to climb the gentle grassy slopes in the direction of the col, keep right of the bulky spur forming the left-hand wall of this corrie. This ascent route is largely trackless, passing a number of small waste piles of slate (much of it 'contaminated' by blocks of white quartz that compromised the slate's perfect cleavage). But the angle of the hillside you have to climb is never severe and in short time you reach the high saddle at **661453**.

> *Your reward here is a bird's-eye view of Moel-yr-Hydd [22-40]. This is a shapely mountain, largely of grass-covered rock, whose South-facing flanks have been totally torn away – partly by nature, but mainly by the nearby Wrysgan Quarry to the West of Tanygrisiau.*
>
> *Even more eye-catching are the enormous pits in the foreground. These mark areas where major underground excavations have collapsed. Recently the entire area adjacent to these pits has been fenced off due to the continuing instability of the ground, and there are notices advising you to keep well clear (this applies particularly to the path running between the two largest holes as shown on the Explorer map).*
>
> *Perversely, the two pits and their unstable environs lie within the boundary of the Snowdonia National Park, but the entire massif of Moel-yr-Hydd is excluded.*
>
> *More of this later.*

**5)**    **(661453)**    →

      **200°**    →

A fence runs the lower length of the saddle with a ladder stile almost directly where you reach the skyline. This gives access to the paths crossing the foot of Moel-yr-Hydd and eventually dropping down either to Cwm Stwlan or Tanygrisiau. Ignore the stile and instead turn right to follow a steep but painless path [22-41], cut clearly into the turf as it zig-zags up the Northern spur of **Moelwyn Mawr** to the summit trig point (at **658448** – 770m/2526ft) [22-42].

> *Scanning the skyline in a clockwise sweep from the summit you take in pretty much all the surrounding peaks. Starting with Moel Hebog, it is easy to identify the Nantlle Ridge [22-43], then further right the Snowdon Horseshoe [22-44], then Moel Siabod [22-45] and finally Moel Penamnen set further back.*
>
> *Closer at hand are the scree-curtained slopes of Cnicht, the lake-studded uplands of Ysgafell Wen to Allt-Fawr, and finally Moel-yr-Hydd beyond which sprawls the built-up area of Blaenau Ffestiniog.*
>
> *In the opposite direction to the high ground two things compete for your attention: Moelwyn Bach, a misshapen brute of a mountain, backed by Llyn Trawsfynydd [22-46] – and the coastline dominated by Traeth Bach where the Afon Glaslyn enters Cardigan Bay with further left the coastal settlements of Porthmadog and Morfa Bychan [22-47].*

**6)**     **(658448)**     →

    **115°**             →

Unless conditions are dire, it is no easy matter dragging yourself off this high summit. If you want to stretch out your time here even further it is well worth following the ridge along its Western arm to where steep crags overlook Cwm Croesor. But the next stage involves dropping down from Moelwyn Mawr's summit onto the fin of rock angling down into Bwlch Stwlan.

The descent of the ridge linking Moelwyn Mawr to Moelwyn Bach can be tricky if iced over, but its roller-coaster quality makes it a pleasant contrast to the ground you have covered so far. Retreat from the summit trig point by retracing your steps across sloping grassland for a few metres before beginning to trend to the right, heading more steeply down convex slopes towards the hidden valley ahead.

    **155°**          →

As you begin to lose height, keep trending to the right across these grassy slopes to join a faint path heading in the direction of Llyn Trawsfynydd to the left of Moelwyn Bach's bulk [22-48]. The Eastern face of Moelwyn Mawr drops away quickly to your left into the massive cirque which now contains the circular, dammed lake of Llyn Stwlan [22-49]. This is the upper reservoir of the pumped storage scheme linked to Tanygrisiau Reservoir on the valley floor.

There is a hydro-electric power station on the shore of Tanygrisiau reservoir which supplies energy to the National Grid when necessary – the first such scheme to be constructed in Britain.

When there is surplus electricity in the Grid, largely generated by the neighbouring nuclear power station on Llyn Trawsfynydd, it is impractical to reduce output from that site – so the surplus power is used to pump water from Tanygrisiau reservoir uphill to Llyn Stwlan. Then when electricity demands cannot be met solely by Trawsfynydd, water from Llyn Stwlan is released to drive the turbines in the Tanygrisiau hydro-electric station, instantly generating an extra supply at minimal cost financially.

Llyn Stwlan is named after the high pass above it, Bwlch Stwlan. This pass was originally named Bwlch Trwstyllon on early maps. Like many Welsh geographical names there is some ambiguity as to its origins. Some authorities suggest it comes from the Welsh word 'trwstan' meaning awkward – describing a pathless ascent perhaps.

But I had a strange experience here one day while resting my bones above the lake. There had been RAF jets flying overhead for much of the morning – black arrows chased by their shadows across the terrain below and the shrieking roar of their passage. I had also heard the whistle of the little steam engine running along Ffestiniog railway many times during the descent of Moelwyn Mawr. Now suddenly there came a deep, throbbing sound that seemed to reverberate off the surrounding rocks. It grew louder and I sat expectantly, waiting for at the very least a Hercules transport plane or a Lancaster bomber to cruise across the open valley below me.

Then suddenly the timbre of the sound changed to the feeble, distant chopping of a small helicopter passing at great height overhead. And within seconds as it disappeared over the skyline there was absolute silence. It seemed as if the rock walls enclosing the cirque had funnelled the sound of the approaching chopper towards the high pass where it was amplified to dramatic effect. I mention this because the word 'trwst' means 'noise' or 'racket' in Welsh…....

There are sheer drops into Cwm Stwlan from these crags making for increasingly dramatic views, but the exposure is at all points easily avoidable. A zig-zagging path leads down to a final, steepish section above the first saddle of the connecting ridge. This side of Moelwyn Mawr has suffered some serious erosion exposing a large scar of unstable white rocks just before the path drops to the 630-metre contour (at **659446**) [22-50 looking back from the floor of the saddle].

After reaching the grassy strip that straddles this little col, you are faced with the soaring crest of Craigysgafn, a pyramid of cinder-like crags blocking the route to the next summit [22-51 from above the col]. The path onto this section of the ridge is intermittent at best as it weaves between bands and knobs of grey rock. But if you relish easy scrambling on solid, grippy rock (a bit like the gabbro on the Coolins of Skye) then this is the bit for you. Your boots will stick to this rock like Velcro.

Keeping as close to the left edge of the cliffs as you choose to, you pass one large cleft through which a slice of Llyn Stwlan and the Tanygrisiau reservoir is visible [22-52]. Then suddenly the path begins its drop to the next col, scrambling down abruptly with ample handholds where needed.

As you descend you cross a prominent band of white quartz before the path bears left and drops more steeply again onto coarse, slate scree [22-53 looking back up]. Keep to the left to by-pass a large outcrop of darker rock on the right before crossing more scree and steep grass where a clear path leads down to Bwlch Stwlan at **661441**. A small cairn, identifying the path's exit point further left from this saddle, comes into play later [22-54 looking back from the col].

Facing you now is the distorted head of Moelwyn Bach [22-55]. Its left flank is a scree slope of slate. To its right a massive, dark bulge of rock swells out of the mountain's base, one particular outcrop near the skyline protruding some distance from the summit's Northern face to form a menacing overhang. The ascent path goes directly up the slate scree slope on the left. To reach this path pass first to the right of a sizeable outcrop of dark, grey rock that sits alongside the obvious track heading North from the cairn [22-56]. A faint path then crosses a grassy ramp before heading straight up the scree slide.

As the merciless angle of ascent finally relents, head to the right across grass to reach the summit area. Outcrops of tilted rock emerge from the turf like fractured or serrated ribs, grey and abrasive [22-57 looking to your right as you reach the summit]. This distinctive grey rock is rhyolite (for more detail refer to **Walk 21**). Walk a short distance South to a rocky overhang topped by a small cairn identifying the summit of **Moelwyn Bach** (at **660437** – 710m/2329ft) [22-58 and 22-59].

> *This perch provides a perfect spot for some refreshment – as well as giving you the opportunity to lay out your map and compare what you see on the ground with what's printed on paper.*
> *There's a lot to pick out – not least the distant peaks of Yr Eifl – Traeth Bach where the Afon Glaslyn joins the Afon Dwyryd just before entering Tremadoc Bay – the flatlands of Morfa Harlech – the dromedary humps of higher ground above Porthmadog – and the sinister concrete buildings on the Northern shoreline of Llyn Trawsfynydd.*
> *Roads, railways lines, rivers, bridges, forest, endless sand banks and the sky stretching far above blue sea if you are fortunate.*

**7)**     **(660437)**     →

      **0°**     →

Moelwyn Bach's summit is another one worth investigating further, particularly at its Northern end. Cross the pavement of grey rock then drop down slightly to its left and you will get a close-up look at the snout of stratified rock overhanging the slopes below [22-60].

---

### OPTION 2
From here you can retrace your steps and follow the slate scree path back to Bwlch Stwlan if you wish. At least you know what to expect, the descent path is clear enough, and your scrambling abilities need never be put to the test.

---

Grassy slopes , scattered here and there with fans of scree, drop from Moelwyn Bach to the lower reaches of Bwlch Stwlan [22-61]. When I first walked this route I figured that this might well provide an alternative route back to lower ground, although there could be a bit of a climb to regain the col and the path into Cwm Stwlan on the other side of the ridge. From this high vantage point there appeared to be no obstacles to a straightforward descent.

However, as you start to contour downslope be aware that there are a couple of crags close to the Eastern end of the mountainside that are best avoided. The angle of slope is such that you are unable to see what lies directly beneath you, and scrambling down easy rock in such a blind fashion could conceivable result in your becoming cragfast.

Look out for a deep furrow cut into the face of the mountain below the rockier section of the summit to your left. The top of this cleft can be crossed by a narrow sheep path. This in turn leads towards outcrops of grey rock that look from a distance like weathered wood-grain or layered onion-skin [22-62]. This is more rhyolite, looking as if the lava flow that formed it only solidified a few months ago.

Beneath these outcrops a faint path leads you most securely down through the rocks and rocky rubble to reach lower ground [22-63]. Once you are close to the foot of the slope you will come upon a prominent pile of rock, partly grass-covered that looks like a small waste heap [22-64]. Cross this, or by-pass either side of it, then turn right and start to circle the base of the mountain, gaining height as you do in order to reach the floor of the col again at **661441** [22-65].

145°            →

With the lip of Cwm Stwlan ahead of you, bear right for a short distance from the aforementioned cairn as if returning onto Moelwyn Bach. But this time keep left of the outcrop of grey rock that you by-passed on the right when approaching the slate scree path. A prominent path leads to a track set upon a low walled causeway.

This track beneath the Eastern flanks of Moelwyn Mawr is the old pack-horse route that was used to carry slate from West Twll Quarry (from the foot of Moel-yr-Hydd). The finished product was transported to market over Bwlch Stwlan to Porthmadog by way of the Afon Dwyryd, close to Maentwrog.

Just before you reach this track you should notice another path dropping down left, doubling back behind you to run beneath the Eastern flanks of Moelwyn Mawr [22-66 looking back].

This route begins as a faint line crossing grassy slopes then develops into a broader path running in a level line along the backwall of Cwm Stwlan, safely crossing a tip of large slate blocks [22-67]. Below you on the right are a set of ruins, the remains of buildings serving yet another quarry nearby [22-68].

---

OPTION 3

There is a faint track that drops down to the right past these ruins below your path to meet the Southern shoreline of Llyn Stwlan.
From there it is an easy matter to continue beneath the dam, connect with the service road (which also serves as a 'scenic drive' for car-bound tourists) and follow it down-valley to **point 11**.

---

Beyond the first heap of waste slate the path is well-constructed as it contours the steep slope along a level embankment of solid blocks.

A green swing-gate (that would look more at home at the end of someone's garden path) lets you through a fence running down the slope ahead [22-69]. If you are fortunate you may spot a couple of choughs which frequent these slopes (only about 230 pairs normally nest in Wales but I have seen some here on two separate occasions).

The path then begins to gain height gradually as it approaches the saddle between Moelwyn Mawr and Moel-yr-Hydd. The final few metres pass across hummocky rocks before emerging at the col where a substantial cairn identifies this as a meeting point of several paths [22-70].

Behind your left shoulder a path begins the gradual ascent of Moelwyn Mawr. Another fragmented path veers off ahead and to your right, dropping down beneath the cliff face and screes below Moel-yr-Hydd to eventually reach Tanygrisiau.

## OPTION 4
If you have decided to give Moel-yr-Hydd a miss today, take this right hand path running beneath the cliff face.
Follow the directions given for those heading back from the summit (**point 9**) once they have reached the lower section of path where it doubles back beneath these cliffs.

### *Time saved about 30 mins*

But directly ahead of you is a faint path climbing the part-grassy/part-rocky slopes to reach the high ground above these cliffs. Follow that path as it heads towards the top of Moel-yr-Hydd.

Incidentally, do not place too much reliance on the path network displayed on the Explorer map for this area. And while you are crossing the low saddle between Moelwyn Mawr and Moel-yr-Hydd keep to the right-hand side of the wire fence you eventually meet. The fence on your left also boasts a rusted gate that ineffectively guards entry to the treacherous ground on the other side – ground subject to subsidence and so strictly off-limits.

Officially no part of this mountain stands within the Snowdonia National Park. This +600-metre hill was excluded when the boundary was drawn up, along with the less striking bookends of Manod Mawr and Graig-Ddu. Undoubtedly the three were rejected due to the scale of the slate-mining nearby. But Moel-yr-Hydd is a shapely mountain, surrounded by striking countryside, and I believe it should be given special status – following a referendum perhaps.

Ironically, the lower ground surrounding Moel-yr-Hydd's base does find itself placed within the National Park despite the two yawning holes cut into it.

One of these huge openings is the 'West Twll' ('West Hole') where several of the underground chambers at the top of Rhosydd mine came up to the surface.

In 1900 a large section of the Rhosydd quarry collapsed, burying several rock-men and creating the second massive crater on the surface; the 'East Twll'.

Both craters are strictly out of bounds to most members of the public unless you are an experienced pot-holer, rock-climber and mine explorer. Indeed, using a combination of wire ropes, rubber dinghies, rope ladders and probably a supply of mind-enhancing drugs industrial speliologists still make the trip from No. 9 adit (at 666463) to emerge at 'West Twll'.

8)      **(666449)**      →

        20°              →

A fence runs alongside the left-hand side of the path, keeping walkers clear of the yawning shafts that penetrate the broad saddle, and probably extend underground even beneath your feet. Both path and fence take a sharp turn left towards a point at which the first crags of Moel-yr-Hydd's Southern cliffs infringe upon the grassy slope [22-71]. At the corner where rock and grass finally meet, the fence turns right again.

You can either cross the fence here in the corner and follow scuffed grass directly to the summit, or keep to the right-hand side of the fence a while longer. A faint path on this side also continues uphill, but a little closer to the cliff edge on your right. You should have no problem crossing the fence closer to the top. Whichever side you choose, it's an easy romp through thick grass and past a couple of small outcrops of steeply-dipping rock to **Moel-yr-Hydd's** domed summit (at **671454** – 648m/2125ft).

*Views are predominantly East and South East to Blaenau Ffestiniog, the reservoir and hydro-electric station at Tanygrisiau, the railway running alongside, and Llyn Trawsfynydd in the distance. There's also the bonus of a retrospective view of the two Moelwyns, and a superb close-up of the path you followed earlier in the day along the valley floor of upper Cwmorthin –*

*with its little chapel, and the lake now shrivelled into its Southern corner where long strands of slate waste invade its dark blue waters like some malignant coral reef [22-72].*

The Eastern flanks of Moel-yr-Hydd overlooking Cwmorthin correspond with a massive outcrop of rhyolite – an igneous rock which is normally associated with lava flows emerging from volcanic vents. But in view of the massive depth of rock here it is possible that part of the outcrop represents a dome or well of subterranean molten rock which solidified before all of its content was able to escape through the overlying strata as lava.

**9)**     **(671454)**    →

       **250°**       →

Retrace your steps, passing the corner of fence where rock meets grassy slope. While you are up above the cliffs you have the chance to study some of the lower ground stretched out far beneath you (what bits are visible). Look out for the tiny, trowel-shaped body of water enclosed in a rocky basin [22-73]. This is the Llyn Wrysgan reservoir along whose shores you should be traipsing before too long – unless of course you intend chickening out and follow Option 5's escape route.

       **90°**       →

Continue to where fence and path take a right-hand turn and double back on yourself to join a faint path running downhill on your left. This path, running beneath the steep face of Moel-yr-Hydd, is Option 4's escape route. Eventually the path trends further right, away from the cliffs, to cross slightly more level terrain [22-74].

The correct line to follow is initially difficult to make out due to the abundance of rocks littering the ground – if in doubt look out for boot-marks in the muddier sections.

The litter of loose boulders thins out eventually and the path becomes quite wet as it begins to cross coarse grassland. Look out on your left for a section of cliff extending from the hillside to tower above the valley below. The path skirts the base of these rounded crags [22-75] although it is easy enough to clamber onto their tops should you be so inclined. Beyond here the path levels out as it runs between a series of angled slabs suspended over the valley away to your right. Llyn Wrysgan with its tiny stone-built dam nestles ahead of you in the angle between these rocks and the mountainside [22-76].

### OPTION 5
If you are at all claustrophobic, now is perhaps the time to keep trending further right, descending untidy slopes to join the roadside below. Once there follow the road left to join the main walk at **point 11**.

If you are not already walking along it, join the track that keeps to the left of the dam. A path of crushed slate now runs parallel to the left-hand shore of the lake, close enough to the mountain's cliff walls to see the tunnels cut into the rock which lead to larger caverns or shafts deeper within the hillside. Keep your head-torch switched off for now – entry into these is not recommended unless you are prepared to crawl through on your belly to gain access.

The slate path runs along a level embankment [22-77] before dropping quite steeply down an old incline constructed of uneven slate steps. At the bottom of the incline lie the ruins of Wrysgan Quarry [22-78]. Once you reach the foot of this ramp, turn right and thread your way along an overgrown trench towards a massive outcrop of smooth rocks [22-79].

### OPTION 6
You still have this one last chance to avoid using your head-torch. Once you reach the base of the ramp, if you continue directly ahead instead of turning right, a faint path trends slightly left as it picks a way

through the mass of slate waste. This path becomes more evident as it loops right, left then right again to skirt the crags on your right before meeting an old track. Turn right and follow this track past a body of water on the left then the 'slate garden' on the right. The main Cwmorthin path lies directly ahead with the car park a short distance downhill to your right.

Keep close to the rock wall on the right. The going can be wet underfoot but there are stepping stones allowing you to cross the larger pools. Ahead of you there are rusted pieces of machinery, thick cable and old winding drums littering the ground – as well as an ominous, black, circular tunnel some 3 metres in height cut into the hillside (at **678455**).

It's too late to check the batteries in your head-torch now.

**10)**  **(678455)**  →

  **155°**  →

As you get closer to this hole in the smooth rock wall and peer into the gloom you will see a bright patch of light low down near the floor – that is actually daylight shining in through the opposite end of the subterranean passageway. This actually provides enough illumination to get through in one piece – and each time I have used this tunnel I managed to pass along it without need of a torch. The tunnel is quite short, but its floor does drop fairly continuously at an uncomfortable angle towards the exit so you need to take adequate care.

At times it is a case of inching your way ahead carefully to avoid slipping on the wet patches. Also the rock-hewn floor is extremely irregular underfoot – which is where a head-torch does come in useful. However, I have managed to get through on more than one occasion without any artificial light as the way ahead does get clearer the closer you get to the far end [22-80].

There is one particularly steep step down which you have to drop (a drop of a metre or so) to reach a lower level. But by keeping close alongside one of the tunnel's walls, rather than trying to cross the step midway between both tunnel walls, you have something solid to fasten your hands onto and aid your balance.

Beyond this obstacle course you emerge at the top of a long incline to the valley below – and into welcome daylight. There is a 'DANGER' sign on the left warning of the possibility of a serious fall – just in case you hadn't figured out the exposure for yourself!

You are indeed perched quite high above a narrow, steep chute of rock where one careless step could result in a bruising tumble – but it is no worse than any scree run I have tiptoed down in my time [22-81 and 22-82 looking back uphill]. The incline drops down to more vegetated slopes below, but its surface in places is extremely rugged, with strands of cable and loose, unstable ballast underfoot. Its descent requires tiny steps, particular along the lowest section where much of the surface hardcore has been eroded away.

However, the relative safety of tarmac is only a few metres down-slope now, and you soon emerge onto the road (at View Point 3 according to the roadside sign) providing the 'scenic' route to Llyn Stwlan and the main Tanygrisiau reservoir. A second 'DANGER' sign at the roadside warning potential walkers of the perils presented by the tramway you have just descended is perhaps superfluous – surely one look uphill tells you it's not your average High Street? How soon before we see every exposed ridge on every hill in Snowdonia bearing 'Warning' signs?

As well as being a 'scenic' route, this road also acts as the access road to the Stwlan dam. On the opposite verge the incline actually continues through a rock cutting to descend along another section of steep slope to the shores of the Tanygrisiau reservoir. That section is probably best left to the sheep and goats.

**70°**          →

Instead turn left and follow the road downhill towards Tanygrisiau village. A dry-stone wall separates the grass verge from steep cliffs on your left – crossed by a ladder stile at one point. Ignore the temptation to investigate further.

Where the road makes a wide bend to the right towards Tanygrisiau village, follow the minor path exiting ahead to the left which crosses deep grass on the right side of a wire fence. This path leads directly to the wooden footbridge crossing the river exiting Cwmorthin beneath the waterslides. On the other side of the footbridge pass through the kissing gate and you will emerge at the parking area beneath the slate tips.

**END**

## WALK 23
# Moel Penamnen <sup>77</sup>

| 9.5 Km (5.94 miles) 500m (1640ft) Time : 3hrs 30min | A remote summit over-looking the exclusion-zone of Blaenau Ffestiniog |
|---|---|

One of the benefits of walking in Snowdonia is the network of tracks and paths that allows access even onto the highest tops within the reach of most fit walkers. Much like the stalkers' paths that penetrate even the most isolated, 'wilderness' parts of Scotland, there is very little of Snowdonia that cannot be reached with a reasonable amount of effort.

Then there are the hills on the Southern side of the Crimea Pass – a few Kilometres from the built-up area of Blaenau Ffestiniog, and clinging tightly to the boundary of the National Park.

There is a conveniently-located car park right at the foot of Moel Farlwyd, the nearest neighbouring summit to Moel Penamnen. Every guide book advertises this car park as the best starting point for the walk. But..... and it's a big but. There is no access from the car park onto the hill. It is circled by a substantial fence, topped by double strands of barbed wire. Not much of a welcome in the hillside. Even if you do manage to negotiate this first obstacle, there's no path visible on the slopes beyond.

This is a walk that follows a good deal of trackless terrain, but don't be put off. Moel Penamnen and the other peaks that surround this forgotten corner of Snowdonia are worth an outing. Just pick your day carefully. The higher ground hereabouts is amongst the wettest in North Wales.

**North**

**Don't forget**

**map/compass whistle/torch**

**suitable footwear + clothing**

**food/drink**

**brain**

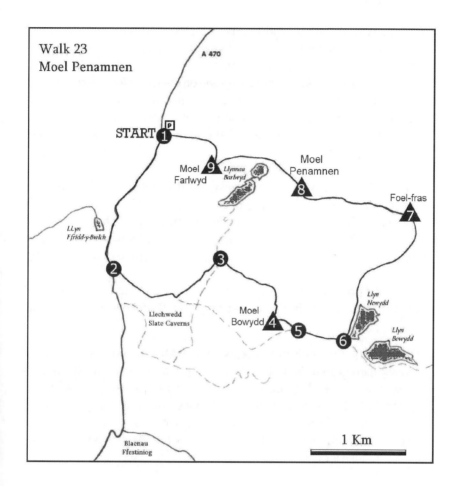

Walk 23
Moel Penamnen

A 470

START — 1 — P

Moel Farlwyd — 9
Llynnau Barlwyd

Moel Penamnen — 8

Foel-fras — 7

LLyn Ffridd-y-Bwlch

2

3

Llechwedd Slate Caverns

Moel Bowydd — 4 — 5

Llyn Newydd

6

Llyn Bewydd

Blaenau Ffestiniog

1 Km

## APPROACH

Despite its shortcomings, the free car park (at **702490**) close to the highest point of the Crimea Pass (Bwlch y Gorddinan) is the best starting point. During 2007-09 this section of road has been much improved (although during the upgrade, the free car park has been temporarily closed to the public – a large lay-by on the opposite side of the road some 200 metres closer to Blaenau Ffestiniog providing alternative parking at the starting point of the 'Ffestiniog Horseshoe' walk).

From the West or South head for Blaenau Ffestiniog then take the steep, twisting A470 uphill out of the town towards Dolwyddelan and Betws-y-Coed. This busy road passes the entrance to the Llechwedd Slate Caverns on the right then the Gloddfa Ganol Slate Mine on the left before reaching open country above the main excavations. The small car park, complete with Snowdonia National Park plaque and fringe of conifer trees, is on your right shortly after you reach the crest of the high pass (which tops out just beneath the 400-metre contour).

From the North or East take the Dolwyddelan/Dolgellau exit off the A5 and drive through the beautiful valley of the Afon Lledr. After passing through the village of Dolwyddelan with its square fortress of a castle beyond on your right, the A470 begins a long and steady climb. The car park is on the left just as the road runs close to the shapely summit of Moel Dyrnogydd on your right.

The summit point of the Crimea Pass is an austere spot during bad weather and the pass is usually the first to be closed to traffic following winter snow.

Although the Crimea Pass shares its name with a famous battle, it was actually named after the 'Crimea' tavern that once stood on the site of the present car park. This isolated hostelry was obviously a popular neighbourhood attraction until its licence was withdrawn in 1910 following local complaints about the behaviour of its regulars. Once the tavern was shut it was quickly demolished before Wetherspoon's had a chance to take it over.

**START**

1)  (702490)  →

    200°  →

As you exit the car park by legitimate means, stepping out onto the A470, turn left and follow the road in the direction of Blaenau Ffestiniog. This is not the best stretch of road to be walking along even after the upgrade – an intermittent pavement, blind corners and enough traffic to deter dawdling. The road soon reaches the highest point of the pass before the long descent towards civilisation, but not as we know it perhaps. On your right you pass a large lay-by (the starting point of the 'Ffestiniog Horseshoe' walk). Further downhill the reservoir of Llyn Ffridd-y-Bwlch lies partially hidden in a dip; its access road just beyond. Then again on your right is the prominent entrance to the upper reaches of the Gloddfa Ganol Slate Mine (the site of the Ffestiniog Slate Quarry).

On your left a sign heralds your arrival at Blaenau Ffestiniog, together with speed camera sign. Just before both signs an over-grown cart-track leads left from the roadside to a fenced-off compound enclosing electrical equipment [23-01]. The real walk starts here.

**2)**     **(696477)**     →

      130°     →

At last the throbbing beat of boots on tarmac is left behind. Follow this track past the fenced-off compound and you reach a metal gate with a ladder stile to its right [23-02]. Cross the stile and continue along the same track – now little more than a pair of ruts in the grass and reeds.

After passing beneath the overhanging branches of a large tree on your right the way ahead narrows [23-03], passing a scree of slate on the left as well as the scanty remains of a stone building. From here the path climbs towards a stub of wall visible on a rise ahead of you [23-04].

Pass this truncated wall on your right [23-05 looking back down the path] and proceed through dense vegetation (tussocky grass, foxgloves and ferns predominantly) where the track has been reinforced by angular blocks of stone [23-06]. The track climbs gradually to greener hillsides above the huge workings of the Llechwedd Slate Caverns on your right.

*Those views to your right are depressing, huge excavations cut into what once was sheep pasture. The extraction here is on a massive scale, nowhere near as stirring as those above Cwmorthin. Here the uniform grey sheds and omnipresent waste heaps give the place a dismal aspect even on the sunniest of days.*

As you pass another abandoned stone building on your left at **701473** the view ahead opens up. Moel Penamnen is the double-topped mountain straight ahead of you.

The track soon becomes overwhelmed by tussocky grass. The best advice is to aim for the collapsed walls set on raised ground to your left where surface runoff has eroded a couple of scars into the terrace on which these walls stand [23-07]. Once you reach this platform continue ahead, passing through the gap in the wall then keeping it on your right-hand side. The Afon Barlwyd sneaks past on your right, hidden in the creases of ground beyond the wall.

As you continue uphill look out for a slimmer-than-average, wooden footbridge crossing the Afon Barlwyd not far beyond the other side of this wall on your right [23-08 and 23-09]. You can get to it by passing through one of several gaps in the wall and crossing a corner of paddock. A fence marks the boundary between this paddock and the deeply incised stream which the footbridge spans. Climb over the small step stile (with two footpath marker posts either side) to reach the footbridge. Cross the stream and ascend uneven grassland with the fence now on your left until you reach a broad, gravelled track.

> *On the other side of the fence Moel Penamnen assumes an even greater presence on the skyline. To its left is the continuation of this track – an access road to the twin reservoirs of Llynnau Barlwyd (hidden from view at present) occupying low ground between Moel Penamnen and Moel Farlwyd further to its left.*

**3)**  **(708477)**  →

  **120°**  →

Turn left onto this roadway and climb over the two gates that block the way ahead [23-10].

Almost immediately, set back from the track on the right-hand verge, is a rusted gate forming part of two fences that meet at the corner of a field [23-11]. Turn right to clamber over this gate and continue across the field, keeping to the left hand side of the main fence on your right.

Ahead of you is a patch of reeds and taller grass with another fence running left to right. In the right-hand corner where both fences meet is another rusty gate in the main fence on your right and a pair of galvanised gates in the fence ahead of you [23-12]. Climb over these galvanised gates onto a short section of track that climbs up a ramp made out of old railway sleepers.

This ramp leads nowhere special – it just crosses a wet bit of ground. Keep heading upslope through more reeds and tall grass with the main fence still on your right-hand side [23-13 looking back downslope]. The next barrier is a bit more substantial – a sheep enclosure constructed out of an assortment of gates, wooden barriers and wire fences [23-14]. Don't let this hinder your progress – the green slopes of Moel Bowydd are within touching distance on the immediate skyline ahead. You can either by-pass the sheepfold on its left, or perform a laboured, slow-motion steeple-chase over the gates and fences to join the faint path continuing uphill on the left-hand side of the fence. But don't rely on this fence for much longer as it has its own agenda, eventually veering left across the lower flanks of Moel Bowydd.

To reach the higher ground beyond, climb over the fence and scale the relatively gentle slopes on your immediate right to the flattish top of **Moel Bowydd** (at **713470** – 493m/1617ft).

*From this inconspicuous summit there are impressive views of Moelwyn Bach and Moelwyn Mawr to the South West with the elongated reservoir of Tanygrisiau at their feet [23-15]. The service road winding its way up to Llyn Stwlan can be picked out, as well as the dam enclosing its waters high up on the hillside beneath Bwlch Stwlan.*

*Skim across the vast scars of the Ffestiniog Slate Quarry and the Snowdon Horseshoe pokes its peaks above the distant ridge-line of Ysgafell Wen with the trough of the Llanberis Pass to its right [23-16].*

*Closer at hand is Moel Farlwyd, then Moel Penamnen (Moel Siabod set back beyond the col between the two) [23-17] and the long descending spur to Foel-fras [23-18].*

*To the South are the Maen-Offeren slate quarries – with the more distant Graig-Ddu quarries scarring the higher skyline – while the Rhinogau and Llyn Trawsfynydd are visible in the hazy distance [23-19].*

**4)      (713470)      →**

**105°          →**

As you study the broad valley of the Afon Bowydd close to the South East, crossing open moorland before sinking into a rocky cleft that marks the outer extremities of the Maen-Offeren quarry, you will see a stone construction in the foreground [23-20]. This once held a large drum or wheel probably linked to heavy-duty wire or chain used to haul wagons up the incline hidden to the right. Heading left from this ruined winching-tower is a track winding across fairly gentle slopes in the direction of two lakes just visible below the Eastern skyline [23-21].

It is easy enough descending the Eastern slopes of Moel Bowydd. Beneath you a faint path appears, flagged in places, that joins the track. It isn't until you reach the lower ground crossed by this path that it becomes clear these slate flagstones are actually covers topping a water-filled culvert, diverting some of the water from the reservoir up-valley to smaller holding tanks below the Southern flanks of Moel Bowydd [23-22].

Some of the slate covers are concealed by vegetation, and others have either been removed or have broken and fallen into the channel, revealing quite a drop to the water below, with only the rusted iron cross-members remaining.

YOU WOULD DO WELL TO AVOID THIS SECTION OF 'PATH' WHEN THERE'S SNOW ON THE GROUND TO AVOID ACCIDENTALLY PLUNGING THROUGH THE GAPS BETWEEN THE SLATES INTO THE CULVERT AND POSSIBLY INJURING YOURSELF.

Once you reach the main track you might like to take a few moments to divert right, following the low causeway to visit the ruined winching-tower and take a closer look at the incline (as well as the massive slate face of the quarry across the valley) [23-23 and 23-24].

**5)     (715470)      →**

**90°            →**

From the top of the incline follow the causeway back up-valley towards a metal gate in a wall. Beyond this gate a track leads uphill, passing another small clutch of ruined buildings on the left. The track draws close to the slate-covered culvert again (now running along the right-hand side of your path).

The headwaters of the Afon Bowydd lie a few metres below the culvert; the stream cutting its way downhill until the remainder of its diminished flow is diverted into a stone-lined channel that crosses an embankment [23-25 looking downstream].

This area yielded an abundance of good quality slate – enough to allow some of the 'reject' slabs to be used to cover the water-culvert or to provide fence-posts. But on the evidence all around you, water seems to have been just as valuable a resource to the quarrying industry. Without easily-harnessed rivers and the skill to control and use their flow economically perhaps the industry might never have thrived in such a remote area on such a vast scale regardless of man's ingenuity.

The track peters out now as it reaches an area of rough ground, littered with rocks and other detritus beneath the low dam wall of the Llyn Newydd reservoir. A path continues to the right beneath the lake's outflow towards the Llyn Bowydd reservoir. But a discarded drainage pipe, set on its end and filled with rubble, has directions on it pointing to the left shore of Llyn Newydd where your route lies [23-26].

It is an easy matter to cross the overflow stream from the reservoir on the left side of the dam and walk across the rocky barrier to investigate the opposite shore if you so wish. There are warning signs of deep water – not something you would expect perhaps in a small lake in such flat terrain. But one look at the drop over the 'dry' side of the dam gives you an idea of the depth that must also exist on the 'wet' side.

*The right-hand shore of Llyn Newydd provides one of the most agreeable spots from which to study Moel Penamnen [23-27]. From this angle the mountain appears as a single, shapely cone with a steep, geometrically perfect slope descending from the left of the rocky summit and a gentler ridge dipping gradually to the right where it meets Foel-fras [23-28].*

The water diverted from this lake has always been a critical component in the slate-finishing industry just downstream of here.

In 2007 the future of slate mining in this region found itself placed under threat (not for the first time) as a result of financial difficulties suffered by the owners at some of their other locations nearby. The local workforce was left fearing for its future.

To aggravate this delicate situation, shortly after an announcement by the company of possible closures, service engineers responsible for the upkeep of the slate-finishing process downstream noted an inexplicable reduction in the flow of water entering the system. When they investigated it was discovered that someone had deliberately tried to empty the lake by opening a sluice-gate in the dam.

These remote hillsides are hardly the kind of setting you would expect to feature industrial sabotage!

The path to Foel-fras keeps to the left of this body of water, but if you do want to investigate the lake's Eastern shoreline before continuing uphill there is relatively easy access. Even if the overflow stream is in spate or the stepping stones look a little slippery there is an alternative crossing point a short distance downstream. A rusted iron girder enables you to make a dry crossing of the stream from the shoreline to the main dam. Although it looks a little shaky, it was secure enough the day I walked across it – all in the cause of research.

**6)**  **(721469)**  →

  **10°**  →

Keep close to the lake's Western shoreline as you head towards the skyline ridge ahead of you. Just be wary of the large patches of sphagnum moss that denote wetter ground where tributaries enter the lake from your left. After particularly heavy rain I imagine this section is better if you have webbed feet. At the lake's North Western corner a pair of streams converge before entering a shallow inlet. Head a few metres left of this last stretch of water and you will find a series of stepping stones making the crossing much easier.

If from a distance you have already studied the terrain ahead and to the right of the lake, you will have noticed a wide streak of yellow grass snaking its way through dense heather towards Foel-fras. Now that you are closer, the way ahead is less easy to pick out. But if you aim for the Eastern end of the spur extending to the right from Moel Penamnen's summit you will avoid the worst of the heather and bog. There are a couple of ups and downs, false ridges that trick you into thinking you are closer to the foot of the main ridge than you really are. But in short time you do reach the grassy saddle right beneath the flanks of Foel-fras [23-29].

A fence can be seen climbing the Southern face of this grassy spur on your right just on the other side of an intermittent section of wall. Directly ahead of you there are a couple of footpaths worn into the turf. These lead straight up the grassy slopes, threaded between insignificant rock outcrops to easily gain the flat, open top of **Foel-fras** (at **728481** – 586m/1922ft).

*There is nothing here to mark the actual summit point, and little of note to see to the North or East. Much of this is due to the fact that the deep valleys of Penamnen and Penmachno to the East are all but hidden by the undulating terrain. Crossing the fence on your right and dropping downslope does give you a glimpse of Cwm Penamnen's forested slopes and the forestry road, but to gain a broader view entails too much descent [23-30]. Close by to the South the two reservoirs (Llyn Newydd and Llyn Bowydd) lie upon a broad plateau beneath the darker slopes of Manod Mawr – a 661 metre mountain, excluded from the Snowdonia National Park due to the proximity of the Graig-Ddu quarry [23-31].*

*The ground to the North is a featureless expanse of moor-land running down in broad swathes to the margins of hill bordering Bwlch y Gorddinan and the Lledr valley. I would discourage anyone from wandering far in that direction. Fortunately to the West the twin tops of Moel Penamnen are now reassuringly close at hand [23-32].*

As well as encircling the town of Blaenau Ffestiniog, the 'black hole' produced by the National Park boundary encloses the entire summit area of Manod Mawr and Manod Bach. Although most of this particular walk strays well into this exclusion zone, at least the three main summits visited are on the boundary line.....just.

Manod Mawr has suffered more than most of Snowdonia's summits from quarrying for slate. The mountain is riddled by a vast system of tunnels and caverns and its slopes still bear the scars of quarrying on a vast scale (see **Walk 24**).

**7)**     **(728482)**     →

        275°         →

At first it appears to be a gentle amble West to the next top – the highest of the day and the raison d'être for this particular excursion. As you descend first to a broad, flat-bottomed col close to the 560-metre contour you should be able to make out a series of slender paths running up onto Moel Penamnen's top [23-33]. One path edges close to its crag-laden Southern face [23-34 looking back], another pair of tram-lines take an easier route further to the right.

After a short, steep climb onto a prominent hump and a drop to a slight dip there is one final slog to the flat summit where a scatter of slates (perhaps a flat-pack cairn that no one figured out how to fit together) mark the highest point of **Moel Penamnen** (at **716482** – 623m/2043ft) [23-35].

*There is a fine view back to Manod Mawr and the two reservoirs that seem to hover above the craggy outcrops that form the Southern face of this grassy mountain.*

*Further right the day's route so far is laid out at your feet – the track from the Llechwedd Slate Mines to Llynnau Barlwyd as conspicuous as a motorway.*

*Moel Farlwyd with the twin lakes at its feet looks deceptively distant from this vantage point [23-36]. Looking down from the summit one can see how the South Eastern slopes of Moel Farlwyd appear to have collapsed in a massive landslip which has effectively split what was once a much larger lake in two. This probably happened close to the end of the last ice age when many of the area's sodden slopes were at their most unstable.*

*To the North the skyline from Snowdon to Moel Siabod is classic but the intervening ground remains fairly featureless – pasture and forest. Perhaps what it needs to liven things up is a little more quarrying.*

8)     **(716482)**     →

        **330°**          →

The shoreline of Llynnau Barlwyd corresponds roughly to the 460-metre contour, some 150 metres below Moel Penamnen's summit. Moel Farlwyd's top is over 100 metres uphill again. Peering down at the intervening ground it looks as if there is a lot of work ahead of you [23-37]. But there is a relatively easy route skirting the Northern shore of the smaller of the two lakes.

The 45° slopes that drop relentlessly from the top of Moel Penamnen to the West have been shaped by a post-glacial process called 'solifluction'. This is often found in sub-Arctic regions where waterlogged soil creeps downslope to form mini-terraces due to the perpetual pattern of freezing and thawing. This occurred after the glaciers retreated, but before more temperate conditions allowed vegetation to colonise the landscape and stabilise the slopes.

Small terraces run across the entire Western face of Moel Penamnen like a series of steps, far too many to count. These make for easy contouring North West and downhill towards the shelf of land sweeping across the headwall of Llynnau Barlwyd [23-38].

There is one erosion scar to cross but again it presents no problem and you should soon find yourself beneath the steepest crags to your right. A small boulder-field of irregular blocks litters these slopes to your right [23-39] and a fence can be seen running along the high point of the saddle separating the two mountains. Weave your way between these blocks and climb gradually right to get as close as you can to the fence-line. Once level with it you should be able to follow it along easier ground above the crags to where it climbs the flanks of Moel Farlwyd.

270°                →

From this point the way ahead is pretty straightforward. The fence guides you a substantial way onto Moel Farlwyd without any need to cross it. But just before the last steep section beneath the summit you are forced to cross over since the fence has other things in mind, preferring to contour left beneath the highest point. Slabs of stone set either side of this fence at a number of places make crossing it no problem.

There now follows a very steep bit of clambering onto the summit, smaller in area than its loftier neighbour with a line of slanted crags skimming the top. Presumably other walkers must visit here as there is a small pile of stones identifying the highest point of **Moel Farlwyd** (at **706486** – 577m/1893ft) [23-40].

*This is your final opportunity today to study the scenery from altitude. On one side is the tangle of service roads and waste tips forming the Gloddfa Ganol Slate Mine and the uppermost corner of the Llechwedd Caverns.*
*Closer at hand the best view is back towards Moel Penamnen with the twin lakes sprawled at its foot [23-41].*
*On the other side lies open moor-land as far as the eye can see – Moel Dyrnogydd (with Yr Aran and Snowdon beyond) and further right Moel*

*Siabod perched above the Lledr valley the only distant points of interest. In a certain light the skyline from this spot featuring Yr Aran and the Snowdon 'Horseshoe' has an aura all its own [23-42].*

**9)**     **(706486)**     →

    **350°**              →

From the summit there are no paths to be seen so the direction of onward progress is largely a matter of personal choice. Dropping down easy slopes, initially across short grass, you will see the A470 below to your left. A series of small humps stands between you and the road itself, hiding the car park from which you set off when you started the walk [23-43].

---

### OPTION 2
If you prefer to return by way of an established path, descend the Southern slopes of Moel Farlwyd to reach the road serving the Llynnau Barlwyd reservoir. Then follow it down-valley as far as the gates at **point 3**. From there it is a case of reversing your approach route back to the A470 – followed by the final uphill roadside walk back to the car park.

***This probably adds 45mins to the walk***

---

Aim for low ground to your left. Signs of a path appear leading down to the valley skirting left of the humps. But these signs are merely sheep trods that in places have cut through the turf to expose the pale soil.

Ignore any temptation to enter this valley on your left and by-pass the humps (although you will reach the roadside eventually). Instead continue ahead towards the slight dip between the two most prominent humps. As you reach this dip the ground falls away more steeply ahead to a line of telegraph poles running along the roadside across the other side of Bwlch y Gorddinan. Beyond this dip you enter onto easier slopes leading you down to the road, and the line of conifers sheltering the car park [23-44].

I would normally discourage anyone from attempting to scale fences specifically designed to deter people from climbing over them. But I am sure

I am not the first walker to have been flummoxed by the National Park's failure to provide a stile giving access to a car park designed for little else except as an obvious start/finish point to a trek in the adjoining hills.

There are two spots at which it is a relatively easy matter to cross the fence – each at either corner of the car park. On the left the fence comes closest to a wall – and on the right the fence forms a corner where the centre post is probably the most stable of the lot.

However, for legality's sake, if you take the trouble to head a few metres to the right (away from the car park) you will find a far more feeble stretch of fence. It is low and flimsy enough to step across without too much damage (to fence or anatomy).

From here it's only a couple of metres back (left) along the main road to that car park.


**END**

# Manod Mawr [78] / Graig-Ddu [79]

**9.5 Km (5.94 miles)**

**785m (2575ft)**

**Time : 4hrs 30min**

**A huge block of slate to the East of Blaenau Ffestiniog – more attractive in the flesh than on paper**

This pair, together with their lowlier neighbour Manod Bach, almost never made it into this volume. Since both summits and indeed the entire route are outwith the Snowdonia National Park I saw that as a good enough excuse to restrict myself to 78 hills. After all, it's my list so I can decide which summits count and which don't. But, having climbed Moel-yr-Hydd a few days earlier and finding it well worth the visit, I relented and made my mind up that the Manods had just as much right to be included in the list.

Not particularly high by Snowdonia standards, the twin bookends of Manod Bach and Manod Mawr may still act as suitable deterrents to anyone choosing to explore the ground beyond them. Their grey, scree-laden slopes are universally steep, promising arduous ascents from most directions. Add the large-scale quarrying that has almost totally obliterated the Southern face of Graig-Ddu and you might decide they hardly warrant the effort.

However, the surrounding countryside promises views as spectacular as many found South of Moel Siabod – and you are guaranteed virtual solitude when you reach these forgotten heights.

**North**

**Don't forget**

**map/compass whistle/torch**

**suitable footwear + clothing**

**food/drink**

**brain**

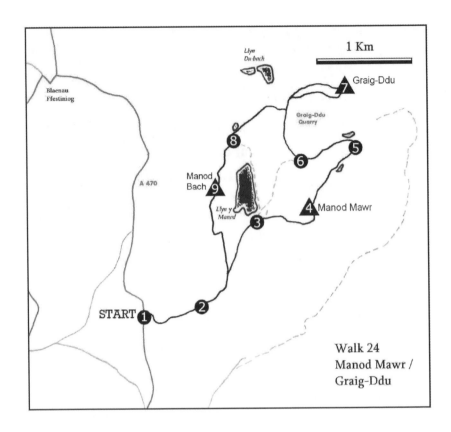

Walk 24
Manod Mawr /
Graig-Ddu

## APPROACH

If travelling from the North – as you reach the bottom of the Crimea Pass into Blaenau Ffestiniog, turn left at the large roundabout heading into the town itself (following the A470). Drive through the town for approximately 3 Km.

The houses lining the roadside grow further apart as you approach the end of the 40-mph zone. Beyond a turning on the left into a gateway (to Ffynnon-Uchaf farm) and the last terrace of cottages, there is a long lay-by on the right-hand side of the road at **706436** (adjacent to the 40-mph sign marking the town's margins) [24-01].

If travelling from the West – take the Blaenau Ffestiniog road (A496) then as the road climbs through woodland look out for the junction on your right – signposted Blaenau Ffestiniog and Manod.

Turn right here and climb steeply uphill, continuing until you enter the town of Blaenau Ffestiniog itself. After passing under a railway bridge you meet a T-junction (with the 'Wynne Arms' pub on your right). Turn right here and continue along the A470 – the long lay-by is on the right-hand side as described above.

If travelling from the South or South East – take the A470 into Llan Ffestiniog village, then turn right (still following the A470 as it doubles back on itself) at the junction signposted Blaenau Ffestiniog). Follow this road for 2 Km to the 40-mph sign identifying the outskirts of town. The long lay-by is on your left-hand side just before the sign.

**START**

1)      (706436)      →

        130°           →

Cross the road to a footpath sign just on the town side of the 40-mph sign. Go through the gate here and follow the path as it climbs a small, fern-clad bank [24-02] to a broad, grassy track leading uphill to the railway line. Signs instruct you to Stop, Look and Listen but the track is disused and overgrown – still, better safe than sorry. Ladder stiles either side of the track lead to a grassy meadow with another ladder stile visible a short way ahead crossing the wall/fence-line on your left at **708435** [24-03].

        50°

Cross this ladder stile and follow a faint path across the rough pasture (wet in places – complete with cunningly-hidden drainage ditches). For much of the way there is a wall on your left in varying stages of collapse [24-04]. A broad track emerges from the left through a gap in this wall and continues South [24-05] – ignore this. After passing a derelict enclosure on your left a ladder stile (again on your left) gives access to another footpath [24-06] – ignore that one as well.

The bulk of Manod Mawr is clearly visible ahead and slightly to your right. A fence emerges from the left to cross the way ahead, but a ladder stile can be seen in the distance almost directly beneath the point of Manod Mawr's summit [24-07].

A sunken wall – possibly an old causeway – takes a short-cut directly to this stile. Follow that now and cross the stile then aim for the ruined buildings in the left-hand corner of the paddock [24-08]. This avoids you having to pick your way through the jumble of rocks and stunted trees directly ahead. Ignore the gateway on your left and facing you as you reach the corner of the paddock. Instead bear right and follow the line of the dry-stone wall along an overgrown track.

**2)**     **(712437)**      →

       **65°**         →

Where this dry-stone wall peters out, the track climbs up a grassy bank [24-09], swinging left to approach a ruined small-holding directly under the dark crags of Manod Mawr [24-10]. From this angle the hill's steep Southern face, Clogwyn y Candryll, looks impregnable. The collapsed walls either side of the track and the remains of a tiny enclosure close to the old house add to the desolation of the scene.

A path runs in front of the house, beneath a stone wall towards a more substantial wall – but to regain the correct route from there involves ploughing through numerous gorse bushes and crossing a deeply-incised stream bed.

It is better to continue along the track that skirts the rear of the house. This track crosses a paddock, climbing to an iron gate in its highest corner ahead on your left (at **715439**) [24-11]. Pass through the gate, cross a slate step (bridging a stream) then follow the path across the next paddock, keeping within spitting distance of the dry-stone wall on its left. This field can be extremely wet in places, but your dry passage is assisted by railway sleepers laid down in bundles of three – five bundles in total – the first two some distance apart, the last three closer together as you reach the next corner on your left (at **715440**) [24-12].

A narrow, rusty gate here leads through a gap in the wall – the path on the other side (particularly close to the gateway) is very wet but you quickly gain drier ground as the gradient increases. Keep close to the fence on your left [24-13]. Ahead of you now is a broad saddle with Manod Mawr's steep slopes reaching down to meet you on the right, and Manod Bach's slopes set further back on your left. A low platform of rock appears to block the way ahead as the grassy slopes finally level out [24-14]. Aim to the right of this outcrop – the path can be picked out heading in the same direction towards the Eastern base of Manod Mawr.

**3)**      **(718445)**      →

         70°            →

A conspicuous pile of grey-brown rubble lies at the foot of the mountainside, with a large scattering of grey boulders covering most of the steep slopes above it [24-15]. Slightly to the left of this boulder-field the outcropping bedrock displays white striations of quartz. Using these as a guideline it is possible to pick a relatively direct line to Manod Mawr's summit. In places the rock is loose and unstable, but it is a steep walk rather than a scramble. The boulders can be avoided by keeping left of them, crossing bare rock in places and loose gravel or steep grass in others. The angle barely relents until you reach the 630-metre contour, but in relative terms the agony is short-lived and soon over.

---

**OPTION 1**

A clear track does continue past the waste tip before splitting in two [24-16, 24-17 and 24-18 from the upper slopes]. The lower of the pair follows the eastern shore of Llyn y Manod to a kissing-gate. Turning right beyond the gate gives access to the steep North Western face of

---

> Manod Mawr.
> The higher of the two tracks slowly contours Manod Mawr's slopes until you find yourself some 100 metres above the lower track by which time you are forced right. From here it is possible to climb the Northern slope of Manod Mawr, although navigation would be difficult in low cloud.
>
> ***There is no time gained by electing to follow either of the two tracks.***

As the gradient finally eases, a triangular pile of rocks marks the summit area – but not the actual top [24-19]. Another smaller cairn just beyond adds to the confusion [24-20]. Head left, and a short distance beyond across a grey boulder-field on slightly higher ground stands a prominent cairn (actually a small windbreak) marking the top of **Manod Mawr** (at **723446** – 661m/2168ft) [24-21]. The remains of its trig point – crushed concrete foundations – lie in a cluster of nettles. Not the most photogenic of spots.

*The summit area of Manod Mawr is quite flat with steepening slopes falling away to the West, South and East some distance from the trig point. To get the best of the views on offer involves mini-detours in all three directions.*

*To the West – Manod Bach, Llyn y Manod at its foot [24-22]. Beyond it Moelwyn Bach and Moelwyn Mawr stand out with Blaenau Ffestiniog further right.*

*To the South – the verdant Vale of Ffestiniog with the high moorland of Migneint on the far horizon and Llyn Trawsfynydd to the right with the Rhinogau beyond.*

*To the West the twin lakes of Llynnau Gamallt and Graig Goch, and further left the forested slopes above Cwm Penmachno [24-23].*

*To the North – avert your eyes unless you are a fan of slate. The descent path soon brings you close enough to witness the splendour of Graig-Ddu Quarry [24-24 and 24-25].*

| 4) | (723446) | → | 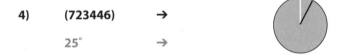 |
| | 25° | → | |

From this high point head across the flat plateau following the faint path. Some guidebooks describe this path as supposedly linking the summit of

Manod Mawr with the neighbouring top of Graig-Ddu (unnamed on the Explorer map). Reality is somewhat different. This path only exists on the ground in transient form, eventually petering out close to the 600-metre contour with the drained remains of a small reservoir on its right (at **726450**) [24-26].

A small, stone embankment acts as a causeway at the reservoir's North Western end [24-27], leading to a path that drops down to the col separating the two summits. However, less than 100 metres along you are confronted by the quarry buildings below. This path drops steeply to meet the main service road that runs from Cwm Teigl to the right (and Llan Ffestiniog beyond) [24-28] – away from the high ground you are aiming for.

This quarry has been in and out of action a number of times over the last 50 years or so – and at the time of writing it was obviously back at work. For this reason, with my own safety in mind (and to avoid trespassing) I opted for a more convoluted approach to a summit a mere 600 metres distant.

*Graig-Ddu slate quarry is a sorry sight from up here – yet one cannot fail to be humbled by the scale of the operation on display. Much of the mining takes place underground (merely intimated by the three enormous cavern-like entrances cut into the rock face).*

*Above the grey cliff is a greenish band of granite that is interbedded with the slate, but of little value. There is not much more to see at the surface apart from the massive spoil heaps (many dating from the mine's heyday), serpentine roadways, and the occasional employee. On the day I was there I saw two tipper wagons, one jeep, one tractor spraying water on the dusty road, and two helmeted/yellow-vested quarrymen escorting four sheep from the premises. Not a hive of activity, but the size of the buildings beneath the main workings and the scale of the excavations suggest otherwise (indeed, this quarry is claimed to be the highest industrial operation in Wales).*

*So not picture-postcard country. But at least this short detour North East gives a spectacular view of the steep crags of Carreg y Fran guarding the upper reaches of Cwm Teigl.*

During World War Two many of the country's art treasures were stored in the bowels of Manod Mawr for safety's sake. About 2000 priceless paintings were originally transferred from the National Gallery to Penrhyn Castle in Bangor, but were moved again when German bombing attacks on Liverpool increased in intensity. These treasures were stored in a special, air-conditioned bunker, 200-feet below ground in a disused part of the quarry.

Still on the subject of bunkers, during the planning stages for the new Snowdon 'café' ("Hafod Eryri") the bizarre suggestion was made that part of the roof be constructed of rock imported from Portugal! There was understandably much public outrage (particularly amongst the local people who had contributed to the Public Appeal for funds – to the tune of almost £250,000). It seemed sacrilegious that such an iconic structure, on a site surrounded by communities once famed for 'roofing the world', be made from imported stone. In the end additional funds of 56,000 were earmarked to ensure the stone was sourced locally and Welsh granite from the Graig-Ddu quarry was used.

**5)**    **(728453)**    →

         340°           →

From the lip of the steep valley beyond the drained reservoir it is advisable to retrace your steps and gradually pick your way directly downslope to join another path running right-to-left between Manod Mawr and the quarry. Once you reach this path turn left, passing a small circular waste tip [24-29], and follow it as it slowly climbs the base of Manod Mawr's Northern face [24-30].

As the massive heaps of slate waste on your right get closer, head downslope along another path that drops down to meet the service road skirting the base of these waste heaps [24-31]. A sign warns you of the dangers of "Quarry Workings" and instructs you to keep to the path (obviously intended for those ascending Manod Mawr from the North). The path in question now follows a dry ditch along the left-hand verge of the service road for a short distance before reaching a large flat expanse of crushed slate (close to **725452**) [24-32].

A few derelict quarry buildings remain standing beyond this flattened area and to your left – including one construction sunk into the ground, complete with underground doorway and domed roof constructed from slate slabs which have now partly collapsed [24-33]. Beyond these ruins a clear path runs beneath the grassy slopes of Manod Mawr [24-34], eventually veering left to head into the valley enclosing Llyn y Manod.

---

**OPTION 2 and 3**

From here you can choose to continue towards Llyn y Manod – bypassing Graig-Ddu altogether – ascending Manod Bach from the lake's Northern end (Option 2)

or

retreating to the lay-by if time or weather conditions warrant a hasty exit (Option 3).

*Time saved –*
*with Manod Bach ascent – 2 hrs*
*without Manod Bach ascent – 3 hrs*

---

*As you emerge into this col's Western end there is a stunning view of Moel Penamnen to your right (although the layers of black, crenulated rock, slate waste and lakes form a less eye-catching foreground) [24-35].*

**6)**　　**(723452)**　　→

　　　　**325°**　　　　→

On your right the stepped heaps of slate waste seem to do their damnedest to hide the approaches to Graig-Ddu. But below on your right where the waste eventually gives way to grass and more natural rock rubble, the remains of an old incline can be clearly seen running downslope [24-36]. Exit the path right and cross fairly level ground, keeping well to the left of the tongues of waste slate on your uphill side, to reach this old incline [24-37 looking downslope].

This incline can be seen dropping down quite steeply to your left until it levels out on the causeway separating the two reservoirs below. From there another old incline ran all the way into Blaenau Ffestiniog.

To your right the remains of the incline can be seen climbing just as steeply to the heart of the quarry workings.

Even though this area lies outside the National Park boundaries it is unlikely that a theme park on the scale of Alton Towers would ever be allowed to be built here. However, a century or so ago the local quarrymen had the next best thing. The more daring miners used to ride down this incline after work (presumably all the way from the workface to their doorstep) in gravity-fed trucks controlled by the most rudimentary braking systems. These kamikaze vehicles were known as "ceir gwylltion" ('wild cars').

Cross the incline (no need to Stop, Look and Listen these days, honestly) and continue over undulating ground beneath the towering heaps on the right. A massive outcrop of rock on your right marks where wet ground spreads from the base of the waste tips onto the slopes below [24-38]. Around the next corner there are yet more waste heaps – now with two or three enormous, angular boulders partially embedded in the grassland some distance from the fringes of the waste [24-39]. Continue past these, gradually climbing to your right as the tips recede into the mountainside [24-40].

As you gain height the double lake of Llyn Du-bach appears in the hollow down to your left while on your right the last of the waste heaps trickles down to meet a large outcrop of dark grey rock [24-41].

The ground approaching this outcrop is again quite wet, although a faint path attempts to pick the driest line. A pair of rusty fence posts surrounded by a plinth of loose stones acts as a cairn of sorts [24-42]. Ahead and to your right are the very steep slopes leading up onto Graig-Ddu's summit, some 200 metres higher. The steepest, rockiest face of Graig-Ddu is immediately to the left of the final waste tip, and the best approach is to follow the bare, grassy slopes up to where the mountain and the slate waste meet [24-43]. The narrow gap between the two is blocked high up by fallen boulders (including one composed almost entirely of grey-white quartz) but with care it is possible to clamber into the V-shaped gap beyond [24-44] and continue to where the top of the waste tip has been levelled to form an extensive platform [24-45]. On your left, less demanding slopes now lead directly to the summit area of Graig-Ddu [24-46]. The flat grassy summit is surrounded by a platform of pale, jointed rock rather like the icing on a cake, with the cherry of a sizeable cairn marking the top of **Graig-Ddu** (at **727458** – 658m/2158ft) [24-47 and 24-48].

*In some ways the view from the summit of Graig-Ddu is an anticlimax. The only consolation is an almost uncontaminated view of Manod Mawr (since the quarry workings lie hidden in the dip between the two) [24-49]. The view North is hardly more impressive – level moorland cut by hidden valleys extending to flat horizons [24-50].*

*Things only get interesting when you turn to face North West and West – towards the familiar Moel Siabod, Glyderau, Snowdon massif and the Moelwyns – the most noteworthy feature being the steep-sided trough of Nant Peris. Moel Penanmen and Moel Farlwyd can also be studied at leisure from up here should you be planning to visit the pair [24-51].*

*To the South East the Arans peer above Y Gamallt [24-52].*

7)      (727458)      →

        295°          →

As I retreated towards the Western lip of Graig-Ddu's summit I stumbled across a faded red metal sign half-buried in the peat –

> "Cwt Y Bugail Slate Quarry Co. Ltd"
> Danger Blasting
>
> Imminent Blasting
> Continuous Siren
>
> All Clear
> Intermittent Siren

I could not imagine how this sign had found its way here, more than a kilometre from Cwt-y-Bugail quarry (now disused) to the North. And – in case you were wondering, I knew that my bearings were spot on. Only on investigating further did I discover that when Alfred McAlpine Slate purchased the Graig-Ddu quarry in the 1980's they renamed it 'Cwt y Bugail' – presumably to confuse anyone who ends up on this summit.

The grassy slopes dropping West from the top are easier on descent. It is a straightforward matter to pick a safe path to lower ground, keeping well to the right of the ascent route. There is even a wide, gravel path part of the way down, but it is steep and very loose underfoot – and not particularly suited to scree-sliding [24-53]. The safest bet is to keep to the grass until you reach the base of the mountain.

The chances are that as you traverse the turfed area beneath the waste heaps on your left you might end up marooned on top of the dark grey outcrop of rock that abuts with the tips. It is, however, possible to manoeuvre a way carefully down the narrow cleft on your left where the loose slate meets solid rock. This block-strewn alley bottoms out only a short distance from the rusted fence-post cairn encountered on the way up.

From here to reach the route onto Manod Bach (or indeed to return to the lay-by) the best option is to retrace your steps. To shorten the journey across difficult ground it is possible to drop down slightly to the right to arrive on lower ground more quickly. Bear in mind that the aim is to eventually reach the twin reservoirs at the Northern foot of Manod Bach [24-54].

I elected to follow my ascent route downhill as far as the large boulders that I passed on the way up. From there I angled off to the right, dropping down into a small incised stream bed. The rock outcrops forming the walls of this miniature valley are composed of a conspicuously dark rock made up of angular fragments cemented together [24-55]. This is breccia – volcanic debris ejected from an exploding vent and laid down on the sea floor several millions of years ago.

Where this small valley emerges, the twin reservoirs are only a short distance away to the right of Manod Bach. The intervening ground is flat and boggy in places, but a stone embankment enclosing the Western end of Llyn Glas (at **718455**) can be used to cross the damper patches [24-56]. Llyn Glas like many of the small lakes hereabouts was once harnessed as a reservoir but has now almost completely dried up, its bed covered in vegetation. A rusted contraption once served to open and close a small sluice gate in the distant past [24-57]. Now this dog-leg of twisted metal seems to be bending over curiously as if searching for its lost reflection.

Whichever line you follow, you will eventually join a path leading along the Eastern side of the reservoirs before reaching the descent ramp of the incline running down from the old Manod Quarry [24-58 looking upslope]. Follow the line of the incline between these two bodies of water. The one on the right still holds a substantial amount of water, but the strand lines on the slate slabs that mark its shoreline attest to a larger mass of water in the past [24-59]. The reservoir on your left has fared less well – most of it now filled in by crushed slate [24-60]. The path circles this lake in an anti-clockwise direction to join the clear track skirting the base of Manod Bach.

---

### OPTION 4

To avoid the ascent of Manod Bach follow this path straight ahead, keeping the fence-line on your right. Then turn right at the bottom of the col to join the path skirting the Eastern shoreline of Llyn y Manod. Go through the kissing-gate and continue along the length of the lake to regain the ascent route below the small rubble tip at **717444**.

*Time saved – approx 30 mins.*

---

**8)**    **(716453)**    →

       200°       →

Manod Bach's summit lies below the magic 600-metre contour, but is still worth visiting. Take the path towards the Northern end of Llyn y Manod for a short distance. The fence on the right-hand side of this path has to be crossed in order to gain the flanks of Manod Bach. Fortunately you will find several rocks laid beside it at strategic locations where the top strand of barbed wire is absent [24-61]. Cross the fence and continue along another path running parallel to it.

Once you reach the small collapsed dry-stone enclosure on your right [24-62], strike off to the right to climb the slopes towards the skyline. The angle is relentless and there is no clear path, but you soon spot the cairn on the summit above. Don't get too excited – that one is not the true summit. A flat, hummocky section of ground with a large wet patch has to be crossed before you reach the second and higher of the two cairns marking the true summit of **Manod Bach** (at **714447** – 511m/1676ft) [24-63 looking back to the first cairn].

*Despite its inferior position, Manod Bach provides a superb spot from which to study its loftier neighbours.*
*There are extraordinary views of Snowdon and Crib Goch [24-64], Cnicht [24-65], and the Moel Farlwyd/Moel Penamnen pair [24-66 and 24-67] – each group of summits resembling flawless islands floating in a menacing ocean of slate workings.*
*In clear conditions this rarely-visited summit is one of those places you never want to leave. Studying the skyline in a 360° scan from this particular spot perhaps gives you an idea of the immensity of Snowdonia*
*You also get to study the route you took up Manod Mawr earlier in the day [24-68].*
*For those familiar with the local community, there are close-up views of much of Tanygrisiau and Blaenau Ffestiniog. From here you get an aerial view of both towns. And just as impressive is the sight of the dam enclosing Llyn Stwlan beneath Moelwyn Mawr [24-69].*

9)    (714447)    →

135°    →

Like Manod Mawr, the Southern slopes of this hill are its steepest and are best avoided, particularly on descent. Instead, aim for the dry-stone wall that runs right to left along Manod Bach's stubby toe. Continue to drop to your left as you navigate the best line through the jumble of rocks and tussocky grass towards the wall [24-70].

As soon as you reach the wall, keep to its uphill side as you follow it quite steeply down to a junction of walls close to the 420-metre contour at **713446** [24-71].

The wall for much of its run from here on is collapsing before your very eyes, and it is quite easy to cross over without dislodging any more stones. Ahead of you now is an area of hummocky ground, littered with patches of loose boulders. This area is quite wet in places – but the stream marked on the map is no longer evident on the ground.

A vague path runs across this rough pasture to a fence that can be seen running left to right ahead of you (parallel to the path you followed on your way up to Manod Mawr's base). The path becomes clearer and easier to follow as it bears right to run alongside the fence in the direction of more fertile pasture in the valley below [24-72 and 24-73].

Eventually you meet a dry-stone wall with a metal gate in it. However, on your left on the other side of the rickety fence is the narrow, rusty gate you passed through earlier in the day (at **715440**) [24-74]. The better option is to cross the fence here in this wet corner, pass through the gate and head downhill (reversing your earlier route).

Continue now across the damp ground below, through the next metal gate and pass behind the ruined small-holding at **715438**.

*Perhaps this is a good spot to take one final look at the hills behind you. The grey mass of Manod Mawr takes on an imposing posture with this small stone ruin tucked beneath its slopes. What a place to live this must once have been – cut off in winter, but blessed in summer with views second to none. On older maps this dwelling is identified as "Bryn-Eithin" ('Gorse Hill') but sadly more recent maps give it no name – one further step to oblivion [24-75]. In absolute contrast, as you reach the final stages of the return leg you are faced by the twin towers of Trawsfynydd Nuclear Power Station (recently decommissioned but with a legacy that is likely to outlive our race). Perhaps another reminder in this battered landscape that large-scale industry will always win the day when pitted against small-scale agriculture.*

Turn your back on the hills one last time and continue along the track downhill – taking note of which stiles you crossed earlier in the day, and which you ignored. Finally you reach the roadside – and hopefully encounter no 'ceir gwylltion' on your drive home.

**END**

# Carnedd Moel Siabod [80]

**10 Km (6.25 miles)**

**775m (2542ft)**

**Time : 4hrs 30min**

**A striking summit, graced by some of the finest views Snowdonia has to offer – but also worth a visit just to sample some easy scrambling**

This is one of the few mountains I have been fortunate enough to visit in a variety of seasons. It's the kind of hill that demands you experience it frozen under a cover of snow, as well as baking beneath sun-parched skies; and its stunning location is enhanced all the more by the russet tints of autumn or the fresh sparkle of spring.

Getting onto Daear Ddu's enthralling ridge is so painless that it's amazing more people don't visit here purely for the scrambling – not to mention the stunning views from this peak's highest point. You could spend an entire afternoon scanning the skyline to savour the wealth of summits laid out at your feet.

Even if you pick a foul day of low cloud and rain when all you can focus on is where your next boot-step is going to land, the exhilarating ascent of Daear Ddu will still make all your efforts worthwhile.

The choice of descent routes allows you to return as the crow flies along Moel Siabod's main ridge, or as the 'tourists' crawl along its Northern flanks to the banks of the Llugwy. The only thing I suggest is that you don't attempt this walk in reverse – the hard slog up the tourist route will do little to establish Moel Siabod's rightful place in your heart.

**North**

**Don't forget**

**map/compass
whistle/torch**

**suitable footwear
+ clothing**

**food/drink**

**brain**

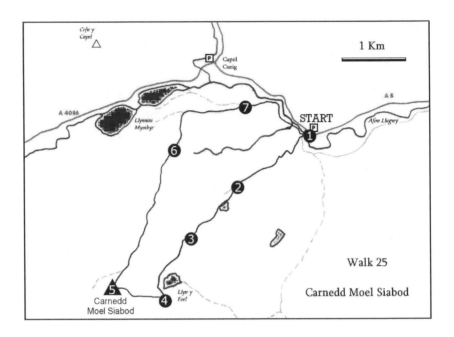

## APPROACH

If travelling from Caernarfon (along the Beddgelert road – A4086) or Bangor (along the Ogwen valley road – A5), at Capel Curig continue East along the A5 all the way through the stretched-out village.

Pass 'Cobden's Hotel' on your left then once you emerge from the 30mph restriction there is a longish lay-by on your right. You can park here, or slightly further along on your left adjacent to the 'Bryn-Glo' café where there is a sizeable parking area (presumably meant for customers rather than walkers though).

If heading from Betws-y-Coed (along the A5), 1½ Km after passing the Capel Curig Training Camp on your left you will see the 'Bryn-Glo' café on your right, and just beyond it a lay-by on the left-hand verge. If you have entered the first section of 30mph restriction on the approaches to Capel Curig village you have driven too far.

**START**

**1)**  **(735571)**  →

**305°**  →

From the long lay-by walk along the pavement (on the same side of the road) heading towards Capel Curig village. Behind the wall on your left you should be able to catch a glimpse of the Cyfyng Falls where the Afon Llugwy cuts through the bedrock in a series of impressive plunge-pools, water-chutes and ice-smoothed steps. From a distance the combination of solid rock and turbulent white water looks an inviting playground for the more daredevil individual.

REGRETTABLY MANY AN INNOCENT TEENAGER HAS DROWNED HERE IN THE PAST – EITHER BY JUMPING INTO THE POOLS FOR A SWIM OR ATTEMPTING TO NAVIGATE THE WATERFALLS IN A CANOE OR MAKESHIFT DINGHY. SUCH TRAGEDY IS ALL THE MORE POIGNANT GIVEN THE NATURAL BEAUTY OF THE SURROUNDINGS AND THE PROXIMITY OF A BUSY ROAD.

**170°**  →

Turn left onto the minor road leading across the bridge spanning the Llugwy river towards Pont Cyfyng village. Remarkably, the river on the upstream side of this bridge consists of wide stretches of placid water ideal for a paddle at the end of a long summer hike.

Continue past the first footpath signposted on your right. This leads to the water meadows beside the river and will feature in the return leg. Beyond the signpost there is a stone building on your right with white garage doors – and a notice board publicising the local community activities [25-01]. Just past this building, again on the right, a narrow tarmac road veers uphill beneath the trees at **734570**.

Follow this private road across the cattle grid then continue steeply uphill. An overgrown track emerges on the left half way up – the exit point of an old incline linked to a disused quarry higher up [25-02].

There were once two slate quarries here dating from the early 19th century – both finally closed in 1940.

This road swings to the right as the gradient eases, by-passing a gravel path on its left that cuts through a bank of ferns. Take this path now (as the road becomes the private access to 'Rhos' farm) [25-03]. There is a marker post and a white arrow painted on the road itself stressing the point that walkers are not welcome any closer to the farm than here!

*As you follow this path the views open up to the Carneddau on your right – dominating the scene are Pen Llithrig y Wrach [25-04] and Pen yr Helgi Du.*

A farm track joins this path from the right – the rear access road to 'Rhos' farm – again strictly out of bounds to the uninvited. The path broadens beyond this junction and starts to gain height again as it approaches a gate with ladder stile alongside (at **731567**) [25-05]. After crossing the stile you pass an abandoned farmhouse on the left, beyond which the track climbs to an area of more open terrain with Moel Siabod visible directly ahead of you. Your path levels off before meeting a second gate with a stile alongside [25-06] which you should also cross (close to **724562**).

---

OPTION 1

For a more direct approach onto Moel Siabod's summit, by-passing the shores of Llyn y Foel and the scramble up Daear Ddu, once across the stile bear right to another ladder stile [25-07] beyond which a faint path picks its way up easy-angled slopes onto the main ridge.

Older OS maps show a track leading to an incline that ran directly to Moel Siabod's summit ridge from the 400- to the 700-metre contours.

**Time saved – approx 45mins.**

---

2)      (724562)        →

        210°            →

Continue ahead along the main track, ignoring a metal gate in the fence on your left. A third metal gate complete with ladder stile bar the way ahead now [25-08] as you approach scattered piles of slate waste close to the path's margins. The ground can be quite wet hereabouts, particularly just beyond this gateway [25-09 looking back towards the gate] before the track makes a gentle descent towards a small lake on your left [25-10 and 25-11]. Despite its size – and undeniable photogenic qualities – the lake is not named on any map past or present.

The clear path skirts this lake's North Western shore then, as it begins a long, slow climb again it is transformed into a series of large stone steps [25-12]. Beyond a massive slab of stone on your right the path narrows and becomes more unstable underfoot.

Ahead of you now stand a slate spoil heap to the left of the path as well as a small selection of ruined buildings on slightly lower ground to your left [25-13]. The path threads a way past the right-hand side of the larger waste heap then cuts across the lower slopes of another on the right as it approaches a disused quarry whose rust-tinted strata can be clearly discerned from a distance [25-14]. Ruined buildings stand on either side of the path as it climbs to the left-hand edge of the flooded quarry. There is a short ramp exiting right directly to the quarry's edge but it is best kept clear of. Better views of this flooded crater can be gained by keeping to the well-trodden path as it climbs steeply to the left of this vast pit. The sight is impressive to behold, largely due to the sheer rock walls and the implied depth of the dark waters [25-15].

The slate mined at this quarry, compared to the rest of the rocks surrounding Dolwyddelan, was of unusually high quality due to its low sulphur content.

Continue along this crushed-slate path as it circles around the upper edge of the quarry [25-16], keeping to the left-hand side of the fence which guards the drop to the depths [25-17].

**3)    (717554)    →**

**210°**              →

Although not displayed on the Explorer map, a clear path (perhaps in places resembling a dry river bed rather than a path) meanders uphill to the immediate skyline. Once you reach level ground [25-18 looking back downhill], passing low outcrops of rock on your right, you face a large, flat hollow containing the much-diminished waters of Llyn y Foel [25-19].

---

OPTION 2

If the ground ahead appears wet, it probably is. In this event the drier route is to the left, skirting the lake's Eastern then Southern shores by way of a series of rocky platforms separated by patches of bog [25-20]. Cross the lake's outflow at **716548** and head uphill towards the obvious trough lying at the base of the Daear Ddu ridge – **Point 4**

**OR**

OPTION 3

Alternatively, a second drier path swings to the right beneath the steep slopes of the corrie wall [25-21]. This makes a large circuit of the corrie floor, keeping well to the West of the lake shore and the wetter ground between the lake and the mountain's rock-strewn slopes. You would be wise to keep clear of the immediate slopes to your right as there is no easy ascent route there, but eventually the path strikes upslope into the trough lying at the base of the Daear Ddu ridge – **Point 4**

---

On one July visit, following three weeks without significant rainfall, I was able to follow the middle way – cutting directly across the low ground by way of a faint path leading to the broad notch in the ridge that drops down from the highest slopes on the right. This steep ridge is the Daear Ddu – your route to the summit.

Even after prolonged drought you will probably find that this ground is still spongy in patches – in particular in the three intervening flat areas between the rockier bits. The final flat patch closest to Llyn y Foel's SouthWest corner is the wettest.

Once you have crossed this level section, a short ramp of grassy ground leads to a broad, distinctly flat-floored trough separating the main ridge on your right from the foothills on the left [25-22].

*For the first time on the walk you are able to see what lies beyond this widescreen gap – Moel Penamnen and Moel Farlwyd, the Manod group just peering over the skyline, and the higher tips of the Rhinogau far beyond [25-23]. Perched on a small mound in the verdant valley of the Lledr below stands the tiny stone fortress of Dolwyddelan Castle [25-24].*

Despite its insignificant size Dolwyddelan has played a major role in the history of Wales since the 13th century. This area is generally accepted as the birthplace of one of Gwynedd's most famous princes, Llywelyn Fawr or Llywelyn the Great (1195-1240). He emerged as ruler after a fierce family struggle and his reign saw the construction of a series of sophisticated stone castles in Wales. Sited at strategic points peripheral to Snowdonia, often on his summer grazing lands, they guarded the store cupboard of his kingdom (e.g. Dolwyddelan, and Dolbadarn near Llanberis). These were built between 1220 and 1230 after the disastrous attack his kingdom suffered from none other than his father-in-law, King John, in 1211.

Llywelyn and his wife Joan (or Siwan) lived much of their lives at Trefriw in the Conwy valley. In 1229-30 his wife had an affair with one of the Marcher lords – William de Braose. As penalty for such a treacherous deed her lover was hanged and Joan was imprisoned for a short time.

Such infidelities were perhaps customary at the time – less than a year later one of William de Braose's daughters, Isabel, married Dafydd, the son of Llywelyn and Joan. When Joan died, she was buried at Llanfaes on Anglesey where Llywelyn founded a Franciscan friary in her memory.

When Llywelyn died in 1240, Wales went through the usual dynastic upheaval until his grandson Llywelyn ein Lliw Olaf or Llywelyn the Last (1246-1282) overcame family rivalry. His position as effective ruler over all Wales as far south as Caerffili was eventually recognised by Henry III in the Treaty of Montgomery (1267) acknowledging the title 'Prince of Wales' and the concept of Wales as a unified state for the first time in its history.

Once you have studied the views ahead, retrace your steps a short distance to meet the faint path leading onto the rocky ridge of Daear Ddu [25-25 and 25-26].

**4)**      **(713546)**      →

         **260°**        →

There are several ways of tackling this exciting ridge – if in doubt look for the rust-coloured rocks flagging the most frequented line [25-27]. If you are looking for more exposure, trend further to the right so that you can make the most of the views into the deep corrie-basin and do a bit of scrambling at the same time. Much of the rock hereabouts has been weathered into a distinctly pock-marked surface – possibly the source of the mountain's name ('Siabod' means scabbed and derives from the same word as "shabby") [25-28].

> Like Cnicht and its lowlier neighbours, most of the Moel Siabod ridge is composed of dolerite. This resistant rock provides Snowdonia with many of its more impressive features – the cliffs of Ysgolion Duon separating Carnedd Dafydd from Carnedd Llywelyn, and the steep backwall of Cwm Dulyn being two fine examples.

In its favour, this rock provides excellent grip for fingers and boot soles. None of the scrambles are particularly lengthy or exposed – each leading onto a sizeable platform where there is a softer escape route round to the left or a new challenge to the right. These hiatuses also provide an opportunity to regain breath and admire the view back down along the spine of the mountain to the shoreline of Llyn y Foel [25-29].

At one point you encounter a massive triangular block of grey rock outcropping from the hillside like the prow of an ice-breaker [25-30]. There is a grassy ramp on its right-hand side leading to higher ground, but if you pass beneath this rock you will find better scrambling prospects just beyond – again eventually climbing to your right and terminating in a small grass-covered viewing platform, hemmed in by a low rocky wall that shelters you from the sheer drop beyond [25-31].

*As you gain height you are rewarded with better views of Moel Siabod's awe-inspiring Southern slopes – the headwall of what undoubtedly was once a massive lake-filled corrie [25-32]. Much of the lower slopes, composed of loose rock and semi-frozen mud, presumably became unstable towards the end of the last Ice Age and collapsed or avalanched into the basin below, shoving the remnants of the lake (now Llyn y Foel) to the SouthEastern edge of the basin.*

From here drop down steeply by way of a series of slabs to a high gap in the ridge. Beyond this low saddle a straightforward scramble, including a small section of bare slab, leads you onto another high shelf. From here cross a mass of boulders by way of an intermittent path to reach the base of one final pile of grey, angular blocks. Again the rustier bits identify the easiest route bringing you ever closer to the summit itself [25-33, and 25-34 looking back downhill].

Finally haul yourself through more boulders towards the cairn perched high up on a rocky platform to your left [25-35]; the flat summit of **Carnedd Moel Siabod** (at **705546** – 872m/2860ft) [25-36].

A few metres North of the trig point stands a large windbreak; useful should the weather turn unfavourable [25-37].

This shelter once acted as an enclosure for the Welsh ponies that carried Victorian tourists onto this summit from the hotels in Capel Curig. While these intrepid travellers took in the wild views, the local boys who tended to the ponies made sure their charges were fed and watered in preparation for the descent. Even in Victorian days Moel Siabod's summit was a popular attraction, heralded as one of the best spots from which to study the classic profile of the Snowdon Horseshoe as well as the South Eastern Carneddau. Day-trippers in their 'Sunday best' were carried up here along the 'tourist' path in order to see for themselves the views on offer [25-38 and 25-39].

**5)**    **(705546)**    →

**40°**    →

A faint path can be picked out as it runs along the lip of the high corrie wall towards the subsidiary top just above 810 metres in height to the North East.

*As you follow this long ridge, its lofty position affords an unequalled view into the corrie basin below with fans of scree tumbling steeply down to the shoreline of Llyn y Foel [25-40].*

### OPTION 4

For a more direct descent you can follow Option 1 in reverse to **Point 2** by continuing along this line to the Northernmost top [25-41]. As the summit plateau drops away to the North search for the old incline (no longer marked on the maps). This descends the mountain's slope quite easily until near the base you negotiate a jumble of crags and grassy hollows before reaching a ladder stile. Cross this and head right to join the main track, reversing the ascent route 300 metres North of the unnamed lake at **724562**.

As you begin to cross the blocky boulders that guard the base of this subsidiary top, bear left downslope in the direction of the valley containing Llynnau Mymbyr, crossing grassy slopes and a boulder-field in the process [25-42]. You quickly meet an unambiguous footpath cut into the turf lower down this slope that continues left and uphill to the summit (along the popular 'tourist route') [25-43] or right, and downhill in the direction of Capel Curig [25-44]. This path is an unrelenting trudge to the summit, with little to recommend it to the peak-bagger apart from the views. However, it does provide a straightforward descent route.

Turn right and follow the eroded path – crossing either of a pair of ladder stiles located where the going is particularly steep and rocky [25-45 looking uphill]. Beyond this point the path narrows as it drops towards a series of grassy humps [25-46]. Where the gradient finally levels at a boggy section, aim slightly left to regain a dry path threading between two grassy rises towards the woodland in the distance. A fence crosses ahead of you with dense heather beyond. Cross the ladder stile to regain a path running slightly left at the boundary between tussocky grass to the left and steeper, heather-clad slopes on your right. This path eventually leads you to the edge of a large coniferous plantation [25-47].

6)      (714568)      →

    25°            →

For a short stretch the path runs through a tunnel of branches before surfacing in open ground again. Ignore the wet and overgrown track beyond on your right. On the left stand a ladder stile and a wooden gate [25-48]. Cross the stile and continue downhill to the right along the banks of a small stream until you reach level ground where your path emerges onto a wide forest track at **716573**. To your left the track eventually meets a dead-end at the forest edge above Llynnau Mymbyr. But a footpath exits this shortly to the right to descend wooded slopes to a large footbridge crossing the outflow of these lakes and emerging on the roadside a few metres West of the Plas y Brenin National Mountain Centre. However, this is a long way from Pont Cyfyng where the walk started.

> Plas y Brenin was originally the site of the 'Royal Hotel', built by Lord Penrhyn at the end of the road he built running along the West side of Nant Ffrancon from his quarry to Capel Curig.

Rather than following this more fashionable exit route, turn right to continue along the forest track. After a few metres you emerge at a wide opening where there is a choice of continuing left or right. Follow the left-hand road as it continues gradually downhill through scrubby woodland.

This road leads to a large swing-gate (one of several along these forest tracks to deter unauthorised vehicle access). Beyond this it joins a better-constructed track emerging from the left which followed the lower forest margins on the broad valley floor East of Llynnau Mymbyr.

**7)** (725575) →

85° →

Continue along the same line for a short distance beyond this junction to where the track splits left and right again. The left spur runs directly downhill to cross the valley opposite Plas Gurig Youth Hostel. Instead take the right spur along a narrowing track which becomes decidedly wet in parts. Eventually the river on your left becomes confined to a narrow chasm (signs on the fence alongside your path warn of dangerous old mine workings). A short stone staircase on your right carries the path upslope slightly [25-49] to cross a tributary stream before emerging into more open woodland at **730575**.

A number of vague paths keep to the edge of the woodland here as it turns sharply to your right where the Afon Llugwy makes a sharp turn South. Whichever path you take you soon find yourself on the river's grassy banks. A ladder stile on your left gives access to a large meadow at the river's edge – often utilised as a vehicle-free camp site in summer, so be prepared to have to pick your way through an assortment of tents.

The next water-meadow you cross runs along the banks of the quieter reaches of the Afon Llugwy [25-50], passing on your right a ruined stone building [25-51], and the classic view of Moel Siabod above the forested slopes [25-52]. Beyond the ruin, ahead, and slightly to your right, you should be able to make out the wooden sides of a footbridge beneath the trees at the edge of the field at **733571**. Cross this footbridge then turn left to pass through a metal gate onto a narrow private road.

Turn left again and follow this road a few metres to emerge at the roadside at **734570**. Follow the road and turn left to cross the stone bridge spanning the Afon Llugwy (smooth rocks and plunge-pools on the downstream side) and at the T-junction with the A5 turn right. The lay-by where the walk began is a few metres beyond on your right.

**END**

# Carnedd Moel Siabod [80]

| 20 Km (12.5 miles)  985m (3231ft)  Time : 6hrs 50min | **Of all the eye-catching summits that adorn Snowdonia, this is the one you are most likely to catch a glimpse of somewhere on the horizon.** |
|---|---|

One relatively sober New Years' Day I set myself the challenge of setting foot on every summit in North Snowdonia that stood above the 600-metre contour. Less than 18 months later the task was done – Moel Penamnen and its neighbours had been visited a fortnight ago. But I felt that my mission deserved a more memorable walk to mark its completion.

What had started off as the 52 highest summits (provisionally four a month) became 64 when I looked closer, then 72 and finally 80. I went up Snowdon four times – from four different directions – for the sake of 'completion'. And an original set of 18 walks had eventually grown to 25. To make it 26 Moel Siabod got the vote for one more outing. This time I intended concentrating on its Southern approaches, starting off from Dolwyddelan in the Lledr valley.

The classic traverse includes the entire length of its Western ridge, an area normally missed out when walking up from Capel Curig. And as has been the case with every other route in this guide, starting and ending the walk from the same point can often make for very long days on the hill. So just this once I made an exception – starting with a railway journey.

Nothing to get too excited about – a five-minute commute followed by the usual seven hours of foot slogging.

**North**

**Don't forget**

**map/compass whistle/torch**

**suitable footwear + clothing**

**food/drink**

**brain**

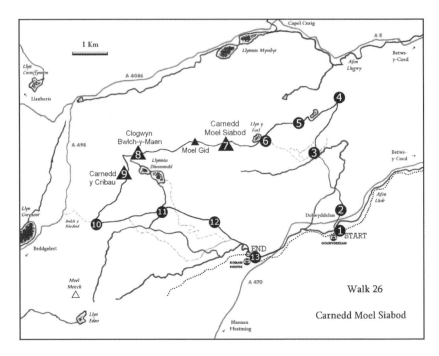

## APPROACH

From the West or South head through Blaenau Ffestiniog then follow the A470 uphill out of the town towards Dolwyddelan and Betws-y-Coed. This busy road crosses the high Crimea Pass (Bwlch y Gorddonin) before dropping down into the Lledr valley. 3Km from the pass's highest point is a minor road to your left signposted for Roman Bridge railway station.

From the North or East take the Dolwyddelan/Dolgellau exit off the A5 and drive through the beautiful valley of the Afon Lledr. After passing through the village of Dolwyddelan with its square fortress of a castle on your right, just under 1.5Km further along again on the right is a minor road signposted for Roman Bridge railway station.

Follow this twisting road for some 300 metres and the station is on the right-hand side of the road with enough room for about four cars. When I was last there trains ran every three hours to the start of the walk (06.04a.m. and 09.05a.m. being the most practical schedules for what turns out to be a full day's trek).

Roman Bridge is a 'request' stop so make sure you are standing on the platform in a visible spot – the train sneaks up on you and there's no warning rattle from the single-track line. From this platform, incidentally, there is a marvellous view of Moel Siabod itself to enliven the wait. Dolwyddelan station is the next stop – about three or four minutes by rail. The morning I took this ride I got a freebie – the conductor had not had the time to collect my fair. And although I offered him payment as I got out of the train at Dolwyddelan station and found him standing beside the rearmost carriage he gave me a little wave and said, "Don't worry about it". Thank you Arriva.

You can travel here directly by train from Llandudno, Llandudno Junction or Blaenau Ffestiniog if you want to leave the car at home (in which case – get off at Dolwyddelan where the actual walk starts). Then time the length of your walk to catch your return train from Roman Bridge station at the end of the day.

**START**

1)　　(738521)　　→

　　　　300°　　　→

Walk out of Dolwyddelan railway station onto Bridge Street that heads left towards Dolwyddelan village centre. You cross the bridge over the Afon Lledr then just after you pass the cemetery on the left you will see a small War memorial on the opposite side of the road with a 'Public Footpath' sign alongside a kissing gate.

　　　35°　　　→

Go through the gate and follow a narrow tarmac path across the water meadows alongside the Lledr. This short-cut avoids the village centre and leads to the main A470 by way of another kissing-gate. Cross the road, head right and almost immediately turn left into a narrow lane (signposted 'Unsuitable for Vehicles') at **738525**.

This lane heads uphill very steeply, passing some nurseries. It takes two left turns (ignore the two exits) before transforming into a track. On the right-hand side of this track is a fence with a drop into untidy woodland. On the left-hand side are fern-covered banks climbing to hidden heights.

The gradient eases for a time as the track reaches level ground then after crossing a trickle of wet ground it climbs towards the right. This is followed by a short section of tarmac leading to a T-junction.

**2)**    **(738527)**    →

20°    →

To your left this track crosses a cattle grid before immediately entering a meadow. Instead continue right, keeping to the sheltering canopy of the trees. On the right-hand side of this track are a wall and a fence, with just a fence on the left.

The angle of ascent levels off again before the track bears left and passes through a gateway (minus gate). Ahead is another T-junction at the edge of denser forest where a broad track runs right to left.

335°    →

The right-hand track is guarded by a wide barrier-type gate at **739529**. Take the left turning instead; this is actually the main forest track which now bears North.

I'm not a big fan of forest tracks, and fortunately there are not many hills in this part of Snowdonia that incorporate wooded areas. Whenever they do, such as on the tourist approach to Moel Hebog, you will notice that I have studiously avoided them. However I make an exception here as this forest track makes for a fairly pleasant walk. The trees are neither dense nor tall enough to entirely blot out the surrounding scenery so there is a welcome sense of openness.

After joining the main forest track ignore the footpath sign a few metres further along pointing to the right. The broad track climbs to another level section. You should also ignore the overgrown track exiting left and shortly you will get your first full view of Moel Siabod (excluding the earlier one overlooking the platform of Roman Bridge station) [26-01].

*From this spot you realise that Moel Siabod is quite a substantial ridge in its own right; beneath its notched skyline the cliff face is scarred with gullies and scree runnels [26-02 and 26-03]. At its highest point on the left end of the ridge is the pyramid of Carnedd Moel Siabod. But a lot of trees lie between you and the distant summit.*

From here the main track bears right with a slight descent then levels off, followed by a left bend (ignore the minor track that continues straight ahead). You then cross a bridge at **736533** (the Afon Ystumiau river beneath it running right to left). From here the track begins to climb gradually, taking a sweeping bend to the right. Ignore the next two overgrown tracks exiting left and right within a short distance of each other. The track levels again with another overgrown track heading off to the left at Beudy Brynbugelyn (**734539**).

Ignore that exit as well. The main track bears left and levels off before descending for a time, bearing left and quickly levelling off yet again. Shortly it crosses the same river as before, now running left to right. After this river crossing the track enters a broad valley with a finger post ahead marking where the track splits in two (shortly after you pass another overgrown track turning off to the right). This section of forest track is marked Sarn yr Offeiriad on the Explorer map ('The Priest's Causeway') and it was undoubtedly an important line of communication sometime in the past.

**3)**     **(731544)**     →

        0°               →

Ahead of you the fingerpost points left towards Moel Siabod, advertising the "Courtesy Path to Moel Siabod". But if, like me, you first want to take a closer look at the terrain to the East, forget your manners, turn right and follow the Capel Curig fork.

This track heading to your right begins a gradual climb, bearing first right then left. It then levels before bearing right again. Ignore the overgrown track on the left then where the track divides take the right fork. A couple of wet patches and a minor stream crossing follow before you reach a metal gate with a ladder stile on the left at **732548** that finally releases you from the forest [26-04 looking back].

> *To your left stretches featureless moorland that extends beyond the low line of Mynydd Cribau to the dense forests South of Betws-y-Coed. The higher forested escarpments to the right mark the junction where the valley of the Lledr meets that of the Conwy at the Southern entrance to the Vale of Conwy. Beyond this gateway there is not much else visible except the low rocky crest of the spur on your left descending from the South Eastern corner of Llyn y Foel [26-05].*

Cross the stile and follow a cart track, muddy in places, past hut circles on the high slopes to the left and the remnants of a group of cairns on the right [26-06]. You then reach another metal gate with a ladder stile on its left [26-07] – go through the gate. The map identifies a second set of hut circles on the slopes above this ladder stile (at **736555**).

The hut circles on these hillsides probably date from the Iron Age and it is likely they were still inhabited during the Roman occupation. When the Romans passed through this region they kept to the low ground where possible, although presumably their presence had some impact on those who occupied the surrounding hills.

*Given the bracken cover on these slopes it is difficult to identify whether you are looking at a significant archaeological site or a natural outcrop of crags. What is more noticeable behind you to the West is the modern A470 climbing the Crimea Pass between the peaks of Moel Penamnen on its left and Moel Dyrnogydd on its right. If you continue a little further along the track and look back again there is a superb head-on view of Cwm Penamnen to the left of Moel Penamnen itself.*

If you keep an eye on the spur of high ground on the left-hand side of the track you will see it gradually dropping towards the skyline ahead. The track itself heads in roughly the same direction, swinging left then right just for a moment to pass through a section of collapsed wall. On the right a grassed-over stone and earth embankment abuts with the track where it reaches this route's highest point.

As the track begins its slow, damp descent through several puddles towards the Llugwy valley the embankment reasserts itself, now running along the right-hand side of the track. Finally it climbs again to one final crest beyond which it begins a steady drop, initially between clumps of trees, to the low ground close to Pont Cyfyng.

On the floor of the Llugwy valley a short distance below this track is the site of Caer Llugwy – a Roman fort (also known as 'Bryn y Gefeiliau' after the farm nearby). There is evidence that the soldiers who camped here played a significant part in mining the nearby hills for lead.

Of more strategic importance was the roadway constructed to link Caerhun, 4 miles South of Conwy, with Caerfyrddin (Carmarthen) in South Wales. This Roman road ran through Caer Llugwy, across the Lledr valley close to Dolwyddelan, up Cwm Penamnen, past Trawsfynydd and Southwards to eventually cross the Dyfi valley. The roadway was named 'Sarn Elen' ('Helen's Causeway') after the legendary Elen, who in Welsh folklore as written in the Mabinogion was the wife of the Roman emperor 'Macsen Wledig' (Maximus)

*This is as good a spot as any from which to study the Southern end of the Creigiau Gleison ridge (the Eastern wall of the trough enclosing the Cowlyd reservoir).* Crimpiau and Craig Wen are easily identified with Pen Llithrig y Wrach towering behind them.

**4)**     **(738559)**     →

       **240°**          →

Soon it is time for an almost complete reversal of direction as Moel Siabod beckons. Turn left as you abandon the track and begin to climb the spur that ran alongside your path for much of the way. Early on you cross a ditch but soon a sheep path can be picked out directing you through the tussocky grass to a nearby rocky slab. After crossing more grassland a clearer path can be seen bearing right towards a ridge [26-08]. The intervening low ground is quite boggy but soon crossed. Now aim for the sand-coloured scar where a dry river course cuts through the grassy slopes [26-09].

Follow this uphill to a low, grassy ridge overlooking an unnamed lake on the right (in the vicinity of **731554**) [26-10]. It's Eastern outflow is held back by a stone wall which suggests it was used as a reservoir; supplying water to the disused quarry above Pont Cyfyng [26-11] (together with the other unnamed lake you pass on **Walk 25** to Moel Siabod).

The Western shore of the lake has a fence separating it from the craggy slopes above [26-12 and 26-13]. Cross this fence to reach a clear footpath running left to right. Follow it to the right, crossing a wet area marking the lake's inflow before climbing up a steep, fern-covered bank ahead and to the right [26-14]. On top of this bank the ground is wet and spongy, with a ladder stile clearly visible to your right (although there is no path marked on the Explorer map) [26-15]. In fact this part of the walk is fairly pathless and the route you follow will pretty much be determined by ground conditions and personal preference. The overall aim is to head towards any higher ground to the right, getting closer to Moel Siabod's ascent ridge in the process.

It is best to head away from the ladder stile, tempting as any path might seem. A rocky cliff stands to your left which is skirted by a faint path running left to right along its base. The path then bears right, crossing a stream and bypassing a large hump of rock and heather which the ladder stile by now is hidden behind. More damp ground needs to be crossed as you trend left again heading towards yet higher ground.

Not many parts of NorthWest Snowdonia are matted by mature heather; the coarse, woody type that reaches up to your waist, hides any irregularities on the ground, and snags your feet at every step. It's fair to say that these formidable slopes beneath the base of Moel Siabod make up for any deficiency there might be elsewhere. The only pleasant distractions were the swarms of bright, blue damsel-flies that seemed to flourish under the hot sun when I was last here.

*As you look towards the West, with the line of Moel Siabod's Daear Ddu ridge barely visible on the skyline descending to the left from the summit, there are two features nearer at hand and beneath it that reward closer scrutiny.*

It is difficult to miss the substantial platform of ground straight ahead that separates you from your goal. And to the left of that is a low hummock of ground with a much larger set of crags further left again.
The best line of approach [26-16] runs beneath this larger set of crags, climbs to the rear of the hummock and attacks the front of the platform to gain the high ground forming the Southern shore of Llyn y Foel.

Even the remarkably detailed Explorer maps give few clues away here, not least because this entire walk is split between one side of OL18 (the Harlech, Porthmadog and Bala map) and both sides of the OL17 (the Snowdon/Conway Valley map). Just pray that the weather keeps visibility sufficiently clear for you to be able to pick your way ahead using your eyes.

From the heather-clad rise it is not particularly difficult to reach the base of the crags on your left – although there is more soggy ground to cross before you reach its base where a stream trickles downslope [26-17]. As you sneak underneath the right-hand side of these damp cliffs, take a line that allows you to climb up the steep slope of overgrown rubble beyond – towards the short section of dry-stone wall half way up the fern bank.

Where the wall meets the cliff face on the left you will see a sheep tunnel built into it (plugged by a slab of rock on the other side when I was last there). Nearby crags enable you to safely cross the wall and follow its left-hand side onto the crags ahead [26-18]. These are best skirted left by clambering over a small heap of enormous boulders to gain a high shelf covered in more ferns close to **725552**.

On your right now the wall reappears in a sweeping arc whilst on your left stand two massive, isolated boulders – the smaller of the two perched on top of the other [26-19 looking back from further upslope].

These boulders are as likely as not erratics dumped by the melting ice sheet that covered this area during the last ice age.
As well as local, mountain glaciers produced by the accumulation of snow falling on Snowdonia's high ground to form ice-caps, there were also ice-sheets that encroached on the area from further afield. The Irish Sea ice-sheet was formed of ice which built up in the sea's basin as larger glaciers fed it from the mountains of Scotland, Ireland and the Isle of Man. This ice became so thick that it impinged on the North Wales coast and the lower slopes of Northern Snowdonia reaching heights of 1500 metres.
Rocks that were broken away by the ice digging away at the Scottish mountains ended up being carried several hundreds of miles before being unceremoniously dumped when the ice-sheets finally melted. Since these boulders bear no geological relation to the surrounding bedrock on which they lie, they are called 'erratics'.

It is not a requirement that you clamber on top of these two boulders, but I bet that once you reach them most of you will be unable to resist the temptation.

Ferns and heather cloak the tricky slopes ahead of you – together with a fairly steep rocky face which presents a more attractive means of ascent onto the platform above than it might under different circumstances. The line you follow is a matter of personal preference. Keep left to join a neighbouring ridge first, or cross the lower ground on the right to seek a way into the gap on the immediate skyline, or aim even further right towards where the skyline of the Daear Ddu ridge meets the high platform.

I hate having to lose altitude when there's still a good deal of climbing ahead unless it's absolutely necessary. So I suggest you keep left, battling against the heather perhaps, but it can actually provide you with something useful to hold onto as you haul yourself up the final rock face onto the top. From there you are given the opportunity to pick an approach line up the next set of cliff faces directly ahead of you at the Southern edge of the next high platform [26-20].

*You also have the opportunity to admire the landscape to the South for the first time since leaving the track high above Pont Cyfyng. Behind you lies a long ridge – from the vast, peat-covered moorland of Migneint on the left [26-21] to the dead-end valley of Cwm Penamnen with its forested ramparts on the right. And tucked in further right is the Crimea Pass providing the only feasible route South.*

**5)**      **(726552)**        →

         **275°**            →

A frontal assault of the platform now facing you is easier than it looks from below. First you have to clamber over the frequent outcrops of grey, pock-marked rock. Beyond these the most direct line involves a hard pull up a grassy cleft to the right of a large fissure (the fissure itself will probably prove to be too sheer on closer inspection for most walkers). Where the cleft levels off at the top the ground opens up with views ahead to Moel Siabod's Southern-facing rock wall.

It's a great feeling to reach the top of this platform at last. The flat ground on top of it is boggy in parts, with an assortment of small pools stippling its surface [26-22]. But the going is distinctly easier as you head left across a gently descending rocky pavement to meet the shores of Llyn y Foel [26-23].

*From the Southern shoreline of Llyn y Foel the steep walls of Moel Siabod are overwhelming. Rugged grey crags crumbling to fans of white scree below look impregnable, while the gullies and slivers of grassy slope give the false impression that there is a wide choice of routes to the top.*

In practice the only safe approach route to the summit from the lake shore is the Daear Ddu ridge – the rocky spur at the left-hand end of the Moel Siabod ridge. Its knife-edge façade hides a relatively easy scramble. Once the peat at the lake's shore has given way to grass and rock you soon reach the stone barrier holding back the waters of Llyn y Foel [26-24]. This is the point at which Option 1 emerges from the gorge below.

**6)**   **(716547)**   →

   **245°**   →

The stone barrier is actually a pair of dry-stone walls. The lower one dips in the middle where the ground drops to the banks of the stream exiting the lake – the headwaters of the Afon Ystumiau. The path bears left to easily cross this stream. A closer look at the stones scattered across the broad, grassy banks here suggests this is a popular 'wild' campsite. Many are soot-covered and stacked in little piles.

On the opposite bank the rocky spur of Daear Ddu thrown down Moel Siabod's South Eastern flanks reaches right to the lake shore. A path begins to climb this spur, circling the ice-carved basin holding Llyn y Foel and sticking to the line of the highest outcrops for most of the ascent.

As you meet the first pyramid of fractured rock you have the choice of flanking its left or right face in order to continue the ascent. There is more opportunity for scrambling along the right-hand path which is the more exposed; although the exposure is low scale. Scrapes on the rocks here attest to the high number of boots (and crampons no doubt) that have followed this same route [26-25, and 26-26 looking back from higher up the ridge]. For a more detailed description of this scramble refer to **Walk 25**.

A line of white gravel runs along the right-hand side of the ridge then bears off left to climb across steeply tilted slabs of rough rock – the rust-coloured line of favoured ascent visible at every step.

From here it is an easy scramble to gain the crest of the ridge again. Handholds are plentiful and secure and the steep angle of ascent is never intimidating. Above and ahead of you now is a straightforward boulder-strewn slope climbing quite sedately to the final set of crags directly beneath the summit point. Short sections of path cross angular boulders and bare rock to where the last set of crags form a slight overhang. Again the scrambling is straightforward up this final obstacle; a simple matter of hauling yourself through a series of blocky outcrops to reach the triangulation pillar (Bench Mark S7317 for those of you who have an appetite for such trivia) marking the summit point of **Carnedd Moel Siabod** (at **705546** – 872m/2860ft).

*The views from Moel Siabod's summit are legendary – one of the few spots where you can see the classic profile of the Snowdon Horseshoe forming the backdrop to Dyffryn Mymbyr but from a loftier perspective. Even Tryfan and the Glyderau look memorable from up here.*
*Then there are the South Eastern Carneddau – Pen yr Helgi Du and Pen Llithrig y Wrach peering over the wind shelter erected a few metres North of the mountain's top.*
*And on the opposite side there's still plenty to ponder over – the wooded slopes of Garnedd y Bont with its tadpole lake wriggling free of the forest margins.*

Unfortunately on the day I chose for this extended walk stifling heat and watery sunshine gave way to gusting winds and increasingly dense cloud by the time I reached the summit. With low cloud closing in from every direction I only lingered long enough to say "Hello" to a couple of walkers who emerged from the East, grab a bite to eat and double-check the compass bearings for the next leg – fresh ground for me as I had never done this section of the walk before.

**7)**    **(705546)**    →

    270°    →

As you start to walk Westwards from Carnedd Moel Siabod's rocky summit you meet a fence that follows the same route, dropping directly across the grassy slopes of Moel Gid towards Bwlch Rhiw'r Ychen [26-37]. Initially I crossed to the left-hand side of this fence in order to gain the small grey outcrops of rock ahead. The fence skirts these by sticking to the grassy slopes below.

It is worth pointing out at this point that this section of path to the left-hand side of the fence was littered with discarded lengths of barbed wire, lying in rusty coils between the boulders and rotting fence-posts. I came across the same on the ascent of Clogwyn Bwlch-y-Maen further along – just keep your eyes peeled, especially if walking your dog.

As you cross over the crags and reach open grass beyond, you can see the fence running in a relentless line along the spur of Moel Gid to your right. There is a ladder stile a short distance along that allows you to re-cross the fence and join the descent path on your right which eventually drops all the way down to Pen-y-Gwryd (a clear footpath which is not shown on the Explorer map).

> As you head West the sheer walls of Clogwyn Du beneath Y Foel Goch on your right across Dyffryn Mymbyr look vast in scale until you see the monolithic hulk of Tryfan towering above.
> Further down the valley Llyn Lockwood and the pine plantation alongside the Pen y Gwryd hotel are visible beside the main road. Perched on a shelf above these is Llyn Cwm Ffynnon which drains by circuitous means into Nant Gwryd – the river which passes through Llynnau Mymbyr before joining the Afon Llugwy close to Plas y Brenin.
> Still largely hidden further to the right behind Moel Berfedd is the Llanberis Pass.

Follow the path down gently undulating slopes. Despite the dropping mist (Moel Siabod's top was already covered in low cloud by now) and the buffeting wind, this part of the walk was easy on the soles and an absolute pleasure. Small tussocks of short grass that covered this spur ebbed and flowed like a vivid emerald tide, each individual blade of grass tipped in red.

Eventually you reach a point almost directly across valley from Llyn Lockwood (at 691544) where small piles of flat rocks form a track of sorts heading eventually down the slopes of Dyffryn Mymbyr [25-38]. These are probably old field enclosures – collapsed walls being all that remain of the small-holdings that once dotted the slopes above Cwm Clorad.

Ahead and to your left the rounded slopes of the ridge begin to change in nature as two rocky bluffs tumble steeply left into the basin holding Llynnau Diwaunydd. The first and steeper outcrop is that of Clogwyn Bwlch-y-Maen – the second and more dominant is that of Carnedd y Cribau [26-29].

The fence takes a direct line onto Clogwyn Bwlch-y-Maen, swinging to the right then crossing steep slabs onto the skyline. But a ladder stile allows you to cross to its left-hand side and follow a steep, sinuous line crossing grassy slopes to the top of the crags, the summit point of **Clogwyn Bwlch-y-Maen** (at **679543** – 548m/1797ft).

*From here there is a picture-postcard view of Llynnau Diwaunydd on your left – actually a single body of water that has been pinched in its middle by a small bracelet of silt and gravel [26-30 and 26-31]. The soft, green, grass-covered shoulders that sweep down on either side to cradle the lake, and the clusters of dark pines on its Northern shoreline alerting one to the forested slopes below give this valley an almost Alpine air.*

**8)**      **(679543)**      →

       **220°**          →

From the crest of Clogwyn Bwlch-y-Maen, continue to follow the fence as it edges towards the deep gash ahead – Bwlch Rhiw'r Ychen [26-32]. But just before the ground starts to fall away ahead of you, this fence makes a right-hand turn towards gentler slopes [26-33]. Keep following the fence as it drops down one very steep, rocky section before bottoming out onto what is still a relatively high part of the pass (close to the 510-metre contour).

*Before you abandon the welcome bit of altitude where the fence takes a right turn above Bwlch Rhiw'r Ychen, take a look ahead (North) into the jaws of the Llanberis Path. From up here you get a bird's-eye view of the Pen y Pass car park [26-34]. All those vehicles; all those walkers tramping up Snowdon – yet I didn't meet another soul between here and Roman Bridge railway station.*

At **676542** there is a junction of fences and stiles that resembles the Gravelly Hill Interchange Assuming you have kept to the left-hand side of the fence, you must first somehow cross to its right-hand side, then climb over the ladder stile a short distance beyond this junction and to your left, then climb over the next ladder stile on your left again to reach a path along the left-hand side of the fence running up the slopes of Carnedd y Cribau! It sounds confusing but it's not really.

The saddle hereabouts is extremely boggy, particularly so close to the fence. Veering further left across firmer ground is wisest before rejoining the fence as it begins to climb the hillside. It leads uphill across grass-covered slopes then small outcrops of rock until you reach the summit area of Carnedd y Cribau. Just before you reach the craggy top there is a small dip in the ridge where a ladder stile invites you to cross over [26-35]. There is nothing to be gained in suddenly changing sides. Concentrate on climbing the final outcrop of grey rock to reach the highest point of the crest – the summit of **Carnedd y Cribau** (at **676536** – 591m/1938ft).

9)      (676536)      →

195°         →

This was the point at which the weather did what it had threatened to do for the preceding hour. The drizzle transformed into a downpour and the wisps of mist became dense cloud. Where the ground fell away sheer to my left I got a fleeting glimpse far below of Llynnau Diwaunydd [26-36] then the entire valley disappeared behind a white mush. This deterioration in the weather meant I was ready to consider any feasible option to reach lower ground and any track that led back to civilisation.

A ladder stile close on my right tried its best to tempt me over it [26-37] – there was even a path clearly visible on the other side of the fence. But that only leads to a large pool surrounded by rock and peat-bog. The ridge running gradually downhill South West from Carnedd y Cribau is a mess of steep, rocky humps, dark pools and muddy bogs. Fortunately the fence takes roughly the same line as the most straightforward descent – just resist the temptation to cross to the right every time you come across a ladder stile. And there are quite a few of those strung along the crest-line.

There are numerous dips in the ridge; some involving clambering between fractured blocks of rock, others a straightforward walk down grassy ramps. But when I reached the first pronounced depression I calculated that this was probably Bwlch Maen Pig at **673531** – still a good way higher than the low col of Bwlch y Rhediad at **666523** which I was aiming for – at an altitude more than 400 metres below the summit. Another steady rise was followed by a jumble of large blocks dropping to more grass – the fence doing its best to keep up with me as I clambered down between the rocks. Then the cloud thinned, the wind pulled it aside like a stage curtain and for an instant I got a clear view of the terrain to my left. Across a large expanse of green beneath ran a faint track (or so I thought) leading to a distinct clump of trees.

When planning this walk in the comfort of an armchair, studying the Explorer map for clues and scanning the lay-out while tramping across Ysgafell Wen [26-38 from **Walk 20**] months beforehand, I had already earmarked this isolated conifer plantation as a noteworthy landmark (at **676524**) – one of the few features lying close to the track running Eastwards from Bwlch y Rhediad.

---

### OPTION 2
If you decide to exit left from this ridge rather than continue the entire trek to Bwlch y Rhediad, this is the time to make a move as it is possible to progress quite safely downslope from **673531**.
Once you begin to drop down from the highest rim of the rocky ridge look out for a tiny ragged pool in a depression on your left with a slightly smaller circle of turf in its middle [25-39]. Boggy ground to the right holds another body of water. Beyond the smaller pool a slight rise in the ground extends left forming a small spur. This in turn leads to a short, rocky lip beyond which gentle slopes descend in a sweep to flatter ground [25-40].
Faint sheep tracks can now be seen crossing the lush pasture below to meet a more definite path heading left to right. Far beyond this extensive tract of grassland are the margins of the forest that cloak the ground South and East of Llynnau Diwaunydd. The best route is to head directly South towards the isolated stand of conifers and from there locate the main path running West to East from Bwlch y Rhediad to the forest track [25-41 looking back up to the ridge].

From the height of Y Cribau (the ridge running South West from Carnedd y Cribau) this grassland looks like normal pastureland. But after heavy rain the ground hereabouts quickly becomes soggy and wading through knee-high grass can have the same effect as paddling through a bog. And it's only when you get closer that you discover the faint track visible from the ridge and heading in a straight line for the trees is actually a ditch.

However, it is possible to pick out firmer ground by keeping close to the sheep paths. Just before you reach that isolated stand of trees with ruined farm buildings to its right, you meet the main path leading East from Bwlch y Rhediad. Turn left along this path and continue to the forest margins at **point 11**.

*Time saved – 30mins.*

OR

OPTION 3

To avoid the forest area altogether, rather than turning left and continuing to the forest margins, cross the main path leading East from Bwlch y Rhediad and continue with **Option 4**.

If you decide to press on along the ridge it is fortunately pretty much all downhill from here.

There is one steep section of grey crag (Clogwyn Pwll-budr) to pick your way down [26-42 from below], trending left to meet a series of low, grass-covered hummocks. As you continue ahead across these mounds you reach a fence that leads the way downhill to a saddle covered in tussocky grass. An antiquated gate and a standard ladder-stile mark the low point of Bwlch y Rhediad [26-43].

The pass of Bwlch y Rhediad has been a significant line of communication since ancient times. For centuries a track crossing this high col provided the shortest route from the valley of Nantgwynant to the West (and feasibly the Llanberis Pass further North) to Dolwyddelan and the Lledr valley to the East.

*If you have ever traversed the distant heights of Ysgafell Wen (during **Walk 20** perhaps) then the lowlands opening out ahead of you might be familiar. To your right, across the open valley of the Afon Cwm Edno, rise the bare slopes of Foel Goch, with the rockier crest of Yr Arddu further right. This pair are poor imitations of the two loftier mountains of the same name.*

**10)**   **(667523)**      →

     85°          →

Cross the ladder stile and follow the path (in places resembling a stream bed) left in the direction of the lower reaches of the Afon Cwm Edno. This clear track is simple to follow as it creeps beneath the grassy slopes of Y Cribau despite there being few if any landmarks to latch onto should low cloud close in [26-44]. Even more helpfully, someone has been considerate enough to erect a series of marker posts pointing the way ahead should the path itself be obscured by snow cover.

Within a short distance you will hopefully be able to pick out a clump of conifers ahead of you and slightly to the right of the path [26-45]. These are the trees that you may have already spotted from the high ridge – the landmark tempting tired walkers to take the Option 2 shortcut from the ridge. Under closer scrutiny there are ruins close to this plantation suggesting there was perhaps a cottage once standing here, the conifers a windbreak in an otherwise treeless expanse of valley [26-46].

The path continues to plough ahead relentlessly, crossing a minor stream using stepping stones laid out for the purpose, and leaving the conifers in its wake a short distance downhill to its right (at **676524**)

---

**OPTION 4**
If you don't fancy 45 minutes of forest, and mud which is where this footpath leads, cross to the right and head towards these conifers. An eroded track descends to the Afon Cwm Edno then crosses it by way of a footbridge.

---

> On the opposite bank continue uphill slightly then turn left along a wider track passing old quarry workings as it skirts the stub-end of Foel Goch's North Eastern spur.
> This track eventually joins the road at **697514**. Turn left and follow the road for just over 1Km through Blaenau Dolwyddelan to **point 13**.
> *Time saved – about 20 minutes*

Beyond, the path soon loses its shape. For the next ½ Km or so it's a case of sticking to the driest parts where possible, and keeping an eye open for the next marker post. I sympathise with the chap whose job it was to plant these in the ground – not the best job in the National Park. But I think he was a bit stingy when he got to this bit.

Ahead of you the path emerges from the undergrowth again before splitting in two – and, of course, with no marker post in sight when you really need one. The left fork actually leads uphill towards the shores of Llynnau Diwaunydd. Take the right fork which soon becomes very wet underfoot as it approaches a river crossing – assisted by large, solid stepping stones – with a ladder stile on the opposite bank at the edge of a large forest [26-47]. Cross this stile and step into the wildwood.

**11)**    **(685527)**    →

   75°    →

You now join the start of another forest track – marker-posted the entire way. However, unlike the forest at the start of the walk, this is primordial territory. Just peer left or right into the gloom beneath the dense forest canopy and you begin to realise that wilderness is not confined to open moor-land or rocky heights. Unfortunately, much of the route is very muddy underfoot as well.

A slate bridge crosses a small stream cut into the bedrock, the pools of water visible on the left a livid rust-red (presumably due to the minerals leached out of the soil upslope). The path then climbs over damp ground to cross a broad forest track.

OPTION 5
It is possible to turn right onto this forestry road and follow it downhill
as it twists and squirms its way in a series of convoluted bends that lead
South to the Eastern outskirts of the village of Blaenau Dolwyddelan.
Once there turn left onto the same road as that encountered in
Option 3 and continue to **point 13.**

You then descend to a wet stream bed which crosses an overgrown track, then descend some more to a relatively large clearing. After such a spell of heavy rain in what had been a warm, dry week, the air in here seemed to be overloaded with scents of greenery and growth. The footpath soon gets muddy again, crosses another stream by way of some rickety rocks, then continues along a pavement of large stone blocks to another muddy section.

Finally the path becomes even wetter as it weaves between low branches to find a better path at the end of which stands a ladder stile. Beyond this stile you cross another river – Ceunant y Garnedd – the outflow from the tadpole-shaped lake beneath Garnedd y Bont seen earlier on your hike. There are two sets of stepping stones to choose from (those on the right looked more secure to me). Then you suddenly find yourself at the forest's Eastern margins where there is a fence with a wooden gate on the right [26-48].

**12)**   **(701525)**   →

     150°      →

You are now on a substantial rocky path, which is still wet in parts until it starts to trend downhill. Shortly it meets a broad track that climbs round to your left – follow this down to the right.

As you drop down towards lower ground you might notice the patches of black shale that make up part of the track. This rock, although much darker, is similar in structure and origin to the slates that made much of North Wales its fortune. But you only have to pick up a piece to discover how brittle it is compared to the top-class slate mined in Blaenau Ffestiniog. Perhaps if the slate here had been of better quality the Lledr valley would today be yet another scarred wilderness.

The black deposit is a sign of high sulphur content which made much of the local slate worthless.

Continue down this track to a metal gate – go through it. There is a farmhouse set back on the left – 'Ffridd' – stone-built with white walls. The path bears right then you meet another metal gate on your left below the farm. Go through this gate to join the road.

115°         →

Turn left onto the road and straight ahead of you on the right-hand verge is a public-footpath signpost. This footpath takes you through the first gate on your right into a pleasant open meadow that drops down to the banks of the Afon Lledr, such a contrast to the terrain higher uphill.

Surprisingly the path is clearly paved for much of the way as it leads to another gate just this side of the river on your left. All rather civilised after what you have suffered during the latter half of the walk.

Go through that gate and bear right as the path runs under some trees. It then crosses a very basic footbridge and continues to the right – paved again – to finally climb up a short ramp to a wooden gate (actually a wooden pallet with hinges attached).

Go through it and you are back on tarmac again. Turn right to follow this road, crossing the river bridge, then shortly after the railway bridge. After these two bridges a track continues straight on into 'Gorddinan' farm but the main road takes a hairpin swing to the left and climbs a short, steep hill.

It then drops down past an overgrown hollow on your left full of stagnant water and felled trees. Beyond this on the left are the white buildings of Roman Bridge railway station and the end of what was hopefully a satisfying day.

**13)     (713514)        →**

Finally, no more walking. Unless you are ready to start all over again.


**END**



If you have followed every walk in this guide and set foot on every hill then you might be surprised to learn that you have walked a total distance of 355.2 Km (222 miles), climbed 23565 metres (77293 feet) and perhaps spent 8730 minutes doing it (a total of 6 days, one and a half hours well spent).

There's no point asking me where passion becomes obsession as far as hill-walking is concerned. All I know is that the 26 walks included here are only the tip of an iceberg. One could easily revisit every one of these 80 hills by routes other than the ones described here. And even following a familiar route time and time again can often prove that no two days are the same. Which is what makes walking the hills such an enthralling pursuit. The more you do it, the more you end up wanting to spend more time doing more of it. So here is where my experiences really do end, and where I trust yours begin…..

**Safe walking**

**Phil Jones**

# GLOSSARY

| | | |
|---|---|---|
| Aber | : | estuary |
| Afon | : | river |
| Allt/Gallt | : | hill or hillside |
| Bach/Bychan/Fach/Fechan: | | small |
| Bera | : | old word for mountain |
| Blaen | : | farthest end, summit or source (plural 'blaenau') |
| Bont/Pont | : | bridge |
| Braich | : | arm or spur of land |
| Bryn | : | hill |
| Bwlch | : | gap or pass (col) |
| Cadair/Cader | : | chair |
| Cae | : | field or enclosure |
| Caer/Gaer | : | castle or citadel |
| Carn/Carnedd | : | cairn |
| Carreg/Craig | : | rock (plural – 'cerrig') |
| Castell | : | castle |
| Cefn | : | back or ridge |
| Clogwyn | : | cliff |
| Coch/Goch | : | red |
| Coed | : | wood or trees |
| Crib | : | ridge or crest (plural 'cribau') |
| Cwm | : | mountain valley or glen |
| Dôl/ Ddôl | : | meadow |
| Drum/Trum | : | ridge |
| Du/Ddu | : | black |
| Dyffryn | : | valley |
| Foel/Moel | : | bare hill |
| Ffordd | : | road |
| Ffridd | : | mountain pasture |
| Ffynnon | : | well or spring |

| | | |
|---|---|---|
| Gallt | : | wooded hillside |
| Garn/Garnedd | : | cairn |
| Garreg/Graig | : | rock |
| Glas/Las | : | blue or green |
| Glyder | : | pile (of rock) |
| Golau/Goleuni | : | light |
| Gwyn/Wyn | : | white |
| Gwynt | : | wind |
| Hafod | : | summer dwelling (plural 'hafodydd') |
| Hendre | : | winter dwelling |
| Llan | : | parish or church |
| Llwybr | : | path |
| Llyn | : | lake (plural 'llynnau') |
| Maen | : | rock |
| Mawr/Fawr | : | large or big |
| Melyn | : | yellow or sallow |
| Mynydd/Fynydd | : | mountain |
| Nant | : | valley |
| Pant | : | valley or hollow |
| Pen | : | head or summit |
| Rhaeadr | : | waterfall |
| Rhyd | : | ford |
| Tal | : | front or end |
| Tan | : | below or beneath |
| Traeth | : | beach |
| Y/Yr | : | the |

# On-line Shop

Our whole catalogue of titles are
available on our website

- Walking and Mountaineering
- Regions of Wales / Local Guides
- Maritime Wales
- Welsh Heritage and Culture
- Art and Photography
- Welsh History and Myths
- Children's Books
✻ BARGAINS ✻

## www.carreg-gwalch.com

# Further enjoyable reading on History and Heritage

Visit our website for further information:

## www.carreg-gwalch.com

Orders can be placed on our

# On-line Shop